Rick Steves'
GREAT
BRITAIN
2004

D1113046

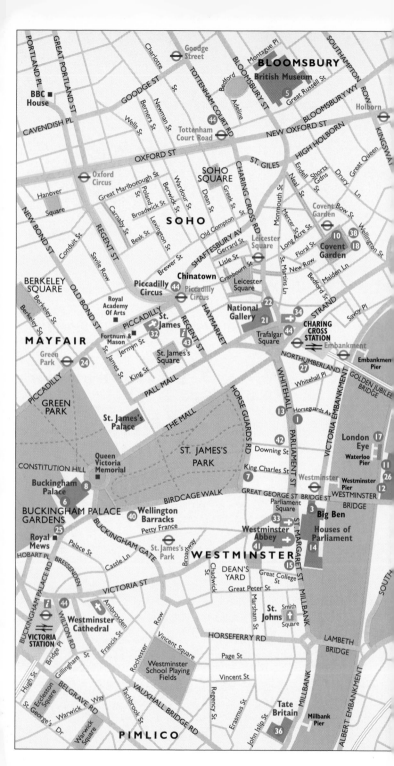

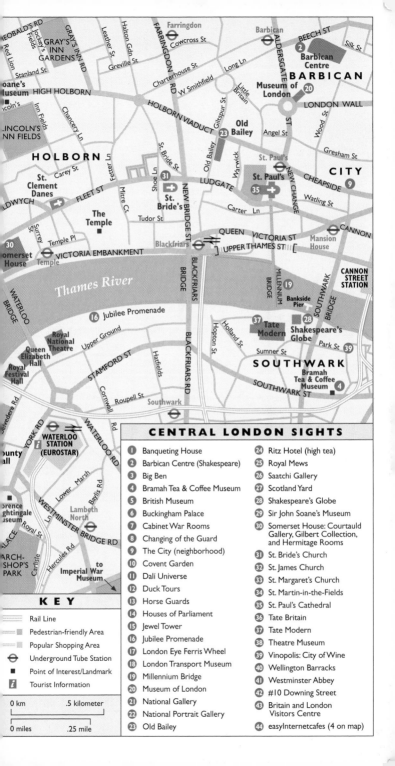

CENTRAL LONDON SIGHTS

1. Banqueting House
2. Barbican Centre (Shakespeare)
3. Big Ben
4. Bramah Tea & Coffee Museum
5. British Museum
6. Buckingham Palace
7. Cabinet War Rooms
8. Changing of the Guard
9. The City (neighborhood)
10. Covent Garden
11. Dalí Universe
12. Duck Tours
13. Horse Guards
14. Houses of Parliament
15. Jewel Tower
16. Jubilee Promenade
17. London Eye Ferris Wheel
18. London Transport Museum
19. Millennium Bridge
20. Museum of London
21. National Gallery
22. National Portrait Gallery
23. Old Bailey
24. Ritz Hotel (high tea)
25. Royal Mews
26. Saatchi Gallery
27. Scotland Yard
28. Shakespeare's Globe
29. Sir John Soane's Museum
30. Somerset House: Courtauld Gallery, Gilbert Collection, and Hermitage Rooms
31. St. Bride's Church
32. St. James Church
33. St. Margaret's Church
34. St. Martin-in-the-Fields
35. St. Paul's Cathedral
36. Tate Britain
37. Tate Modern
38. Theatre Museum
39. Vinopolis: City of Wine
40. Wellington Barracks
41. Westminster Abbey
42. #10 Downing Street
43. Britain and London Visitors Centre
44. easyInternetcafes (4 on map)

KEY

- Rail Line
- Pedestrian-friendly Area
- Popular Shopping Area
- Underground Tube Station
- Point of Interest/Landmark
- Tourist Information

| 0 km | .5 kilometer |
| 0 miles | .25 mile |

© Transport for London

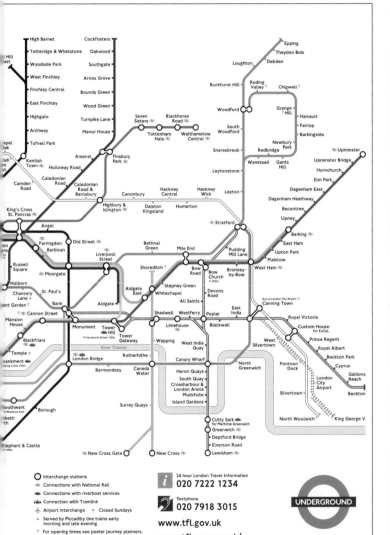

High Barnet
Cockfosters
Totteridge & Whetstone
Oakwood
Woodside Park
Southgate
West Finchley
Arnos Grove
Finchley Central
Bounds Green
East Finchley
Wood Green
Highgate
Turnpike Lane
Archway
Manor House
Tufnell Park

Epping
Theydon Bois
Loughton
Debden
Buckhurst Hill
Roding Valley
Chigwell †
Woodford
Grange † Hill
Hainault
South Woodford
Fairlop
Barkingside
Newbury Park
Snaresbrook
Redbridge
Upminster
Wanstead
Gants Hill
Upminster Bridge
Leytonstone
Hornchurch
Elm Park
Leyton
Dagenham East
Dagenham Heathway
Becontree
Upney
Stratford
Barking
East Ham
Upton Park
Plaistow
West Ham

Seven Sisters
Blackhorse Road
Tottenham Hale
Walthamstow Central

Arsenal
Finsbury Park
Kentish Town
Holloway Road
Caledonian Road
Camden Road
Caledonian Road & Barnsbury
Canonbury
Hackney Central
Hackney Wick
King's Cross St. Pancras
Highbury & Islington
Dalston Kingsland
Homerton
Angel
Old Street
Farringdon
Barbican
Bethnal Green
Mile End
Pudding Mill Lane
Russell Square
Liverpool Street
Moorgate
Shoreditch †
Bow Road
Bow Church
Bromley-by-Bow
Holborn
St. Paul's
Aldgate East
Stepney Green
Devons Road
Chancery Lane *
Whitechapel
All Saints
Cannon Street
Bank
Aldgate
Shadwell
Westferry
Poplar
East India
Mansion House
Monument
Tower Hill
Tower Gateway
Limehouse
Blackwall
Canning Town
Bus to London City Airport
Royal Victoria
Custom House for ExCeL
Blackfriars
Wapping
West India Quay
West Silvertown
Prince Regent
Royal Albert
Temple *
River Thames
Beckton Park
Embankment
London Bridge
Rotherhithe
Canary Wharf
North Greenwich
Pontoon Dock
Cyprus
Gallions Reach
Bermondsey
Canada Water
Heron Quays
South Quay
Crossharbour & London Arena
Mudchute
London City Airport
Beckton
Southwark
Silvertown
Borough
Surrey Quays
Island Gardens
North Woolwich
King George V
Elephant & Castle
Cutty Sark for Maritime Greenwich
Greenwich
New Cross Gate
New Cross
Deptford Bridge
Elverson Road
Lewisham

○ Interchange stations
⇌ Connections with National Rail
⚓ Connections with riverboat services
🚋 Connection with Tramlink
✈ Airport interchange   ★ Closed Sundays
▲ Served by Piccadilly line trains early morning and late evening
† For opening times see poster journey planners.
Certain stations are closed on public holidays.

ℹ 24 hour London Travel Information
020 7222 1234

Textphone
020 7918 3015

www.tfl.gov.uk
www.tflwap.gov.uk/

LTM FA(a) 04.03

UNDERGROUND

Reg. user No. 03/4010

Rick Steves'
GREAT
BRITAIN
2004

AVALON
TRAVEL

For a complete list of Rick Steves' guidebooks, see page 12.

Thanks to my wife, Anne, for making home my favorite travel destination. Thanks also to Roy and Jodi Nicholls for their research help, to our readers for their input, and to local friends listed in this book who put the "Great" in Britain.

Avalon Travel Publishing
1400 65th Street, Suite 250
Emeryville, CA 94608
Avalon Travel Publishing is a division of Avalon Publishing Group.

Printed in the USA by Worzalla. First printing January 2004.

ISSN 1090-6843
ISBN 1-56691-527-9

For the latest on Rick's lectures, guidebooks, tours, and public television series, contact Europe Through the Back Door, Box 2009, Edmonds, WA 98020, 425/771-8303, fax 425/771-0833, www.ricksteves.com, rick@ricksteves.com.

Europe Through the Back Door Managing Editor: Risa Laib
Europe Through the Back Door Editors: Jill Hodges, Cameron Hewitt
Avalon Travel Publishing Series Manager & Editor: Laura Mazer
Avalon Travel Publishing Project Editor: Patrick Collins
Research Assistance: Jill Hodges
Copy Editor: Matthew Reed Baker
Production and Layout: PDBD
Interior Design: Jane Musser, Laura Mazer, Amber Pirker
Cover Design: Kari Gim, Laura Mazer
Maps and Graphics: David C. Hoerlein, Rhonda Pelikan, Zoey Platt, Mike Morgenfeld
Front matter color photos: p. i, Village of Stanton, © Nik Wheeler; p. viii, Bagpipe player in Loch Ness, © Randy Wells
Front Cover Photos: Front image: Wales, © Royalty-Free/CORBIS; Back image: Hampton Court Palace, © Royalty-Free/CORBIS
Avalon Travel Graphics Coordinator: Susan Snyder

CONTENTS

Top Destinations in Great Britain

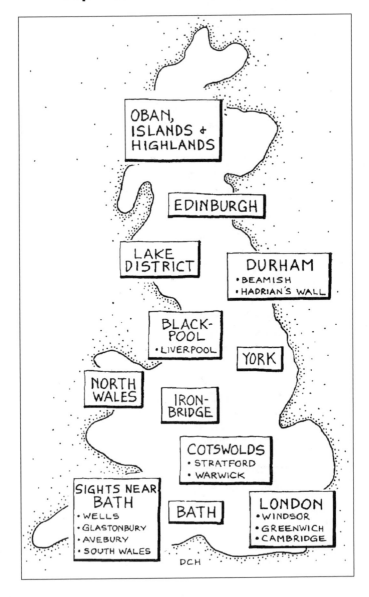

INTRODUCTION

This book breaks Britain into its top big-city, small-town, and rural destinations. It gives you all the information and opinions necessary to wring the maximum value out of your limited time and money in each of these destinations. If you plan a month or less for Britain and have a normal appetite for information, this lean and mean little book is all you need. If you're a travel-info fiend, this book sorts through all the superlatives and provides a handy rack upon which to hang your supplemental information.

Experiencing British culture, people, and natural wonders economically and hassle-free has been my goal for more than 25 years of traveling, tour guiding, and travel writing. With this new edition I pass on to you the lessons I've learned, updated for your trip in 2004. Note that Northern Ireland—part of the United Kingdom—is covered in my book *Rick Steves' Ireland*.

Rick Steves' Great Britain is a personal tour guide in your pocket. The places I cover are balanced to include a comfortable mix of exciting big cities and great-to-be-alive-in small towns. While including the predictable biggies (such as Big Ben, Stratford-upon-Avon, and Stonehenge), the book also mixes in a healthy dose of Back Door intimacy (windswept Roman lookouts, angelic boys' choirs, and nearly edible Cotswold villages). I've been selective. On a short trip, visiting both Oxford and Cambridge is redundant; I cover just the best (Cambridge). There are plenty of great countryside palaces; again, I recommend just the best (Blenheim).

The best is, of course, only my opinion. But after more than two busy decades of researching Europe, I've developed a sixth sense for what travelers enjoy. The places featured in this book will knock your spots off.

This Information Is Accurate and Up-to-Date

Most publishers of guidebooks that cover a country from top to bottom can afford an update only every two or three years. Since this book is selective, covering only the top month of sightseeing, I'm able to update it each year. Even with annual updates, prices and key information change. Travel with the current edition of this book; I guarantee it's the most up-to-date information available (for the latest, see www.ricksteves .com/update). Also at our Web site, check our Graffiti Wall (select "Rick Steves' guidebooks," then "Great Britain" or "London") for a huge, valuable list of reports and experiences—good and bad—from fellow travelers. If you're packing an old book, you'll learn the seriousness of your mistake...in Britain. Your trip costs about $10 per waking hour. Your time is valuable. This guidebook saves you lots of time.

Planning Your Trip

This book is organized by destinations, each one a mini-vacation on its own, filled with exciting sights and homey, affordable places to stay. In each chapter, you'll find the following:

Planning Your Time, a suggested schedule with thoughts on how to best use your limited time.

Orientation, including tourist information, city transportation, and an easy-to-read map designed to make the text clear and your arrival smooth.

Sights, with ratings: ▲▲▲—Don't miss; ▲▲—Try hard to see; ▲—Worthwhile if you can make it; No rating—Worth knowing about.

Sleeping and Eating, with addresses and phone numbers of my favorite good-value hotels and restaurants.

Transportation Connections to nearby destinations by train or bus and route tips for drivers.

The **appendix** is a traveler's tool kit, with information on history, architecture, TV, climate, telephoning, and a British-Yankee vocabulary list.

Browse through this book, choose your favorite destinations, and link them up. Then have a great trip! You'll travel like a temporary local, getting the absolute most out of every mile, minute, and dollar. You won't waste time on mediocre sights, because, unlike others, this guidebook covers only the best. Since your major financial pitfall is lousy, expensive hotels, I've worked hard to assemble the top accommodation values for each stop. And as you travel the route I know and love, I'm happy you'll be meeting some of my favorite British people.

Trip Costs

Five components make up your trip costs: airfare, surface transportation, room and board, sightseeing/entertainment, and shopping/miscellany.

Airfare: Don't try to sort through the mess. Find a good travel agent. A round-trip U.S.A.-to-London flight costs $350 to $1,000 (even cheaper in winter), depending on where you fly from and when. Consider saving time and money by flying "open-jaw" (into one city and out of another; for instance, into London and out of Edinburgh).

Surface Transportation: For a three-week whirlwind trip of all my recommended British destinations, allow $500 per person for public transportation (train pass and key buses) or for car rental (based on two people sharing a three-week rental), including gas and insurance. Car rental is cheapest if arranged from the United States. Train passes are normally available only outside of Europe. You may save money by simply buying tickets as you go (see "Transportation" section below).

Room and Board: You can thrive in Britain on $70 per day per person for room and board (allow $90 per day for London). A $70-per-day budget allows $10 for lunch, $15 for dinner, and $45 for lodging (based on two people splitting a $90 double room that includes break-fast). That's doable, particularly outside London. Students and tight-wads can do it on $40 ($20 for a bed, $20 per day for meals and snacks). But budget sleeping and eating require the skills and information covered below (and in greater detail in my book, *Rick Steves' Europe Through the Back Door*).

Sightseeing and Entertainment: In big cities, figure $5 to $15 per major sight (Westminster Abbey-$10, Edinburgh Castle-$13.50), $3 for minor ones (climbing church towers), $10 for guided walks, and $25 for bus tours and splurge experiences (Welsh and Scottish folk evenings). An overall average of $15 a day works for most. Don't skimp here. After all, this category directly powers most of the experiences all the other expenses are designed to make possible.

You will be tempted to buy the British Heritage Pass, which gets you into more than 500 British Heritage and National Trust properties: £22/$35 for 4 days, £35/$54 for 7 days, £46/$75 for 15 days, £60/$102 for 30 days (sold at Heathrow Airport TI and the Britain Visitors Centre on Regent Street in London; if you're bringing children, don't buy passes for them, since kids get in free or cheap at most sights).

Of the 600 sights included or discounted (a list comes with the pass, www.visitbritain.com/world/heritagepass), here are the sights I describe and recommend for a three-week tour of Britain, along with their adult admission prices. A typical sightseer with three weeks will probably pay to see nearly all of these: Tower of London-£13.50 (with pass, price drops to £6.75); Shakespeare's Birthplace-£6.50 (Stratford); Anne Hathaway's Cottage-£5 (Stratford); Warwick Castle-£13.50 (near Stratford); Blenheim Palace-£11.50 (near the Cotswolds and Oxford); Roman and Medieval Baths-£8.50 (Bath); Stonehenge-£5 (near Bath); Caerphilly Castle-£3 and Tintern Abbey-£2.50 (South Wales); Caernarfon Castle-£4.50 (North Wales); Wordsworth's Dove Cottage-£5.80 (Lake District); Housesteads Roman Fort-£3.10 (Hadrian's

Wall); Edinburgh Castle-£8.50, Georgian House-£5, Gladstone's Land-£3.50, and Holyrood Palace-£7.50 (Edinburgh); Culloden Battlefield-£5 (near Inverness); and Urquhart Castle-£5.10 (near Loch Ness). This totals £117; a pass takes the pain out of all these admissions with one big pill. People traveling by car—easily able to get to the more remote sights—are more likely to get their money's worth out of the pass if traveling in peak season (Easter–Oct). The British Heritage Pass is a lesser value off-season (Nov–Easter) when many of the smaller, out-of-the-way sights are closed.

Garden-and-estate enthusiasts might consider a one-year National Trust membership, which gains you access to over 300 historic houses and 200 gardens throughout Britain (£34/yr, www.nationaltrust.org.uk).

Shopping and Miscellany: Figure $1 per postcard, tea, or ice-cream cone and $4 per beer. Shopping can vary in cost from nearly nothing to a small fortune. Good budget travelers find that this category has little to do with assembling a trip full of lifelong and wonderful memories.

Exchange Rates

I list prices in pounds (£) throughout this book.

One British pound (£1) = about $1.60

While the euro is now the currency of most of Europe, Britain is sticking with its pound sterling. The British pound (£), also called a "quid," is broken into 100 pence (p). Pence means "cents." You'll find coins ranging from 1p to £2 and bills from £5 to £50. To roughly convert pounds to dollars, add 50 percent to British prices: £6 is about $9 (actually $9.60), £3 is about $4.50, and 80p is about $1.20. Scotland and Northern Ireland issue their own currency in pounds, worth the same as an English pound. English, Scottish, and Northern Ireland's Ulster pounds are technically interchangeable in each region, although Scottish and Ulster pounds are "undesirable" in England. Banks in any of the three regions will convert your Scottish or Ulster pounds into English pounds at no charge. Don't worry about the coins, which are accepted throughout Britain.

Prices and Discounts

The prices in this book, as well as the hours and telephone numbers, are accurate as of mid-2003. The economy is flat and inflation is low, so these prices should be more or less accurate in 2004. But Britain is always changing, and I know you'll understand that this guidebook, like any other, starts to yellow even before it's printed.

While discounts (called "concessions" in Britain) are not listed in this book, nearly all British sights are discounted for seniors (loosely defined as anyone retired or willing to call themselves a "senior"), youths (ages 8–18), students, groups of 10 or more, and families (two full-price parents take kids in for about half price).

Red Tape and Times

You need a passport, but no visa or shots, to travel in Britain.

Hours: In Britain you'll be using the 24-hour clock. After 12:00 noon, keep going—13:00, 14:00, and so on. For anything over 12, subtract 12 and add p.m. (14:00 is 2 p.m.).

Stores: Most shops are open Monday through Saturday from (roughly 10:00–18:00), with a late night on Wednesday or Thursday (until 19:00 or 20:00), depending on the neighborhood. On Sunday, when some stores are closed, street markets are lively with shoppers.

Watt's up? If you're bringing electrical gear, you'll need an adapter plug (sold cheap at travel stores like ours, www.ricksteves.com). Britain's plugs have three square-shaped prongs (not the two round prongs used by continental Europe). You may also need a converter to deal with the increased voltage. Travel appliances often have convenient, built-in converters; look for a voltage switch marked 120V (U.S.) and 240V (Europe). If your gear doesn't have a built-in converter, you'll pay around $20 to get an external one.

VAT Refunds and Customs Regulations

VAT Refunds for Shoppers: Wrapped into the purchase price of your British souvenirs is a Value Added Tax (VAT) that's generally about 15 percent. If you make a purchase of more than £30 at a store that participates in the VAT refund scheme, you're entitled to get most of that tax back. Personally I've never felt that VAT refunds are worth the hassle, but if you do, here's the scoop.

If you're lucky, the merchant will subtract the tax when you make your purchase (this is more likely to occur if the store ships the goods to your home). Otherwise, you'll need to:

Get the paperwork. Have the merchant completely fill out the necessary refund document, called a "Tax-Free Shopping Cheque." You'll have to present your passport at the store.

Have your cheque(s) stamped at your last stop in the European Union by the customs agent who deals with VAT refunds. It's best to keep your purchases in your carry-on for viewing, but if they're too large or dangerous to carry on, then track down the proper customs agent to inspect them before you check your bag. You're not supposed to use your purchased goods before you leave. If you show up at customs wearing your new kilt, officials might look the other way—or deny you a refund.

To collect your refund, you'll need to return your stamped documents to the retailer or its representative. Many merchants work with a service, such as Global Refund or Cashback (also called Vatback), which have offices at major airports, ports, or border crossings. These services, which extract a 4 percent fee, can refund your money immediately in your currency of choice or credit your card (within two billing cycles). If you have to deal directly with the retailer, mail the store your stamped documents and then wait. It could take months.

Customs Regulations: You can take home $800 in souvenirs per person duty-free. The next $1,000 is taxed at a flat 3 percent. After that, you pay the individual item's duty rate. You can also bring in duty-free a liter of alcohol (slightly more than a standard-sized bottle of wine), a carton of cigarettes, and up to 100 cigars. To check customs rules and duty rates, visit www.customs.gov.

Banking

Throughout Britain, cash machines are the way to go. Bring an ATM or debit card (with a PIN code) to withdraw funds from cash machines as you travel, and carry a couple hundred dollars in American cash as a backup. Since fees are charged per exchange and most ATM screens top out at £200, save money by pushing the "other amount" button and asking for a higher amount.

Bring a credit card, handy for booking rooms and theater and transportation tickets over the phone, and necessary for renting a car. For cash advances, you'll find that Barclays, National Westminster, and places displaying an Access or Eurocard sign accept MasterCard. Visa is accepted at Barclays and Midland banks. In general, Visa and MasterCard are far more widely accepted than American Express.

Traveler's checks work fine in Britain, but banks commonly charge a commission fee of £2 to £4, or even more.

Even in jolly olde England, you should use a money belt (for our free newsletter/catalog, call 425/771-8303 or visit www.ricksteves.com). Thieves target tourists. A money belt provides peace of mind. You can carry lots of cash safely in a money belt—and, given the high bank fees, you should.

Bank holidays bring most businesses to a grinding halt on Good Friday, Easter Monday, the first and last Monday in May, the last Monday in August, Christmas, December 26, and New Year's Day.

When to Go

July and August are peak season—my favorite time—with very long days, the best weather, and the busiest schedule of tourist fun. Prices and crowds don't go up as dramatically in Britain as they do in much of Europe. Still, travel during "shoulder season" (May, early June, Sept, and early Oct) is easier and a bit less expensive. Shoulder-season travelers get minimal crowds, decent weather, the full range of sights and tourist fun spots, and the joy of being able to just grab a room almost whenever and wherever they like—often at a flexible price.

Winter travelers find absolutely no crowds and soft room prices, but shorter sightseeing hours and fewer activities. Some attractions are open only on weekends or are closed entirely in the winter (Nov–Feb). Confirm your sightseeing plans locally, especially when traveling outside of peak season. The weather can be cold and dreary, and nightfall draws the shades on sightseeing well before dinnertime. While England's rural charm falls with the leaves, city sightseeing is fine in the winter.

Plan for rain no matter when you go. Just keep going and take full advantage of "bright spells." Conditions can change several times in a day, but rarely is the weather extreme. Daily averages throughout the year range between 42 and 70 degrees Fahrenheit. Temperatures below 32 or over 80 degrees are cause for headlines (see the climate chart in the appendix). July and August are not much better than shoulder months. May and June can be lovely. While sunshine may be rare, summer days are very long. The summer sun is up from 6:30 until 22:30. It's not uncommon to have a gray day, eat dinner, and enjoy hours of sunshine afterward.

Sightseeing Priorities

Depending on the length of your trip, here are my recommended priorities:

3 days:	London
5 days, add:	Bath, Cotswolds, Blenheim
7 days, add:	York
9 days, add:	Edinburgh
11 days, add:	Stratford, Warwick, Cambridge
14 days, add:	North Wales, Wells/Glastonbury/Avebury
17 days, add:	Lake District, Hadrian's Wall, Durham
21 days, add:	Ironbridge Gorge, Blackpool, Scottish Highlands
24 days, add:	South Wales

(The Whirlwind Tour map and three-week itinerary on pages 8 and 9 include everything in the above 24 days.)

Itinerary Tips

Most people fly into London and remain there for a few days. Instead, consider a gentler small-town start in Bath, and visit London at the end of your trip. You'll be more rested and ready to tackle Britain's greatest city. Heathrow Airport has direct connections to Bath and other cities.

To give yourself a little rootedness, minimize one-night stands. It's worth a long drive after dinner to be settled into a town for two nights. B&Bs are also more likely to give a good price to someone staying more than one night.

Many people save a couple of days and a lot of miles by going directly from the Lake District to Edinburgh and skipping the long joyride through Scotland. If it's Celtic Britain you're after, visit Wales rather than Scotland.

Whirlwind Three-Week Tour of Great Britain

BEST THREE-WEEK TRIP IN BRITAIN BY CAR

Day	Plan	Sleep in
1	Arrive in London, bus to Bath	Bath
2	Bath	Bath
3	Pick up car, Avebury, Wells, Glastonbury	Bath
4	South Wales, St. Fagans, Tintern	Chipping Campden
5	Explore the Cotswolds, Blenheim	Chipping Campden
6	Stratford, Warwick, Coventry	Ironbridge Gorge
7	Ironbridge Gorge, Ruthin banquet	Ruthin (if banquet) or Conwy
8	Highlights of North Wales	Ruthin or Conwy
9	Liverpool, Blackpool	Blackpool
10	Southern Lake District	Keswick area
11	Northern Lake District	Keswick area
12	Drive up west coast of Scotland	Oban
13	Highlands, Loch Ness, Scenic Highlands Drive	Edinburgh
14	More Highlands or Edinburgh	Edinburgh
15	Edinburgh	Edinburgh
16	Hadrian's Wall, Beamish, Durham evensong	Durham
17	North York Moors, York, turn in car	York
18	York	York
19	Early train to London	London
20	London	London
21	London	London
22	Side trip to Cambridge or Greenwich, London	Whew!

While this three-week itinerary is designed to be done by car, it can be done by train and bus or, better yet, with a rail 'n' drive pass (best car days: Cotswolds, North Wales, Lake District, Scottish Highlands, Hadrian's Wall). For three weeks without a car, I'd probably cut back on the recommended sights with the most frustrating public transportation (South and North Wales, Ironbridge Gorge, the Highlands). Lacing together the cities by train is very slick. With more time, everything is workable without a car.

Travel Smart

Your trip is like a complex play—easier to follow and to really appreciate on a second viewing. While no one does the same trip twice to gain that advantage, reading this book in its entirety before your trip accomplishes much the same thing.

Reread entire chapters as you travel, and visit local tourist information offices. Upon arrival in a new town, lay the groundwork for a smooth departure. Buy a phone card and use it for reservations and confirmations. You speak the language—use it! Enjoy the friendliness of the local people. Ask questions. Most locals are eager to point you in their idea of the right direction. Those who expect to travel smart, do. Bring along a pocket-size notebook to organize your thoughts. Plan ahead for banking, laundry, post office chores, and picnics. Mix intense and relaxed periods. Every trip (and every traveler) needs at least a few slack days. Pace yourself. Assume you will return.

As you read this book, make note of festivals, colorful market days, and days when sights are closed. Sundays have pros and cons, as they do for travelers in the United States (special events, limited hours, closed shops and banks, limited public transportation, no rush hours). Saturdays are virtually weekdays. Popular places are even more popular on weekends—especially sunny weekends, which are sufficient cause for an impromptu holiday in this soggy corner of Europe.

Consider making the travel arrangements and reservations listed below before your trip or within a few days of arrival.

Before You Go

• Reserve a room for your first night.
• If you'll be traveling in late June, July, or August and want to sleep in my lead listings, book your B&Bs as soon as you're ready to commit to a date.
• Confirm car rental and pick-up plans with your rental agency (picking up a car on Saturday afternoon or Sunday may be difficult).
• If you'll be attending the Edinburgh Festival (August 15–Sept 4 in 2004), you can book tickets in advance (from mid-April on) by calling the festival office at 0131/473-2000 or ordering online (www.eif.co.uk). And while you're at it, book your Edinburgh room.
• If you want to attend the pageantry-filled Ceremony of the Keys at the Tower of London, write for tickets (see details in the London chapter, under "Sights—East London").

Within a Day or Two of Arrival

• If you'll be in London the last night of your trip, reserve a room and book tickets for a London play or concert. You can book a play from home (see details in the London chapter, under "Entertainment and Theater"), but for simplicity, I book plays while in London.

• If the Royal Shakespeare Company will be performing at the Stratford theater when you're in or near Stratford, consider reserving a ticket (tel. 01789/403-403, www.rsc.org.uk).

Tourist Information

Virtually every town in Britain has a tourist information center (abbreviated "TI" in this book). Take full advantage of this service. Arrive (or telephone) with a list of questions and a proposed sightseeing plan. Pick up maps, brochures, and walking-tour information. In London, you can pick up everything you'll need for Britain in one stop at the Britain and London Visitors Centre.

While TIs can be good resources, remember that they are money-making enterprises. Each year they become more of a shop and ticket-and-advertising agency than a true information service. If a hotel or activity doesn't pay its dues and follow tourist-board dictates, it disappears from their material. This is a particular problem with room-finding services offered by TIs. Getting a room through the TI can be handy in a jam, but it comes with bloated prices and fees—and the TI takes a cut from your host. Many of my best listings are blacklisted by the tourist boards for their independence. Skip the TI's room-finding services and call direct.

Britain's national tourist office—**Visit Britain**—in the United States has a wealth of information (551 Fifth Avenue, 7th floor, New York, NY 10176, 800/462-2748, www.visitbritain.com, travelinfo @visitbritain.org). Before your trip, request any information you may want, such as city maps and schedules of upcoming festivals. Ask for the Britain Vacation Planner and free maps of London and Britain. You can get regional information, an updated garden-tour map, an urban cultural activities brochure, and more.

Recommended Guidebooks

You may want some supplemental travel guidebooks, especially if you're traveling beyond my recommended destinations. I know it hurts to spend $25 or $35 on extra books and maps, but when you consider the money they'll save you and the improvements they'll make in your $3,000 vacation, not buying them would be penny-wise and pound-foolish.

While this book offers everything you'll need for the structure of your trip, each place you will visit has plenty of great little guidebooks to fill you in on local history. For cultural and sightseeing background in bigger chunks, Michelin and Cadogan guides to London, England, and Britain are good. The best budget travel guides to Britain are the Lonely Planet and Let's Go guidebooks. Lonely Planet's guidebook is more thorough and informative, but it's not annually updated. Let's Go is annually updated and youth oriented, with good coverage of nightlife, hostels, and cheap transportation deals.

RICK STEVES' GUIDEBOOKS

Country Guides

Rick Steves' Best of Europe
Rick Steves' Best of Eastern Europe
Rick Steves' France
Rick Steves' Germany, Austria & Switzerland
Rick Steves' Great Britain
Rick Steves' Ireland
Rick Steves' Italy
Rick Steves' Scandinavia
Rick Steves' Spain & Portugal

City and Regional Guides

Rick Steves' Amsterdam, Bruges & Brussels
Rick Steves' Florence & Tuscany
Rick Steves' London
Rick Steves' Paris
Rick Steves' Provence & the French Riviera
Rick Steves' Rome
Rick Steves' Venice
Rick Steves' Easy Access Europe
    (with a focus on London, Paris, Bruges, Amsterdam, and
    the Rhine)

(Avalon Travel Publishing)

Rick Steves' Books, Videos, and DVDs

Rick Steves' Europe Through the Back Door 2004 gives you budget travel skills, such as minimizing jet lag, packing light, planning your itinerary, traveling by car or train, finding beds, changing money, avoiding rip-offs, staying healthy, taking great photographs, using mobile phones, and much more. The book also includes chapters on 38 of Rick's favorite "Back Doors," six of which are in Great Britain.

Rick Steves' Country Guides, an annually-updated series that covers Europe, offer you the latest on the top sights and destinations, with tips on how to make your trip efficient and fun. You'll learn the best places to stay, eat, enjoy, and explore.

My **City and Regional Guides,** freshly updated every year, focus on Europe's most compelling destinations. Along with specifics on sights, restaurants, hotels, and nightlife, you'll get self-guided, illustrated tours of the outstanding museums and most characteristic neighborhoods. With the sleek Eurostar train, Paris is just 2.5 hours from London. Consider combining these two exciting cities (and city guides) for a great visit.

New for 2004, *Rick Steves' Easy Access Europe* is written for travelers with limited mobility and covers London, Paris, Bruges, Amsterdam, and the Rhine River.

Rick Steves' Europe 101: History and Art for the Traveler (with Gene Openshaw) gives you the story of Europe's people, history, and art. Written for smart people who were sleeping in their history and art classes before they knew they were going to Europe, *101* really helps Europe's sights come alive. However, this book has far more coverage of the European continent than of Britain.

Rick Steves' Mona Winks (with Gene Openshaw) provides fun, easy-to-follow, self-guided tours of Europe's top 25 museums. All of the *Mona Winks* chapters on London are included in this London guidebook. But if you'd like similar coverage for the great museums in Paris, Amsterdam, Madrid, Venice, Florence, and Rome, *Mona's* for you.

My new public television series, *Rick Steves' Europe,* keeps churning out shows. Of 82 episodes (including the new series and *Travels in Europe with Rick Steves*), two shows are on London and eight are on other parts of Great Britain. These air nationally on public television and the Travel Channel. They are also available in information-packed home videos and DVDs (order online at www.ricksteves.com or call us at 425/771-8303 for our free newsletter/catalog).

Rick Steves' Postcards from Europe, my autobiographical book, packs more than 25 years of travel anecdotes and insights into the ultimate 2,000-mile European adventure. Through his guidebooks, Rick shares his favorite European discoveries with you. *Postcards* introduces you to Rick's favorite European friends.

All of Rick's books are published by Avalon Travel Publishing (www.travelmatters.com).

Maps

The black-and-white maps in this book, designed and drawn by Dave Hoerlein, are concise and simple. Dave, who is well traveled in Britain, has designed the maps to help you locate recommended places and get to the tourist information office, where you'll find more in-depth, cheap (or free) maps. The color maps at the front of the book will help you navigate from town to town.

For even more detail, consider our Rick Steves' Britain Planning Map. Designed for the traveler, it lists sightseeing destinations prominently, with Britain on one side and London on the other (can order online at www.ricksteves.com).

Maps to buy in England: Train travelers can do fine with a simple rail map and city maps from TIs. (Get a free map of London and Britain from Visit Britain before you go; see "Tourist Information," page 11.) If you're driving, get a road atlas (one inch equals three miles) covering all of Britain. Ordnance Survey, AA, and Bartholomew editions are available for about £7 at TIs, gas stations, and bookstores. Drivers, hikers, and bikers may want more detailed maps for the Cotswolds, North Wales, and Lake District (easy to buy locally).

Tours of London and Britain

Travel agents will tell you about all the mainstream tours of London and Britain, but they won't tell you about ours. At Europe Through the Back Door, we organize and lead one-week getaway tours of London (departures Jan–Dec, maximum 24 people). We also offer 17-day tours of Britain featuring just the right mix of thatch-happy villages and big-city thrills. Our Britain tours depart each year from May through September, are limited to 26 people per group, and come with a great guide and a big, roomy bus. For details, call 425/771-8303 or check www.ricksteves.com.

Transportation in Britain

By Car or Train?

Cars are best for three or more traveling together (especially families with small kids), those packing heavy, and those scouring the countryside. Trains and buses are best for solo travelers, blitz tourists, and city-to-city travelers.

Britain has a great train-and-bus system, and travelers who don't want (or can't afford) to drive a rental car can enjoy an excellent tour using public transportation. Britain's 100-mph train system is one of Europe's best. Buses pick you up when the trains let you down.

In Britain, my choice is to connect big cities by train and to explore rural areas (the Cotswolds, North Wales, Lake District, and the Highlands) footloose and fancy-free by rental car. The mix works quite efficiently (e.g., London, Bath, Edinburgh, and York by train with a rental car for the rest). You might consider a BritRail Pass + Drive, which gives you various combinations of rail days and car days to use within a month's time.

Deals on Rails, Wheels, and Wings in Britain

Regular tickets on Britain's great train system (15,000 departures from 2,400 stations daily) are the most expensive per mile in all of Europe. Those who save big are those who go round-trip (leaving after 9:30 in the morning), buy in advance, avoid travel on Fridays, or ride the bus.

Buying Train Tickets in Advance: Either go direct to any station or call and book your ticket with a credit card. To book ahead, call 08457-484-950 (from the U.S., call 011/44/8457-484-950, phone answered 24 hours) to find out the schedule and best fare for your journey; then you'll be referred to the appropriate number to call—depending

SAMPLE TRAIN JOURNEY

Here is a typical example of a personalized train schedule printed out by Britain's train stations. At the Llandudno Junction station in North Wales, I told the clerk I wanted to leave after 16:30 for Moreton-in-Marsh, in the Cotswolds.

Stations	Arrive	Depart	Class
Llandudno Junction	——	16:41	Standard
Crewe	17:56	18:11	Standard
Smethwick	19:20	19:33	Standard
Worcester	20:20	20:58	1st/Standard
Moreton-in-Marsh	21:37	——	

Even though the trip involved three transfers, this schedule allowed me to easily navigate the rails. It's helpful to ask at the information desk (or any conductor) for the final destination of your next train so you'll be able to figure out quickly which platform it's departing from (e.g., upon arrival at Worcester, I looked for "Oxford" on the station's overhead train schedule to determine where to catch my train to Moreton-in-Marsh; often the conductor on your previous train can even tell you the platform your next train will depart from, but it's wise to confirm). Note that on the smaller runs, only standard (second) class is available. If you're exploring Britain's backcountry with a BritRail pass, rather than invest the extra money in first class, buy standard class—because that's how you'll travel.

Lately Britain's train system has experienced a lot of delays, causing more and more travelers to miss their connections. Don't schedule your connections too tightly if you have to be at your destination at a specific time.

on the particular rail company—to book your ticket (or book online at www.thetrainline.com). For schedules, visit http://bahn.hafas.de/english.html (Germany's excellent all-Europe timetable), www.nationalrail.co.uk, or www.pti.org.uk.

Here are a few of the many deals:

Bargain fares offer the greatest savings but must be booked at least seven days in advance and usually apply to journeys of about 250 miles (i.e., London-Edinburgh) or longer (sometimes shorter journeys qualify—ask). If the Bargain Single seats are sold out, use half of a Bargain Return ticket—which usually costs only a pound or two more. **Apex** fares, which must be booked at least seven days in advance, apply to

Railpasses

Prices listed are for 2003. My free *Rick Steves' Guide to European Railpasses* has the latest details. To get the railpass guide or an order form, call us at 425/771-8303 or visit www.ricksteves.com/rail.

BRITRAIL CLASSIC PASS

	Adult first class	Adult standard	Senior (60+) first class	16-25 youth standard
4 consecutive days	$285	$189	$245	$155
8 consecutive days	405	269	345	219
15 consecutive days	609	405	519	285
22 consecutive days	769	515	659	359
1 month	915	609	779	429

"Standard" is the polite British term for "second" class. No senior discounts for standard class. For each adult pass you buy, one child (5-15) travels free with you (ask for the "Family Pass"). Additional kids pay the normal half-adult rate. Kids under 5: free. These rules also apply to the Flexipasses listed below.

BRITRAIL FLEXIPASS

	Adult first class	Adult standard	Senior (60+) first class	16-25 youth standard
4 days in 2 months	$355	$239	$305	$189
8 days in 2 months	519	349	439	245
15 days in 2 months	779	525	669	429

BRITRAIL PASS 'N DRIVE

Any 3 rail days and 2 car days in 2 months.

	1st class	2nd class	extra car day
Mini car	$359	$259	$49
Compact car	369	269	61
Intermediate car	379	279	71

Prices are approximate per person for 2 traveling together. 3rd and 4th person sharing car pay $295 in 1st or $199 in 2nd class. Senior, child, and single adult rates also available. To order Britrail Pass 'N Drive, call your travel agent or Rail Europe at 800/438-7245.

Britain:

The map shows approximate point-to-point one-way 2nd-class fares in $US by rail (solid line) and bus (dashed line). 1st class costs 50% more. Add up fares for your itinerary to see whether a railpass will save you money.

BRITRAIL DAYS OUT OF LONDON

	First class	Standard class
2 out of 8 days	$89	$59
4 out of 8 days	145	109
7 out of 15 days	195	145

Covers trips to much of southeast England including London, Oxford, Cambridge, and Salisbury. Not valid for Bath or Exeter, on service via Reading, on Great Western trains, Heathrow Express, or for discounts on the Chunnel. The pass is valid on the Gatwick and Stansted Express. Kids 5-15 pay $31 (1st class) or $21 (2nd class) flat fare per pass.

FREEDOM OF WALES FLEXIPASS

Any 4 rail days within 8 consecutive bus days	$89
Any 8 rail days within 15 consecutive bus days	$149

Standard class on rail and major bus routes. Children 5-15 $59 or $99.

FREEDOM OF SCOTLAND TRAVELPASS

4 days out of 8 flexi	$139
8 days out of 15 flexi	179

Good on all trains in Scotland, standard class only, and covers Caledonian MacBrayne and Strathclyde ferry service to Scotland's most popular islands, some Citylink buses & more. Kids 5-15 half fare. Children under 5 free. Also available in Scotland.

BRITRAIL PLUS IRELAND PASS

	First class	Standard class
5 days out of 1 month	$479	$359
10 days out of 1 month	755	545

This pass covers the entire British Isles (England, Wales, Scotland, Northern Ireland and the Republic of Ireland) including a round-trip Stena Line ferry crossing between Wales or Scotland and the Emerald Isle during the pass's validity (okay to leave via one port and return via another). Reserve boat crossings a day or so in advance—sooner for holidays. One child (5-15) travels along free with each pass. Extra kiddies pay half fare; under 5 free. For cheaper deals in Ireland see our railpass guide or *Rick Steves' Ireland*.

journeys of about 100 miles (i.e., London-York) or longer. (You can book Apex and Bargain tickets as early as six to eight weeks before your journey; be warned that these first-come, first-served cheap fares go fast in summer, tickets have refund restrictions, and you'll need to pin down specific dates and times for your journeys.)

To save a few pounds without booking so far ahead, buy a **Super Advance** ticket before 18:00 the day before your journey (you must specify the specific dates and times for your outbound and, if applicable, return journeys when you buy the ticket). To save a little less and have even fewer restrictions, consider one of the same-day Saver tickets (you can buy on the day of travel, don't need to specify a date or time, and the return trip is valid for one month from purchase). **Super Saver** tickets require you to leave after 9:30 if you're traveling from London, and avoid traveling on Fridays year-round and on Saturdays in July and August (not available on many heavy-demand commuter trains between big cities). A **Saver** ticket, a bit pricier, is good for any day of the week—but you can't start your trip from London before 9:30 Monday through Friday. If you're traveling from somewhere other than London, the morning rush-hour restriction does not apply for the Saver tickets— however, if you're traveling *to* London, you can qualify for the reduced fares on weekdays only if you arrive at 10:00 or later.

There can be up to 30 different prices for the same journey. All of the above discount fares come with restrictions and are available on a first-come, first-served basis. A clerk at any station (or the helpful folks at tel. 08457-484-950, 24 hours daily) can figure out the cheapest fare for your trip. Savings can be significant. For a London–Edinburgh round-trip (standard class), the regular fare is £90, Super Advance is £64, Apex is £50, and Bargain Return is £36. For a York–London round-trip ticket, the regular fare is £134, Saver is £62 (no Super Saver option exists for this trip), Super Advance is £48, Apex is £36, and Bargain Return is £34.

You can book rail tickets online at www.thetrainline.com, but ordering by phone is more foolproof. If you order online, be sure you know what you want; it's tough to reach a person if you want to change a ticket later. You pick up your ticket at the station (unless your order was lost—this service still has some glitches). If you want your ticket mailed to you in the United States, you need to allow a couple of weeks and cover the shipping costs. Note that BritRail passholders cannot use this Web site to make reservations.

Railpasses: Consider getting a railpass. The BritRail pass comes in "consecutive day" and "flexi" versions, with price breaks for youths, seniors, and second class ("standard" class, available to anyone). Standard class is a good choice since many of the smaller train lines don't even offer first-class cars. BritRail passes cover England, Scotland, and Wales. There are now Scotland or Wales passes, England/Ireland passes, "Days Out of London" passes, and BritRail Pass + Drive passes (which offer you some rail days and some car-rental days). BritRail Classic, Flexi, and Plus Ireland passes, as well as Eurailpasses, get you a discount on the Eurostar train that zips you to continental Europe under the English Channel. These passes are sold outside of Europe only. For specifics, contact your travel agent or Europe Through the Back Door (425/771-8303, www.ricksteves.com).

Senior, Youth, and Family Deals: To get a third off the price of most point-to-point rail tickets, seniors can buy a Senior Railcard (for age 60 and over, www.senior-railcard.co.uk), and young people can buy

Britrail Routes

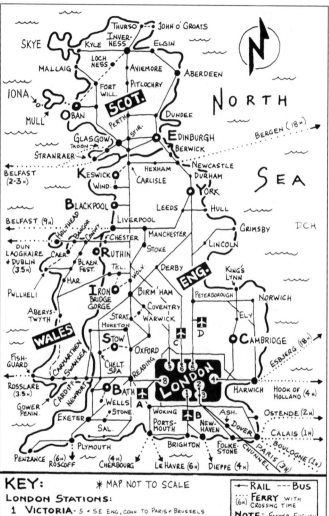

KEY: ✳ MAP NOT TO SCALE

London Stations:

1 **VICTORIA** - S. • S.E. Eng., conn. to Paris & Brussels
2 **CHARING CROSS** - S.E. Eng
3 **WATERLOO** - S. England, Paris & Bruss. (Chunnel)
4 **LIVERPOOL ST.** - East Anglia, Amsterdam
5 **KING'S CROSS** - Midlands, N.E. Eng., E. Scotland
6 **ST. PANCRAS** - E. Midlands
7 **EUSTON** - Midlands, N. Wales, N.W. Eng., W. Scot.
8 **PADDINGTON** - W. Eng, S Wales

━• RAIL ‐‐‐ BUS
⋮⋮ FERRY with **(6H)** CROSSING TIME
NOTE: Faster English Channel crossings with Hovercraft & Hydrofoil on some runs. Check! The Chunnel is faster still...

LONDON AIRPORTS: ✈
A- HEATHROW   B- GATWICK
C- LUTON   D- STANSTED

a Young Persons Railcard (for ages 16–25, or full-time students 26 and over with a valid ISIC card, www.youngpersons-railcard.co.uk). Each card costs £18. A Family Railcard allows adults to travel cheaper (about 33 percent) while their kids age 5 to 15 receive a 60 percent discount for most trips (£20, maximum of four adults and four kids, www .family-railcard.co.uk). Any of these cards are valid for a year on virtually all trains except special runs like the Heathrow Express and Eurostar (fill out application at station, brochures on racks in info center, need to show passport). Youth also need to submit a passport-type photo for the Young Persons Card and have to pay a minimal fare for journeys starting before 10:00 on weekdays.

Buses: Although buses are about 33 percent slower than trains, they're also a lot cheaper. Round-trip bus tickets usually cost less than two one-way fares (e.g., London–York one way costs £21; round trip costs £27.50). And buses go many places that trains don't. Budget travelers can save a wad with a bus pass. The National Express sells Tourist Trail bus passes (over the counter, tel. 0870-580-8080, www.national express.com); passes cost £49 (any 2 days out of 3 consecutive days), £85 (any 5 days within 30), £135 (any 8 days within 30), £190 (any 15 days within 30), and £205 (any 15 days within 60). If you want to take a bus from your last destination to Heathrow or Gatwick airport, ask about the many National Express Flight Link and Jet Link buses. Bus stations are normally at or near train stations (in London, the bus station is a block southwest of Victoria Station). The British distinguish between "buses" (for local runs with lots of stops) and "coaches" (long-distance express runs).

A couple of companies offer **backpacker's bus circuits.** These hop-on, hop-off bus circuits take mostly youth hostelers around the country super cheap and easy with the assumption that they'll be sleeping in the hostels along the way. For instance, **Stray Travel** network does a six-day-or-more tour, making a 1,000-mile circle connecting London, Bath, Stratford, the lakes, Edinburgh, York, Cambridge, and London hostels (£159/6 days, pass good for four months, three buses weekly, driver provides commentary and books passengers' rooms at hostels; also offers loop trips of Ireland and Europe; tel. 020/7373-7737, www.straytravel .com). **Haggis Backpacker** offers a similar deal, with buses circling Scotland (from £80/3 days, £140/6 days; 2-4 buses weekly, ticket good for three months, tel. 0131/557-9393, www.radicaltravel.com, haggis @radicaltravel.com).

Flights: Before buying a ticket for a long train trip, consider a flight offered by one of the discount airlines such as Ryanair (British tel. 0871-246-0000, www.ryanair.com), Virgin Express (British tel. 020/7744-0004, www.virgin-express.com), Easy Jet (British tel. 0870-600-0000, www.easyjet.com), or bmi britishmidland (British tel. 0870-607-0555 or U.S. tel. 800/788-0555, U.S. office sells "Discover Europe

STOP AND LEARN THESE ROAD SIGNS

Speed Limit (km/hr)

Yield

No Passing

End of No Passing Zone

One Way

Intersection

Main Road

Freeway

Danger

No Entry

No Entry for cars

All Vehicles Prohibited

Parking

No Parking

Customs

Peace

Air Pass," www.flybmi.com, also check subsidiary, bmi baby, at www .bmibaby.com). Visit www.cheapflights.co.uk for more.

Returns can be cheaper than one-way. To get the best prices, book in advance, as soon as you have a date set. Each flight has an allotment of cheap seats; these sell fast, leaving the higher-priced seats for latecomers.

Car Rental

To save money, arrange your car rental from the States (either on your own or through your travel agent) rather than in Britain. The best rates are weekly with unlimited mileage or leasing (possible for rentals of over three weeks). You can pick up and drop off just about anywhere, anytime. For a trip covering both Britain and Ireland, you're better off with two separate car rentals. If you pick up the car in a smaller city, such as Bath, you'll more likely survive your first day on the British roads. If you drop the car off early or keep it longer, you'll be credited or charged at a fair, prorated price. Big companies have offices in most cities. (Ask to be picked up at your hotel.) Small local rental companies can be cheaper but aren't as flexible.

The 1.3-liter Ford Escort-category car costs about $50 more per week more than the smallest cars but feels better on the motorways and safer on the small roads. Remember, minibuses are a great budget way to go for five to nine people.

When shopping around, consider Newcomer easyCar.com (a distant relative of the easyInternet café chain), the Southwest Airlines of car rentals. They eliminate the extras (you clean the car and fill it with gas) and offer cheap rates in return. They don't do cancellations or refunds, so this is worth pursuing only if your plans are certain (offices throughout London, in Liverpool and Glasgow, toll tel. 0906-333-3333, 60p/min, www.easycar.com).

For peace of mind when renting a car, spring for the CDW insurance (Collision Damage Waiver, about $15 per day), which gives a zero (or low) deductible rather than the standard value-of-the-car deductible. A few "gold" credit cards cover CDW insurance; quiz your credit-card company on the worst-case scenario.

Driving
Your U.S. license is all you need to drive in Britain. Driving in Britain is basically wonderful—once you remember to stay on the left and after you've mastered the roundabouts. Traffic in roundabouts has the right-of-way; entering traffic yields (look to your right as you merge). It helps to remember that the driver is always in the center of the road. But be warned: Every year I get a few cards from traveling readers advising me that, for them, trying to drive Britain was a nerve-racking and regrettable mistake. If you want to get a little slack on the roads, drop by a gas station or auto shop and buy a green "L" (new driver with license) sign to put in your window (don't get the red "L" sign, which means you're a student driver without a license and thus prohibited from driving on motorways).

A British Automobile Association membership comes with most rentals. Understand its towing and emergency-road-service benefits. Gas (petrol) costs more than $5 per gallon and is self-serve. Green pumps are unleaded. Seat belts are required by law. Speed limits are 30 mph in town, 70 mph on the motorways, and 50 or 60 mph elsewhere. The national sign for 60 mph is a white circle with a black slash. Note that road-surveillance cameras strictly enforce speed limits. Any driver

Britain by Car: Mileage and Time

(including foreigners renting cars) photographed speeding will get a nasty bill in the mail. (Cameras—you'll see the foreboding gray boxes—flash on your rear license plate in order not to invade the privacy of anyone sharing the front seat with someone they shouldn't be with.) Avoid driving in big cities whenever possible. Most have modern ring roads to skirt the congestion. The shortest distance between any two points is usually the motorway. Road signs can be confusing, too few, and too late. Study your map before taking off. Know the cities you'll be lacing together, since road numbers are inconsistent. Miss a motorway exit and you can lose 30 minutes. A Britain road atlas (sold at gas stations and bookstores) is $10 well spent.

Parking is confusing. One yellow line marked on the pavement means no parking Monday through Saturday during work hours. Double yellow lines mean no parking at any time. Broken yellow lines mean short stops are OK, but you should always look for explicit signs or ask a passerby. White lines mean you're free to park.

Even in small towns, rather than fight it, I just pull into the most central and handy "pay and display" car park I can find. Rates are reasonable by U.S. standards. Locals love to share "pay and display" stickers. If you stand by the machine, invariably someone on their way out with time left on their sticker will give it to you. Keep a bag of coins in the ashtray for parking meters.

Set your car up for a fun road trip. Establish a cardboard-box munchies pantry. Buy a rack of liter boxes of juice for the trunk. Buy some Windex and a roll of paper towels for cleaner sightseeing.

Telephones, Mail, and E-mail

Use the telephone routinely. You can make long-distance calls directly, cheaply, and easily, and there's no language barrier. Call ahead to reserve or reconfirm rooms, check opening hours, confirm tour times, and reserve theater tickets.

Public Pay Phones: The British telephone system is great. Easy-to-use public phone booths are everywhere. Phones clearly list which coins they'll take (usually from 10p to £1), and a display shows how your money supply is doing. Only completely unused coins will be returned, so put in biggies with caution. (If money's left over, rather than hanging up, push the "make another call" button.)

British Telecom (BT) used to sell phone cards that could be inserted into the phone to pay for the call, but they have phased these out. Now to avoid the hassle of carrying enough coins, you have the following two options: 1) Use a scratch-off PIN card (these cards work from most phones, including the one in your hotel room—see "International Calling Cards," on the next page), or 2) insert a major credit card and dial away. If you use a credit card to make a call from a BT phone booth, the minimum charge is 50p.

The only tricky public pay phones you'll use are the expensive, Mickey Mouse coin-op ones in bars and B&Bs. Some require money before you dial, while others wait until after you've connected. Many have a button you must push before you begin talking. But all have clear instructions.

Calling Long Distance within Britain: To call long distance, you'll need the correct area code. You'll find area codes listed throughout this book, listed by city on phone-booth walls, or available from directory assistance (dial 192 in Britain). To make a call, first dial the area code (which starts with zero), then dial the local number. Note that phone numbers and area codes rarely have a standard number of digits.

It's most expensive to call from 8:00 to 13:00 and cheapest from 17:00 to 8:00. Still, a short call across the country is inexpensive; don't hesitate to call long distance. Remember that Northern Ireland is part of Britain and just a long-distance call away (simply dial the area code and the local number).

Making International Calls: For a listing of **international access codes and country codes,** see the appendix. Britain's time is five/eight hours ahead of the east/west coasts of the United States.

When making an international call to Britain, first dial the international access code of the country you're in (011 from the United States or Canada, 00 if you're calling from Europe), then Britain's country code (44), then the area code (without its initial zero) and the local number. For example, London's area code is 020. To call one of our listed London B&Bs from the States, dial 011 (U.S. international access code), 44 (Britain's country code), 20 (London's area code without its initial zero), then 7730-8191 (the B&B's number).

To call my office from Britain, I dial 00 (Britain's international access code), 1 (U.S. country code), 425 (Edmonds' area code), then 771-8303.

International Calling Cards: The easiest, cheapest way to make international calls from Britain (under 10 cents a minute to the States) is with an international calling card. There are many different brands, so just ask for an "international calling card" (sold for £5, £10, and £20 at most newsstands, exchange bureaus, and mini-marts; Unity has a reputation for having some of the cheapest per-minute rates). Because cards are occasionally duds, avoid the high denominations.

Since you don't insert international calling cards into the phone, you can use them from any phone, even from your hotel room. Just follow the instructions on the card: dial an access number, listen to the prompts, dial your PIN code, and the number you want to call. Be aware that if you use one of the calling cards at a BT phone booth, you'll typically pay a hefty surcharge (18–25p/min).

If you're using an international calling card to make a long-distance call within Britain, you need to dial the area code even if you're calling across the street. To make numerous calls with an international calling card without having to redial the long access number each time, press the keys (see instructions on card) that allow you to launch directly into your next call.

Phone cards work only within the country of purchase (e.g., one bought in Britain won't work in France).

Calling Cards from American Companies: Calling cards offered by AT&T, MCI, and Sprint used to be a good value until direct-dialing rates dropped and international calling cards appeared. It's much cheaper to dial direct by using coins or any international calling card.

Mobile Phones: Many travelers now buy cheap mobile phones in Europe to make both local and international calls. (Typical American mobile phones don't work in Europe, and those that do work have horrendous per-minute costs.) For about $75 you can get a phone with $20 worth of calls that will work in the country where you purchased it. (You can buy more time at newsstands or mobile-phone shops.) For about $100 you can get a phone that will work in most countries once you pick up the necessary chip per country (about $25). If you're interested, stop by any European shop that sells mobile phones; you'll see prominent store window displays. Depending on your trip and budget, ask for a phone that works only in that country or one that can be used throughout Europe.

The latest trend among small hotels is loaner mobile phones (free, but you pay the 50 cents a minute usage, which is easy to track). Ask your hotel about this if you'd like to be connected.

If you're on a tight budget, skip mobile phones and buy cheap international calling cards instead.

Mail: You can get stamps at the neighborhood post office, at newsstands within fancy hotels, and at some mini-marts and card shops (if you purchase postcards at the store). To arrange for mail delivery, reserve a few hotels along your route in advance and give their addresses to friends, or use American Express mail services (free to AmEx cardholders and for a minimal fee to others). Allow 10 days for a letter to arrive. Phoning is so easy that I've dispensed with mail stops altogether.

E-mail: E-mail is getting more common among hoteliers and Internet access points are available in most cities. Many libraries offer free access, but they also tend to have limited opening hours. Look for the places listed in this book, or ask the local TI, computer store, or your B&B host. Some hotels have a dedicated computer for guests' e-mail needs. Small places are accustomed to letting guests (who've asked politely) sit at their desk for a few minutes just to check their e-mail.

Sleeping

In the interest of smart use of your time, I favor accommodations (and restaurants) handy to your sightseeing activities. Rather than list hotels scattered throughout a city, I choose two or three favorite neighbor-

SLEEP CODE

To help you easily sort through the accomodations listed, I've divided the rooms into three categories based on the price for a standard double room with bath.

$$$	**Higher Priced**
$$	**Moderately Priced**
$	**Lower Priced**

To give maximum information with a minimum of space, I use this code to describe accommodations listed in this book. Prices are listed per room, not per person. Breakfast is included.

S = Single room, or price for one person in a double.

D = Double or twin room. (I specify double- and twin-bed rooms only if they are priced differently, or if a place has only one or the other. When reserving, you should specify.)

T = Three-person room (often a double bed with a single).

Q = Four-person room (adding an extra child's bed to a triple is usually cheaper).

b = Private bathroom with toilet and shower or tub.

s = Private shower or tub only. (The toilet is down the hall.)

no CC = Does not accept credit cards; pay in local cash.

Non-smoking—With this edition, about 80 percent of my recommended B&Bs prohibit smoking. While some places allow smoking in the sleeping rooms, breakfast rooms are nearly always smoke free.

Family deal—Indicates that parents with young children can easily get a room with an extra child's bed or a discount for larger rooms. Call to negotiate the price. Teenage kids are generally charged as adults. Little kids sleep almost free.

According to this code, a couple staying at a "Db-£60" hotel would pay a total of £60 (about $95) per night for a room with a private toilet and shower (or tub). The hotel accepts credit cards or cash. You can assume credit cards are accepted unless otherwise noted.

hoods and recommend the best accommodations values in each, from $15 bunk beds to fancy-for-my-book $200 doubles. Outside of London you can expect to find good doubles for $60 to $100, including cooked breakfasts and tax.

I've described my recommended hotels and B&Bs with a standard code. Prices listed are for one-night stays in peak season, include a hearty breakfast (unless otherwise noted), and assume you're booking direct and not through a TI. Prices can soften off-season, for stays of two nights or longer, or for payment in cash (rather than credit card). Particularly at nicer hotels, ask about deals (usually offered for two-night stays, sometimes mid-week or weekends, often called Leisure Breaks); the room price doesn't drop dramatically, but the pricey breakfasts are usually included. Booking a big hotel in advance usually gets you the highest-priced "rack rate." Calling the same day often gets you a deeply discounted rate.

When establishing prices with a hotelier or B&B owner, confirm if the charge is per person or per room (if a price is too good to be true, it's probably per person). Because many places in Britain charge per person, small groups often pay the same for a single and a double as they would for a triple. Note: In this book, room prices are listed per room, not per person.

Most places I list have three floors of rooms, steep stairs, and no elevator. If you're concerned about stairs, call and ask about ground-floor rooms.

Virtually all rooms have sinks. Rooms with a private bathroom (toilet plus shower and/or tub) are called "en suite"; rooms that lack private plumbing are "standard." As more rooms go en suite, the hallway bathroom is shared with fewer standard rooms. If money's tight, ask for standard rooms.

Britain has a rating system for hotels and B&Bs. These diamonds and stars are supposed to imply quality, but I find that they mean only that the place sporting these symbols is paying dues to the tourist board. Rating systems often have little to do with value.

For listings of more accommodations, particularly if you travel beyond my recommended destinations, visit www.smoothhound.co.uk, which offers a range of accommodations for towns throughout Britain and Northern Ireland (searchable by town, airport, hotel name, or price range).

Bed-and-Breakfasts (B&Bs)

Compared to hotels, bed-and-breakfast places give you double the cultural intimacy for half the price. In 2004, you'll pay £20 to £35 (about $30–55) per person for a B&B. Prices include a big cooked breakfast. The amounts of coziness, tea, and biscuits that are tossed in varies tremendously.

If you have a reasonable but limited budget, skip hotels. Go the B&B way. If you can use a telephone and speak English, you'll enjoy homey, friendly, clean rooms at a great price by sticking to my listings. Always call first.

If you're traveling beyond my recommended destinations, you'll find B&Bs where you need them. Any town with tourists has a TI that books rooms or can give you a list and point you in the right direction. In the absence of a TI, ask people on the street for help.

"Twin" means two single beds, and "double" means one double bed. If you'll take either one, let them know or you might be needlessly turned away. "Standard" rooms come with just a sink (many better places have standard rooms that they don't even advertise). If you want a room that contains a private bathroom, specify "en suite"; B&B owners sometimes use the term "private bathroom" for a bathroom down the hall that only your room has the key for.

B&Bs range from large guest houses with 15 to 20 rooms to small homes renting out a spare bedroom. The philosophy of the management determines the character of a place more than its size and facilities offered. Avoid places run as a business by absentee owners. My top listings are run by people who enjoy welcoming the world to their breakfast table.

The B&Bs I've recommended are nearly all stocking-feet comfortable and "homely," as they say in England. I look for a place that has friendly hosts (i.e., they enjoy Americans); a location in a central, safe, quiet neighborhood; clean rooms, with firm beds; a good value; and no mention in other guidebooks (and therefore it's filled mostly by English travelers). In certain cases, my recommendations don't meet all of these prerequisites. I'm more impressed by a handy location and a fun-loving philosophy than hair driers and shoe-shine machines.

A few tips: B&B proprietors are selective as to whom they invite in for the night. At some B&Bs, children are not welcome. Risky-looking people (two or more single men are often assumed to be troublemakers) find many places suddenly full. If you'll be staying for more than one night you are a "desirable." Sometimes staying several nights earns you a better price—ask about it. If you book through a TI, it takes a 10 percent commission and may charge you an extra pound or two. If you book direct, the B&B gets it all (and you'll have a better chance of getting a discount). I have negotiated special prices with this book (often for cash). You should find prices quoted here to be good through 2004 (except for major holidays and festivals). In popular weekend-getaway spots, you're unlikely to find a place to take you for Saturday night only. If my listings are full, ask for guidance. (Mentioning this book can help.) Owners usually work together and can call up an ally to land you a bed.

B&Bs are not hotels: If you want to ruin your relationship with your hostess, treat her like a hotel clerk. Americans often assume they'll get new towels each day. The British don't, and neither will you. Hang them up to dry and reuse.

B&Bs have plenty of stairs. Expect good exercise and be happy you packed light. Some B&Bs stock rooms with a hot-water pot, cups, tea bags, and coffee packets (if you prefer decaf, buy a jar at a grocery, and dump into a baggie for easy packing). Electrical outlets sometimes come with switches on the outlet to turn the current on or off; if your electrical appliance isn't working, flip the switch.

In B&Bs, no two showers are alike. Sometimes you'll encounter "telephone" showers—a handheld nozzle in a bathtub. Many B&Bs have been retrofitted with plumbing, and water is heated individually for each shower rather than by one central heating system. While the switch is generally left on, in some rooms you'll have a hot-water switch to consider. Any cord hanging from the ceiling is for lights or fans (not emergencies). Once in the shower, you'll find a multitude of overly clever mechanisms designed to somehow get the right amount and temperature of water. Good luck.

Cheap, Modern Hotels

Hotel chains, offering predictably comfortable accommodations at reasonable prices, are popping up in the center of big cities in Britain. The biggies are Travelodge (reservations tel. 0870-085-0950, also has freeway locations for tired drivers, www.travelodge.co.uk), Travel Inn (reservations tel. 0870-242-8000, www.travelinn.co.uk), and Premier Lodge (their older ones are a little scruffy but OK, reservations tel. 0870-201-0203, www.premierlodge.co.uk). The Irish chain Jurys Inn also has some hotels in Britain (reserve at Irish tel. 01/607-0000 or U.S. tel. 800/423-6953, call their hotels directly, or book online at www.jurys.com).

These super-convenient hotels are ideal for families, offering simple, clean, and modern rooms for up to four people (2 adults/2 children) for £50 to £90, depending on the location. Note that couples or families (up to 4) pay the same price for a room. Most rooms have a double bed, single bed, five-foot trundle bed, private shower, WC, and TV. Hotels usually have an attached restaurant, good security, and a 24-hour staffed reception desk. Of course they are as cozy as a Motel 6, but many travelers love them. You can book over the phone (or online) with a credit card, then pay when you check in. When you check out, just drop off the key, Lee.

Couples could also consider Holiday Inn Express, spreading throughout Britain. These are like a Holiday Inn Lite, with cheaper prices and no restaurant. Many of their hotels allow only two per room, but some take up to four (doubles cost about £60–100, make sure Express is part of the name or you'll pay more for a regular Holiday Inn, reservations tel. 0800-897-121, www.hiexpress.co.uk).

Making Reservations

It's possible to travel at any time of year without reservations, but given the high stakes, erratic accommodations values, number of people traveling with this book, and the quality of the gems I've listed, I highly recommend calling ahead for rooms at least a few days in advance as you travel.

When tourist crowds are down and you're traveling without reservations, you might make a habit of calling your hotel between 9:00 and 10:00 on the day you plan to arrive, when the hotel knows who'll be checking out and just which rooms will be available. I've taken great pains to list telephone numbers with long-distance instructions (see "Telephones, Mail, and E-mail" above; also see the appendix). Get a phone card and use it to confirm and reconfirm as you travel. A hotel receptionist will trust you and hold a room until 16:00 without a deposit, though some will ask for a credit-card number.

Honor your reservations or cancel by phone: Trusting travelers to show up is a huge, stressful issue and a financial risk for small B&B owners. I promised the owners of the places I list that you will be reliable when you make a telephone reservation; please don't let them (or me) down. If you'll be delayed or won't make it, simply call in. Americans are notorious for reserving B&Bs long in advance and never showing up (causing B&B owners to lose money—and respect for Americans). Being late is no problem if you are in telephone contact. Long-distance calls are cheap and easy from public phone booths.

Note that B&B owners will likely ask you the approximate time you'll arrive. Unlike hotels, most B&Bs don't have staff available to receive guests when they're out, so it helps them plan their days if they know when you're likely to show up.

While it's generally easy to find a room, a few national holidays jam things up (especially bank holiday Mondays) and merit your making reservations long in advance. Mark these dates in red on your travel calendar for 2004: Good Friday through Easter Monday (April 9–12 in 2004), the first and last Monday in May (May 4 and 31), the last Monday in August (Aug 30), Christmas, December 26, and New Year's Day. Monday bank holidays are preceded by busy weekends; book the entire weekend in advance.

If you know exactly which dates you need and really want a particular place, reserve a room before you leave home. To reserve from home, contact the hotel by e-mail, phone, or fax. To e-mail or fax, use the form in the appendix (online at www.ricksteves.com/reservation). A two-night stay in August would be "two nights, 16/8/04 to 18/8/04"— Europeans write the date day/month/year, and hotel jargon uses your day of departure. You'll often be asked for one night's deposit. Your credit-card number and expiration date will usually be accepted as a deposit, though you may need to send a signed traveler's check or a bank draft in the local currency. If your credit card is the deposit, you can pay with your card or cash when you settle up the bill. If you don't show up (or if you cancel with short notice), you'll be billed for one night.

Hotels in larger cities sometimes have strict cancellation policies (you might lose, say, a deposit if you cancel within two weeks of your reserved stay, or you might be billed for the entire visit if you leave early);

ask about cancellation policies before you book.

On the road, reconfirm your reservations a day or two in advance for safety (or you may be bumped—really). Also, don't just assume you can extend. Take the time to consider in advance how long you'll stay.

Hostels

If you're traveling alone, hosteling is the best way to conquer hotel loneliness. Hostels are also a tremendous source of local and budget travel information. You'll pay an average of £11.50 for a bed and £3 for breakfast. Anyone of any age can hostel in Britain. While there are no membership concerns for private hostels, IYHF hostels require membership. Those without cards simply buy one-night guest memberships for £1.50.

Britain has hundreds of hostels of all shapes and sizes. Choose your hostel selectively. Hostels can be historic castles or depressing huts, serene and comfy or overrun by noisy children. Unfortunately, many of the international youth hostels have become overpriced, and, in general, I no longer recommend them. The only time I do recommend them is if you're on a very tight budget, want to cook your own meals, or are traveling with a group that likes to sleep on bunk beds in big rooms. The informal private hostels are often more fun, easygoing, and cheaper. These alternatives to the International Youth Hostel Federation (IYHF) hostels are more common than ever. Hostels of Europe (www .hostelseurope.com) and Hostels.com have good listings. You can book online for many hostels (for London: www.hostellondon.com, for England and Wales: www.yha.org.uk, and for Scotland: www .hostel-scotland.co.uk).

Eating

England's reputation for miserable food is now dated, and the British cuisine scene is lively, trendy, and pleasantly surprising. (Unfortunately, it can also be expensive.) Even the basic, traditional pub grub has gone "upmarket," and you'll generally find fresh vegetables rather than soggy fries and mushy peas.

Your £7 budget choices are "early bird" restaurant specials, bakeries, ethnic eateries, cafeterias, fast food, picnics, fish and chips, pizza, pubs, or greasy spoon cafés. Here are a few tips on budget eating.

The hearty British **breakfast** can tide many travelers over until dinner. This traditional "fry," also known as a "heart attack on a plate," is especially feast-like if you've just come from the land of the skimpy continental breakfast across the Channel.

Your standard fry gets off to a healthy start with juice and cereal or porridge. (Try Weetabix, a soggy English cousin of shredded wheat.) Next, with tea or coffee, you get a heated plate with a fried egg, lean Canadian-style bacon, a bad sausage, a grilled tomato, and often a slice of delightfully greasy pan toast and sautéed mushrooms. Toast comes

ENGLISH CHOCOLATE

My chocoholic readers are enthusiastic about English choco-
lates. Their favorites include Cadbury Wispa Gold bars (filled
with liquid caramel), Cadbury Crunchie bars, Nestle's Lion
bars, Cadbury's Boost bars (a shortcake biscuit with caramel in
milk chocolate), and Galaxy chocolate bars (especially the ones
with hazelnuts). Thornton shops (in larger train stations) sell a
box of sweets called the Continental Assortment, which comes
with a tasting guide. The highlight is the mocha white-choco-
late truffle. British M&Ms (Smarties) are better than American
ones. For a few extra pence, adorn your ice cream cone with a
"flake"—a chocolate bar stuck right into the middle.

on a rack (to cool quickly and crisply) with butter and marmalade. Try
kippers (herring fillets smoked in an oak fire). Order only what you'll
eat. Hoteliers and B&B hostesses don't like to see food wasted. And
there's nothing wrong with skipping the "fry"—few locals actually start
their day with this heavy traditional breakfast.

These days, the best coffee is served in a *cafetière* (also called a
"French press"). When your coffee has steeped as long as you like, plunge
down the filter and pour. To revitalize your brew, pump the plunger again.

Many B&Bs don't serve breakfast until 8:00. If you need an early
start, ask politely if it's possible. While they may not make you a cooked
breakfast, they can usually put out cereal, toast, juice, and coffee.

Picnicking saves time and money. Fine park benches and polite
pigeons abound in most neighborhoods. You can easily get prepared
food to go. Bakeries sell yogurt, cartons of "semi-skimmed" milk, pastries, and pasties (PAST-eez). Pasties are "savory" (not sweet) meat pies
that originated in the mining country; they had big crust handles so
miners with filthy hands could eat them and toss the crust.

Good sandwich shops (try curry-flavored "*tikka* chicken") and
corner grocery stores are a hit with local workers eating on the run.
Decent packaged sandwiches (£2–3) are sold everywhere. Try boxes of
orange juice (pure, by the liter), fresh bread, tasty English cheese, meat,
a tube of Colman's English mustard, local eatin' apples, bananas, small
tomatoes, a small tub of yogurt (they're drinkable), gorp or nuts, plain or
chocolate-covered "Digestive Biscuits," and any local specialties. At
open-air markets and supermarkets, you can get produce in small quan-
tities (three tomatoes and two bananas cost me 50p). Supermarkets often
have good deli sections, even offering Indian dishes, and sometimes

salad bars. I often munch a relaxed "meal on wheels" in a car or train, or on an open-top bus tour or river cruise, to save 30 precious minutes for sightseeing. If you're planning a picnic dinner in a smaller town, buy ahead, because groceries can close as early as 17:00.

At classier restaurants, look for **"early bird specials,"** allowing you to eat well and affordably, but early (around 17:30–19:00, last order by 19:00). A top-end, £25-for-dinner-type restaurant often serves the same quality two-course lunch deals for £10.

Ethnic restaurants from all over the world add spice to England's cuisine scene. Eating Indian or Chinese is cheap (even cheaper if you take it out). Sampling Indian food is "going local" in cosmopolitan, multiethnic Britain.

Afternoon Tea

People of leisure punctuate their afternoon with a "cream tea" at a tearoom. You'll get a pot of tea, small finger foods (like cucumber sandwiches), homemade scones, jam, and thick clotted cream. For maximum pinkie-waving taste per calorie, slice your scone thin like a miniature loaf of bread. Tearooms, which often serve appealing light meals, are usually open for lunch and close around 17:00, just before dinner.

Pub Grub and Beer

Pubs are a basic part of the British social scene, and, whether you are a teetotaler or a beer guzzler, they should be a part of your travel here. Pub is short for "public house." It's an extended living room where, if you don't mind the stickiness, you can feel the pulse of Britain. Most traditional atmospheric pubs are in the countryside and smaller towns. Unfortunately, many city pubs have been afflicted with an excess of brass, ferns, and video games. Many others have found that selling beer is more profitable than selling meals and only cook at lunchtime. In any case, smart travelers use the pubs to eat, drink, get out of the rain, watch the latest sporting event, and make new friends.

Pub grub gets better each year. For £6 to £8, you'll get a basic budget hot lunch or dinner in friendly surroundings. The *Good Pub Guide,* published annually by the British Consumers Association, is excellent. Pubs attached to restaurants often have fresher food and a chef who knows how to cook.

Pubs generally serve traditional dishes, like fish and chips, vegetables, "bangers and mash" (sausages and mashed potatoes), roast beef with Yorkshire pudding (batter baked in the oven), and assorted meat pies, such as steak-and-kidney pie or shepherd's pie (stewed lamb topped with mashed potatoes). Side dishes include salads (sometimes even a nice self-serve salad bar), vegetables (especially soggy peas), and—invariably—"chips" (French fries). "Crisps" are potato chips. A "jacket potato" (baked potato stuffed with fillings of your choice) can almost be a meal in itself. A "ploughman's lunch" is a modern "traditional English meal" of bread, cheese, and sweet pickles that nearly every tourist tries...once. These days, you'll likely find more Italian pasta, curried dishes, and quiche on the menu than "traditional" fare.

Meals are usually served from 12:00 to 14:00 and from 18:00 to 20:00, not throughout the day. Typically, there's no table service. Order at the bar, then take a seat and they'll bring the food when it's ready (or sometimes you pick it up at the bar). Pay at the bar (sometimes when you order, sometimes after you eat). In general, don't tip at pubs. Tip (up to 10 percent) only if you're in the pub's restaurant section and you order off a menu from a waiter who takes your order at your table (but look at the bill first; if it lists a service charge, there's no need to tip beyond that).

Servings are hearty, service is quick, and you'll rarely spend more than £8. Your beer or cider adds another couple of pounds. (Free tap water is always available.) Pubs that advertise their food and are crowded with locals are less likely to be the kind that serve only lousy microwaved snacks.

The British take great pride in their beer. Many Brits think that drinking beer cold and carbonated, as Americans do, ruins the taste. Most pubs will have **lagers** (cold, refreshing, American-style beer), **ales** (amber-colored, room-temperature beer), **bitters** (hop-flavored ale, perhaps the most typical British beer), and **stouts** (dark and somewhat bitter, such as Guinness). At pubs, long hand pulls are used to pull the traditional, rich-flavored "real ales" up from the cellar. These are the connoisseur's favorites: fermented naturally, varying from sweet to bitter, often with a hoppy or nutty flavor. Notice the fun names. Short hand pulls at the bar mean colder, fizzier, mass-produced, and less interesting keg beers. Mild beers are sweeter, with a creamy malt flavoring. Irish cream ale is a smooth, sweet experience. Try the draft cider (sweet or dry).

Order your beer at the bar and pay as you go. An average beer costs £2.50. Part of the experience is standing before a line of "hand pulls," or taps, and wondering which beer to choose.

Drinks are served by the pint (20-ounce imperial size) or the half-pint. (It's almost feminine for a man to order just a half; I order mine with quiche.) Proper English ladies like a half-beer and half-lemonade **shandy.**

Besides beer, many pubs actually have a good selection of wines by the glass, a fully stocked bar for the gentleman's "G and T" (gin and tonic), and the increasingly popular bottles of alcohol-plus-sugar (e.g. Bacardi Breezers) for the younger, working-class set. Teetotalers can order from a wide variety of soft drinks.

Pub hours vary. The strict wartime hours (designed to keep the wartime working force sober and productive) finally ended a few years ago, and now pubs can serve beer daily from 11:00 to 23:00 (Sun 12:00–22:30). As it nears 23:00, you'll hear shouts of "Last orders" to order a beer. Then comes the 10-minute warning bell. Finally, they'll call "Time!" to pick up your glass, finished or not, sometime before 23:25, when the pub closes. Children are served food and soft drinks in pubs (sometimes in a courtyard or the restaurant section), but you must be 18 to order a beer. A cup of darts is free for the asking. People go to a "public house" to be social. They want to talk. Get vocal with a local. Sitting or standing at the bar indicates you're interested in a conversation (while sitting at a table, you're likely to be left alone). The pub is the next best thing to having relatives in town. Cheers!

Tipping

Tipping in Britain isn't as automatic and generous as it is in the United States, but for special service, tips are appreciated, if not expected. As in the United States, the proper amount depends on your resources, tipping philosophy, and the circumstances, but some general guidelines apply.

Restaurants: Tipping is an issue only at restaurants and fancy pubs that have waiters and waitresses. If you order your food at a counter, don't tip.

If the menu states that service is included, there's no need to tip beyond that. If service isn't included, tip about 10 percent by rounding up. The discreet English don't like big deals made of anything. Leave the tip on the table or hand it to your server with your payment for the meal and say, "Keep the rest, please."

Taxis: To tip the cabbie, round up. For a typical ride, round up to a maximum of 10 percent (to pay a £4.50 fare, give £5; or for a £28 fare, give £30). If the cabbie hauls your bags and zips you to the airport to help you catch your flight, you might want to toss in a little more. But if you feel like you're being driven in circles or otherwise ripped off, skip the tip.

Special Services: Tour guides at public sites might hold out their hands for tips after they give their spiel; if I've already paid for the tour, I don't tip extra, though some tourists do give a pound, particularly for a job well done. I don't tip at hotels, but if you do, give the porter about 50p for carrying bags and leave a pound in your room at the end of your stay for the maid if the room was kept clean. In general, if someone in the service industry does a super job for you, a tip of a pound or two is appropriate.

When in doubt, ask. If you're not sure whether (or how much) to tip for a service, ask your hotelier or the TI; they'll fill you in on how it's done on their turf.

Stranger in a Strange Land

We travel all the way to Europe to enjoy differences—to become temporary locals. You'll experience frustrations. There are certain truths that we find God-given and self-evident, such as cold beer, ice in drinks, bottomless cups of coffee, easy shower faucets, and driving on the right side of the road. One of the benefits of travel is the eye-opening realization that there are logical, civil, and even better alternatives. A willingness to go local ensures that you'll enjoy a full dose of hospitality.

Back Door Manners

While updating this book, I heard over and over again that my readers are considerate and fun to have as guests. Thank you for traveling as temporary locals who are sensitive to the culture. It's a joy to follow you in my travels.

Send Me a Postcard, Drop Me a Line

If you enjoy a successful trip with the help of this book and would like to share your discoveries, please fill out and send the survey at the end of this book to me at Europe Through the Back Door, Box 2009, Edmonds, WA 98020. I personally read and value all feedback. Thanks in advance—it helps a lot.

For our latest travel information, tap into www.ricksteves.com. To check on any updates for this book, visit www.ricksteves.com/update. My e-mail address is rick@ricksteves.com. Anyone can request a free issue of our newsletter.

Judging from the happy postcards I receive from travelers, it's safe to assume you're on your way to a great, affordable vacation—with the finesse of an independent, experienced traveler. Thanks, and happy travels!

BACK DOOR TRAVEL PHILOSOPHY
from Rick Steves' *Europe Through the Back Door*

Travel is intensified living—maximum thrills per minute and one of the last great sources of legal adventure. Travel is freedom. It's recess, and we need it.

Experiencing the real Europe requires catching it by surprise, going casual..."through the Back Door."

Affording travel is a matter of priorities. (Make do with the old car.) You can travel—simply, safely, and comfortably—anywhere in Europe for $80 a day plus transportation costs. In many ways, spending more money only builds a thicker wall between you and what you came to see. Europe is a cultural carnival, and, time after time, you'll find that its best acts are free and the best seats are the cheap ones.

A tight budget forces you to travel close to the ground, meeting and communicating with the people, not relying on service with a purchased smile. Never sacrifice sleep, nutrition, safety, or cleanliness in the name of budget. Simply enjoy the local-style alternatives to expensive hotels and restaurants.

Extroverts have more fun. If your trip is low on magic moments, kick yourself and make things happen. If you don't enjoy a place, maybe you don't know enough about it. Seek the truth. Recognize tourist traps. Give a culture the benefit of your open mind. See things as different but not better or worse. Any culture has much to share.

Of course, travel, like the world, is a series of hills and valleys. Be fanatically positive and militantly optimistic. If something's not to your liking, change your liking. Travel is addictive. It can make you a happier American as well as a citizen of the world. Our Earth is home to six billion equally important people. It's humbling to travel and find that people don't envy Americans. They like us, but, with all due respect, they wouldn't trade passports.

Globe-trotting destroys ethnocentricity. It helps you understand and appreciate different cultures. Travel changes people. It broadens perspectives and teaches new ways to measure quality of life. Many travelers toss aside their hometown blinders. Their prized souvenirs are the strands of different cultures they decide to knit into their own character. The world is a cultural yarn shop. And Back Door travelers are weaving the ultimate tapestry.

Come on, join in!

LONDON

London is more than 600 square miles of urban jungle. Teeming with nine million people—many of whom don't speak English—it's a world in itself and a barrage on all the senses. On my first visit, I felt very, very small. London is much more than its museums and famous landmarks. It's a living, breathing, thriving organism.

London has changed dramatically in recent years, and many visitors are surprised to find how "un-English" it is. Whites are now a minority in major parts of the city that once symbolized white imperialism. Arabs have nearly bought out the area north of Hyde Park. Chinese take-outs outnumber fish-and-chips shops. Many hotels are run by people with foreign accents (who hire English chambermaids), while outlying suburbs are home to huge communities of Indians and Pakistanis. London is learning—sometimes fitfully—to live as a microcosm of its formerly vast empire. Many see the English Channel Tunnel as another foreign threat to the Britishness of Britain.

With just a few days here, you'll get no more than a quick splash in this teeming human tidal pool. But, with a quick orientation, you'll get a good look at its top sights, history, and cultural entertainment, as well as its ever-changing human face.

Have fun in London. Blow through the city on the open deck of a double-decker orientation tour bus, and take a pinch-me-I'm-in-Britain walk through downtown. Ogle the crown jewels at the Tower of London, hear the chimes of Big Ben, and see the Houses of Parliament in action. Hobnob with the tombstones in Westminster Abbey, duck WWII bombs in Churchill's underground Cabinet War Rooms, and brave the earthshaking Imperial War Museum. Visit with Leonardo, Botticelli, and Rembrandt in the National Gallery. Whisper across the dome of St. Paul's Cathedral and rummage through our civilization's attic at the British Museum. Cruise down the Thames River. You'll enjoy some of Europe's best people-watching at Covent Garden, and you'll snap to at Buckingham Palace's Changing of the Guard. Just sit in Victoria Station, at a major Tube station, at Piccadilly Circus, or in Trafalgar Square, and observe. Spend one evening at a theater and the others catching your breath.

Planning Your Time

The sights of London alone could easily fill a trip to Britain. It's a great one-week getaway. On a three-week tour of Britain I'd give it three busy days. If you're flying in, consider starting your trip in Bath and making London your British finale. Especially if you hope to enjoy a play or concert, a night or two of jet lag is bad news.

Here's a suggested schedule:

Day 1: 9:00-Tower of London (Beefeater tour, crown jewels), 12:00-Munch a sandwich on the Thames while cruising from the Tower to Westminster Bridge, 13:00-Follow the self-guided Westminster Walk (see below) with a quick visit to the Cabinet War Rooms, 15:30-Trafalgar Square and National Gallery, 17:30-Visit the Britain and London Visitors Centre near Piccadilly, planning ahead for your trip, 18:30-Dinner in Soho. Take in a play or 19:30 concert at St. Martin-in-the-Fields.

Day 2: 8:30-If traveling around Britain, spend 30 minutes in a phone booth getting all essential elements of your trip nailed down. If you know where you'll be and when, call those B&Bs now. 9:00-Take a hop-on, hop-off bus tour (consider hopping off near the end for the 11:30 Changing of the Guard at Buckingham Palace), 12:30-Covent Garden for lunch and people-watching, 14:00-Tour the British Museum. Have a pub dinner before a play, concert, or evening walking tour.

Days 3 and 4: Choose among these remaining London highlights: Tour Westminster Abbey, British Library, Imperial War Museum, the two Tates (Tate Modern on the south bank for modern art, Tate Britain on the north bank for British art), St. Paul's Cathedral, or the Museum of London; take a spin on the London Eye Ferris Wheel or a cruise to Kew or Greenwich; do some serious shopping at one of London's elegant department stores or open-air markets; or take another historic walking tour.

After considering nearly all of London's tourist sights, I have pruned them down to just the most important (or fun) for a first visit of up to seven days. You won't be able to see all of these, so don't try. You'll keep coming back to London. After 25 visits myself, I still enjoy a healthy list of excuses to return.

ORIENTATION

(area code: 020)

To grasp London comfortably, see it as the old town in the city center, without the modern, congested sprawl. The River Thames runs roughly west to east through the city, with most of the visitor's sights on the north bank. Mentally, maybe even physically, trim down your map to include only the area between the Tower of London (to the east), Hyde Park (west), Regent's Park (north), and the Thames (south). (This is roughly the area bordered by the Tube's Circle Line.) This three-mile stretch between the Tower and Hyde Park (about a 90-min walk) holds 80 percent of the sights mentioned in this chapter.

London is a collection of neighborhoods:

Westminster: This neighborhood includes Big Ben, Parliament, Westminster Abbey, and Buckingham Palace, the grand government buildings from which Britain is ruled.

The City: Shakespeare's London was a walled town clustered around St. Paul's Cathedral. Today it's the modern financial district.

The West End: Lying between Westminster and the City (that is, at the "west end" of the original walled town), this is the center of London cultural life. Trafalgar Square has major museums. Piccadilly Circus and Leicester Square host tourist traps, cinemas, and nighttime glitz. Soho and Covent Garden are thriving people-zones that house theaters, restaurants, pubs, and boutiques.

The South Bank: Until recently, the entire south bank of the Thames River was a run-down, generally ignored area, but now it's the hottest real estate in town, with upscale restaurants, major new sight-seeing attractions, and pedestrian bridges that allow easy access from the rest of London.

Residential neighborhoods to the west: Though they lack major tourist sights, South Kensington, Notting Hill, Chelsea, and Belgravia are home to London's wealthy and trendy, as well as many shopping streets and enticing restaurants.

With this focus and a good orientation, you'll find London manageable and even fun. You'll get a sampling of the city's top sights, history, and cultural entertainment, and a good look at its ever-changing human face.

Tourist Information

The **Britain and London Visitors Centre** is the best tourist information service in town (Mon–Fri 9:00–18:30, Sat–Sun 10:00–16:00, phone not answered after 17:00 Mon–Fri and not at all Sat–Sun, booking service, just off Piccadilly Circus at 1 Lower Regent Street, tel. 020/8846-9000, www.visitbritain.com, www.visitlondon.com). If you're traveling beyond London, take advantage of the Centre's well-equipped England desk. Bring your itinerary and a checklist of questions. Pick up these publications: *London Planner* (a great free monthly that lists all the sights, events, and hours), walking-tour schedule fliers, a theater guide, "Central London Bus Guide," and the Thames River Services brochure.

The Britain and London Visitors Centre sells long-distance bus tickets and passes, train tickets (can also make reservations for you), British Heritage Passes, and tickets to plays (20 percent booking fee). In addition, they sell **Fast Track tickets** to some of London's attractions (at no extra cost), allowing you to skip the queue at the sights. These can be worthwhile for places that sometimes have long ticket lines, such as the Tower of London, London Eye Ferris Wheel, and Madame Tussaud's Wax Museum. While the Visitors Centre books rooms, you can avoid their £5 booking fee by calling hotels direct.

The **London Pass** provides free entrance to most of the city's sights, but since many museums are free, it's hard to justify the purchase. Still, fervent sightseers can check the list of covered sights and do the arithmetic (1 day-£27, 2 days-£42, 3 days-£52, 6 days-£72, includes 128-page guidebook, tel. 0870-242-9988 for purchase instructions, www.londonpass.com).

Nearby you'll find the **Scottish Tourist Centre** (May–Sept Mon–Fri 9:30–18:30, Sat 10:00–17:00, off-season Mon–Fri 10:00–18:00, Sat 12:00–17:00, Cockspur Street, tel. 0845-225-5121, www.visitscotland.com) and the slick **French National Tourist Office** (Mon–Fri 10:00–18:00, Sat until 17:00, closed Sun, 178 Piccadilly, tel. 0906-824-4123).

Unfortunately, **London's Tourist Information Centres** (which present themselves as TIs at major train and bus stations and airports) are now simply businesses selling advertising space to companies with fliers to distribute.

Local bookstores sell London guides and maps; **Bensons Mapguide** is the best (£2.25, also sold at newsstands).

Helpful Hints

U.S. Embassy: 24 Grosvenor Square (for passport concerns, open Mon–Fri 8:30–11:00 plus Mon and Fri 14:00–16:00, Tube: Bond Street, tel. 020/7499-9000).

Theft Alert: The Artful Dodger is alive and well in London. Be on guard, particularly on public transportation and in places crowded with tourists. Tourists, considered naive and rich, are targeted. Each year, more than 7,500 handbags are stolen at Covent Garden alone.

Pedestrian Safety: Cars drive on the right side of the road, so before crossing a street, I always look right, look left, then look right again just to be sure.

Changing Money: ATMs are the way to go. While regular banks charge several pounds to change traveler's checks, American

Express offices offer a fair rate and will change any brand of traveler's checks for no fee. Handy AmEx offices are at Heathrow's Terminal 4 Tube station (daily 7:00–19:00) and near Piccadilly (June-Sept Mon–Sat 9:00–18:00, Sun 10:00–17:00; Oct–May Mon–Sat 9:00–17:30, Sun 10:00–17:00; 30 Haymarket, tel. 020/7484-9610; refund office 24-hr tel. 0800-521-313). Marks & Spencer department stores give good rates with no fees.

Avoid changing money at exchange bureaus. Their latest scam: They advertise very good rates with a same-as-the-banks fee of 2 percent. But the fine print explains that the fee of 2 percent is for buying pounds. The fee for *selling* pounds is 9.5 percent. Ouch!

What's Up?: For the best list of what's happening and a look at the trendy London scene, pick up a current copy of *Time Out* (£2.20, www.timeout.com) or *What's On* at any newsstand. The TI's free, monthly *London Planner* covers sights, events, and plays at least as well. For plays, also visit www.officiallondontheatre.co.uk. For a chatty, *People Magazine*-type Web site on London's entertainment, look up www.thisislondon.com.

Sights: Free museums include the British Museum, British Library, National Gallery, National Portrait Gallery, Tate Britain (British art), Tate Modern (modern art), Imperial War Museum, Natural History Museum, Science Museum, Victoria and Albert Museum, and the Royal Air Force Museum Hendon. Special exhibitions cost extra. Telephoning first to check hours and confirm plans is always smart, especially off-season, when hours can shrink.

Internet Access: The astonishing easyInternetcafé offers up to 500 computers per store and is open long hours daily. Depending on the time of day, a £2 ticket buys anywhere from 80 minutes to six hours of computer time. The ticket is valid for four weeks and multiple visits at any of their five branches: Victoria Station (across from front of station, near taxis and buses, long lines), Trafalgar Square (456 Strand), Tottenham Court Road (#9-16), Oxford Street (#358, opposite Bond Street Tube station), and Kensington High Street (#160–166). They also sell 24-hour, seven-day, and 30-day passes (www.easyinternetcafe.com).

Travel Bookstores: Stanfords Travel Bookstore is good and stocks current editions of my books at Covent Garden (Mon–Fri 9:00–19:30, Sat 10:00–19:00, Sun 12:00–18:00, 12 Long Acre, tel. 020/7836-1321). There are two impressive Waterstone's bookstores: the biggest in Europe on Piccadilly (Mon–Sat 10:00–22:00, Sun 12:00–18:00, 203 Piccadilly, tel. 020/7851-2400) and one on the corner of Trafalgar Square (Mon–Sat 9:30–21:00, Sun 12:00–18:00, next to Costa Café, tel. 020/7839-4411).

Left Luggage: As security concerns heighten, train stations have replaced their lockers with left-luggage counters. Each bag must go through a scanner (just like at the airport), so lines can be long. Expect a wait to pick up your bags, too (each item-£5/24 hrs, daily 7:00–24:00). You can also check bags at the airports (£4/day). If leaving London and returning later, you may be able to leave a box or bag at your hotel for free—assuming you'll be staying there again.

Medical Problems: Local hospitals have 24-hour-a-day emergency care centers where any tourist who needs help can drop in and, after a wait, be seen by a doctor. The quality is good and the price is right (free). Your hotel has details. St. Thomas' Hospital, immediately across the river from Big Ben, has a fine reputation.

Arrival in London

By Train: London has eight train stations, all connected by the Tube (subway) and all with exchange offices and luggage storage (see above). From any station, ride the Tube or taxi to your hotel.

By Bus: The bus station is one block southwest of Victoria Station, which has a TI and Tube entrance.

By Plane: For detailed information on getting from London's airports to downtown London, see "Transportation Connections" at the end of this chapter.

Getting around London

To travel smart in a city this size, you must get comfortable with public transportation. London's excellent taxis, buses, and subway system make a private car unnecessary. In fact, the new "congestion charge" of £5 levied on any private car entering the city center has been effective in cutting down traffic jam delays and bolstering London's public transit. The new revenue subsidizes the buses, which are now more inexpensive, frequent, and user-friendly than before. Today the vast majority of vehicles in the city center are buses, taxis, and service trucks. (Drivers: For all the details on the congestion charge, see www.cclondon.com.)

By Taxi: London is the best taxi town in Europe. Big, black, carefully regulated cabs are everywhere. I never met a crabby cabbie in London. They love to talk, and they know every nook and cranny in town. I ride in one each day just to get my London questions answered. Rides start at £2 and cost about £1.50 per Tube stop. Connecting downtown sights is quick and easy and will cost you about £4 (e.g., St. Paul's to the Tower of London). For a short ride, three people in a cab travel at Tube prices. Groups of four or five should taxi everywhere. If a cab's top light is on, just wave it down. (Drivers flash lights when they see you.) They have a tiny turning radius, so you can wave at cabs going in either direction. If waving doesn't work, ask someone where you can find a taxi stand. While telephoning a cab gets one in minutes, it's generally not necessary and adds to the cost. London is such a great wave-'em-down taxi town that most cabs don't even have a radio phone.

London

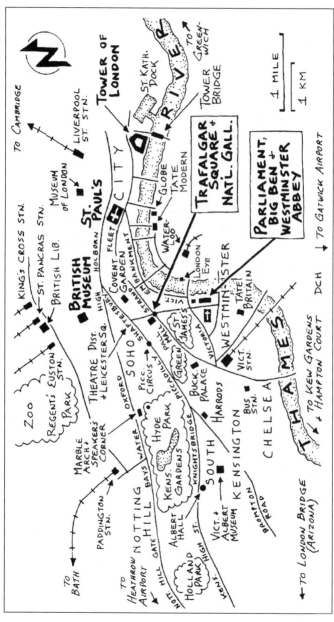

HANDY BUSES

Since the institution of London's "congestion charge" for cars, the bus system is faster, easier, and cheaper than ever. Tube-oriented travelers need to make a point to get over their tunnel vision, learn the bus system, and get around fast and easy.

Here are some of the most useful routes:

Route #9: Harrods to Hyde Park Corner to Piccadilly Circus to Trafalgar Square.

Routes #11 and #24: Victoria Station to Westminster Abbey to Trafalgar Square (#11 continues to St. Paul's).

Route #RV1: Tower of London to Tower Bridge to Tate Modern/Shakespeare's Globe to London Eye/Waterloo Station/County Hall Travel Inn to Trafalgar Square to Covent Garden (a scenic joyride).

Route #15: Paddington Station to Oxford Circus to Regent Street/TI to Piccadilly Circus to Trafalgar Square to Fleet Street to St. Paul's to Tower of London.

Route #188: Waterloo Station/London Eye to Trafalgar Square to Covent Garden to British Museum.

In addition, several buses (including #6, #12, #13, #15, #23, #139, and #159) make the corridor run from Trafalgar Square, Piccadilly Circus, and Oxford Circus to Marble Arch.

Don't worry about meter cheating. British cab meters come with a sealed computer chip and clock that ensures you'll get the regular tariff #1 most of the time, tariff #2 during "unsociable hours" (18:00-6:00 and Sat–Sun), and tariff #3 only on holidays. All extra charges are explained in writing on the cab wall. The only way a cabbie can cheat you is to take a needlessly long route. There are alternative cab companies driving normal-looking, non-metered cars that charge fixed rates based on the postal codes of your start and end points. These are generally honest and can actually be cheaper when snarled traffic drives up the cost of a metered cab. Tip a cabbie by rounding up (maximum 10 percent).

By Bus: London's extensive bus system is easy to follow. Just pick up a free "Central London Bus Guide" map from a TI or Tube station. Signs at stops list routes clearly. On most buses (marked on sign), you'll pay at a machine at the bus stop (exact change only), then show your ticket as you board. On other buses, you can pay the conductor (take a seat, and he'll come and collect £1). Any ride in downtown London costs £1. (The best views are upstairs.) If you have a Travel Card (see below), get in the habit of hopping buses for quick little straight shots, even just to get to a Tube stop. During bump-and-grind rush hours (8:00–10:00 and 16:00–19:00), you'll go faster by Tube. Consider two special bus deals: all day for £2 and a ticket six-pack for £4 (also see "London Tube and Bus Passes," page 48).

By Tube: London's subway system (called the Tube or Underground, but never "subway") is one of this planet's great people-movers and the fastest (and cheapest) long-distance transport in town (runs Mon–Sat about 5:00–24:00, Sun about 7:00–23:00).

Survey a Tube map. At the front of this book, you'll find a complete Tube map with color-coded lines and names. You can also pick up a free Tube map at any station window. Each line has a name (such as Circle, Northern, or Bakerloo) and two directions (indicated by the end-of-the-line stop). Find the line that will take you to your destination, and figure out roughly what direction (north, south, east, west) you'll need to go to get there.

In the Tube station, feed your ticket into the turnstile, reclaim it, and hang onto the ticket—you'll need it to get through the turnstile at the end of your journey. Find your train by following signs to your line and the (general) direction it's headed (e.g., Central Line: East).

Since some tracks are shared by several lines, you'll need to double-check before boarding a train: First, make sure your destination is one of the stops listed on the sign at the platform. Also, check the electronic signboards that announce which train is next, and make sure the destination (the end-of-the-line stop) is the one you want. Each train has its final destination above its windshield. When in doubt, ask a local or a blue-vested staff person for help.

Trains run roughly every three to 10 minutes. If one train is absolutely packed and you notice another to the same destination is coming in three minutes, you can wait to avoid the sardine experience. The system can be fraught with construction delays and breakdowns, so pay attention to signs and announcements explaining necessary detours, etc. The Circle Line is notorious for problems. Bring something to do to make your waiting time productive.

You can't leave the system without feeding your ticket to the turnstile. (The turnstile will either eat your now-expired single-trip ticket, or spit your still-valid pass back out.) Save walking time by choosing the best street exit—check the maps on the walls or ask any station personnel. "Subway" means "pedestrian underpass" in "English." For Tube and bus information 24 hours a day, call 020/7222-1234 (www.transportforlondon .gov.uk). And always...mind the gap.

Cost: Any ride in Zone 1 (on or within the Circle Line, including virtually all my recommended sights and hotels) costs £1.60. Tube tickets are also valid on city buses. You can avoid ticket-window lines in Tube stations by buying tickets from coin-op machines; practice on the punchboard to see how the system works (hit Adult Single and your destination); these tickets are valid only on the day of purchase. Again, nearly every ride will be £1.60. Beware: Overshooting your zone nets you a £10 fine.

Carnet of 10 tickets: If you want to travel a little each day or if you're part of a group, an £11.50 *carnet* (pron. CAR-net) is a great deal: You get 10 separate tickets for Tube travel in Zone 1, paying £1.15 per ride rather than £1.60. Wait for the machine to lay all 10 tickets.

London Tube and Bus Passes: Consider using these passes, valid on both the Tube and buses (all passes are available for more zones, can be purchased as easily as a normal ticket at any station, and can get you a 33 percent discount on most Thames cruises):

One-Day pass: If you figure you'll take three rides in a day, a day pass is a good deal. The One Day Travel Card, covering Zones 1 and 2, gives you unlimited "off-peak" travel for a day, starting after 9:30 on weekdays and anytime on weekends (£4.10). The all-zone version of this card costs £5.10 (and includes Heathrow Airport). The unrestricted version, covering six zones (including Heathrow) at all times, costs £10.70. Families save with the One Day Family Travel Card (price varies depending on number in family). For details, including a handy journey planner, see www.thetube.com.

Weekend pass: The Weekend Travel Card, covering Saturday, Sunday, and Zones 1 and 2 for £6.10, costs 25 percent less than two one-day cards.

Seven-Day pass: The 7-Day Travel Card costs £19.60 and covers Zones 1 and 2.

Group deals: Groups of 10 or more can travel all day on the Tube for £3.10 each (but not on buses).

TOURS

▲▲▲**Hop-on, Hop-off Double-Decker Bus Tours**—Two competitive companies (Original and Big Bus) offer essentially the same tours with buses that have either live (English-only) guides or a tape-recorded, dial-a-language narration. This two-hour, once-over-lightly bus tour drives by all the famous sights, providing a stress-free way to get your bearings and at least see the biggies. You can sit back and enjoy the entire two-hour orientation tour (a good idea if you like the guide and the weather) or hop on and hop off at any of the nearly 30 stops and catch a later bus. Buses run about every 10–15 minutes in summer, every 20 minutes in winter. It's an inexpensive form of transport as well as an informative tour. Buses operate daily (from about 9:00 until early evening in summer, until late afternoon in winter) and stop at Victoria Street (1 block north of Victoria Station), Marble Arch, Piccadilly Circus, Trafalgar Square, and elsewhere.

Each company offers a core two-hour overview tour, two other routes, and a narrated Thames boat tour covered by the same ticket (buy ticket from driver, credit cards accepted at major stops such as Victoria Station, ticket good for 24 hrs, bring a sweater and extra film). Pick up a map from any flier rack or from one of the countless salespeople and study the complex system. Note: If you start at Victoria Station at 9:00, you'll finish near Buckingham Palace in time to see the Changing of the Guard (at 11:30); ask your driver for the best place to hop off. Sunday morning is a fine time for a tour; traffic is light and many museums are closed. The last full loop leaves Victoria at 17:00. Both companies have entertaining as well as boring guides. The narration is important. If you don't like your guide, jump off and find another. If you like your guide, settle in for the entire loop.

Original London Sightseeing Bus Tour: Live guided buses have a Union Jack flag and a yellow triangle on the front of the bus. If the front has many flags or a green or red triangle, it's a tape-recorded multilingual tour—avoid it, unless you have kids who'd enjoy the entertaining tape-recorded kids' tour (£15, £2.50 discount with this book, limit 2 discounts per book, they'll rip off the corner of this page, raise bloody hell if they don't honor this discount, ticket good for 24 hours, tel. 020/8877-1722, www.theoriginaltour.com). Your ticket includes a 50-minute-long round-trip boat tour from Westminster Pier or Waterloo Pier (departs hourly, tape-recorded narration).

Big Bus Hop-on, Hop-off London Tours: These are also good. For £17, you get the same basic tour plus coupons for three different one-hour London walks, as well as the scenic and usually entertainingly guided Thames boat ride (normally £5) between Westminster Pier and the Tower of London. The pass and extras are valid for 24 hours. Buses with live guides are marked in front with a picture of an orange bus; buses with tape-recorded spiels display a picture of a blue bus and headphones. While the price is steeper, Big Bus guides seem more dynamic than the Original guides (daily 8:30–18:00, July–Aug until 18:00, winter until 16:30, from Victoria Station, tel. 020/7233-9533, www.bigbus .co.uk).

At Night: The London by Night Sightseeing Tour runs basically the same circuit as the other companies, but after hours. While the narration is pretty lame (the driver does little more than call out the names of famous places as you roll by), the views at twilight are grand (£9.50, pay driver or buy tickets at Victoria Station or Paddington Station TI, April–Oct only, 2-hr tour with live guide, departs at 19:30, and 21:30 from Victoria Station, Taxi Road, at front of station near end of Wilton Road, tel. 020/8646-1747, www.london-by-night.net).

▲▲**Walking Tours**—Several times a day, top-notch local guides lead (often big) groups through specific slices of London's past. Schedule fliers litter the desks of TIs, hotels, and pubs. *Time Out* lists many scheduled walks, but not all. Simply show up at the announced loca-

DAILY REMINDER

Sunday: Some sights don't open until noon. The Tower of London is especially crowded today. Hyde Park Speakers' Corner rants from early afternoon until early evening. These are closed: Banqueting House, Sir John Soane's Museum, and legal sights (Houses of Parliament, Old Bailey, the City is dead). Evensong is at 15:00 at Westminster Abbey (plus organ recital at 17:45 for a fee) and 15:15 at St. Paul's (plus free organ recital at 17:00); both churches are open during the day for worship but closed to sightseers. Many stores and theaters are closed. Street markets flourish: Camden Lock, Spitalfields, Greenwich, and Petticoat Lane.

Monday: Virtually all sights are open except for Apsley House, the Theatre Museum, Sir John Soane's Museum, and a few others. The St. Martin-in-the-Fields church offers a free 13:05 concert. At Somerset House, the Courtauld Gallery is free until 14:00. Vinopolis is open until 21:00.

Tuesday: All sights are open; the British Library is open until 20:00. St. Martin-in-the-Fields has a free 13:05 concert.

Wednesday: All sights are open, plus evening hours at Westminster Abbey (until 19:45), the National Gallery (until 21:00), and Victoria and Albert Museum (until 22:00).

tion, pay £5, and enjoy two chatty hours about Charles Dickens, the Plague, William Shakespeare, Legal London, the Beatles, Jack the Ripper, or whatever is on the agenda. Original London Walks, the dominant company, lists its extensive daily schedule in a beefy, plain, black-and-white *The Original London Walks* brochure—which you'll see at the TI and on racks in every hotel (walks offered year-round—even Christmas, private tours for £90, tel. 020/7624-3978, for a recorded listing of today's walks call 020/7624-9255, www.walks.com). They also run **Explorer day trips,** a good option for those with limited time and transportation (different trip daily: Stonehenge/Salisbury, Oxford/Cotswolds, York, Bath, and so on).

The Beatles: Fans of the still-Fabulous Four can take one of the Beatles walks (5/week, offered by Original London Walks, above), visit the Beatles Shop (daily, 231 Baker Street, next to Sherlock Holmes Museum, Tube: Baker Street, tel. 020/7935-4464), or go to Abbey Road and walk the famous crosswalk (at intersection with Grove End, Tube: St. John's Wood).

Private Guides: Standard rates for London's registered guides are

Thursday: All sights are open, British Museum until 20:30 (selected galleries), National Portrait Gallery until 21:00. St. Martin-in-the-Fields hosts a 19:30 evening concert (for a fee).

Friday: All sights are open, British Museum until 20:30 (selected galleries only), National Portrait Gallery until 21:00, Tate Modern until 22:00. Best street market: Spitalfields. St. Martin-in-the-Fields offers two concerts (13:05-free, 19:30-fee).

Saturday: Most sights are open except legal ones (Old Bailey; Houses of Parliament—open summer Sat for tours only; skip the City). Vinopolis is open until 21:00, Tate Modern until 22:00. Best street markets: Portobello, Camden Lock, Greenwich. Evensong is at 15:00 at Westminster Abbey, 17:00 at St. Paul's. St. Martin-in-the-Fields hosts a concert at 19:30 (fee).

Notes: Evensong occurs daily at St. Paul's (Mon–Sat at 17:00 and Sun at 15:15) and daily except Wednesday at Westminster Abbey (Mon–Tue and Thu–Fri at 17:00, Sat–Sun at 15:00). London by Night Sightseeing Tour buses leave from Victoria Station every evening at 20:00, 21:00, and 22:00. The London Eye Ferris Wheel spins nightly until 22:00 in summer, until 20:00 in winter (closed Jan).

£97 for four hours, £146 for eight hours (tel. 020/7403-2962, www.touristguides.org.uk). Robina Brown leads tours with small groups in her Toyota Previa (£200/3 hrs, £300-450/day, tel. 020/7228-2238, www.driverguidetours.com, robina@driverguidetours.com). Britt Lonsdale, an energetic mother of twins, is another registered London guide (half day-£89, full day-£142, tel. 020/7386-9907, brittl@ntlworld.com).

▲▲**Cruises**—Boat tours with entertaining commentaries sail regularly from many points along the Thames. It's confusing, since there are several companies offering essentially the same thing. Your basic options are downstream (to the Tower and Greenwich), upstream (to Kew Gardens and Hampton Court), and round-trip scenic tour cruises. Most people depart from the Westminster Pier (at the base of Westminster Bridge under Big Ben). You can catch most of the same boats (with less waiting) from Waterloo Pier at the London Eye Ferris Wheel across the river. For pleasure and efficiency, consider combining a one-way cruise (to Kew, Greenwich, or wherever) with a Tube ride back. While Tube and bus tickets don't work on the boats, a Travel Card can snare you a 33 percent discount on most cruises. Buy boat tickets at the small ticket offices on the docks. Children and seniors get discounts. You can buy drinks and scant, pricey snacks on board. Clever budget travelers pack along a small picnic and munch while they cruise.

Here are some of the most popular cruise options.

To Tower of London: City Cruises boats sail 30 minutes to the Tower from Westminster Pier (one way-£5.20, round-trip-£6.30, one-way included with Big Bus London tour; covered by £8.50 "River Red Rover" ticket that includes Greenwich—see next paragraph; 3/hr during June–Aug daily 10:00–20:40, 2/hr and shorter hours rest of year).

To Greenwich: Two companies head to Greenwich from Westminster Pier. Choose between **City Cruises** (one way-£6.50, round-trip-£8; or get their £8.50 all-day, hop-on, hop-off "River Red Rover" ticket to have option of getting off at London Eye and Tower of London; June–Aug daily 10:00–17:00, fewer off-season, every 40 min, 70 min to Greenwich, usually narrated only downstream—to Greenwich, tel. 020/7740-0400, www.citycruises.com) and **Thames River Services** (one way-£6.50, round-trip-£8, April-Oct daily 10:00–16:00, July–Aug until 17:00, 2/hr, 50 min, has shorter hours and runs every 40 min rest of year, usually narrated only to Greenwich, tel. 020/7930-4097, www.royalriverthames.com).

To Kew Gardens: Westminster Passenger Services Association leaves for Kew Gardens from Westminster Pier (one way-£9, round-trip-£15, 4/day, generally departing 10:30–14:00, 90 min, narrated for 30 min, tel. 020/7930–2062, www.wpsa.co.uk). Some boats continue on to **Hampton Court Palace** for an additional £3 (and 90 min). Because of the river current, you'll save 30 minutes cruising from Hampton Court back into town.

Round-Trip Cruises: Fifty-minute round-trip cruises of the Thames leave hourly from Westminster and Embankment Piers (£7.50, included with Original London Bus tour—listed above, tape-recorded narration, Catamaran Circular Cruises, tel. 020/7987-1185). The London Eye Ferris Wheel operates its own "River Cruise Experience," offering a similar 45-minute circular tour from Waterloo Pier (must be done in combination with Ferris wheel, £20 includes both, reservations recommended and cost 50p, tel. 0870-443-9185, www.ba-londoneye.com).

From Tate to Tate: This new boat service for art-lovers connects the Tate Modern and Tate British galleries in 18 scenic minutes (departing every 40 min from 10:00–17:00, also stops at London Eye Ferris Wheel, £4.50, £10 per family, buy ticket at gallery desk or on board, tel. 020/7887-8008).

On Regent's Canal: Consider exploring London's canals by taking a cruise on historic Regent's Canal in north London. The good ship *Jenny Wren* offers 90-minute guided canal boat cruises from Walker's Quay in Camden Town to Little Venice (£6.50, March–Oct daily

THAMES BOAT PIERS

While Westminster Pier is the most popular, it's not the only dock in town. Consider all the options:

Westminster Pier, at the base of Big Ben, offers round-trip sightseeing cruises and lots of departures in both directions.

Waterloo Pier, at the base of London Eye Ferris Wheel, is a good, less-crowded alternative to Westminster, with many of the same cruise options.

Embankment Pier is near Covent Garden, Trafalgar Square, and Cleopatra's Needle (the obelisk on the Thames). You can take a round-trip cruise from here, or catch a boat to the Tower of London and Greenwich.

Tower Millennium Pier is at the Tower of London. Boats sail west to Westminster Pier or east to Greenwich.

Bankside Pier (near Tate Modern and Shakespeare's Globe) and **Millbank Millennium Pier** (near Tate Britain) are connected to each other by the new "Tate to Tate" ferry service.

12:30, 14:30, Sat–Sun also 10:30, 16:30, Walker's Quay, 250 Camden High Street, Tube: Camden Town, tel. 020/7485-4433 or 020/7485-6210, www .walkersquay.com). While in Camden Town, stop by the popular Camden Lock Market to browse through trendy arts and crafts (daily 10:00–18:00, busiest on weekends, a block from Walker's Quay).

London Duck Tours—A bright-yellow amphibious vehicle takes a gang of 30 tourists past some famous sights on land (Big Ben, Buckingham Palace, Piccadilly Circus), then splashes into the Thames for a 30-minute cruise (£17, 2/hr, daily 10:00–18:00, 75 min, live commentary, these book up in advance, departs from Chicheley Street behind County Hall near London Eye Ferris Wheel, Tube: Waterloo or Westminster, tel. 020/7928-3132, www.londonducktours.com).

SIGHTS

From Westminster Abbey to Trafalgar Square

▲▲**Westminster Walk**—Just about every visitor to London strolls the historic Whitehall boulevard from Big Ben to Trafalgar Square. Beneath London's modern traffic and big-city bustle lies 2,000 fascinating years of history. This three-quarter-mile, self-guided orientation walk (see map on page 57) gives you a whirlwind tour and connects the sights listed in this section.

LONDON AT A GLANCE

▲▲▲**British Museum** The world's greatest collection of artifacts from Western Civilization, including the Rosetta Stone and the Parthenon's Elgin Marbles. **Hours:** Daily 10:00–17:30, Thu–Fri until 20:30, but only a few galleries open after 17:30.

▲▲▲**National Gallery** Remarkable collection of European paintings (1250–1900), including Leonardo da Vinci, Sandro Botticelli, Diego Velázquez, Rembrandt, J.M.W. Turner, Vincent van Gogh, and the Impressionists. **Hours:** Daily 10:00–18:00, Wed until 21:00.

▲▲▲**British Library** Impressive array of the most important literary treasures of the Western world, from the Magna Carta to Handel's *Messiah.* **Hours:** Mon–Fri 9:30–18:00, Tue until 20:00, Sat 9:30–17:00, Sun 11:00–17:00.

▲▲▲**Westminster Abbey** Britain's finest church, and the site of royal coronations and burials since 1066. **Hours:** Mon–Fri 9:00–16:45, Wed also 18:00–-19:45, Sat 9:30–14:45, closed Sun to sightseers but open for services.

▲▲▲**St. Paul's Cathedral** The main cathedral of the Anglican Church, designed by Christopher Wren, with a climbable dome and daily evensong services. **Hours:** Mon–Sat 8:30–16:30, closed Sun except for worship.

▲▲▲**Tower of London** Historic castle, palace, and prison, today housing the crown jewels and a witty band of Beefeaters. **Hours:** March-Oct Mon–Sat 9:00–18:00, Sun 10:00–18:00; Nov–Feb Tue–Sat 9:00–17:00, Sun–Mon 10:00–17:00.

▲▲▲**London Eye Ferris Wheel** Enormous observation wheel, dominating London's skyline and offering commanding views. **Hours:** April–mid-Sept daily 9:30–22:00, mid-Sept–March 9:30–20:00, closed Jan.

▲▲▲**Tate Modern** Art by Claude Monet, Henri Matisse, Salvador Dalí, Pablo Picasso, and Andy Warhol, displayed in a converted power house. **Hours:** Daily 10:00–18:00, Fri–Sat until 22:00.

▲▲**Tate Britain** Collection of British painting from the 16th century through modern times, including works by William Blake, the Pre-Raphaelites, and Turner. **Hours:** Daily 10:00–17:50.

▲▲Houses of Parliament London's famous neo-Gothic landmark, topped by Big Ben and occupied by the Houses of Lords and Commons. **Hours:** House of Commons—Mon 14:30–22:30, Tue–Thu 11:30–19:30, Fri 9:30–15:00; House of Lords—Mon–Wed 14:30–22:30 or until they finish, Thu from 12:00 on, sometimes Fri from 10:00.

▲▲Imperial War Museum Examines the military history of the bloody 20th century. **Hours:** Daily 10:00–18:00.

▲▲Cabinet War Rooms Underground WWII headquarters of Churchill's war effort. **Hours:** Daily April—Sept 9:30–18:00, Oct–March 10:00–18:00.

▲▲National Portrait Gallery A pictorial *Who's Who* of British history, featuring portraits of this nation's most important historical figures. **Hours:** Daily 10:00–18:00, Thu–Fri until 21:00.

▲▲Buckingham Palace Britain's royal residence with the famous changing of the guard. **Hours:** Palace—Aug-Sept only, daily 9:30-17:00; Guard—Almost daily in summer at 11:30, every other day all year long.

▲▲Shakespeare's Globe Timbered, thatch-roofed reconstruction of the Bard's original wooden "O." **Hours:** Actor-led tours mid-May–Sept Mon–Sat 9:30–12:00, Sun 9:30–11:30; virtual tours daily 12:30–16:00; actor tours also Oct–mid-May daily 10:30-17:00; also regular performances (see "Entertainment and Theater," page 90).

▲▲Victoria and Albert Museum The best collection of decorative arts anywhere. **Hours:** Daily 10:00–17:45, Wed until 21:30.

▲▲Somerset House Grand 18th-century civic palace housing three fine art museums: Courtauld Gallery (decent painting collection), Hermitage Rooms (rotating exhibits from famous St. Petersburg musuem), and the Gilbert Collection (decorative arts). **Hours:** Daily 10:00–18:00.

▲▲Old Operating Theatre Museum 19th-century hall where surgeons performed amputations for an audience of aspiring med students. **Hours:** Daily 10:30–17:00.

▲▲Vinopolis: City of Wine Offers a breezy history of wine with plenty of tasting opportunities. **Hours:** Daily 11:00–18:00, Sat and Mon until 21:00.

Start halfway across **Westminster Bridge** (#1 on map) for that "Wow, I'm really in London!" feeling. Get a close-up view of the **Houses of Parliament** and **Big Ben** (floodlit at night). Downstream you'll see the **London Eye Ferris Wheel.** Down the stairs to Westminster Pier are boats to the Tower of London and Greenwich.

En route to Parliament Square, you'll pass a statue of **Boadicea** (#2), the Celtic queen defeated by Roman invaders in A.D. 60.

To thrill your loved ones (or bug the envious), call home from a pay phone near Big Ben at about three minutes before the hour. You'll find a phone on Great George Street, across from Parliament Square. As Big Ben chimes, stick the receiver outside the booth and prove you're in London: Ding dong ding dong...dong ding ding dong.

Wave hello to Churchill in Parliament Square (#3). To his right is **Westminster Abbey** with its two stubby, elegant towers.

Walk north up Parliament Street (which turns into Whitehall) toward Trafalgar Square. You'll see the thought-provoking **Cenotaph** (#5) in the middle of the street, reminding passersby of Britain's many war dead. To visit the Cabinet War Rooms (see below) take a left before the Cenotaph, on King Charles Street (#4).

Continuing on Whitehall, stop at the barricaded and guarded little **10 Downing Street** to see the British "White House" (#6), home of the prime minister. Break the bobby's boredom and ask him a question.

Nearing Trafalgar Square, look for the **Horse Guards** behind the gated fence (11:00 inspection Mon–Sat, 10:00 on Sun; dismounting ceremony daily at 16:00) and the 17th-century **Banqueting House** across the street (#7; see below).

The column topped by Lord Nelson marks **Trafalgar Square** (#8). The stately domed building on the far side of the square is the **National Gallery** (free), which has a classy café (upstairs in the Sainsbury wing). To the right of the National Gallery is **St. Martin-in-the-Fields Church** and its Café in the Crypt.

To get to Piccadilly from Trafalgar Square, walk up Cockspur Street to Haymarket, then take a short left on Coventry Street to colorful **Piccadilly Circus.**

Near Piccadilly you'll find the **Britain and London Visitors Centre** and piles of theaters. **Leicester Square** (with its half-price ticket booth for plays) thrives just a few blocks away. Walk through gritty **Soho** (north of Shaftesbury Avenue) for its fun pubs (see "Food is Fun" Dinner Crawl, page 106). From Piccadilly or Oxford Circus, you can taxi, bus, or Tube home.

▲▲▲**Westminster Abbey**—As the greatest church in the English-speaking world, Westminster Abbey has been the place where England's kings and queens have been crowned and buried since 1066. A thousand years of English history—3,000 tombs, the remains of 29 kings and queens, and hundreds of memorials—lie within its walls and under

Westminster Walk

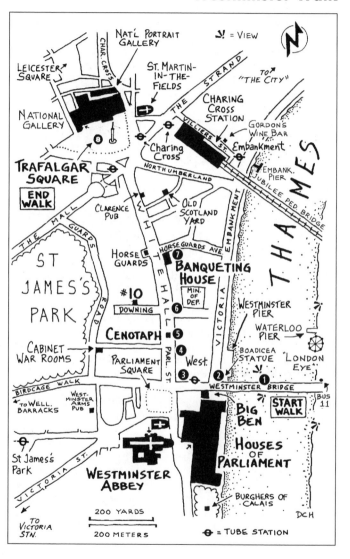

↘! = VIEW

Nat'l PORTRAIT GALLERY

LEICESTER SQUARE

CHAR. CROSS ROAD

ST. MARTIN-IN-THE-FIELDS

THE STRAND

TO "THE CITY"

CHARING CROSS STATION

GORDON'S WINE BAR

NATIONAL GALLERY

VILLIERS ST.

Charing Cross

Embankment

THAMES

8

TRAFALGAR SQUARE

NORTHUMBERLAND

EMBANK. PIER

JUBILEE PED. BRIDGE

END WALK

CLARENCE PUB

OLD SCOTLAND YARD

THE MALL

GUARDS

ST JAMES'S PARK

Horse GUARDS

GUARDS ROAD

HORSEGUARDS AVE.

7

BANQUETING HOUSE

EMBANKMENT

WHITEHALL

#10 DOWNING

MIN. OF DEF.

6

WESTMINSTER PIER

VICTORIA

WATERLOO PIER

CABINET WAR ROOMS

CENOTAPH

5

4

West.

BOADICEA STATUE

"LONDON EYE"

PARL. ST.

3

2

PARLIAMENT SQUARE

PARLIAMENT SQUARE

BIRDCAGE WALK

1

WESTMINSTER BRIDGE

TO WELL. BARRACKS

WEST-MINSTER ARMS PUB

St James's Park

BIG BEN

START WALK

BUS 11

VICTORIA ST.

HOUSES OF PARLIAMENT

WESTMINSTER ABBEY

BURGHERS OF CALAIS

TO VICTORIA STN.

DCH

200 YARDS

200 METERS

⊖ = TUBE STATION

its stone slabs. Like a stony refugee camp huddled outside St. Peter's gates, this place has a story to tell and the best way to enjoy it is with a **tour** (audioguide-£2, live-£3; many prefer the audioguide because it's self-paced, both tours include entry to cloister museums). Experience an **evensong** service—awesome in a nearly empty church (weekdays except Wed at 17:00, Sat–Sun at 15:00). The **organ recital** on Sunday at 17:45 is another highlight (fee, 40 min). Organ concerts here are great and inexpensive; look for signs with schedule details (or visit www.westminster -abbey.org).

Three tiny **museums** ring the cloister (£1 covers all, on top of your abbey ticket; or free with either the audioguide or live tour): the Chapter House (where the monks held their daily meetings, notable for its fine architecture and well-described but faded medieval art), the Pyx Chamber (containing an exhibit on the king's treasury), and the Abbey Museum (which tells of the abbey's history, royal coronations, and burials). Look into the impressively realistic eyes of Henry VII's funeral effigy (one of a fascinating series of wax-and-wood statues that graced royal coffins during funeral processions for three centuries).

Enter the abbey on the Big Ben side (often with a sizable line, visit early to avoid crowds) and then follow a one-way route through this English hall of fame around the church and cloisters (with the three small museums), back through the nave, and out (£6 for abbey entry, Mon–Fri 9:00–16:45, Wed also 18:00–19:45, Sat 9:30–14:45, last admission 60 min before closing, closed Sun to sightseers but open for services and organ recital, photography prohibited, coffee in cloister, Tube: Westminster or St. James's Park, call for tour schedule, tel. 020/7222-7110). Since the church is often closed to the public for special services, it's wise to call first.

For a free peek inside and a quiet sit in the nave, you can tell a guard at the west end (where the tourists exit) that you'd like to pay your respects to Britain's Unknown Soldier. If the guard is nice, he might let you slip in.

▲▲**Houses of Parliament (Palace of Westminster)**—This neo-Gothic icon of London, the royal residence from 1042 to 1547, is now the meeting place of the legislative branch of government. Tourists are welcome to view debates in either the bickering House of Commons or the genteel House of Lords (when in session—indicated by a flag flying atop the Victoria Tower). While the actual debates are generally extremely dull, it is a thrill to be inside and see the British government inaction (House of Commons: Mon 14:30–22:30, Tue, Wed, Thu 11:30–19:30, Fri 9:30–15:00, generally less action and no lines after 18:00, use St. Stephen's entrance, Tube: Westminster, tel. 020/7219-4272 for schedule, www.parliament.uk). The House of Lords has more pageantry, shorter lines, and less interesting debates (Mon–Wed 14:30–22:30 or until they finish, Thu from 12:00 on, sometimes Fri from 10:00 on, tel.

020/7219-3107 for schedule). If there's only one line outside, it's for the House of Commons. Go to the gate and tell the guard you want the Lords (that's the second "line" with no people in it). You may pop right in—that is, after you've cleared the security gauntlet. Once you've seen the Lords (hide your House of Lords flier), you can often slip directly over to the House of Commons and join the gang waiting in the lobby. Inside the lobby, you'll find an announcement board with the day's line-up for both houses.

Just past security to the left, study the big dark **Westminster Hall,** which survived the 1834 fire. The hall was built in the 11th century, and its famous self-supporting hammer-beam roof was added in 1397. The Houses of Parliament are located in what was once the Palace of Westminster, long the palace of England's medieval kings, until it was largely destroyed by fire in 1834. The palace was rebuilt in Victorian Gothic style (a move away from neo-classicism back to England's Christian and medieval heritage, true to the Romantic Age). It was completed in 1860.

Houses of Parliament tours are offered in August and September (£7; 75 min, roughly Mon, Tue, Fri, and Sat 9:15–16:30; Wed and Thu 13:15–16:30; to avoid waits, book in advance through First Call, tel. 0870-906-3773, www.firstcalltickets.com, no booking fee). Meet your Blue Badge guide (at the Sovereign's Entrance—far south end) for a behind-the-scenes peek at the royal chambers and both Houses.

The **Jewel Tower** is the only other part of the old Palace of Westminster to survive (besides Westminster Hall). It contains a fine little exhibit on Parliament (first floor—history, second floor—Parliament today) with a 25-minute video and lonely, picnic-friendly benches (£2, April–Sept daily 10:00–18:00, Oct daily 10:00–17:00, Nov–March daily 10:00–16:00, across street from St. Stephen's Gate, tel. 020/7222-2219).

Big Ben, the clock tower (315 feet high), is named for its 13-ton bell, Ben. The light above the clock is lit when the House of Commons is sitting. The face of the clock is huge—you can actually see the minute hand moving. For a hip view of it, walk halfway over Westminster Bridge.

▲▲**Cabinet War Rooms**—This is a fascinating walk through the underground headquarters of the British government's fight against the Nazis in the darkest days of the Battle for Britain. The 27-room nerve center of the British war effort was used from 1939 to 1945. Churchill's room, the map room, and other rooms are just as they were in 1945. For all the blood, sweat, toil, and tears details, pick up an audioguide at the entry and follow the included and excellent 60-minute tour. Be patient—it's worth it (£7, April–Sept daily 9:30–18:00, Oct-March daily 10:00–18:00, last entry 45 min before closing, on King Charles Street 200 yards off Whitehall, follow the signs, Tube: Westminster, tel. 020/ 7930-6961, www.iwm.org.uk).

For a nearby pub lunch, try the Westminster Arms (food served downstairs, on Storey's Gate, a couple of blocks south of Cabinet War Rooms).

Horse Guards—The Horse Guards change daily at 11:00 (10:00 on Sun), and there's a colorful dismounting ceremony daily at 16:00. The rest of the day, they just stand there—terrible for camcorders (on Whitehall, between Trafalgar Square and #10 Downing Street, Tube: Westminster). While Buckingham Palace pageantry is canceled when it rains, the horse guards change regardless of the weather.

▲**Banqueting House**—England's first Renaissance building was designed by Inigo Jones around 1620. It's one of the few London landmarks spared by the 1666 fire and the only surviving part of the original Palace of Whitehall. Don't miss its Peter Paul Rubens ceiling, which, at Charles I's request, drove home the doctrine of the legitimacy of the divine right of kings. In 1649—divine right ignored—Charles I was beheaded on the balcony of this building by a Cromwellian parliament. Admission includes a restful 20-minute audiovisual history, which shows the place in banqueting action; a 30-minute audio tour—interesting only to history buffs; and a look at the exquisite banqueting hall (£4, Mon–Sat 10:00–17:00, closed Sun, last entry at 16:30, subject to closure for government functions, aristocratic WC, immediately across Whitehall from the Horse Guards, Tube: Westminster, tel. 020/7930-4179). Just up the street is Trafalgar Square.

Trafalgar Square

▲▲**Trafalgar Square**—London's central square, the climax of most marches and demonstrations, is a thrilling place to simply hang out. Lord Nelson stands atop his 185-foot-tall fluted granite column, gazing out to Trafalgar, where he lost his life but defeated the French fleet. Part of this 1842 memorial is made from his victims' melted-down cannons. He's surrounded by giant lions, hordes of people, and—until recently—even more pigeons. London's mayor, Ken Livingstone (nicknamed "Red Ken" for his passion for an activist government), decided that London's "flying rats" were a public nuisance and evicted the venerable seed salesmen (Tube: Charing Cross).

▲▲▲**National Gallery**—Displaying Britain's top collection of European paintings from 1250 to 1900 (works by Leonardo, Botticelli, Velázquez, Rembrandt, Turner, van Gogh, and the Impressionists), this is one of Europe's great galleries. While the collection is huge, following the route suggested on the map (on page 62) will give you my best quick visit. The audioguide tours are the best I've used in Europe (suggested £4 donation). Don't miss the Micro Gallery, a computer room even your dad could have fun in (closes 30 min earlier than museum); you can study any artist, style, or topic in the museum and even print out a tailor-made tour map (free, daily 10:00–18:00, Wed until 21:00, free one-hour overview tours daily at 11:30 and 14:30 plus Wed at 18:30, photography prohibited, on Trafalgar Square, Tube: Charing Cross or Leicester Square, tel. 020/7747-2885, www.nationalgallery.org.uk).

▲▲National Portrait Gallery—Put off by halls of 19th-century characters who meant nothing to me, I used to call this "as interesting as someone else's yearbook." But a selective walk through this 500-year-long *Who's Who* of British history is quick and free and puts faces on the story of England. A bonus is the chance to admire some great art by painters such as Hans Holbein, Sir Anthony Van Dyck, William Hogarth, Sir Joshua Reynolds, and Thomas Gainsborough. The collection is well described, not huge, and in historical sequence, from the 16th century on the second floor to today's royal family on the ground floor.

Some highlights: Henry VIII and wives; several fascinating portraits of the "Virgin Queen" Elizabeth I, Sir Francis Drake, and Sir Walter Raleigh; the only real-life portrait of William Shakespeare; Oliver Cromwell and Charles I with his head on; self-portraits and other portraits by Gainsborough and Reynolds; the Romantics (William Blake, Lord Byron, William Wordsworth, and company); Queen Victoria and her era; and the present royal family, including the late Princess Diana.

The excellent audioguide tours (£3 donation requested) describe each room (or era in British history) and more than 300 paintings. You'll learn more about British history than art and actually hear interviews with 20th-century subjects as you stare at their faces (free, daily 10:00–18:00, Thu–Fri until 21:00, entry 100 yards off Trafalgar Square, around corner from National Gallery, opposite Church of St. Martin-in-the-Fields, tel. 020/7306-0055, recorded info tel. 020/7312-2463, www.npg.org.uk). The elegant Portrait Restaurant on the top floor comes with views and high prices (cheaper Portrait Café in basement).

▲St. Martin-in-the-Fields—This church, built in the 1720s with a Gothic spire atop a Greek-type temple, is an oasis of peace on the wild and noisy Trafalgar Square (free, donations welcome, open daily, www.stmartin-in-the-fields.org). St. Martin cared for the poor. "In the fields" was where the first church stood on this spot (in the 13th century), between Westminster and the City. Stepping inside, you still feel a compassion for the needs of the people in this community. A free flier provides a brief yet worthwhile self-guided tour. The church is famous for its concerts. Consider a free lunchtime concert (Mon, Tue, and Fri at 13:05) or an evening concert (£6-18, Thu–Sat at 19:30, box office tel. 020/7839-8362, church tel. 020/7766-1100). Downstairs, you'll find a ticket office for concerts, a gift shop, a brass-rubbing center, and a fine support-the-church cafeteria (see "Eating," page 103).

National Gallery Highlights

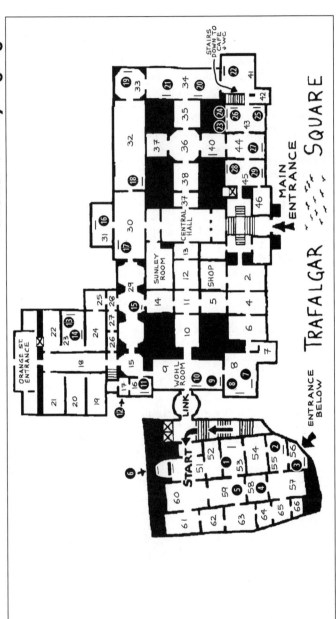

MEDIEVAL & EARLY RENAISSANCE

1 Wilton Diptych
2 UCCELLO Battle of San Romano
3 VAN EYCK Arnolfini Marriage
4 BOTTICELLI Venus and Mars
5 CRIVELLI Annunciation with St. Emidius

HIGH RENAISSANCE

6 LEONARDO DA VINCI Virgin and Child (painting and cartoon)

NATIONAL GALLERY MAIN
BUILDING - HIGH RENAISSANCE

7 MICHELANGELO Entombment
8 RAPHAEL Pope Julius II

VENETIAN RENAISSANCE

9 TITIAN Bacchus and Ariadne
10 TINTORETTO Origin of the Milky Way

NORTHERN PROTESTANT ART

11 VERMEER Young Woman
12 "A PEEPSHOW"
13 REMBRANDT Belshazzar's Feast
14 REMBRANDT Self-Portrait

BAROQUE & ROCOCO

15 RUBENS The Judgment of Paris
16 VAN DYCK Charles I on Horseback
17 VELAZQUEZ The Rokeby Venus
18 CARAVAGGIO Supper at Emmaus
19 BOUCHER Pan and Syrinx

BRITISH

20 CONSTABLE The Hay Wain
21 TURNER The Fighting Temeraire
22 DELAROCHE The Execution of Lady Jane Grey

IMPRESSIONISM & BEYOND

23 MONET Gare St. Lazare
24 MONET The Water Lily Pond
25 MANET The Waitress (Corner of a Café-Concert)
26 RENOIR Boating on the Seine
27 SEURAT Bathers at Asnières
28 VAN GOGH Sunflowers
29 CEZANNE Bathers

London's Top Squares

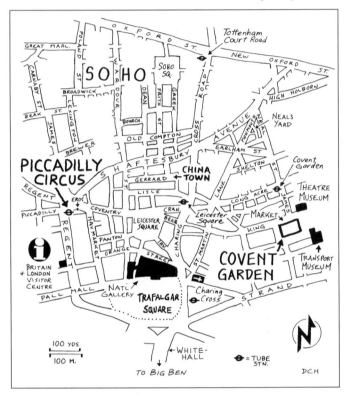

London's Top Squares

SOHO

PICCADILLY CIRCUS

CHINA TOWN

COVENT GARDEN

TRAFALGAR SQUARE

BRITAIN & LONDON VISITOR CENTRE

NAT'L GALLERY

100 YDS.
100 M.

←WHITE-HALL

TO BIG BEN

●=TUBE STN.

DCH

More Top Squares: Piccadilly, Soho, and Covent Garden

For a "Food Is Fun" dinner crawl from Covent Garden to Soho, see page 106.

▲▲**Piccadilly Circus**—London's most touristy square got its name from the fancy ruffled shirts—*picadils*—made in the neighborhood long ago. Today the square is surrounded by fascinating streets swimming with youth on the rampage. For overstimulation, drop by the extremely trashy **Pepsi Trocadero Center**'s "theme park of the future" for its Segaworld virtual-reality games, nine-screen cinema, and thundering IMAX theater (admission to Trocadero is free; individual attractions cost £2-8; before paying full price for IMAX, look for a discount ticket at brochure racks at the TI or hotels; located between Coventry Street and Shaftesbury Avenue, just off Piccadilly). Chinatown, to the east, has swollen since Hong Kong lost its independence. Nearby Shaftesbury

Avenue and Leicester Square teem with fun-seekers, theaters, Chinese restaurants, and street singers.

Soho—North of Piccadilly, trendy and motley Soho is well worth a gawk. But Soho is also London's red light district, where "friendly models" wait in tiny rooms up dreary stairways and voluptuous con artists sell strip shows. While venturing up a stairway to check out a model is interesting, anyone who goes into any one of the shows will be ripped off. Every time. Even a £5 show in a "licensed bar" comes with a £100 cover or minimum (as it's printed on the drink menu) and a "security man." You may accidentally buy a £200 bottle of bubbly. And suddenly, the door has no handle.

Telephone sex is hard to avoid these days in London. Phone booths are littered with racy fliers of busty ladies "new in town." Some travelers gather six or eight phone booths' worth of fliers and take them home for kinky wallpaper.

▲▲**Covent Garden**—This boutique-ish shopping district is a people-watcher's delight, with cigarette eaters, Punch-and-Judy acts, food that's good for you (but not your wallet), trendy crafts, sweet whiffs of marijuana, two-tone hair (neither natural), and faces that could set off a metal detector (Tube: Covent Garden). For better Covent Garden lunch deals, walk a block or two away from the eye of this touristic hurricane (check out the places north of the Tube station along Endell and Neal streets).

Museums near Covent Garden

▲▲**Somerset House**—This grand 18th-century civic palace offers a marvelous public space, three fine art collections, and a riverside terrace (between the Strand and the Thames). The palace once housed the national registry that records Britain's births, marriages, and deaths ("where they hatched 'em, latched 'em, and dispatched 'em"). Step into the courtyard to enjoy the fountain. Go ahead...walk through it. The 55 jets get playful twice an hour.

Surrounding you are three small and sumptuous sights: the Courtauld Gallery (paintings), the Gilbert Collection (fine arts), and the Hermitage Rooms (the finest art of czarist Russia). All three are open the same hours (daily 10:00–18:00, buy a ticket at one gallery and get a £1 discount off admission to either or both of the other two on the same day, easy bus #6, #9, #11, #13, #15, or #23 from Trafalgar Square, Tube: Temple or Covent Garden, tel. 020/7848-2526 or 020/7845-4600, www.somerset-house.org.uk). The Web site lists a busy schedule of tours, kids' events, and concerts. The riverside terrace is picnic-friendly (deli inside lobby).

The **Courtauld Gallery** is less impressive than the National Gallery, but its wonderful collection of paintings is still a joy. The gallery is part of the Courtauld Institute of Art, and the thoughtful description

Central London

NOT TO SCALE
BIG BEN TO TRAFALGAR
IS ABOUT ¾ MILE

of each piece of art reminds visitors that the gallery is still used for teaching. You'll see medieval European paintings and works by Rubens, the Impressionists (Edouard Manet, Claude Monet, Edgar Degas, Georges Seurat), Post-Impressionists (such as Paul Cézanne), and more (£5, free Mon until 14:00, last admission 17:15, downstairs cafeteria, cloak room, lockers, and WC).

The **Hermitage Rooms** offer a taste of Romanov imperial splendor. As Russia struggles and tourists are staying away, someone had the bright idea of sending the best of its art to London to raise some hard cash. These five rooms host a different collection every six months, with a standard intro to the czar's winter palace in St. Petersburg (£6, includes unmissable live video of the square, tel. 020/7420-9410). To see what's on, visit www.hermitagerooms.org.uk.

The **Gilbert Collection** displays 800 pieces of the finest in European decorative arts, from diamond-studded gold snuffboxes to intricate Italian mosaics. Maybe you've seen Raphael paintings and Botticelli frescoes...but this lush collection is refreshingly different (£5, includes free audioguide with a highlights tour and a helpful loaner magnifying glass, free after 16:30, last admission 17:30).

▲**London Transport Museum**—This wonderful museum is a delight for kids. Whether you're cursing or marveling at the buses and Tube, the growth of Europe's biggest city has been made possible by its public transit system. Watch the growth of the Tube, then sit in the simulator to "drive" a train (£6, kids under 16 free, Sat–Thu 10:00–18:00, Fri 11:00–18:00, 30 yards southeast of Covent Garden's marketplace, tel. 020/7565-7299).

Theatre Museum—This earnest museum, worthwhile for theater buffs, traces the development of British theater from Shakespeare to today (free, Tue–Sun 10:00–18:00, closed Mon, free guided tours at 11:00, 12:00, and 16:00, a block east of Covent Garden's marketplace down Russell Street, tel. 020/7943-4700, www.theatremuseum.org).

North London

▲▲▲**British Museum, Great Court, and Reading Room**—Simply put, this is the greatest chronicle of civilization...anywhere. A visit here is like taking a long hike through Encyclopedia Britannica National Park. Entering on Great Russell Street, you'll step into the Great Court, the glass-domed hub of a two-acre cultural complex, containing restaurants, shops, and lecture halls plus the Round Reading Room.

The most popular sections of the museum fill the ground floor: Egyptian, Mesopotamian, and ancient Greek—with the famous Elgin Marbles from the Athenian Parthenon. Huge winged lions (which guarded Assyrian palaces 800 years before Christ) guard these great ancient galleries. For a brief tour, connect these ancient dots:

Start with the **Egyptian.** Wander from the Rosetta Stone past the many statues. At the end of the hall, climb the stairs to mummy land.

Back at the winged lions, wander through the dark, violent, and mysterious **Assyrian** rooms. The Nimrud Gallery is lined with royal propaganda reliefs and wounded lions.

The most modern of the ancient art fills the **Greek** section. Find room 11 behind the winged lions and start your walk through Greek art history with the simple and primitive Cycladic fertility figures. Later, painted vases show a culture really into partying. The finale is the Elgin Marbles. The much-wrangled-over bits of the Athenian Parthenon (from 450 B.C.) are even more impressive than they look. To best appreciate these ancient carvings, take the audioguide tour (available in this gallery).

Be sure to venture upstairs to see artifacts from **Roman Britain** (Room 50) that surpass anything you'll see at Hadrian's Wall or elsewhere in Britain. Nearby, the Dark Age Britain exhibits offer a worthwhile peek at that bleak era; look for the Sutton Hoo Ship Burial artifacts from a seventh-century royal burial on the east coast of England (Room 41). A rare Michelangelo cartoon is in Room 90.

British Museum

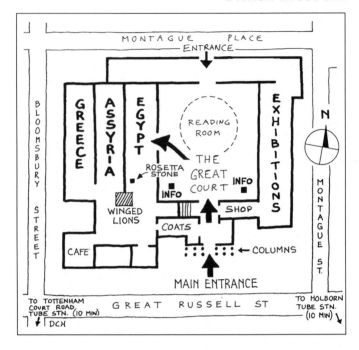

The **Queen Elizabeth II Great Court** is Europe's largest covered square—bigger than a football field. This people-friendly court—delightfully out of the London rain—was for 150 years one of London's great lost spaces...closed off and gathering dust. While the vast British Museum wraps around the court, its centerpiece is the stately **Reading Room**—famous as the place where Karl Marx hung out while formulating his ideas on communism and writing *Das Kapital*. The Reading Room—one of the fine cast-iron buildings of the 19th century—is free for you to wander, but there's little to see that you can't see from the doorway.

Hours and Location: The British Museum is free (£2 donation requested, daily 10:00–17:30, Thu–Fri until 20:30—but only a few galleries open after 17:30, least crowded weekday late afternoons, Great Russell Street, Tube: Tottenham Court Road, tel. 020/7323-8000 or recorded information 020/7388-2227, www.thebritishmuseum.ac.uk). The Reading Room is free and open daily 10:00–17:30 (Thu until 20:30). Computer terminals within the Reading Room offer COMPASS, a database of information about selected museum items. The Great Court has longer opening hours than the museum (daily 9:00–18:00, Thu–Sat until 23:00).

Tours: Guided **eyeOpener tours** (free, nearly hrly, 50 min) are each different, focusing on one particular subject within the museum. These leave throughout the day and can make the visit much more meaningful. There are also three types of **audioguide tours:** Top 50 highlights (90 min, pick up at Great Court information desks), the Parthenon Sculptures (60 min, get at desk outside Parthenon Galleries), and the family tour, with themes such as "bodies, boardgames, and beasts" (length varies, pick up at Great Court information desks). To rent an audioguide (£3.50), you'll need to leave a photo ID and £10 for a deposit.

▲▲▲**British Library**—The British Empire built its greatest monuments out of paper. And it's in literature that England made her lasting contribution to civilization and the arts. Britain's national archives has more than 12 million books, 180 miles of shelving, and the deepest basement in London. But everything that matters for your visit is in one delightful room labeled "The Treasures." This room is filled with literary and historical documents that changed the course of history. You'll trace the evolution of European maps over 800 years. Follow the course of the Bible—from the earliest known gospels (written on scraps of papyrus) to the first complete Bible to the original King James version and the Gutenberg Bible. You'll see Leonardo's doodles, the Magna Carta, Shakespeare's First Folio, the original *Alice in Wonderland* in Lewis Carroll's handwriting, and manuscripts by Ludwig van Beethoven, Wolfgang Amadeus Mozart, John Lennon, and Paul McCartney. Finish in the fascinating *Turning the Pages* exhibit, which lets you actually browse through virtual manuscripts of a few of these treasures on a computer (free, Mon–Fri 9:30–18:00, Tue until 20:00, Sat 9:30–17:00, Sun 11:00–17:00; 60-min tours for £5 usually offered Mon, Wed, and Fri–Sun at 15:00, also Tue 18:30, Sat 10:30, and Sun 11:30; call 020/7412-7332 to confirm schedule and reserve; £3.50 audioguide, £1 lockers, Tube: King's Cross, turn right out of station and walk a block to 96 Euston Road, library tel. 020/7412-7000, www.bl.uk). The ground-floor café is next to a vast and fun pull-out stamp collection, and the cafeteria upstairs serves good hot meals.

▲**Madame Tussaud's Waxworks**—This is expensive but dang good. The original Madame Tussaud did wax casts of heads lopped off during the French Revolution (such as Marie-Antoinette's). She took her show on the road and ended up in London. And now it's much easier to be featured. The gallery is one big *Who's Who* photo-op—a huge hit with the kind of travelers who skip the British Museum. Don't miss the gallery of has-been heads that no longer merit a body (such as Sammy Davis Jr. and Nikita Khrushchev). After looking a hundred famous people in their glassy eyes and surviving a silly hall of horror, you'll board a Disney-type ride and cruise through a kid-pleasing "Spirit of London" time trip (£20, children-£15, under 5 free, tickets include entrance to

British Library Highlights

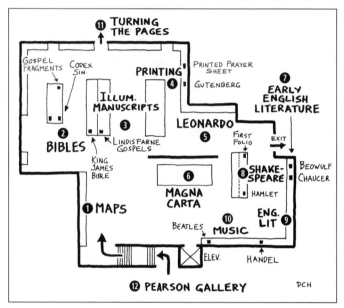

the London Planetarium, Jan–Sept daily 9:00–17:30, Oct–Dec Mon–Fri 10:00–17:30, Sat–Sun 9:30–17:30, last entry 30 min before closing, Marylebone Road, Tube: Baker Street). The waxworks are popular. Avoid a wait by either booking ahead to get a ticket with an entry time (tel. 0870-400-3000, online at www.madame-tussauds.com for a £2 fee, or at no extra cost at the Britain and London Visitors Centre or the TIs at Victoria and Waterloo train stations) or arriving late in the day—90 minutes is plenty of time for the exhibit.

Sir John Soane's Museum—Architects and fans of eclectic knickknacks love this quirky place (free, Tue–Sat 10:00–17:00, first Tue of the month also 18:00–21:00, closed Sun-Mon, £3 guided tours Sat at 14:30, five blocks east of British Museum, Tube: Holborn, 13 Lincoln's Inn Fields, tel. 020/7405-2107).

Buckingham Palace

▲**Buckingham Palace**—This lavish home has been Britain's royal residence since 1837. When the queen is at home, the royal standard flies; otherwise the Union Jack flaps in the wind (£12 for state apartments and throne room, open Aug–Sept only, daily 9:30–17:00, only 8,000 visitors a day—to get an entry time, come early or for £1 extra book ahead by phone or online, Tube: Victoria, tel. 020/7321-2233, www.the-royal -collection.com, buckinghampalace@royalcollection.org.uk).

Buckingham Palace

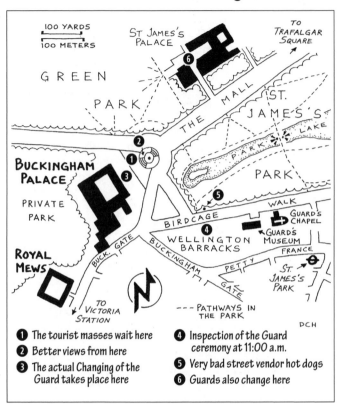

100 YARDS
100 METERS

ST JAMES'S PALACE

TO TRAFALGAR SQUARE

GREEN

PARK

THE MALL

ST. JAMES'S

LAKE

PARK

BUCKINGHAM PALACE

PRIVATE PARK

ROYAL MEWS

WALK

BIRDCAGE

WELLINGTON BARRACKS

GUARD'S CHAPEL

GUARD'S MUSEUM

FRANCE

ST. JAMES'S PARK

BUCK. GATE

BUCKINGHAM GATE

PETTY

TO VICTORIA STATION

- - - PATHWAYS IN THE PARK

DCH

❶ The tourist masses wait here

❷ Better views from here

❸ The actual Changing of the Guard takes place here

❹ Inspection of the Guard ceremony at 11:00 a.m.

❺ Very bad street vendor hot dogs

❻ Guards also change here

Royal Mews—Actually the queen's working stables, the "mews" are open to visitors to wander, talk to the horse-keeper, and see the well-groomed horses. Marvel at the gilded coaches paraded during royal festivals, see fancy horse gear—all well-described—and learn how skeptical the attendants were when the royals first parked a car in the stables (£5, April–Oct 11:00–16:00, closed Nov–March, Buckingham Palace Road, tel. 020/7321-2233).

▲▲**Changing of the Guard at Buckingham Palace**—The guards change with much fanfare at 11:30 almost daily in the summer and at a minimum, every other day all year long (no band when wet). Each month it's either daily or on odd or even days. Call 020/7321-2233 or check www.royalresidences.com for the day's plan. Join the mob behind the palace (the front faces a huge and extremely private park). You'll need to be early or tall to see much of the actual Changing of the Guard, but for the pageantry in the street you can pop by at 11:30. Stake out the high ground on the circular Victoria Monument for the best overall view. The marching troops and bands are colorful and even stirring, but the actual Changing of the Guard is a nonevent. It is interesting, however, to see nearly every tourist in London gathered in one place at the same time. Hop into a big black taxi and say, "Buck House, please." The show lasts about 30 minutes: Three troops parade by, the guard changes with much shouting, the band plays a happy little concert, and then they march out. On a balmy day, it's a fun happening.

For all the pomp with none of the crowds, see the colorful **Inspection of the Guard** ceremony at 11:00 in front of the **Wellington Barracks,** 500 yards east of the palace on Birdcage Walk. Afterward, stroll through nearby St. James's Park (Tube: Victoria, St. James's Park, or Green Park).

West London

▲**Hyde Park and Speakers' Corner**—London's "Central Park," originally Henry VIII's hunting grounds, has more than 600 acres of lush greenery, a huge man-made lake, the royal Kensington Palace (not worth touring), and the ornate neo-Gothic Albert Memorial across from the Royal Albert Hall. Early afternoons on Sunday (until early evening), Speakers' Corner offers soapbox oratory at its best (Tube: Marble Arch). "The grass roots of democracy" is actually a holdover from when the gallows stood here, and the criminal was allowed to say just about anything he wanted to before he swung. I dare you to raise your voice and gather a crowd—it's easy to do.

▲**Apsley House (Wellington Museum)**—Having beaten Napoleon at Waterloo, the Duke of Wellington was once the most famous man in Europe. He was given London's ultimate address, #1 London. His newly refurbished mansion offers one of London's best palace experiences. An 11-foot-tall marble statue (by Antonio Canova) of Napoleon, clad only in a fig leaf, greets you. Downstairs is a small gallery of Wellington memorabilia (including a pair of Wellington boots). The lavish upstairs shows off the duke's fine collection of paintings, including works by Velázquez and Jan Steen (£4.50, Tue–Sun 11:00–17:00, closed Mon, well-described by included audioguide, 20 yards from Hyde Park Corner Tube station, tel. 020/7499-5676, www.apsleyhouse.org.uk). Hyde Park's pleasant and picnic-wonderful rose garden is nearby.

▲▲**Victoria and Albert Museum**—The world's top collection of decorative arts (vases, stained glass, fine furniture, clothing, jewelry, carpets, and more) is a surprisingly interesting assortment of crafts from the West as well as Asian and Islamic cultures.

The V&A, which grew out of the Great Exhibition of 1851—that ultimate festival celebrating the Industrial Revolution and the greatness of Britain—was originally for manufactured art, but fine art sculptures

West London

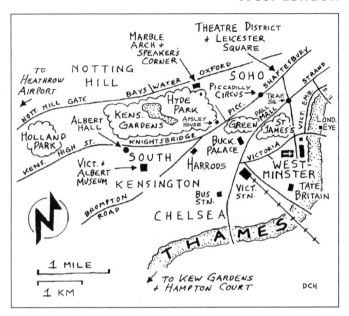

Map labels: THEATRE DISTRICT & LEICESTER SQUARE; MARBLE ARCH & SPEAKER'S CORNER; NOTTING HILL; TO HEATHROW AIRPORT; NOTT. HILL GATE; BAYSWATER; OXFORD; SOHO; SHAFTESBURY; STRAND; PICCADILLY CIRCUS; TRAF. SQ.; VICT. EMB.; HYDE PARK; KENS. GARDENS; ALBERT HALL; APSLEY HOUSE; PICC.; PALL MALL; GREEN PARK; ST. JAMES'S; LOND. EYE; HOLLAND PARK; KENS. HIGH ST.; KNIGHTSBRIDGE; BUCK. PALACE; VICT. & ALBERT MUSEUM; SOUTH KENSINGTON; HARRODS; VICTORIA; WESTMINSTER; BROMPTON ROAD; BUS STN.; VICT. STN.; TATE BRITAIN; CHELSEA; THAMES; N; 1 MILE; 1 KM; TO KEW GARDENS & HAMPTON COURT; DCH

(and copies) were soon added. After much support from Queen Victoria and Prince Albert, it was renamed after the royal couple, and its present building was opened in 1909. The idealistic Victorian notion that anyone can be continually improved by education and example remains the driving force behind this museum.

Cost, Hours, and Location: Free, possible fee for special exhibits, daily 10:00–17:45, Wed until 21:30 (Tube: South Kensington, a long tunnel leads directly from the Tube station to the museum, tel. 020/7942-2000, www.vam.ac.uk).

Museum Overview and Tours: The museum is large and gangly, with 150 rooms and over 12 miles of corridors. While just wandering works well here, consider catching one of the free 60-minute orientation tours (daily, on the half-hour from 10:30–15:30, also daily at 13:00, Wed at 16:30, and a half-hour version at 19:30) or buying the fine £5 *Hundred Highlights* guidebook, or the handy £1 *What to See at the V&A* brochure (outlines five self-guided, speedy tours).

To tour this museum on your own, grab a museum map and start with these ground-floor highlights:

Near the Entrance: The **Medieval Treasury** (room 43) has stained glass, bishops' robes, old columns, and good descriptions. Statues by **Antonio Canova** (room 50A)—white, polished, and pretty

Greek graces, minotaurs, and nymphs—are rare originals by the neo-classical master.

Southeast Corner (to the right of entrance, at the end of the hall): Plaster casts of **Trajan's Column** (room 46A) are a copy of Rome's 140-foot spiral relief telling the story of the conquest of Romania. (The V&A's casts are copies made for the benefit of 19th-century art students who couldn't afford a railpass.) Plaster casts of **Renaissance sculptures** (room 46B) let you compare Michelangelo's monumental *David* with Donatello's girlish *David;* see also Lorenzo Ghiberti's bronze Baptistery doors that inspired the Florentine Renaissance. The hall of **Great Fakes and Forgeries** (room 46) chronicles concocted art and historical objects passed off as originals.

Southwest Corner (left of entrance, end of hall): **Raphael's "cartoons"** (room 48A) are seven huge watercolor designs by the Renaissance master for tapestries meant for the Sistine Chapel. The cartoons were sent to Brussels, cut into strips (see the lines), and placed on the looms. Notice that the scenes, the Acts of Peter and Paul, are the reverse of the final product (lots of left-handed saints). The **Dress Gallery** (in room 40) has 400 years of English fashion corseted into 40 display cases. The **Musical Instruments** section displays lutes, harpsichords, early flutes, big violins, and strange, curly horns—some recognizable, some obsolete (room 40A, up the staircase in the center of the Dress Gallery).

The Rest of the Ground Floor: Room 41 has the finest collection of **Indian** decorative art outside India. There's medieval **stained glass** in room 28 (and much more upstairs).

Upstairs you can walk through the **British Galleries** for centuries of British furniture, clothing, glass, jewelry, and sculpture.

▲**Natural History Museum**—Across the street from Victoria and Albert, this mammoth museum is housed in a giant and wonderful Victorian, neo-Romanesque building. Built in the 1870s specifically to house the huge collection (50 million specimens), it has two halves: the Life Galleries (creepy-crawlies, human biology, the origin of species, "our place in evolution," and awesome dinosaurs) and the Earth Galleries (meteors, volcanoes, earthquakes, and so on). Exhibits are wonderfully explained, with lots of creative interactive displays. Pop in, if only for the wild collection of dinosaurs and the roaring *Tyrannosaurus rex.* Free 45-minute highlights tours occur daily about every hour from 11:00 to 16:00 (free, possible fee for special exhibits, Mon–Sat 10:00–18:00, Sun 11:00–18:00, last entrance 17:30, a long tunnel leads directly from South Kensington Tube station to museum, tel. 020/7942-5000, exhibit info and reservations tel. 020/7942-5011, www.nhm.ac.uk).

Science Museum—A sister to the Natural History museum, next door, this sprawling wonderland for curious minds is kid-perfect. It offers

East London: The City

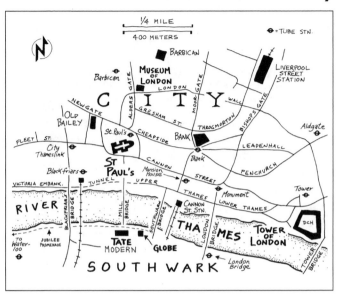

hands-on fun, from moon walks to deep-sea exploration, with trendy technology exhibits, an IMAX theater, and a kids' zone in the basement (free, daily 10:00–18:00, Exhibition Road, tel. 0870-870-4868).

East London: The City

▲▲The City of London—When Londoners say "The City," they mean the one-square-mile business, banking, and journalism center that 2,000 years ago was Roman Londinium. The outline of the Roman city walls can still be seen in the arc of roads from Blackfriars Bridge to Tower Bridge. Within the City are 24 churches designed by Christopher Wren, mostly just ornamentation around St. Paul's Cathedral. Today, while home to only 5,000 residents, the City thrives with over 500,000 office workers coming and going daily. It's a fascinating district to wander on weekdays, but since almost nobody actually lives there, it's dull in the evenings and on Saturday and Sunday.

▲Old Bailey—To view the British legal system in action—lawyers in little blond wigs speaking legalese with a British accent—spend a few minutes in the visitors' gallery at the Old Bailey (free, no kids under 14, Mon–Fri 10:30–13:00 & 14:00–16:30 most weeks, closed Sat–Sun, reduced hours in Aug; no bags, mobile phones, or cameras, but small purses OK; you can check your bag at the bagel shop next door—or any other entrepreneurial place nearby—for £1; Tube: St. Paul's, two blocks

St Paul's Cathedral

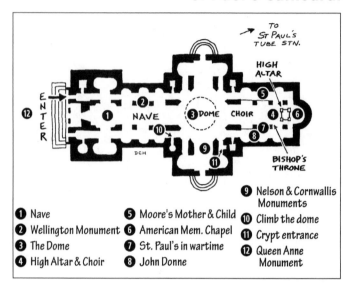

TO
St Paul's
TUBE STN.

HIGH
ALTAR

BISHOP'S
THRONE

❶ Nave
❷ Wellington Monument
❸ The Dome
❹ High Altar & Choir
❺ Moore's Mother & Child
❻ American Mem. Chapel
❼ St. Paul's in wartime
❽ John Donne
❾ Nelson & Cornwallis Monuments
❿ Climb the dome
⓫ Crypt entrance
⓬ Queen Anne Monument

northwest of St. Paul's on Old Bailey street, follow signs to public entrance, tel. 020/7248-3277).

▲▲▲St. Paul's Cathedral—Wren's most famous church is the great St. Paul's, its elaborate interior capped by a 365-foot dome. The crypt (included with admission) is a world of historic bones and memorials, including Admiral Nelson's tomb and interesting cathedral models. The great West Door is opened only for great occasions, such as the wedding of Prince Charles and the late Princess Diana in 1981. Stand in the back of the church and imagine how Diana felt before making the hike to the altar with the world watching. Sit under the second-largest dome in the world and eavesdrop on guided tours.

Since World War II, St. Paul's has been Britain's symbol of resistance. Despite 57 nights of bombing, the Nazis failed to destroy the cathedral, thanks to the St. Paul's volunteer fire watchmen, who stayed on the dome. Climb the dome for a great city view and some fun in the Whispering Gallery—where the precisely designed barrel of the dome lets sweet nothings circle audibly around to the opposite side (£6, includes church entry and dome climb, Mon–Sat 8:30–16:30, last entry 16:00, closed Sun except for worship and organ recital, no photography allowed, £2.50 for guided 90-min "super tours" of cathedral and crypt Mon–Sat at 11:00, 11:30, 13:30, and 14:00, confirm schedule at church or call 020/7236-4128; £3.50 for audioguide tour available Mon–Sat 8:45–15:00; Tube: St. Paul's). Sunday services are at 8:00, 10:15, 11:30

(sung Eucharist), 15:15 (evensong), and 18:00, with a free organ recital at 17:00. The **evensong** services are free, but nonpaying visitors are not allowed to linger afterward (Mon–Sat at 17:00, Sun at 15:15, 40 min). You'll find an inexpensive and cheery café in the crypt.

▲**Museum of London**—London, a 2,000-year-old city, is so littered with Roman ruins that when a London builder finds Roman antiquities, he doesn't stop work. He simply documents the finds, moves the artifacts to a museum, and builds on. If you're asking, "Why did the Romans build their cities underground?" a trip to the creative and entertaining London Museum is a must. Stroll through London history from pre-Roman times through the 1920s. This regular stop for the local school kids gives the best overview of London history in town (free, Mon–Sat 10:00–18:00, Sun 12:00–18:00, Tube: Barbican or St. Paul's, tel. 020/7600-3699).

Geffrye Decorative Arts Museum—Walk through a dozen English front rooms from 1600 to 1990 (free, Tue–Sat 10:00–17:00, Sun 12:00–17:00, closed Mon, Tube: Liverpool Street, then bus #149 or #242 north, tel. 020/7739-9893).

▲▲▲**Tower of London**—The tower has served as a castle in wartime, a king's residence in peace, and, most notoriously, as the prison and execution site of rebels. This historic fortress is host to more than three million visitors a year. Enjoy the free and entertaining 50-minute Beefeater tour (leaves regularly from inside the gate, first one usually at 9:30, last one usually at 15:30, 14:30 off-season). The crown jewels, dating from the Restoration, are the best on Earth—and come with hour-long lines for most of the day. To avoid the crowds, arrive when the Tower opens and go straight for the jewels, doing the Beefeater tour and White Tower later—or do the jewels after 16:30 (£13.50, one-day combo-ticket with Hampton Court Palace-£18, March–Oct Mon–Sat 9:00–18:00, Sun 10:00–18:00; Nov–Feb Tue–Sat 9:00–17:00, Sun–Mon 10:00–17:00; last entry 60 min before closing, the long but fast-moving ticket line is worst on Sun, no photography allowed of jewels or in chapels, skip the £3 audioguide, Tube: Tower Hill, tel. 0870-751-5177, recorded info: 020/7680-9004, booking: 020/7488-5681). You can avoid the long lines by picking up your ticket at any London TI or the Tower Hill Tube station ticket office.

Ceremony of the Keys—Every night at precisely 21:30, with pageantry-filled ceremony, the Tower of London is locked up, as it has been for the last 700 years. To attend this free 30-minute event (which some find dull and others thrilling), you need to request an invitation at least two months before your visit. Write to Ceremony of the Keys, H.M. Tower of London, London EC3N 4AB. Include your name; the addresses, names, and ages of all people attending (up to 6 people, nontransferable, no kids under age 8 allowed); requested date; alternative dates; and two international reply coupons (buy at U.S. post office—if your post

Tower of London

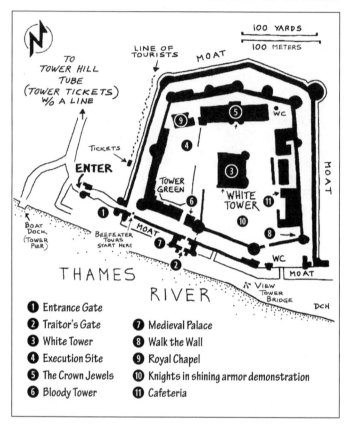

1 Entrance Gate

2 Traitor's Gate

3 White Tower

4 Execution Site

5 The Crown Jewels

6 Bloody Tower

7 Medieval Palace

8 Walk the Wall

9 Royal Chapel

10 Knights in shining armor demonstration

11 Cafeteria

office doesn't have the $1.75 coupons in stock, they can order them; the turn-around time is a few days).

Sights next to the Tower—The best remaining bit of London's **Roman Wall** is just north of the tower (at the Tower Hill Tube station). The impressive Tower Bridge is freshly painted and restored; for more information on this neo-Gothic maritime gateway to London, you can visit the **Tower Bridge Experience** for its 1894–1994 history exhibit and a peek at its Victorian engine room (£4.50, family-£14 and up, daily 9:30–18:00, last entry at 17:00, good view, poor value, enter at the northwest tower, tel. 020/7403-3761). The chic **St. Katherine Yacht Harbor,** just east of the Tower Bridge, has mod shops and the classic old Dickens Inn, fun for a drink or pub lunch. Across the bridge is the South Bank, with the upscale Butlers Wharf area, museums, and promenade.

South London, on the South Bank

The South Bank is a thriving arts and cultural center tied together by a riverside path. This popular, pub-crawling walk—called the Jubilee Promenade—stretches from the Tower Bridge past Westminster Bridge, where it offers grand views of the Houses of Parliament. (The promenade hugs the river except just east of London Bridge, where it cuts inland for a couple of blocks.)

▲▲▲**London Eye Ferris Wheel**—Built by British Airways, the wheel towers above London opposite Big Ben. This is the world's highest observational wheel, giving you a chance to fly British Airways without leaving London. Designed like a giant bicycle wheel, it's a pan-European undertaking: British steel and Dutch engineering, with Czech, German, French, and Italian mechanical parts. It's also very "green," running extremely efficiently and virtually silently. Twenty-five people ride in each of its 32 air-conditioned capsules for the 30-minute rotation (each capsule has a bench, but most people stand). From the top of this 450-foot-high wheel—the highest public viewpoint in the city—Big Ben looks small. You only go around once; save a shot on top for the glass capsule next to yours. Its original five-year lease has been extended to 25 years and it looks like this will become a permanent fixture on the London skyline. Thames boats come and go from here; they use the Waterloo Pier at the foot of the Wheel.

Cost, Hours, and Location: £11, April–mid-Sept daily 9:30–22:00, mid-Sept-March 9:30–20:00, closed Jan for maintenance, Tube: Waterloo or Westminster, www.ba-londoneye.com.

Crowd-Beating Tips: While huge lines made advance booking smart in past years, today you can generally just buy your ticket and walk on (never more than a 30-min wait, worst weekends and on school holidays). To book a ticket (with an assigned time) in advance, buy one at a London TI, call, or go online (50p charge, automated booking tel. 0870-500-0600 or www.ba-londoneye.com). Upon arrival, you either pick up your pre-booked ticket (if you've reserved ahead) or wait in the line inside to buy tickets. Then you join the ticket-holders' line at the wheel (starting 10 min before your assigned a half-hour time slot).

Dalí Universe—Cleverly located next to the hugely popular London Eye Ferris Wheel, this exhibit features 500 works of mind-bending art by Salvador Dalí. While pricey, it's entertaining if you like Surrealism and want to learn about Dalí (£8.50, daily 10:00–18:30, generally summer eves until 20:00, last entry 1 hr before closing, tel. 020/7620–2720).

▲**Saatchi Gallery**—The new contemporary art gallery at the base of the London Eye features "YBAs"—young British artists. Rather than halls of staid canvases, the collection displays many installations, each in their own room, giving the place a kind of funhouse atmosphere.

Ponder mortality at Damien Hirst's glass case, watching flies breed, feed on a rotting cow's head, then die on the bug zapper (the

The South Bank

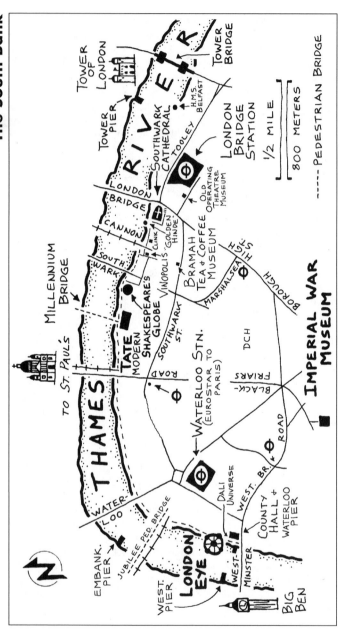

"insectocuter" in Brit-speak). Or gawk at Hirst's (real, dead) cows, pigs, sheep, and sharks sliced into sections and displayed in formaldehyde in glass cases. Ron Mueck's "Dead Dad" is an ultra-realistic (half-size) corpse in silicon and acrylic. Tracey Emin reveals herself by installing her messy bedroom in the main rotunda. And Chris Ofili scandalized New York City with a Virgin Mary splattered with elephant dung.

Much of the Saatchi's art is morbid, and visitors may be off-put or simply grossed out. It's "just conceptual art," but the concepts are realized on a large scale, with big money and ultra-modern technical know-how, and displayed in a wood-paneled Edwardian-era setting. You may not like it, you may be offended, you may find it passé—but it's something to e-mail home about (£8.50, daily 10:00–18:00, Fri–Sat until 22:00, last entry 45 min before closing, located next to London Eye, Tube: Waterloo or Westminster).

▲▲Imperial War Museum—This impressive museum covers the wars of the last century, from heavy weaponry to love notes and Vargas Girls, from Monty's Africa campaign tank to Schwarzkopf's Desert Storm uniform. You can trace the development of the machine gun, watch footage of the first tank battles, see one of more than a thousand V2 rockets Hitler rained on Britain in 1944 (each with more than a ton of explosives), hold your breath through the gruesome WWI trench experience, and buy WWII-era toys in the fun museum shop. The "Secret War" section gives a fascinating peek into the intrigues of espionage in World Wars I and II. The section on the Holocaust is one of the best on the subject anywhere. Rather than glorify war, the museum does its best to shine a light on the powerful human side of one of mankind's most persistent traits (free, daily 10:00–18:00, 90 min is enough time for most visitors, Tube: Lambeth North or bus #12 from Westminster, tel. 020/7416-5000).

The museum is housed in what was once the Royal Bethlam Hospital. Also known as "the Bedlam asylum," the place was so wild it gave the world a new word for chaos: "bedlam." Back in Victorian times, locals—without trash-talk shows and cable TV—came here for their entertainment. The asylum actually opened the place to the paying public on weekends.

▲▲▲Tate Modern—Dedicated in the spring of 2000, this striking museum across the river from St. Paul's opened the new century with art from the old one. Its powerhouse collection of Monet, Matisse, Dalí, Picasso, Warhol, and much more is displayed in a converted power house surrounded by picnic-friendly grounds. The art is exhibited by genre rather than chronologically or by artist (free, fee for special exhibitions, daily 10:00–18:00, Fri–Sat until 22:00—a good time to visit, audioguide-£1, free 1-hr guided tours at 11:00 and 14:00, call to confirm schedule, view café on top floor; cross the Millennium Bridge from St. Paul's; or Tube: Southwark plus a 10-min walk; or hop on the new

CROSSING THE THAMES ON FOOT

You can cross the Thames on any of the bridges that carry car traffic over the river, but pedestrian bridges are more fun. The **Millennium Bridge,** connecting the sedate St. Paul's Cathedral and the great Tate Modern, is now open, apparently for good. The new **Golden Jubilee Bridge** (consisting of two walkways that flank a railway trestle) links bustling Trafalgar Square on the North Bank with the London Eye Ferris Wheel and Waterloo Station on the South Bank. Replacing an old, run-down bridge, the Golden Jubilee Bridge—well lit with a sleek, futuristic look—makes this busy route safer and more popular.

Tate-to-Tate ferry from Tate Britain for £4.50; tel. 020/7887-8008, www.tate.org.uk).

▲**Millennium Bridge**—The pedestrian bridge links St. Paul's Cathedral and the Tate Modern across the Thames. This is London's first new bridge in a century. When it first opened, the $25 million bridge wiggled when people walked on it, so it promptly closed for a long $7 million stabilization; now it's finally stable and back open (free). Nicknamed "a blade of light" for its sleek minimalist design—370 yards long, four yards wide, stainless steel with teak planks—the bridge includes clever aerodynamic handrails to deflect wind over the heads of pedestrians.

▲▲**Shakespeare's Globe**—The original Globe Theater has been rebuilt—half-timbered and thatched—as it was in Shakespeare's time. (This is the first thatched roof in London since they were outlawed after the great fire of 1666.) The Globe originally accommodated 2,000 seated and another 1,000 standing. (Today, leaving space for reasonable aisles, the theater holds 900 seated and 600 groundlings.) Its promoters brag that the theater melds "the three A's"—actors, audience, and architecture—with each contributing to the play. Open as a museum and a working theater, it hosts authentic old-time performances of Shakespeare's plays. The theater can be toured when there are no plays. The Globe's exhibition on Shakespeare is the world's largest, with interactive displays and film presentations, a sound lab, a script factory, and costumes (£8, mid-May–Sept Mon–Sat 9:30–12:00, Sun 9:30–11:30, free 30-min actor-led tour offered on the half-hour; also open daily 12:30–16:00 but only for disappointing virtual tours; Oct–mid-May daily 10:30–17:00, free 30-min tour offered on the half-hour, on the South Bank directly across Thames over Southwark Bridge from St. Paul's, Tube: London Bridge plus a 10-min walk, tel. 020/7902-1500, www.shakespeares-globe.org). For details on seeing a play, see "Entertainment and Theater," below. The Globe Café is open daily (10:00–18:00, tel. 020/7902-1433).

Bramah Tea and Coffee Museum—Aficionados of tea or coffee will find this small museum fascinating. It tells the story of each drink almost passionately. The owner, Mr. Bramah, comes from a big tea family and wants the world to know how the advent of commercial television, with breaks not long enough to brew a proper pot of tea, required a faster hot drink. In came the horrible English instant coffee. Tea countered with finely chopped leaves in tea bags, and it's gone downhill ever since (£4, daily 10:00–18:00, 40 Southwark Street, Tube: London Bridge plus 3-min walk, tel. 020/7403-5650, www.bramahmuseum.co.uk). Its café, which serves more kinds of coffees and teas than cakes, is open to the public (same hours as museum). The #RV1 bus zips you to the museum easily and scenically from Covent Garden.

▲▲**Old Operating Theatre Museum and Herb Garret**—Climb a tight and creaky wooden spiral staircase to a church attic where you'll find a garret used to dry medicinal herbs, a fascinating exhibit on Victorian surgery, cases of well-described 19th-century medical paraphernalia, and a special look at "anesthesia, the defeat of pain." Then you stumble upon Britain's oldest operating theater, where limbs were sawed off way back in 1821 (£3.75, daily 10:30–17:00, Tube: London Bridge, 9a St. Thomas Street, tel. 020/8806-4325, www.thegarret.org.uk).

▲▲**Vinopolis: City of Wine**—While it seems illogical to have a huge wine museum in London, Vinopolis makes a good case. Built over a Roman wine store and filling the massive vaults of an old wine ware-house, the museum offers an excellent audioguide with a light yet earnest history of wine. Sipping various reds and whites, ports, and champagnes, you're immersed in your headset as you stroll and learn about the libation, such as its Georgian origins and the Chilean industry, as well as a Vespa ride through Chianti country in Tuscany. Allow some time, as the audioguide takes 90 minutes—the sipping can slow things down wonderfully (£11.50 with 5 tastes, £14 with 10 tastes, don't worry...for £2.50 you can buy 5 more tastes inside, daily 11:00–18:00, Sat and Mon until 21:00, last entry 2 hrs before closing, Tube: London Bridge, between the Globe and Southwark Cathedral at 1 Bank End, tel. 0870-241-4040 or 020/7940-8301, www.vinopolis.co.uk).

More South Bank Sights, in Southwark

These sights are mediocre but worth knowing about. The area stretching from the Tate Modern to London Bridge, known as Southwark (SUTH-uck), was for centuries the place Londoners would go to escape the rules and decency of the city and let their hair down. Bear-baiting, brothels, rollicking pubs and theater—you name the dream, and it could be fulfilled just across the Thames. A run-down warehouse district

Greater London

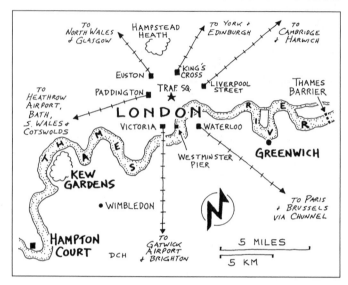

through the 20th century, it's been gentrified with classy restaurants, office parks, pedestrian promenades, major sights (such as the Tate Modern and Shakespeare's Globe), and this colorful collection of lesser sights. The area is easy on foot and a scenic—though circuitous—way to connect the Tower of London with St. Paul's.

Southwark Cathedral—While made a cathedral only in 1905, it's been the neighborhood church since the 13th century and comes with some interesting history (Mon–Sat 10:00–18:00, Sun 11:00–17:00, last admission 30 min before close, evensong services weekdays at 17:30, Sun at 15:00, audioguide–£2.50, tel. 020/7367-6711).

The adjacent church-run **Long View of London Exhibition** tells the story of Southwark (£3, same hours as church).

The Clink Prison—Proudly the "original clink," this was where law-abiding citizens threw Southwark troublemakers until 1780. Today, it's a low-tech torture museum filling grotty old rooms with papier-mâché gore. Unfortunately, there's little to seriously deal with the fascinating problem of law and order in Southwark, where 18th-century Londoners went for a good time (overpriced at £4, daily 10:00–18:00, 1 Clink Street, tel. 020/7378-1558, www.clink.co.uk).

Golden Hinde **Replica**—This is a full-size replica of the 16th-century warship in which Sir Francis Drake circumnavigated the globe from 1577 to 1580. Commanding this ship, Drake earned the reputation as history's most successful pirate. The original is long gone, but this boat has logged more than 100,000 miles, including its own voyage around the world. While the ship is fun to see, its interior is not worth touring (£2.50, daily 9:30–17:30, may be closed if rented out for birthday parties, school groups, or weddings, tel. 0870-011-8700, www.goldenhinde .co.uk).

HMS *Belfast*—"The last big-gun armored warship of World War II" clogs the Thames just upstream from the Tower Bridge. This huge vessel—now manned with wax sailors—thrills kids who always dreamed of sitting in a turret shooting off their imaginary guns. If you're into WWII warships, this is the ultimate...otherwise, it's just lots of exercise with a nice view of the Tower Bridge (£6, March–Oct daily 10:00–18:00, Nov–Feb daily 10:00–17:00, tel. 020/7940-6300).

South London, on the North Bank

▲▲**Tate Britain**—One of Europe's great art houses, Tate Britain specializes in British painting from the 16th century through modern times. The museum has a good representation of William Blake's religious sketches, the Pre-Raphaelites' realistic art, and J.M.W. Turner's swirling works (free, daily 10:00–17:50, last admission 17:00, fine audioguide-£3, free tours: normally Mon–Fri at 11:00—16th, 17th, and 18th centuries; at noon—19th century; at 14:00—Turner; at 15:00—20th century; Sat–Sun at noon and 15:00—highlights; call to confirm schedule; no photography allowed, Tube: Pimlico, then 7-min walk; or arrive directly at museum by taking bus #88 from Oxford Circus or #77A from National Gallery; or catch the Tate-to-Tate ferry from Tate Modern for £4.50, tel. 020/7887-8000, recorded info tel. 020/7887-8008, www.tate.org.uk).

Greater London

▲**Kew Gardens**—For a fine riverside park and a palatial greenhouse jungle to swing through, take the Tube or the boat to every botanist's favorite escape, Kew Gardens. While to most visitors the Royal Botanic Gardens of Kew are simply a delightful opportunity to wander among 33,000 different types of plants, to the hardworking organization that runs the gardens, it's a way to promote understanding and preservation of the botanical diversity of our planet. The Kew Tube station drops you in an little herbal business community a two-block walk from Victoria Gate (the main garden entrance). Pick up a map brochure and check at the gate for a monthly listing of best blooms.

Garden-lovers could spend days exploring Kew's 300 acres. For a quick visit, spend a fragrant hour wandering through three buildings: the Palm House, a humid Victorian world of iron, glass, and tropical plants built in 1844; a Waterlily House that would impress Monet; and the Princess of Wales Conservatory, a modern greenhouse with many different climate zones that grows countless cacti, bug-munching carnivorous plants, and more (£7.50, £5.50 at 16:45 or later, Mon–Fri 9:30–18:30, Sat–Sun 9:30–19:30, until 16:30 or sunset off-season, galleries and conservatories close at 17:30, consider £3 narrated floral 35-min joyride on little train departing on the hour until 16:00 from Victoria Gate, Tube: Kew Gardens, tel. 020/8332-5000). For a sun-dappled lunch, walk 10 minutes from the Palm House to the Orangery (hot meals-£6, daily 10:00–17:30).

▲**Hampton Court Palace**—Fifteen miles up the Thames from downtown (£15 taxi ride from Kew Gardens) is the 500-year-old palace of Henry VIII. Actually, it was the palace of his minister, Cardinal Wolsey. When Wolsey, a clever man, realized Henry VIII was experiencing a little palace envy, he gave the mansion to his king. The Tudor palace was also home to Elizabeth I and Charles I. Sections were updated by Christopher Wren for William and Mary. The stately palace stands overlooking the Thames and includes some impressive Tudor rooms, including a Great Hall with a magnificent hammer-beam ceiling. The industrial-strength Tudor kitchen was capable of keeping 600 schmoozing courtesans thoroughly—if not well—fed. The sculpted garden features a rare Tudor tennis court and a popular maze.

The palace, fully restored after a 1986 fire, tries hard to please, but it doesn't quite sparkle. From the information center in the main courtyard, visitors book times for tours with tired costumed guides or pick up audioguides for self-guided tours of various wings of the palace (all free). The Tudor Kitchens, Henry VIII's Apartments, and the King's Apartments are most interesting. The Georgian Rooms are pretty dull. The maze in the nearby garden is a curiosity some find fun (maze free with palace ticket, otherwise £3). The train (2/hr, 30 min) from London's Waterloo station drops you just across the river from the palace (£12, 1-day combo-ticket with Tower of London-£18, Mon 10:15–18:00, Tue–Sun 9:30–18:00, Nov-March until 16:30, tel. 020/8781-9500).

Royal Air Force Museum Hendon—A hit with aviation enthusiasts, this huge aerodrome and airfield contain planes from World War II's Battle of Britain up through the Gulf War. You can climb inside some of the planes, try your luck in a cockpit, and fly with the Red Arrows in a flight simulator (free, daily 10:00–18:00, café, shop, parking, Tube: Colindale—top of Northern Line Edgware branch, Grahame Park Way, tel. 020/8205-2266, www.rafmuseum.org.uk).

Disappointments of London

The venerable BBC broadcasts from the Broadcasting House. Of all its productions, its "BBC Experience" tour for visitors is among the worst. On the South Bank, the London Dungeon, a much-visited but amateurish attraction, is just a highly advertised, overpriced haunted house—certainly not worth the £12 admission, much less your valuable

London time. It comes with long and rude lines. Wait for Halloween and see one in your hometown to support a better cause. "Winston Churchill's Britain at War Experience" (next to the London Dungeon) wastes your time. The Kensington Palace State Apartments are lifeless and not worth a visit.

SHOPPING

Harrods—Harrods is London's most famous and touristy department store. With a million square feet of retail space on seven floors, it's a place where some shoppers could spend all day. (To me, it's a department store.) Big yet classy, Harrods has everything from elephants to toothbrushes (Mon–Sat 10:00–19:00, closed Sun, mandatory storage for big backpacks-£2.50, on Brompton Road, Tube: Knightsbridge, tel. 020/7730–1234).

Sightseers should pick up the free Store Guide at any info post. Here's what I enjoyed: On the Ground and Lower Ground Floors, find the Food Halls, with their Edwardian tiled walls, creative and exuberant displays, and staff in period costumes—not quite like your local supermarket back home.

Descend to the Lower Ground Floor and follow signs to the Egyptian Escalator, where you'll find a memorial to Dodi Fayed and Princess Diana. Photos and flowers honor the late Princess and her fiancé (the son of Harrods' owner), who both died in a car crash in Paris in 1997. See the wine glass from their last dinner and the engagement ring that Dodi purchased the day before they died.

Ride the Egyptian Escalator—lined with pharaoh-headed sconces, papyrus-plant lamps, and hieroglyphic balconies (Harrods' owner is from Egypt)—to the 4th Floor. From the escalator, make a U-turn left and head to the far corner of the store (toys) to find child-size luxury cars that actually work. A junior Jaguar or Mercedes will set you back about $13,000. The child's Hummer ($30,000) is as big as my car.

Also on the 4th Floor is The Georgian Restaurant. Enjoy a fancy tea under a skylight as a pianist tickles the keys of a Bösendorfer, the world's most expensive piano (tea-£19, includes finger sandwiches and pastries, served after 15:45).

Many of my readers report that Harrods is overpriced (its £1 toilets are the most expensive in Europe), snooty, and teeming with American and Japanese tourists. Still, it's the palace of department stores. The nearby Beauchamp Place is lined with classy and fascinating shops.

Harvey Nichols—Once Princess Diana's favorite, "Harvey Nick's" remains the department store *du jour* (Mon, Tue, Sat 10:00–19:00, Wed–Fri until 20:00, Sun 12:00–18:00, near Harrods, Tube: Knightsbridge, 109 Knightsbridge, www.harveynichols.com). Want to pick up a little £20 scarf for the wife? You won't do it here, where they're more

WHAT'S ON IN THE WEST END

Here are some of the perennial favorites that you're likely to find among the West End's evening offerings. If spending the time and money for a London play, I like a full-fledged high-energy musical.

Generally you can book tickets for free at the box office or for a £2 fee by telephone or online.

Musicals

Chicago—A chorus-girl-gone-bad forms a nightclub act with another murderess to bring in the bucks (£15–40, Mon–Thu and Sat 20:00, Fri 20:30, matinees Fri 17:00 and Sat 15:00, Adelphi Theatre, Strand, Tube: Covent Garden or Charing Cross, booking tel. 020/7344-0055, www.chicagothemusical.com).

Mamma Mia—This high-energy spandex-and-platform-boots musical weaves together 20 or 30 ABBA hits to tell the story of a bride in search of her real dad as her promiscuous mom plans her Greek Isle wedding. The production has the audience dancing by its happy ending (£19–40, Mon–Thu and Sat 19:30, Fri 20:30, matinees Fri 17:00 and Sat 15:00, Prince Edward Theatre, Old Compton Street, Tube: Leicester Square, booking tel. 020/7447-5400).

Les Misérables—Claude-Michel Schönberg's musical adaptation of Victor Hugo's epic follows the life of Jean Valjean as he struggles with the social and political realities of 19th-century France. This inspiring mega-hit takes you back to the days of France's struggle for a just and modern society (£9–40, Mon–Sat 19:30, matinees Thu and Sat 14:30, Palace Theatre, Cambridge Circus, Tube: Leicester Square, box office tel. 0870-160-2878, www.lesmis.com).

like £200. The store's fifth floor is a veritable food fest, with a gourmet grocery store, a fancy (smoky) restaurant, a Yo! Sushi bar, and a lively café. Consider a take-away tray of sushi to eat on a bench in the Hyde Park rose garden two blocks away.

Toys—The biggest toy store in Britain is **Hamleys,** with seven floors buzzing with 28,000 toys and managed by a staff of 200. At the "Bear Factory," kids can get a made-to-order teddy bear by picking out a "bear skin" and watch while it's stuffed and sewn (Mon–Fri 10:00–20:00, Sat 9:30–20:00, Sun 12:00–18:00, 188 Regent Street, tel. 0870-333-2455, www.hamleys.com).

Street Markets—Antique buffs, people-watchers, and folks who brake for garage sales love to haggle at London's street markets. There's good early-morning market activity somewhere any day of the week. The best

The Phantom of the Opera—A mysterious masked man falls in love with a singer in this haunting Andrew Lloyd Webber musical about life beneath the stage of the Paris Opera (£10–40, Mon–Sat 19:30, matinees Wed and Sat 15:00, Her Majesty's Theatre, Haymarket, Tube: Piccadilly Circus, booking tel. 0870-160-2878, www.the phantomoftheopera.com).

The Lion King—In this Disney extravaganza featuring music by Elton John, Simba the lion learns about the delicately-balanced circle of life on the savanna (£18–43, Mon–Sat 19:30, matinees Wed and Sat 14:00 and Sun 15:00, Lyceum Theatre, Wellington Street, Tube: Charing Cross or Covent Garden, booking tel. 0870-243-9000 or 0161/228-1953, theater info tel. 020/7420-8112, www.thelionking .co.uk).

Thrillers

The Mousetrap—Agatha Christie's whodunit about a murder in a country house continues to stump audiences after 50 years (£11.50–30, Mon–Sat 20:00, matinees Tue 14:45 and Sat 17:00, St. Martin's Theatre, West Street, Tube: Leicester Square, box office tel. 0870-162-2878).

The Woman in Black—The chilling tale of a solicitor who is haunted by what he learns when he closes a reclusive woman's affairs (£10–30, Mon-Sat 20:00, matinees Tue 15:00 and Sat 16:00, Fortune Theatre, Russell Street, Tube: Covent Garden, box office tel. 020/7369-1737, www.thewomaninblack.com).

are **Portobello Road** (roughly Mon–Sat 10:00–17:00, closed Sun, go on Sat for antiques—plus the regular junk, clothes, and produce; Tube: Notting Hill Gate, tel. 020/7229-8354) and **Camden Lock Market** (daily 10:00–18:00, arts and crafts, Tube: Camden Town, tel. 020/7284-2084, www.camdenlock.net). The TI has a complete, up-to-date list. Warning: Markets attract two kinds of people—tourists and pickpockets. **Famous Auctions**—London's famous auctioneers welcome the curious public for viewing and bidding. For schedules, call **Sotheby's** (Mon–Fri 9:00–16:30, closed Sat–Sun, 34-35 New Bond Street, Tube: Oxford Circus, tel. 020/7293-5000, www.sothebys.com) or **Christie's** (Mon–Fri 9:00–17:00, Tue until 20:00, closed Sat–Sun, 8 King Street, Tube: Green Park, tel. 020/7839-9060, www.christies.com).

ENTERTAINMENT AND THEATER

London bubbles with top-notch entertainment seven days a week. Everything's listed in the weekly entertainment magazines (e.g., *Time Out*), available at newsstands. Choose from classical, jazz, rock, and far-out music, Gilbert and Sullivan, dance, comedy, Baha'i meetings, poetry readings, spectator sports, film, and theater. In Leicester Square, you'll find movies that have yet to be released in the States; if Hugh Grant is attending an opening-night premiere in London, it will likely be at one of the big movie houses here.

London's theater rivals Broadway's in quality and beats it in price. Choose from the Royal Shakespeare Company, top musicals, comedy, thrillers, sex farces, and more. I prefer big, glitzy—even bombastic—musicals over serious chamber dramas, simply because London can deliver the lights, sound, dancers, and multimedia spectacle I rarely get back home. Performances are nightly except Sunday, usually with one matinee a week. Matinees, usually held on Wednesday, Thursday, or Saturday, are cheaper and rarely sell out. Tickets range from about £8 to £40.

Most theaters, marked on tourist maps, are in the Piccadilly/ Trafalgar Square area. Box offices, hotels, and TIs offer a handy *Theatre Guide.* To book a seat, simply call the theater box office directly, ask about seats and available dates, and for a £2 fee, buy a ticket with your credit card. (To avoid the fee, buy the ticket in person at the box office.) You can call from the United States as easily as from England; check www.officiallondontheatre.co.uk, the American magazine *Variety,* or photocopy your hometown library's London newspaper theater section. Pick up your ticket 15 minutes before the show.

For a booking fee, you can reserve online (www.ticketmaster.co.uk or www.firstcalltickets.com) or call Global Tickets (U.S. tel. 800/223-6108). While booking through an agency is quick and easy, prices are inflated by a standard 25 percent fee. Ticket agencies (whether in the U.S., at London's TIs, or scattered throughout the city) are scalpers with an address. If you're buying from an agency, look at the ticket carefully (your price should be no more than 30 percent over the printed face value; the 15 percent VAT is already included in the face value) and understand where you're sitting according to the floor plan (if your view is restricted, it will state this on the ticket; for floor plans of the various theaters, see www.theatremonkey.com). Agencies are worthwhile only if a show you've just got to see is sold out at the box office. They scarf up hot tickets, planning to make a killing after the show is sold out. U.S. booking agencies get their tickets from another agency, adding even more to your expense by involving yet another middleman. Many tickets sold on the street are forgeries. Although some theatres have booking agencies handle their advance sales, you'll stand a good chance of saving money and avoiding the middleman by simply calling the box office directly to book your tickets (international phone calls are cheap and credit cards make booking a snap).

Theater Lingo: stalls (ground floor), dress circle (first balcony), upper circle (second balcony), balcony (sky-high third balcony), slips (cheap seats on the fringes). Many cheap seats have a restricted view (behind a pillar).

Cheap Theater Tricks: Most theaters offer cheap returned tickets, standing-room, matinee, and senior or student stand-by deals. These "concessions" are indicated with a "conc" or "s" in the listings. Picking up a late return can get you a great seat at a cheap-seat price. If a show is "sold out," there's usually a way to get a seat. Call the theater box office and ask how.

Half-Price "tkts" Booth at Leicester Square: This famous ticket booth sells discounted tickets for top-price seats to shows on the push list the day of the show only (£2.50 service charge per ticket, Mon–Sat 10:00–19:00, Sun 12:00–15:30, matinee tickets from noon, lines often form early, list of shows available online, www.tkts.co.uk).

Here are some sample prices: A top-notch seat to the long-running *Les Misérables* (which rarely sells out) costs £40 bought directly from the theater, but only £22.50 at Leicester (LESS-ter) Square. The cheapest balcony seat (bought from the theater) is £15.

Half-price tickets can be a good deal, unless you want the cheapest seats or the hottest shows. But check the board; occasionally they sell cheap tickets to good shows. Note that the real half-price booth (with its new "tkts" name) is a freestanding kiosk at the edge of the garden in Leicester Square. Several dishonest outfits nearby advertise "official half-price tickets." Avoid these.

Many theaters are so small that there's hardly a bad seat. After the lights go down, scooting up is less than a capital offense. Shakespeare did it.

West End Theaters—The commercial (non-subsidized) theaters cluster around Soho (especially along Shaftesbury Avenue) and Covent Garden. With a centuries-old tradition of pleasing the masses, these present London theater at its glitziest. See the "What's On in the West End" sidebar.

Royal Shakespeare Company—If you'll ever enjoy Shakespeare, it'll be in Britain. The RSC performs at various theaters around London and in Stratford year-round. To get a schedule, contact the RSC (Royal Shakespeare Theatre, Stratford-upon-Avon, tel. 01789/403-403, ticket hotline tel. 0870-609-1110, www.rsc.org.uk).

Shakespeare's Globe—To see Shakespeare in a replica of the theater for which he wrote his plays, attend a play at the Globe. This thatch-roofed, open-air round theater does the plays much as Shakespeare intended (with no amplification). The play's the thing from mid-May through September (usually Tue–Sat 14:00 and 19:30, Sun at either

13:00 and 18:30 or 16:00 only, no plays on Mon, tickets can be sold out months in advance). You'll pay £5 to stand and £13–29 to sit (usually on a backless bench; only a few rows and the pricier Gentlemen's Rooms have seats with backs). The £5 "groundling" tickets—while the only ones open to rain—are most fun. Scurry in early to stake out a spot on the stage-edge leaning rail, where the most interaction with the actors occurs. You're a crude peasant. You can lean your elbows on the stage, munch a picnic dinner, or walk around. I've never enjoyed Shakespeare as much as here, performed as it was meant to be in the "wooden O." Plays can be long. Many groundlings leave before the end. If you like, hang out an hour before the finish and beg or buy a ticket from someone leaving early (groundlings are allowed to come and go).

The theater is on the South Bank directly across the Thames over the Millennium Bridge from St. Paul's Cathedral (Tube: Mansion House or London Bridge, tel. 020/7902-1500, box office tel. 020/7401-9919, www.shakespeares-globe.org). The Globe is inconvenient for public transport, but the courtesy phone in the lobby gets a minicab in minutes. (These have set fees—e.g., £8 to South Kensington—but generally cost less than a metered cab and provide fine and honest service.)

Fringe Theatre—London's rougher evening-entertainment scene is thriving, filling pages in *Time Out*. Choose from a wide range of fringe theater and comedy acts (generally £5).

Music—For easy, cheap, or free concerts in historic churches, check the TIs' listings for lunch concerts (especially Wren's St. Bride's Church; St. James at Piccadilly—free lunch concerts on Mon, Wed, and Fri at 13:10, info tel. 020/7381-0441; and St. Martin-in-the-Fields—free lunch concerts on Mon, Tue, and Fri at 13:05, church tel. 020/7766-1100). St. Martin-in-the-Fields also hosts fine evening concerts by candlelight (£6–18, Thu–Sat at 19:30, box office tel. 020/7839-8362).

At St. Paul's Cathedral, evensong is held Monday through Saturday at 17:00 and on Sunday at 15:15. At Westminster Abbey, it's sung weekdays at 17:00 (but not on Wed) and Saturday and Sunday at 15:00. Organ recitals are held on Sunday at Westminster Abbey (17:45, 40 min, small fee, tel. 020/7798-9055) and at St. Paul's (17:00, 30 min, free, tel. 020/7236-4128).

For a fun classical event (mid-July–early Sept), attend a "Prom Concert" during the annual festival at the Royal Albert Hall. Nightly concerts are offered at give-a-peasant-some-culture prices (standing-room spots sold at the door-£4, restricted-view seats-£7, most seats-£22, depending on performance, Tube: South Kensington, tel. 020/7589-8212, www.royalalberthall.com).

Some of the world's best opera is belted out at the prestigious Royal Opera House, near Covent Garden (box office tel. 020/7304-4000, www.royalopera.org) and at the less-formal Sadler's Wells Theatre (Rosebery Avenue, Islington, Tube: Angel, box office tel. 020/7863-8000, www.sadlers-wells.com).

Walks, Bus Tour, and Cruises—See "Tours" on page 48 for information on walking tours (some are held in the evening), the London by Night bus tour, and Regent's Canal cruise.

A handful of outfits run Thames River evening cruises with four-course meals and dancing. London Showboat offers the best value (£53, April-Oct Wed-Sun, departs 19:00 from Westminster Pier, Thu-Sat evening cruises through the winter, 3.5 hrs, tel. 020/7740-0400, www.citycruises.com). For more on cruising, get the Thames River Services brochure from a London TI.

SLEEPING

Victoria Station Neighborhood, Belgravia

The streets behind Victoria Station teem with budget B&Bs. It's a safe, surprisingly tidy, and decent area without a hint of the trashy, touristy glitz of the streets in front of the station. Here in Belgravia, your neighbors include Andrew Lloyd Webber and Margaret Thatcher (her policeman stands outside 73 Chester Square). Decent eateries abound (see "Eating," page 103). Cheaper rooms are relatively dumpy. Don't expect £90 cheeriness in a £60 room. Off-season, it's possible to save money by arriving late without a reservation and looking around. Competition softens prices, especially for multinight stays. On hot summer nights, request a quiet back room. All are within a five-minute walk of the Victoria Tube, bus, and train stations. There's a £15-per-day (with a hotel voucher) garage, a nearby **launderette** (daily 8:00–20:30, self-service or full service, past Warwick Square at 3 Westmoreland Terrace, tel. 020/7821-8692), and a little dance club (music from 23:30, Club D'Jan, £8 includes drink, Thu–Sat, 63 Wilton Road).

$$$ Lime Tree Hotel, enthusiastically run by David and Marilyn Davies and their daughter Charlotte, comes with spacious and thoughtfully decorated rooms and a fun-loving breakfast room. While priced a bit steep, the place has character and is a good value (30 rooms, Sb-£80, Db-£110–120, Tb-£150, family room-£160, possible discount with cash, all rooms non-smoking, quiet garden, David deals in slow times and is creative at helping travelers in a bind, 135 Ebury Street, tel. 020/7730-8191, fax 020/7730-7865, www.limetreehotel.co.uk, info @limetreehotel.co.uk).

$$$ Quality Hotel Eccleston is big, modern (but with tired carpets), well-located, and a fine value for no-nonsense comfort (Db-£130, on slow days drop-ins can ask for "saver prices," if booking in advance check various specials on the Web, breakfast extra or bargained in, non-smoking floor, elevator, 82 Eccleston Square, tel. 020/7834-8042, fax 020/7630-8942, www.qualityinn.com/hotel/gb614, admin@gb614 .u-net.com).

SLEEP CODE

(£1 = about $1.60, country code: 44, area code: 020)
Sleep Code: **S** = Single, **D** = Double/Twin, **T** = Triple, **Q** = Quad, **b** = bathroom, **s** = shower only, **no CC** = Credit Cards not accepted. Unless otherwise noted, credit cards are accepted.

To help you sort easily through these listings, I've divided the rooms into three categories based on the price for a standard double room with bath:

$$$ **Higher Priced**—Most rooms £100 or more.
  $$ **Moderately Priced**—Most rooms between £70-100.
    $ **Lower Priced**—Most rooms £70 or less.

London is expensive. For £70 ($110), you'll get a double with breakfast in a safe, cramped, and dreary place with minimal service and the bathroom down the hall. For £90 ($145), you'll get a basic, clean, reasonably cheery double in a usually cramped, cracked-plaster building with a private bath, or a soulless but comfortable room without breakfast in a huge Motel 6-type place. My London splurges, at £100-150 ($160-240), are spacious, thoughtfully appointed places you'd be happy to entertain or make love in. Hearty English or generous buffet breakfasts are included unless otherwise noted, and TVs are standard in rooms.

Reserve your London room with a phone call or e-mail as soon as you can commit to a date. To call a London hotel from the United States or Canada, dial 011-44-20 (London's area code without the initial zero), then the local eight-digit number. Some hotels will hold a room until 16:00 without a deposit, although most places will ask you for a credit-card number. The pricier ones have expensive cancellation policies (such as no refund if you cancel with less than two weeks' notice). Some fancy £120 rooms rent for a third off if you arrive late on a slow day and ask for a deal.

$$ Winchester Hotel is family-run and perhaps the best value, with 18 fine rooms, no claustrophobia, and a wise and caring management (Db-£85, Tb-£110, Qb-£140, no CC, no groups, no infants, 17 Belgrave Road, tel. 020/7828-2972, fax 020/7828-5191, www.winchester -hotel.net, enquiry@winchester-hotel.net, commanded by Jimmy with

Victoria Station Neighborhood

1. Lime Tree Hotel
2. Quality Hotel Eccleston
3. Winchester Hotel
4. James House & Cartref House Hotels
5. Elizabeth Hotel
6. To Holiday Inn Express
7. Morgan House
8. Collin House Hotel
9. Harcourt House
10. Georgian House Hotel
11. Cherry Court Hotel
12. La Campagnola Rest.
13. Ebury Wine Bar
14. To Duke of Wellington Pub
15. Jenny Lo's Rest.
16. To La Poule au Pot Rest.
17. Grumbles Rest.
18. Jugged Hare Pub
19. Sainsbury's Local Grocery
20. Internet Café
21. Bus Tours (Day)
22. Bus Tours (Night)
23. TI, Tube, Taxis, City Buses

his able first mates: Juanita, Ian, and Paul). The Winchester also rents apartments—with kitchenettes, sitting rooms, and beds on the quiet back side—around the corner (£125–230).

$$ James House and **Cartref House** are two nearly identical, well-run, smoke-free, 10-room places on either side of Ebury Street (S-£55, Sb-£65, D-£74, Db-£90, T-£100, Tb-£120, family bunk-bed Qb-£140, 5 percent discount with cash, all rooms with fans, no smoking, James House at 108 Ebury Street, tel. 020/7730-7338; Cartref House at 129 Ebury Street, tel. 020/7730-6176, fax for both: 020/7730-7338, www.jamesandcartref.co.uk, jandchouse@aol.com, run by Derek and Sharon).

$$ Elizabeth Hotel is a stately old place overlooking Eccleston Square, with fine public spaces and 38 well-worn but spacious and decent rooms (D-£72, small Db-£88, big Db-£99, Tb-£110, Qb-£120, Quint/b-£125, 37 Eccleston Square, tel. 020/7828-6812, fax 020/7828-6814, www.elizabethhotel.com, info@elizabethhotel.com). Be careful not to confuse this hotel with the nearby Elizabeth House. This one is big and comfy, the other small and dumpy.

$$ Holiday Inn Express fills an old building with 52 fresh, modern, and efficient rooms (Db-£105, Tb-£120, family rooms, up to 2 kids free, some discounts on Web site, non-smoking floor, elevator, Tube: Pimlico, 106 Belgrave Road, tel. 020/7630-8888 or 0800-897-121, fax 020/7828-0441, www.hiexpressvictoria.co.uk, info@hiexpressvictoria.co.uk).

$ Morgan House rents 11 good rooms and is entertainingly run, with lots of travel tips and friendly chat—especially about the local rich and famous—by Rachel Joplin (S-£46, D-£66, Db-£86, T-£86, family suites-£110–122 for 3-4 people, 120 Ebury Street, tel. 020/7730-2384, fax 020/7730-8442, www.morganhouse.co.uk, morganhouse@btclick.com).

$ Collin House Hotel, clean, simple and efficiently-run, offers 12 basic rooms with woody, modern furnishings (Sb-£55, D-£68, Db-£82, T-£95, non-smoking rooms, 104 Ebury St, tel.& fax 020/7730-8031, www.collinhouse.co.uk, booking@collinhouse.co.uk, absentee owner).

$ Harcourt House rents 10 decent smoke-free rooms (Db-£75, 50 Ebury Street, tel. 020/7730-2722, www.harcourthousehotel.co.uk, harcourthouse@talk21.com, David and Glesni Wood).

$ Georgian House Hotel has 50 once-grand, now basic rooms and a cheaper top floor that works well for backpackers (S-£29, tiny D on fourth floor-£45, Db-£69, top floor Db-£59, Tb-£86, Qb-£94, Internet access, 35 St. George's Drive, tel. 020/7834-1438, fax 020/7976-6085, www.georgianhousehotel.co.uk, reception@georgianhousehotel.co.uk).

$ Cherry Court Hotel, run by the friendly and industrious Patel family, rents 12 small, basic rooms for good value in a central location (Sb-£42, Db-£48, Tb-£70, Qb-£85, Quint/b-£100, prices promised with this book through 2004, paying with credit card costs 5 percent extra, fruit-basket breakfast in room, non-smoking, free Internet access, peaceful garden patio, 23 Hugh Street, tel. 020/7828-2840, fax 020/ 7828-0393, www.cherrycourthotel.co.uk, bookings@cherrycourthotel .co.uk).

Big, Cheap, Modern Hotels

These places—popular with budget tour groups—are well-run and offer elevators and all the modern comforts in a no-frills, practical package. The doubles for £65–94 are a great value for London. Mid-week prices are generally higher than weekend rates.

$$ Jurys Inn rents 200 modern, compact, and comfy rooms near King's Cross station (Db/Tb-£104, 2 adults and 2 kids—under age 12— can share 1 room, breakfast extra, non-smoking floors, 60 Pentonville Road, Tube: Angel, tel. 020/7282-5500, fax 020/7282-5511, www .jurysdoyle.com).

$$ London County Hall Travel Inn, literally down the hall from a $400-a-night Marriott Hotel, fills one end of London's massive former County Hall building. This place is wonderfully located near the base of the London Eye Ferris Wheel and across the Thames from Big Ben. Its 300 slick, no-frills rooms come with all the necessary comforts (Db-£82 for 2 adults and up to 2 kids under age 15, couples can request a bigger family room—same price, breakfast extra, book in advance, no-show rooms are released at 16:00, elevator, some smoke-free and easy-access rooms, 500 yards from Westminster Tube stop and Waterloo Station, Belvedere Road, you can call central reservations at 0870-242-8000 or 0870-238-3300, you can fax 020/7902-1619 but you might not get a response, it's easiest to book online at www.travelinn.co.uk).

Other **$$ London Travel Inns** charging £70-80 per room include **London Euston** (big, blue, Lego-type building on handy but noisy street packed with Benny Hill families on vacation, 141 Euston Road, Tube: Euston, tel. 0870-238-3301), **Tower Bridge** (Tower Bridge Road, Tube: London Bridge, tel. 0870-238-3303), and **London Putney Bridge** (farther out, 3 Putney Bridge Approach, Tube: Putney Bridge, tel. 0870-238-3302). For any of these, call 0870-242-8000, fax 0870-241-9000, or best, book online at www.travelinn.co.uk.

$ Hotel Ibis London Euston, which feels classier than a Travel Inn, is located on a quiet street a block behind Euston Station (380 rooms, Db-£80, breakfast-£5, no family rooms, non-smoking floor, 3 Cardington Street, tel. 020/7388-7777, fax 020/7388-0001, www .ibishotel.com, h0921@accor-hotels.com).

$ Premier Lodge is near Shakespeare's Globe on the South Bank (55 rooms, Db for up to 2 adults and 2 kids-£70, Bankside, 34 Park Street, tel. 0870-700–1456, www.premierlodge.co.uk).

South Kensington Neighborhood

● Aster House, Five Sumner Place
   & Sixteen Sumner Place Hotels
❷ Jurys Kensington Hotel
❸ Claverley Hotel
❹ La Bouchee Bistro Café
❺ Daquise Restaurant
❻ Khyber Pass Tandoori Rest.
❼ La Brasserie Restaurant
❽ PJ's Bar and Grill
❾ Launderette

"South Kensington," She Said, Loosening His Cummerbund

To live on a quiet street so classy it doesn't allow hotel signs, surrounded by trendy shops and colorful restaurants, call "South Ken" your London home. Shoppers like being a short walk from Harrods and the designer shops of King's Road and Chelsea. When I splurge, I splurge here. Sumner Place is just off Old Brompton Road, 200 yards from the handy South Kensington Tube station (on Circle Line, 2 stops from Victoria Station, direct Heathrow connection). There's a taxi rank in the median strip at the end of Harrington Road. The handy Wash & Dry **launderette** is on the corner of Queensberry Place and Harrington Road (daily 8:00–21:00, bring 20p and £1 coins).

$$$ **Aster House,** run by friendly and accommodating Simon and Leona Tan, has won the "best B&B in London" award for the last two years. It has a sumptuous lobby, lounge, and breakfast room. Its rooms

are comfy and quiet, with TV, phone, and air-conditioning. Enjoy breakfast or just lounge in the whisper-elegant Orangery, a Victorian greenhouse (Sb-£75–99, Db-£135, bigger Db-£150, deluxe four-poster Db-£180, entirely non-smoking, 3 Sumner Place, tel. 020/7581-5888, fax 020/7584-4925, www.asterhouse.com, asterhouse@btinternet.com). Simon and Leona offer free loaner mobile phones to their guests.

$$$ **Five Sumner Place Hotel** has received several "best small hotel in London" awards. The rooms in this 150-year-old building are tastefully decorated, and the breakfast room is a conservatory/greenhouse (13 rooms, Sb-£100, Db-£153, third bed-£22, ask for Rick Steves discount; TV, phones, and fridge in rooms by request; non-smoking rooms, elevator, 5 Sumner Place, tel. 020/7584-7586, fax 020/7823-9962, www.sumnerplace.com, reservations@sumnerplace.com, run by John and Barbara Palgan).

$$$ **Sixteen Sumner Place,** for well-heeled travelers, has over-the-top formality and class packed into its 40 rooms, plush lounges, and quiet garden. It's in a labyrinthine building, with modern Italian decor throughout (Db-£165–200—but squishy, breakfast in your room, elevator, 16 Sumner Place, tel. 020/7589-5232, fax 020/7584-8615, U.S. tel. 800/553-6674, www.numbersixteenhotel.co.uk, reservations @numbersixteenhotel.co.uk).

$$$ **Jurys Kensington Hotel** is big, stately, and impersonal, with a greedy pricing scheme (Sb/Db/Tb-£100–220 depending on "availability," ask for a deal, breakfast extra, piano lounge, non-smoking floor, elevator, Queen's Gate, tel. 020/7589-6300, fax 020/7581-1492, www.jurysdoyle.com, kensington@jurysdoyle.com).

$$$ **The Claverley,** two blocks from Harrods, is on a quiet street similar to Sumner Place. The 30 fancy, dark-wood-and-marble rooms come with all the comforts (S-£70, Sb-£85–100, Db-£120–190 depending on size, sofa-bed Tb-£190–215, ask for Rick Steves discount, plush lounge, non-smoking rooms, elevator, 13-14 Beaufort Gardens, Tube: Knightsbridge, tel. 020/7589-8541, fax 020/7584-3410, U.S. tel. 800/747-0398, www.claverleyhotel.co.uk, reservations @claverleyhotel.co.uk).

Notting Hill Gate Neighborhood

Residential Notting Hill Gate has quick bus and Tube access to down-town, is on the A2 Airbus line from Heathrow, and, for London, is very "homely." It has a self-serve launderette on Moscow Road, an artsy theater, a late-hours supermarket, and lots of fun budget eateries (see "Eating," page 103).

$$$ **Westland Hotel** is comfortable, convenient, and hotelesque, with a fine lounge and spacious rooms. Cheaper rooms are old and simple; others are quite plush (Sb-£80-90, Db-£95-105, cavernous deluxe Db-£110–125, sprawling Tb-£120–140, gargantuan Qb-£135-

Notting Hill Gate Neighborhood

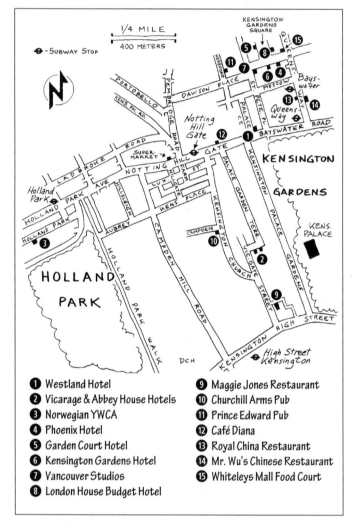

1. Westland Hotel
2. Vicarage & Abbey House Hotels
3. Norwegian YWCA
4. Phoenix Hotel
5. Garden Court Hotel
6. Kensington Gardens Hotel
7. Vancouver Studios
8. London House Budget Hotel
9. Maggie Jones Restaurant
10. Churchill Arms Pub
11. Prince Edward Pub
12. Café Diana
13. Royal China Restaurant
14. Mr. Wu's Chinese Restaurant
15. Whiteleys Mall Food Court

160, Quint/b–£150–170, 10 percent discount with this book for first visit if claimed upon arrival, elevator, free garage with six spaces, between Notting Hill Gate and Queensway Tube stations, 154 Bayswater Road, tel. 020/7229-9191, fax 020/7727-1054, www.westlandhotel.co.uk, reservations@westlandhotel.co.uk).

$$ **Vicarage Private Hotel,** understandably popular, is family-run

and elegantly British in a quiet, classy neighborhood. It has 17 rooms furnished with taste and quality, a TV lounge, and facilities on each floor. Mandy, Richard, and Krassi maintain a homey and caring atmosphere (S-£46, Sb-£75, D-£76, Db-£102, T-£93, Tb-£130, Q-£100, Qb-£140, no CC, 6-min walk from Notting Hill Gate and High Street Kensington Tube stations, near Kensington Palace at 10 Vicarage Gate, tel. 020/7229-4030, fax 020/7792-5989, www.londonvicaragehotel.com, reception@londonvicaragehotel.com).

   $$ Abbey House Hotel, next door, is basic but sleepable (16 rooms, S-£45, D-£74, T-£90, Q-£100, Quint-£110, no CC, 11 Vicarage Gate, tel. 020/7727-2594, fax 020/7727-1873, www.abbeyhousekensington.com, abbeyhousedesk@btconnect.com, Rodrigo).

   $ Norwegian YWCA (Norsk K.F.U.K.) is for women under 30 only (and men with Norwegian passports). Located on a quiet, stately street, it offers non-smoking rooms, a study, TV room, piano lounge, and an open-face Norwegian ambience. They have mostly quads, so those willing to share with strangers are most likely to get a bed (July–Aug: Ss-£30, shared double-£28/bed, shared triple-£24/bed, shared quad-£21/bed, includes breakfast and sack lunch; Sept–June: same prices also include dinner; 52 Holland Park, tel. 020/7727-9897, fax 020/7727-8718, www.kfuk.dial.pipex.com, kfuk.hjemmet@kfuk -kfum.no). With each visit, I wonder which is easier to get—a sex change or a Norwegian passport?

Near Kensington Gardens

Several big old hotels line the quiet Kensington Gardens, a block off the bustling Queensway shopping street near the Bayswater Tube station. Popular with young international travelers, Queensway is a multicultural festival of commerce and eateries (such as Mr. Wu's Chinese Restaurant and the Whiteleys Mall Food Court—see "Eating," page 103). These hotels are very quiet for central London. One of several **launderettes** in the neighborhood is Brookford Wash & Dry, at Queensway and Bishop's Bridge Road (daily 7:00–19:30, service from 9:00–17:30, computerized pay point takes all coins).

   $$$ Phoenix Hotel, a Best Western modernization of a 125-room hotel, offers American business-class comforts; spacious, plush public spaces; and big, fresh, modern-feeling rooms (Sb-£99, Db-£130, Tb-£165, Qb-£185, flaky "negotiable" pricing list, elevator, 1-8 Kensington Gardens Square, tel. 020/7229-2494, fax 020/7727-1419, U.S. tel. 800/528-1234, www.phoenixhotel.co.uk, info@phoenixhotel.co.uk).

   $$ Garden Court rents 34 comfortable, smoke-free rooms and is a fine value. It's friendly and has a garden (S-£39, Sb-£58, D-£58, Db-£88, T-£72, Tb-£99, Q-£82, Qb-£120, 5 percent discount with this book, elevator, 30 Kensington Gardens Square, tel. 020/7229-2553, fax 020/7727-2749, www.gardencourthotel.co.uk, info@gardencourthotel.co.uk).

$$ Kensington Gardens Hotel laces 16 decent rooms together in a tall, skinny place with lots of stairs and no lift (Ss-£45–50, Sb-£50-55, Db-£75, Tb-£95, 9 Kensington Gardens Square, tel. 020/7221-7790, fax 020/7792-8612, www.kensingtongardenshotel.co.uk, info@kensingtongardenshotel.co.uk, charming Rowshanak).

$$ Vancouver Studios offers 45 modern rooms with all the amenities, and gives you a fully-equipped kitchenette (utensils, stove, microwave, and fridge) rather than breakfast (small Sb-£57, big Sb-£77, small Db-£97, big Db-£112, Tb-£132, extra bed-£10, 10 percent discount with week-long stay or more, welcoming staff, homey lounge and private garden, 30 Prince's Square, tel. 020/7243-1270, fax 020/7221-8678, www.vancouverstudios.co.uk, info@vancouverstudios.co.uk).

$ London House Budget Hotel is a threadbare, nose-ringed slumber mill renting 240 beds in 93 stark rooms (S-£40, Sb-£45, twin-£54, Db-£68, dorm bed-£15, prices flex downward with demand, includes continental breakfast, lots of school groups, 81 Kensington Gardens Square, tel. 020/7243-1810, fax 020/7243-1723, londonhousehotel @yahoo.co.uk).

Other Neighborhoods

Near Covent Garden: $$$ Fielding House Hotel, located on a charming, quiet, pedestrian street just two blocks east of Covent Garden, offers 24 no-nonsense rooms, bright orange hallways, and lots of stairs (Db-£100–115, Db with sitting room-£130, no smoking, no kids under 13, no breakfast, 4 Broad Court, Bow Street, tel. 020/7836-8305, fax 020/7497-0064, www.the-fielding-hotel.co.uk).

Downtown near Baker Street: $$$ The 22 York Street B&B offers a less hotelesque alternative in the center, renting 18 stark, hardwood, comfortable rooms (Db-£100, Tb-£141, strictly smoke-free, inviting lounge, social breakfast, from Baker Street Tube station walk 2 blocks down Baker Street and take a right, 22 York Street, tel. 020/7224-3990, fax 020/7224-1990, www.22yorkstreet.co.uk, michael @22yorkstreet.co.uk, energetically run by Liz and Michael).

Near Buckingham Palace: $$ Vandon House Hotel, formerly run by the Salvation Army, is now run by the Central University of Iowa. Filled with students most of the year, the 33 rooms are rented to travelers from late May through August at great prices. The rooms, while institutional, are comfy, and the location is excellent (S-£40, D-£62, Db-£80, Tb-£114, Qb-£145, only single beds, non-smoking, elevator, on a tiny road 2 blocks west of St. James's Park Tube station, near east end of Petty France street at 1 Vandon Street, tel. 020/7799-6780, fax 020/7799-1464, www.vandonhouse.com, info@vandonhouse.com).

Euston Station: The **$$ Methodist International Centre,** a modern, youthful, Christian residence, fills its lower floors with international students and its top floor with travelers. Rooms are modern and simple yet comfortable, with fine bathrooms, phones, and desks. The atmosphere is friendly, safe, clean, and controlled; it also has a spacious lounge and game room (Sb-£48, Db-£74, two-course buffet dinner-£11, non-smoking rooms, elevator, on a quiet street a block west of Euston Station, 81-103 Euston Street—not Euston Road, Tube: Euston, tel. 020/7380-0001, fax 020/7387-5300, www.micentre.com, acc@micentre .com). In June, July, and August, when the students are gone, they rent simple £38 singles.

Near St. Paul's: $ The City of London Youth Hostel is clean, modern, friendly, and well-run. You'll pay £15 per bed in 11-bed dorm, about £25 for a bed in their three- to eight-bed rooms, or £30 for a single room (£2 extra if you have no hostel card, 193 beds, cheap meals, open 24 hrs, Tube: St. Paul's, 36 Carter Lane, tel. 020/7236-4965, fax 020/7236-7681, www.yha.org.uk, city@yha.org.uk).

Near Gatwick and Heathrow Airports

Near Gatwick Airport: The **$ London Gatwick Airport Travel Inn** rents cheap rooms at the airport (Db-£50, tel. 0870-238-3305, www.travelinn.co.uk). The **$ Gatwick Travelodge,** also a budget hotel, is two miles from the airport (Db-£50, breakfast extra, Church Road, Lowfield Heath, Crawley, tel. 0870-905-6343, www.travelodge.co.uk).

$ Barn Cottage, a converted 16th-century barn, sits in the peaceful countryside, with a tennis court, small swimming pool, and a good pub within walking distance. It has two wood-beamed rooms, antique furniture, and a large garden that makes you forget Gatwick is 10 minutes away (S-£45, D-£55, no CC, can drive you to airport or train station for £8, Leigh, Reigate, Surrey, tel. 01306/611-347, www.barn-cottage.com, bookings@barn-cottage.com, warmly run by Pat and Mike Comer).

$ Wayside Manor Farm is another rural alternative to a bland airport hotel. This four-bedroom countryside place is a 10-minute drive from Gatwick (Db-£60, Norwood Hill, near Charlwood, tel. 01293/862-692, www.wayside-manor.com, info@wayside-manor.com).

Near Heathrow Airport: It's so easy to get to Heathrow from central London, I see no reason to sleep there. But for budget beds near the airport, consider **$ Heathrow Ibis** (Db-£69, Db-£49 on Fri–Sun nights, breakfast extra, cheap shuttle bus to/from terminals except T-4, 112 Bath Road, tel. 020/8759-4888, fax 020/8564-7894, www.ibishotel .com, h0794@accor-hotels.com).

EATING

If you want to dine (as opposed to eat), check out the extensive listings in the weekly entertainment guides sold at London newsstands (or catch a train for Paris). The thought of a £30 meal in Britain generally ruins my appetite, so my London dining is limited mostly to easygoing, fun, but inexpensive alternatives. I've listed places by neighborhood—handy to your sightseeing or hotel.

Pub grub is the most atmospheric budget option. Many of London's 7,000 pubs serve fresh, tasty buffets under ancient timbers, with hearty lunches and dinners for £6–8. (While pubs are going strong, the new phenomenon is coffee shops: Starbucks and its competitors have sprouted up all over town, providing cushy and social watering holes with comfy chairs, easy WCs, £2 lattes, and a nice break between sights.)

Ethnic restaurants—especially Indian and Chinese—are popular, plentiful, and cheap. Most large museums (and many churches) have inexpensive, cheery cafeterias. Of course, picnicking is the fastest and cheapest way to go. Good grocery stores and sandwich shops, fine park benches, and polite pigeons abound in Britain's most expensive city.

Near Trafalgar Square

To locate the following restaurants, see the map on page 107.

St. Martin-in-the-Fields Café in the Crypt is just right for a tasty meal on a monk's budget, sitting on somebody's tomb in an ancient crypt (£6-7 cafeteria plates, cheaper sandwich bar, Mon–Wed 10:00–20:00, Thu–Sat 10:00–23:00, Sun 12:00–20:00, profits go to the church, no CC, underneath St. Martin-in-the-Fields church on Trafalgar Square, tel. 020/7839-4342).

Chandos Pub's Opera Room floats amazingly apart from the tacky crush of tourism around Trafalgar Square. Look for it opposite the National Portrait Gallery (corner of William Street and St. Martin's Lane) and climb the stairs to the Opera Room. This is a fine Trafalgar Square rendezvous point—smoky, but wonderfully local. They serve traditional, plain-tasting, £6–7 pub lunches and dinners (kitchen open 11:00–19:00, until 18:00 on weekends, order and pay at the bar, tel. 020/7836-1401).

The International is a mod complement to Chandos (just across the street), offering a bright and spacious retreat for local office workers oblivious to all the touristic hubbub nearby. The ground-floor bar has two-for-one bar meals daily (noon to 17:00). The classy restaurant upstairs serves modern European cuisine (daily, two-course menu-£10, three courses-£13, 116 St. Martin's Lane, tel. 020/7257-8626).

At **Gordon's Wine Bar,** a simple, steep staircase leads into a candlelit 15th-century wine cellar filled with dusty old bottles, faded British memorabilia, and local nine-to-fivers. At the buffet, choose a hot meal or a fine plate of cheeses and various cold cuts. (One £7 cold plate and a couple of glasses of wine provide a light meal for two economically.) Then step up to the wine bar and consider the many varieties of wine and port available by the glass—at great prices. The low, carbon-crusted vaulting deeper in the back seems to intensify the Hogarth-painting atmosphere. While it's crowded, you can normally corral two chairs and grab the corner of a table (arrive before 17:30 to get a seat, Mon–Sat 11:00–23:00, Sun 12:00–22:00, 2 blocks from Trafalgar Square, bottom of Villiers Street at #47, Tube: Embankment, tel. 020/7930–1408). On hot days, the crowd spills out into a leafy back patio.

The Clarence Pub, down Whitehall, a block south of Trafalgar Square toward Big Ben, is touristy but atmospheric with decent grub (indoor/outdoor seating, meals-£8, daily 11:00–22:00). Nearby are several cheaper cafeterias and pizza joints.

Sherlock Holmes Pub, a block from Trafalgar Square, sounds touristy but is the haunt of government workers and locals awaiting trains at Charing Cross Station. Fans of the fictional detective will appreciate the pub's location in the former Northumberland Hotel (featured in Holmes stories) and the fact that Old Scotland Yard was just across the street. Upstairs in the restaurant area is a replica of 221-B Baker Street (Mon–Sat 11:00–23:00, Sun 12:00–22:30, pub fare downstairs, restaurant meals served upstairs at lunch and dinnertime, 10 Northumberland Street, Tube: Charing Cross or Embankment, tel. 020/7930-2644.)

Crivelli's Garden Restaurant, serving a classy lunch in the National Gallery, is a good place to treat your palate to pricey, light Mediterranean cuisine (lunches-£15, daily 10:00–17:00, first floor of Sainsbury Wing). For something more Dickensian, try Hampton's Wine Bar (Mon–Fri 11:30–23:00, closed Sat-Sun, around the corner at 15 Whitcomb Street, tel. 020-7839-2823).

Near Piccadilly

Hungry and broke in the theater district? Head for Panton Street (off Haymarket, 2 blocks southeast of Piccadilly Circus) for cheap Thai, Chinese, and two famous London eateries. **Stockpot** is a mushy-peas kind of place, famous and rightly popular for its edible, cheap meals (daily 7:00–22:00, 38 Panton Street); see map on page 107. The **West End Kitchen** (across the street at #5, same hours and menu) is a direct competitor that's just as good. Vegetarians prefer the **Woodland South Indian Vegetarian Restaurant,** across from the West End Kitchen. For a £5 Chinese meal, **Mr. Wu's** buffet is on Old Compton Street. And **Pizza Express** has many branches offering a gut busting £5 buffet.

The palatial **Criterion Brasserie** serves a special £15 two-course "Anglo-French" menu (or £18 for three courses) under gilded tiles and chandeliers in a dreamy Byzantine church setting from 1880. It's right on Piccadilly Circus but a world away from the punk junk. The house wine is great and so is the food (specials available Mon–Sat 12:00–14:30 & 17:30–19:00, closed Sun lunch, tel. 020/7930-0488). After 19:00, the menu becomes really expensive. Anyone can drop in for coffee or a drink.

The "Food Is Fun" Dinner Crawl: From Covent Garden to Soho

London has a trendy, Generation-X scene that most Beefeater-seekers miss entirely. For a multicultural, movable feast, consider exploring these. Start around 18:00 to avoid lines, get in on early specials, and find waiters willing to let you split a meal. Prices, while reasonable by London standards, add up. Servings are large enough to share. All are open nightly.

Suggested nibbler's dinner crawl for two: Arrive before 18:00 at **Belgo Centraal** and split the early-bird dinner special: a kilo of mussels, fries, and dark Belgian beer. At **Yo! Sushi,** have beer or sake and a few dishes. Slurp your last course at **Wagamama Noodle Bar.** Then, for dessert, people-watch at Leicester Square, where the serf's always up.

Belgo Centraal serves hearty Belgian specialties. It's a seafood, chips, and beer emporium dressed up as a mod monastic refectory—with noisy acoustics and waiters garbed as Trappist monks. The classy restaurant section requires reservations, but just grabbing a bench in the boisterous beer hall (no reservations possible) is more fun. The same menu and specials work on both sides. Belgians claim they eat as well as the French and as heartily as the Germans. Specialties include mussels, great fries, and a stunning array of dark, blond, and fruity Belgian beers. Belgo actually makes Belgian things trendy—a formidable feat (meals-£10–14; open daily until 23:00; Mon–Fri 17:30–19:00 "beat the clock" meal specials for £5.30-7.00, and you get mussels, fries, and beer; no meal-splitting after 18:30, and you must buy food with beer; daily £6 lunch special 12:00–17:30; 1 block north of Covent Garden Tube station at intersection of Neal and Shelton streets, 50 Earlham Street, tel. 020/7813-2233).

Yo! Sushi is a futuristic Japanese-food-extravaganza experience. With thumping rock, Japanese cable TV, a 195-foot-long conveyor belt, the world's longest sushi bar, a robotic drink trolley, and automated sushi machines, just sipping a sake on a bar stool here is a trip. For £1 each you get unlimited tea, water (from spigot at bar, with or without gas), or miso soup. Grab dishes as they rattle by (priced by color of dish; check the chart: £1.50-3.50 per dish, daily 12:00–24:00, 2 blocks south of Oxford Street, where Lexington Street becomes Poland Street, 52 Poland Street, tel. 020/7287-0443). For more serious drinking on tatami mats, go downstairs into "Yo Below." (If you like Yo, there's a handy branch a block from the London Eye on Belvedere Road.)

Wagamama Noodle Bar is a noisy, pan-Asian, organic slurpathon. As you enter, check out the kitchen and listen to the roar of the basement, where benches rock with happy eaters. Everybody sucks. Stand against the wall to feel the energy of all this "positive eating" (meals-£10, daily 12:00–24:00, crowded after 20:00, non-smoking, 10-A

From Covent Garden to Soho: Food is Fun

1. St. Martin-in-the-Fields Café in the Crypt
2. The Chandos Pub
3. The International Pub & Rest.
4. Gordon's Wine Bar
5. The Clarence Pub
6. Crivelli's Garden Rest.
7. Stockpot & West End Kitchen
8. Woodland South Indian Vegetarian Rest.
9. Criterion Brasserie
10. Belgo Centraal
11. Yo! Sushi
12. Wagamama Noodle Bar
13. Soho Spice Indian Rest.
14. Y Ming Chinese Rest.
15. Andrew Edmunds & Mildred's Vegetarian Rest.
16. To Zilly Fish Too Rest.
17. Neal's Yard Rest.
18. Food for Thought Café

Lexington Street, tel. 020/7292-0990 but no reservations taken). If you like this place, there are now handy branches all over town, including near the British Museum (Streatham Street), High Street Kensington (#26), in Harvey Nichols (109 Knightsbridge), Covent Garden (Tavistock Street), Leicester Square (Irving Street), Piccadilly Circus (Norris Street), Fleet Street (#109), and between St. Paul's and the Tower of London (22 Old Broad Street).

Soho Spice Indian is where modern Britain meets Indian tradition—fine cuisine in a trendy, jewel-tone ambience. Unlike many Indian restaurants, when you order an entrée here (£10–15), it comes with side dishes (nan, dal, rice, vegetables). The £15 "tandoori selections" meal is the best "variety" dish and big enough for two (Mon–Sat 11:30–24:00, Sun 12:30–22:30, non-smoking section, 5 blocks north of Piccadilly Circus at 124 Wardour Street, tel. 020/7434-0808).

Y Ming Chinese Restaurant is across Shaftesbury Avenue from the ornate gates, clatter, and dim sum of Chinatown, and it has clean European decor, serious but helpful service, and authentic Northern Chinese cooking (good £10 meal deal offered 12:00–18:00—last order at 18:00, Mon–Sat 12:00–23:30, closed Sun, 35 Greek Street, tel. 020/7734-2721, www.yming.com).

Andrew Edmunds Restaurant is a tiny, candlelit place where you'll want to hide your camera and guidebook and act as local as possible. This great little place—with a jealous and loyal clientele—is the closest I found to Parisian quality in a cozy restaurant in London. The modern European cooking with a creative seasonal menu is worth the splurge (three-course meal-£25, daily 12:30–15:00 & 18:00–22:45, reservations are generally necessary—request ground floor rather than the basement, 46 Lexington Street in Soho, tel. 020/7437-5708).

Mildred's Vegetarian Restaurant, across from Andrew Edmunds, has cheap prices, an enjoyable menu, and a plain-yet-pleasant interior filled with happy eaters (meals-£6, Mon–Sat 12:00–23:00, closed Sun, 45 Lexington Street, tel. 020/7494-1634).

The fun **Zilli Fish Too,** with a modern, bright setting near Covent Garden, serves up fresh seafood with a twist of Italy (two-course meal-£15, three courses-£19, daily 12:00–15:00 & 17:30–23:30, 8 Wild Street, at corner of Great Queen Street, two blocks north of Covent Garden, tel. 020/7240-0011).

Neal's Yard is *the* place for cheap, hip, and healthy eateries near Covent Garden. The neighborhood is a tabbouleh of fun, hippie-type cafés. One of the best is **Food for Thought,** packed with local health nuts (good vegetarian meals-£5, Mon–Sat 12:00–20:30, Sun 12:00–17:00, non-smoking, 2 blocks north of Covent Garden Tube station, 31 Neal Street, tel. 020/7836-0239).

Near Recommended Victoria Station Accommodations

Here are places a couple of blocks southwest of Victoria Station where I've enjoyed eating (see map on page 95).

La Campagnola, small and seriously Italian, is Belgravia's favorite budget Italian restaurant (£8–16, Mon–Sat 12:00–15:00 & 18:00–23:30, closed Sun, 10 Lower Belgrave Street, tel. 020/7730-2057).

Ebury Wine Bar, filled with young professionals, provides a classy atmosphere, delicious meals, and a £13 two-course special from 18:00–19:30 (£15–18, open Mon–Fri 11:00–23:00, Sat 12:00–23:00, Sun 18:00–23:00, 139 Ebury Street, at intersection with Elizabeth Street, near bus station, tel. 020/7730-5447). Several cheap places are around the corner on Elizabeth Street (#23 for take-out or eat-in, super-absorbent fish and chips, and a Spanish tapas place across from that).

Duke of Wellington pub is good, if somewhat smoky, and dominated by local drinkers. It's the neighborhood place for dinner (meals-£6, daily 11:00–15:00 & 18:00–21:00, 63 Eaton Terrace, at intersection with Chester Row, tel. 020/7730–1782).

Jenny Lo's Tea House is a simple, budget place serving up reliably tasty £5-8 eclectic Chinese-style meals to locals in the know (Mon–Fri 11:30–15:00 & 18:00–22:00, Sat 12:00–15:00 & 18:00–22:00, closed Sun, no CC, 14 Eccleston Street, tel. 020/7259-0399).

La Poule au Pot, ideal for a romantic splurge, offers a classy, candlelit ambience with well-dressed patrons and expensive but fine country-style French cuisine (lunch-£15, dinner-£25, daily 12:30–14:30 & 18:45–23:00, Sun until 22:00, leafy patio dining, reservations smart, end of Ebury at intersection with Pimlico, 231 Ebury Street, tel. 020/7730-7763).

Grumbles brags that it's been serving "good food and wine at non-scary prices since 1964." Offering a delicious mix of "modern eclectic French and traditional English," this hip and cozy little place is *the* spot to eat well in this otherwise workaday neighborhood (meals-£12–22, lunch specials-£12, reservations wise, self-serve launderette across the street open evenings, two nice sidewalk tables, daily 12:00–14:30 & 18:00–22:30, half a block north of Belgrave Road at 35 Churton Street, tel. 020/7834-0149).

The Jugged Hare Pub is in a lavish old bank building, its vaults replaced by kegs of beer and a fine kitchen. They have a fun, traditional menu with more fresh veggies than fries, and a plush and vivid pub scene good for a meal or just a drink (meals-£7, daily 12:00–21:00, 172 Vauxhall Bridge Road, tel. 020/7828-1543).

If you miss America, there's a mall-type **food court** at Victoria Place, upstairs in Victoria Station; **Café Rouge** seems to be the most popular here (£8–11 dinners, daily 9:30–22:30).

Groceries in and near Victoria Station: A large grocery, **Sainsbury's Local,** is on Victoria Street in front of the station, just past the buses (daily 6:00–24:00). In the station you'll find another, smaller Sainsbury's (at rear entrance, on Eccleston Street) and a couple other late-hours mini-markets.

Near Recommended Notting Hill Gate B&Bs and Bayswater Hotels

Queensway is lined with lively and inexpensive eateries. See the map on page 100.

Maggie Jones, exuberantly rustic and very English, serves my favorite £20 London dinner. You'll get fun-loving if brash service, solid English cuisine, including huge plates of crunchy vegetables—by candlelight. Avoid the stuffy basement on hot summer nights, and request upstairs seating for the noisy but less-cramped section. If you eat well once in London, eat here—and do it quick, before it burns down (daily 12:30–14:30 & 18:30–23:00, less-expensive lunch menu, reservations recommended, friendly staff, 6 Old Court Place, just east of Kensington Church Street, near High Street Kensington Tube stop, tel. 020/7937-6462).

Churchill Arms pub and **Thai Kitchens** is a local hangout, with good beer and old-English ambience in front and hearty £6 Thai plates in an enclosed patio in the back. You can eat the Thai food in this tropical hideaway or in the smoky but wonderfully atmospheric pub section. Arrive by 18:00 to avoid a line (Mon–Sat 12:00–21:30, Sun 12:00–16:00, 119 Kensington Church Street, tel. 020/7792-1246).

Prince Edward Pub serves good pub grub in a quintessential pub setting (meals-£8, Mon–Sat 12:00–14:30 & 18:00–21:00, Sun 12:00–18:00, indoor/outdoor seating, 2 blocks north of Bayswater Road at the corner of Dawson Place and Hereford Road, 73 Prince's Square, tel. 020/7727-2221).

Café Diana is a healthy little eatery serving sandwiches and Middle Eastern food. It's decorated with photos of Princess Diana, who used to drop by for pita sandwiches (daily 8:00–22:30, 5 Wellington Terrace, on Bayswater Road, opposite Kensington Palace Garden Gates—where Di once lived, tel. 020/7792-9606).

Royal China Restaurant is filled with London's Chinese, who consider this one of the city's best eateries. It's dressy in black, white, and chrome, with candles, brisk waiters, and fine food (£7–9 dishes, dim sum until 17:00, Mon–Thu 12:00–23:00, Fri–Sat 12:00–23:30, Sun 11:00–22:00, 13 Queensway, tel. 020/7221-2535).

Mr. Wu's Chinese Restaurant serves a 10-course buffet in a cramped little cafeteria. Just grab a plate and help yourself (£5, daily 12:00–23:00, check quality of buffet—right inside entrance—before committing, pickings can get slim, across from Bayswater Tube station, 54 Queensway, tel. 020/7243-1017).

Whiteleys Mall Food Court offers a fun selection of ethnic and fast-food eateries in a delightful mall (good salads at Café Rouge, second floor, corner of Porchester Gardens and Queensway).

Supermarket: Europa is a half-block from the Notting Hill Gate Tube stop (Mon–Fri 8:00–23:00, Sun 12:00–18:00, 112 Notting Hill Gate, near intersection with Pembridge Road).

Near Recommended Accommodations in South Kensington

Popular eateries line Old Brompton Road and Thurloe Street (Tube: South Kensington). See the map on page 98.

La Bouchee Bistro Café is a classy, hole-in-the-wall touch of France serving early-bird, three-course £12 meals before 19:00 and *plats du jour* for £8 all *jour* (daily 12:00–23:00, Sun until 22:00, 56 Old Brompton Road, tel. 020/7589-1929).

Daquise, a 1930s Polish time-warp, is ideal if you're in the mood for kielbasa and kraut. It's likeably dreary—fast, cheap, family-run, and a part of the neighborhood (meals-£10, daily 11:00–23:00, non-smoking, 20 Thurloe Street, tel. 020/7589-6117).

The **Khyber Pass Tandoori Restaurant** is a nondescript but handy place serving great Indian cuisine. Locals in the know travel to eat here (dinner-£10, daily 12:00–14:30 & 18:00–23:30, 21 Bute Street, tel. 020/7589-7311).

La Brasserie fills a big, plain room painted "nicotine yellow," with ceiling fans, a Parisian ambience, and good, traditional French cooking at reasonable prices (salads and veggie plates-£10, two-course menus-£15–£18, nightly until 23:00, 272 Brompton Road, tel. 020/7581-3089).

PJ's Bar and Grill is lively with the yuppie Chelsea crowd for a good reason. Traditional "New York Brasserie"-style, yet trendy, it has dressy tables surrounding a centerpiece bar. It serves pricey, cosmopolitan cuisine from a menu that changes with the seasons (meals-£20, nightly until 24:00, 52 Fulham Road, at intersection with Sydney Street, tel. 020/7581-0025).

Elsewhere in London

Between St. Paul's and the Tower: The **Counting House,** formerly an elegant old bank, offers great £7 meals, nice homemade meat pies, fish, and fresh vegetables (Mon–Fri 12:00–20:00, closed Sat–Sun, gets really busy with the buttoned-down 9-to-5 crowd after 12:15, near Mansion House in the City, 50 Cornhill, tel. 020/7283-7123).

Near St. Paul's: Degustibus Sandwiches is where a top-notch "artisan bakery" meets the public, offering fresh you-design-it sandwiches, salads, and soups with simple seating or take-out picnic sacks (great parks nearby) just a block below St. Paul's (Mon–Fri 7:00–17:00, closed Sat–Sun, from church steps follow signs to youth hostel a block downhill, 53 Carter Lane, tel. 020/723-60056, Claire).

Near the British Library: Drummond Street (running just west of Euston Station) is famous in London for very cheap and good Indian and vegetarian food. Consider **Chutneys** and **Ravi Shankar** for a good *thali.*

TRANSPORTATION CONNECTIONS

London's Heathrow Airport

Heathrow Airport is the world's fourth busiest. Think about it: 60 million passengers a year on 425,000 flights from 200 destinations riding 90 airlines...some kind of global maypole dance. While many complain about Heathrow, I think it's a great airport. It's user-friendly. Read signs, ask questions. For Heathrow's airport, flight, and transfers information, call the switchboard at 0870-000-0123 (www.baa.co.uk). It has four terminals: T-1 (mostly domestic flights, with some European), T-2 (mainly European flights), T-3 (mostly flights from the United States), and T-4 (British Airways transatlantic flights and BA flights to Paris, Amsterdam, and Athens). Taxis know which terminal you'll need.

Each terminal has an airport information desk, car-rental agencies, exchange bureaus, ATMs, a pharmacy, a **VAT refund desk** (T-4 VAT info tel. 020/8910-3682, you must present the VAT claim form from the retailer here to get your 15 percent tax rebate on items purchased in Britain, see page 5 in this book's Introduction for details), and a £4/day **baggage-check desk** (T-1 and T-2 desks open daily 6:00–23:00, T-3 desk opens at 5:15, and T-4 at 5:30). Heathrow's **Internet Exchange** provides access 24 hours a day (T-3). There are **post offices** in T-2 and T-4. Each terminal has cheap **eateries** (such as the cheery Food Village self-service cafeteria in T-3). The **American Express** desk, in the Tube station at Terminal 4 (daily 7:00–19:00), has rates similar to the exchange bureaus upstairs, but doesn't charge a commission (typically 1.5 percent) for cashing any type of traveler's check.

Heathrow's small **TI,** even though it's a for-profit business, is worth a visit to pick up free information: a simple map, the London Planner, and brochures (daily 8:30–18:00, 5-min walk from Terminal 3 in Tube station, follow signs to Underground; bypass queue for transit info to reach window for London questions). If you're riding the Airbus into London, have your partner stay with the bags at the terminal while you head over to the TI.

If you're taking the Tube into London, buy a one-day Travel Card pass to cover the ride (see below).

Transportation to London from Heathrow Airport

By Tube (Subway): For £3.70, the Tube takes you the 14 miles to downtown London in 50 minutes (6/hr, depending on your destination, may require a change). Even better, buy a £5 one-day Travel Card that covers your trip into London and all your Tube travel for the day (starting at 9:30). Buy it at the ticket window at the Tube. You can hop on the Tube at any terminal.

By Airport Bus: The Airbus, running between the airport and London's King's Cross station, serves the Notting Hill Gate and Bayswater neighborhoods (£10, round trip-£15, 2/hr, 60 min, runs 5:00–21:15, departs from each terminal, buy ticket from driver, tel. 08705-757-747). The Tube works fine, but with baggage, I prefer the Airbus (assuming it serves my hotel neighborhood) because there are no connections underground and there's a lovely view from the top of the double-decker bus. Ask the driver to remind you when to get off. For people heading to the airport, exact pickup times are clearly posted at each bus stop.

By Taxi: Taxis from the airport cost about £45. For four people traveling together, this can be a deal. Hotels can often line up a cab back to the airport for about £30. For the cheapest taxi to the airport, don't order one from your hotel. Simply flag down a few and ask them for their best "off-meter" rate.

Another good option is Hotelink, a door-to-door airport shuttle (Heathrow-£15 per person, Gatwick-£22 per person, book the day before departure, buy online and save £1-2, tel. 01293/532-244, www.hotelink.co.uk, reservations@hotelink.co.uk).

By Heathrow Express Train: This slick train service zips you between Heathrow Airport and London's Paddington Station. At Paddington Station, you're in the thick of the Tube system, with easy access to any of my recommended neighborhoods—Notting Hill Gate is just two stops away. It's only 15 minutes to downtown from Terminals 1, 2, and 3 and 20 minutes from Terminal 4 (at the airport, you can use the Express as a free transfer between terminals). Buy your ticket to London before you board or pay a £2 surcharge to buy it on the train (£13, but ask about discount promos at Heathrow ticket desk, kids under 16 ride half-price, under 5 ride free, covered by Britrail pass, 4/hr, daily 5:10–23:30, tel. 0845-600–1515, www.heathrowexpress.co.uk). A "Go Further" ticket (£14.60) includes one Tube ride from Paddington to get you to your hotel (valid only on same day and in Zone 1, saves time). For one person on a budget, combining the Heathrow Express with either a Tube or taxi ride (between your hotel and Paddington) is nearly as fast and half the cost of taking a cab directly to (or from) the airport.

Buses from Heathrow to Destinations beyond London

The **National Express Central Bus Station** offers direct Jetlink bus connections to **Gatwick Airport** (2/hr, 70 min or more, depending on traffic), departing just outside arrivals at all terminals (one way-£15, round trip-£20). To **Bath,** direct buses run daily from Heathrow

(11/day, 2.5 hrs, £14, tel. 08705-757-747). BritRail passholders may prefer the 2.5-hour Heathrow-Bath bus/train connection via Reading (£9 for bus, rail portion free with pass, otherwise £29.20 total, payable at desk in terminal); first catch the twice-hourly RailAir Link shuttle bus to Reading (RED-ding), then hop on the hourly express train to Bath. Most Heathrow buses depart from the common area serving Terminals 1, 2, and 3 (a 5-min walk from any of these terminals), although some depart from T-4 (bus tel. 08705-747-777).

London's Gatwick Airport

More and more flights, especially charters, land at Gatwick Airport, halfway between London and the southern coast (recorded airport info tel. 0870-000-2468). Express trains—clearly the best way into London from here—shuttle conveniently between Gatwick and London's Victoria Station (£11, round trip-£21.50, children under 5 free, 4/hr during day, 1-2/hr at night, 30 min, runs 24 hrs daily, can purchase tickets on train at no extra charge, tel. 0845-850–1530, www.gatwickexpress .co.uk). You can save a few pounds by taking South Central rail line's slower and less-frequent shuttle between Victoria Station and Gatwick (£8.20, 3/hr, 1/hr midnight-4:00, 45 min, tel. 08457-484-950, www .southcentraltrains.co.uk).

To get to Bath from Gatwick, you can catch a bus to Heathrow and the bus to Bath from there. By train, the best Gatwick-Bath connection involves a transfer in Reading (2.5 hrs, irregular schedule; avoid transfer in London, where you'll have to change stations).

To make a flight connection between Heathrow and Gatwick (see "Buses," above), allow three hours between your arrival at one airport and departure at the other.

London's Other Airports

If you're flying into or out of **Stansted** (airport tel. 0870-0000-303), you can take the Airbus to or from downtown London's Victoria Coach Station (£10, 2/hr, 1.5 hrs, runs 4:00–24:00, picks up and stops throughout London, tel. 0845-850-0150) or take the Stansted Airport Rail Link (£13, departs London's Liverpool Street Station, 40 min, 2-4/hr, 5:00–23:00, tel. 08705-301-530, www.stanstedexpress.com).

For **Luton** (airport tel. 01582/405-100, www.london-luton.com), take Green Line's bus #757, which runs between the airport and London's Victoria Station at Buckingham Palace Road—stop 6 (£8, £7 for easyJet passengers, 2/hr, 1-1.25 hrs depending on time of day, runs 4:30–24:00, tel. 0870-608-7261, www.greenline.co.uk).

Discounted Flights from London

Although bmi british midland has been around the longest, the others generally offer cheaper flights.

With **bmi british midland,** you can fly inexpensively to destinations in the U.K. and beyond (fares start around £30 one-way to Edinburgh, Paris, Brussels, or Amsterdam; or around £50 one-way to Dublin; prices can be higher, but there can also be much cheaper Internet specials—check online). For the latest, call British tel. 0870-607-0555 or U.S. tel. 800/788-0555 (check www.flybmi.com and their subsidiary, bmibaby, at www.bmibaby.com). Book in advance. Although you can book right up until the flight departs, the cheap seats will have sold out long before, leaving the most expensive seats for latecomers.

With no frills and cheap fares, **easyJet** flies mostly from Luton and Gatwick. Prices are based on demand, so the least popular routes make for the cheapest fares, especially if you book early (tel. 0870-600-0000, www.easyjet.com).

Ryanair is a creative Irish airline that prides itself on offering the lowest fares. It flies from London (mostly Stansted airport) to often obscure airports in Dublin, Glasgow, Frankfurt, Stockholm, Oslo, Venice, Turin, and many others. Sample fares: London-Dublin round trip-£78 (sometimes as low as £25), London-Frankfurt round trip-£67 (Irish tel. 01/609-7881, British tel. 0871-246-0000, www.ryanair.com). Because they offer promotional deals any time of year, it's not essential that you book long in advance to get the best deals.

Virgin Express is a British-owned company with good rates (book by phone and pick up ticket at airport an hour before your flight, tel. 020/7744-0004, www.virgin-express.com). Virgin Express flies from London Heathrow and Brussels. From its hub in Brussels, you can connect cheaply to Barcelona, Madrid, Nice, Malaga, Copenhagen, Rome, or Milan (round trip from Brussels to Rome for as little as £105). Their prices stay the same whether or not you book in advance.

Trains and Buses

London, Britain's major transportation hub, has a different train station for each region. Waterloo handles the Eurostar to Paris. King's Cross covers northeast England and Scotland (tel. 08457-225-225). Paddington covers west and southwest England (Bath) and South Wales (tel. 08457-000-125). For the others, call 08457-484-950. Also see the BritRail Routes map on page 19 of this book's Introduction. Note that for security reasons, stations offer a left-luggage service (£5/day) rather than lockers.

National Express' excellent bus service is considerably cheaper than trains. (For a busy signal, call 08705-808-080, or visit www.nationalexpress .com or the bus station a block southwest of Victoria Station.)

To Bath by train: Trains leave London's Paddington Station every hour between 7:00 and 19:00 (at :15 after each hour) for the 90-min ride to Bath (costs £33 if you leave after 9:30 any day but Fri, when it's £40).

To Bath by bus via Stonehenge: To get to Bath and see Stonehenge to boot, consider taking a guided bus tour from London to Stonehenge and Bath and abandoning the tour in Bath. Several bus-tour companies take London-based travelers out and back every day. If you're going to Bath and want to stay overnight, consider taking a day tour to Bath and skipping the trip back to London. Depending on the type and availability of tour, you'll pay about £50, which also includes a visit to Stonehenge (compare to a £33 one-way second-class train ticket from London to Bath). Evan Evans' tour is fully guided for £50 (includes admissions). The tour leaves from Victoria Coach Station , a block from the Victoria train station every morning at 8:45 (you can stow your bag under the bus), stops in Stonehenge (45 min), and then stops in Bath for lunch and a city tour before returning to London (offered year-round). You can book the tour at Victoria Coach Station, the Evan Evans' office (258 Vauxhall Bridge Road, near Victoria Coach Station, tel. 020/7950–1777, U.S. tel. 866/382-6868, www.evanevans .co.uk, reservations@evanevanstours.co.uk), or the Green Line Travel Office (4a Fountain Square, across from Victoria Coach Station, tel. 020/7950–1777). Golden Tours also runs a fully guided Stonehenge-Bath tour for a similar price (departs from Fountain Square, located across from Victoria Coach Station, tel. 020/7233-6668, U.S. tel. 800/456-6303, www.goldentours.co.uk, reservations@goldentours.co.uk).

To Points North: Trains run hourly from London's King's Cross Station, stopping in York (2 hrs), Durham (3 hrs), and Edinburgh (5 hrs).

To Dublin, Ireland: The boat/bus journey takes between 10 and 11 hours and goes all day or all night (£29–57, 2/day, tel. 08705-143-219, www.eurolines.com). Consider a cheap 70-minute Ryanair flight instead (see above).

Crossing the English Channel
By Eurostar Train
The fastest and most convenient way to get from Big Ben to the Eiffel Tower is by rail. In London, advertisements claim "more businessmen travel from London to Paris on the Eurostar than on all airlines combined."

Eurostar is the speedy passenger train that zips you (and up to 800 others in 18 sleek cars) from downtown London to downtown Paris (12-15/day, last departure 19:23, 2.5 hrs) or Brussels (8/day, 2.5 hrs) faster and easier than flying. The train goes 80 mph in England and 190 mph on the Continent. (When the English segment gets up to speed, the journey time will shrink to 2 hours.) The actual tunnel crossing is a 20-minute, black, silent, 100-mile-per-hour non-event. Your ears won't even pop. You can go direct to Disneyland Paris (1/day, more frequent with transfer at Lille) or change at Lille to catch a TGV to Paris'

Charles de Gaulle Airport.

Channel fares (essentially the same to Paris or Brussels) are reasonable but complicated. Prices vary depending on when you travel; whether you can live with restrictions; and whether you're eligible for any discounts (youth, seniors, and railpass holders all qualify). Rates are lower for round-trip and off-peak (mid-day, mid-week, low-season, and low-interest) travel.

As with airfares, the most expensive and flexible option is a **full-fare ticket** with no restrictions on refundability (even refundable after the departure date; one way in second class-$223, one way in first-class-$312). A first-class ticket comes with a meal (a dinner departure nets you more grub than breakfast)—but it's not worth the extra expense.

Also like the airlines, **cheaper tickets** come with more restrictions—and are limited in number (so they sell out more quickly). Non-full-fare tickets have severe restrictions on refundability (best-case scenario: you'll get 25 percent back, but with many you'll get nothing). But several do allow you to change the specifics of your trip once before departure. For specifics, see "Standard Eurostar Fares" on the next page.

Those traveling with a railpass for Britain, France, or Belgium should look first at the **passholder** fare, an especially good value for one-way Eurostar trips. In Britain, passholder tickets can be issued only at the Eurostar office in Waterloo Station or the American Express office in Victoria Station—not at any other stations. You can also order them by phone, then pick them up at Waterloo Station.

Refund and exchange restrictions are serious, so don't reserve until you're sure of your plans. If you are confident of the time and date of your crossing, order ahead from the U.S. Only the most expensive ticket (full fare) is fully refundable, so if you want to have more flexibility, hold off. On the other hand, keep in mind that the longer you wait, the more likely the cheapest tickets will be sold out.

You can check and book fares by phone or online in the United States (order online at www.ricksteves.com/eurostar, prices listed in dollars; order by phone at U.S. tel. 800/EUROSTAR) or in Britain (British tel. 08705-186-186, www.eurostar.com, prices listed in euros). These are different companies, often with slightly different prices and discount deals on similar tickets (see below)—if you order from the United States, check out both. (If you buy from a U.S. company, you'll pay for ticket delivery in the United States; if you book with the British company, you'll pick up your ticket at Waterloo Station.) In Europe, you can get your Eurostar ticket at any major train station in any country or at any travel agency that handles train tickets (expect a booking fee).

Note that Britain's time zone is one hour earlier than the Continent's. Times listed on tickets are local times.

STANDARD EUROSTAR FARES

I've listed only standard (second-class) prices between London and Paris or Brussels. Standard class is comfortable, making first class an unnecessary luxury. Compare one-way fares with cheap round-trip fares (especially the Leisure RT Same Day; you can forget to return).

The following fares are accurate as of mid-2003 and subject to change. Note that the ticket names, restrictions, and prices listed here are for tickets purchased in the U.S. If you buy your ticket in Europe, your options are similar, though rarely identical. Sometimes it's a better deal to buy your ticket in Britain instead of the United States, and sometimes it's not. Compare. For European fares, go to www.eurostar.com and input your travel date and time to see the available rates and restrictions. For U.S. fares (including first-class prices), visit www.ricksteves.com/eurostar. A Premier Train Fee of $7 per order applies.

Standard Class	Major Restrictions	One-Way	Round-Trip
Full Fare	None (fully refundable even after departure date).	$223	$446
Leisure Flexi	One exchange in Europe before departure; 25 percent refund up to three days before departure. Round-trip discount based on seat availability.	$195	$210/300/390
Leisure	No refund or exchange.	$90	$180
Leisure RT	No refund or exchange. Round-trip travel and minimum one-night stay required.	N/A	$150

Without Eurostar

By bus and boat or by train and boat: The old-fashioned way of crossing the Channel is cheaper than crossing by Eurostar. It's also twice as romantic, complicated, and time-consuming. You'll get better prices arranging your trip in London than you would in the United States. Taking the bus is cheapest, and round-trips are a bargain.

By **bus** to Paris, Brussels, or Amsterdam from Victoria Coach Station (via boat or Chunnel): one way-£35, round trip-£47 for economy fares booked at least two days in advance; 8 hrs to Paris—5/day; 9 hrs to Brussels—5/day; 12 hrs to Amsterdam—4/day; day or overnight, on Eurolines (tel. 08705-143-219, www.eurolines.com).

The **Hoverspeed ferry** runs between Dover, England, and Calais, France (tel. 08705-240-241 or 0870-240-8070, www.hoverspeed.com).

Standard Class	Major Restrictions	One-Way	Round-Trip
Leisure RT Midweek	No refund or exchange. Round-trip travel and minimum one-night stay required. Travel Mon—Thu only. Round-trip discount based on seat availability.	N/A	$90/$120
Leisure RT Same Day	No refund or exchange. Travel round-trip within one day (ideal for Paris day trip from London).	N/A	$94
Passholder	No refund. One exchange in Europe before departure. Trip must occur during the validity period of a railpass including Britain, France, or Belgium.	$75	$150
Senior	Age 60+. No refund. One exchange in Europe before departure.	$90	$180
Youth Peak	Age under 26. No refund, one exchange.	$75	$150
Youth Off-Peak	Age under 26. No refund, one exchange.	$45	$90
Child Age 4-11.	No refund, one exchange.	$38	$76

Hoverspeed sells London-Paris rail and ferry packages: one way-£44, round trip with five-day return-£56; and round trip over more than five days-£67. You can buy this package deal in person at Waterloo and Charing Cross stations. If you book by phone (number listed above), you must book at least two weeks in advance, and the ticket will be mailed to you (no ticket pickup at station for bookings by phone).

By **P&O Stena Line ferry** from Dover to Calais: one way or round trip with five-day return-£17, round-trip over more than five days-£34 (tel. 0870-600-0613, www.posl.com). Prices are for the ferry only; you need to book your own train tickets—see P&O's Web site for details.

By Plane: Typical fares are £110 regular, less for student standby. Check with the budget airlines for cheap round-trip fares to Paris (see "Discounted Flights from London," page 114).

London Day Trips

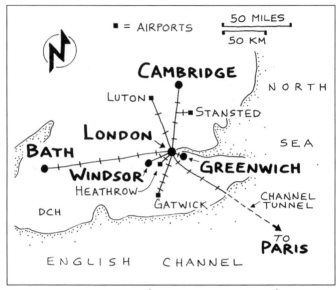

Near London: Greenwich, Windsor, and Cambridge

Greenwich, Windsor, and Cambridge—listed from nearest to farthest—are three of the best day-trip possibilities near London. (Bath, another great choice, is covered in the next chapter.) Greenwich is England's maritime capital; Windsor has the famous castle; and Cambridge is England's finest university town.

You could fill a book with the many easy and exciting day trips from London (Earl Steinbicker did: *Daytrips London: 50 One-Day Adventures by Rail or Car, in and around London and Southern England*).

Getting Around

By Train: The British rail system uses London as a hub and normally offers round-trip fares (after 9:30) that cost virtually the same as one-way fares. For day trips, "day return" tickets are best (and cheapest). You can save a little money if you purchase Super Advance tickets before 18:00 on the day before your trip.

By Train Tour: Original London Walks offers a variety of Explorer day trips year-round via train for about £10 plus transportation costs (pick up their walking-tour brochures at the TI or hotels, tel. 020/7624-3978, www.walks.com).

By Tube or Cruise: You can reach Greenwich by Tube or boat (see Greenwich below).

Greenwich

The palace at Greenwich was favored by the Tudor kings. Henry VIII was born here. Later kings commissioned Inigo Jones and Christopher Wren to beautify the town and palace. In spite of Greenwich's architectural and royal treats, this is England's maritime capital, and visitors go for things salty. Greenwich hosts historic ships, nautical shops, and hordes of tourists.

Planning Your Time

See the two ships—*Cutty Sark* and *Gipsy Moth IV*—upon arrival. Then walk the shoreline promenade, with a possible lunch or drink in the venerable Trafalgar Tavern, before heading up to the National Maritime Museum and the Royal Observatory Greenwich.

The town throbs with day-trippers on weekends because of its arts-and-crafts and antique markets. To avoid crowds, visit on a weekday.

Tourist Information

The TI faces the riverside square a few paces from the *Cutty Sark* (daily 10:00–17:00, 2 Cutty Sark Gardens, Pepys House, tel. 0870-608-2000, www.greenwich.gov.uk). Guided walks cover the big sights (£4, daily 12:15 and 14:15). A shuttle bus runs from Greenwich Pier to the observatory on top of the hill (£1.50, ticket good all day, daily 11:00–17:00, every 15 min, erratic in winter).

SIGHTS

▲▲*Cutty Sark*—The Scottish-built *Cutty Sark* was the last of the great China tea clippers. Handsomely restored, she was the queen of the seas when first launched in 1869. With 32,000 square feet of sail, she could blow with the wind 300 miles in a day. Below deck, you'll see the best collection of merchant-ship figureheads in Britain and exhibits giving a vivid peek into the lives of Victorian sailors back when Britain ruled the waves. Stand at the big wheel and look up at the still-rigged main mast towering 150 feet above. You may meet costumed storytellers spinning yarns of the high seas and local old salts giving knot-tying demonstrations (£4, daily 10:00–17:00, tel. 020/8858-3445, www .cuttysark.org.uk).

▲*Gipsy Moth IV*—Tiny next to the *Cutty Sark,* the 54-foot *Gipsy Moth IV* is the boat Sir Francis Chichester used for the first solo circumnavigation of the world in 1966 and 1967. Upon Chichester's return, Queen

Greenwich

Elizabeth II knighted him in Greenwich, using the same sword Elizabeth I had used to knight Francis Drake in 1581 (free, viewable anytime, but interior not open to public).

Stroll the Thames to Trafalgar Tavern—From the *Cutty Sark* and *Gipsy Moth IV*, pass the pier and wander east along the Thames on Five Foot Walk (the width of the path) for grand views in front of the Old Royal Naval College (see below). Founded by William III as a naval hospital and designed by Wren, the college was split in two because Queen Mary didn't want the view from Queen's House blocked. The riverside view is good, too, with the twin-domed towers of the college (one giving the time, the other the direction of the wind) framing Queen's House, and the Royal Observatory Greenwich crowning the hill beyond.

Continuing downstream, just past the college, you'll see the **Trafalgar Tavern.** Dickens knew the pub well and even used it as the setting for the wedding breakfast in *Our Mutual Friend.* Built in 1837 in the Regency style to attract Londoners downriver, the tavern is still popular with Londoners (and tourists) for its fine lunches. The upstairs Nelson Room is still used for weddings. Its formal moldings and elegant windows with balconies over the Thames are a step back in time (daily 12:00–15:00 & 18:00–22:00, Sun lunch only, Park Row, tel. 020/8858-2437). From the pub, enjoy views of the white-elephant Millennium Dome a mile downstream.

From the Trafalgar Tavern, you can walk the two long blocks up Park Row and turn right onto the park leading up to the Royal Observatory Greenwich.

Old Royal Naval College—Now that the Royal Navy has moved out, the public is invited in to see the elaborate Painted Hall and Chapel, grandly designed by Wren and completed by other architects in the 1700s (free, Mon–Sat 10:00–17:00, Sun 12:30–17:00, in the two college buildings farthest from river, choral service Sun at 11:00 in chapel—all are welcome).

Queen's House—This building, the first Palladian-style villa in Britain, was designed in 1616 by Inigo Jones for James I's wife, Anne of Denmark. All traces of the queen are now gone, and the Great Hall and Royal Apartments serve as an art gallery for rotating exhibits (free, daily 10:00–17:00, July–Aug 10:00–18:00, tel. 020/8858-4422).

▲▲**National Maritime Museum**—Great for anyone remotely interested in the sea, this museum holds everything from *Titanic* tickets and Captain Scott's reindeer-hide sleeping bag (from his 1910 Antarctic expedition) to the uniform Admiral Nelson wore when he was killed at Trafalgar. Under a big glass roof, accompanied by the sound of creaking wooden ships and crashing waves, slick, modern displays depict lighthouse technology, a whaling cannon, and a Greenpeace "survival pod."

The Nelson Gallery, while taking up just a fraction of the floor space, deserves at least half your time here. It offers an intimate look at Nelson's life, the Napoleonic threat, Nelson's rise to power, and his victory and death at Trafalgar. Don't miss Turner's *Battle of Trafalgar*—his largest painting and only royal commission.

Kids love the All Hands Gallery, where they can send secret messages by Morse code and operate a miniature dockside crane (free, daily 10:00–17:00, July–Aug 10:00–18:00; look for the events board at entrance—singing, treasure hunts, storytelling—particularly on weekends; tel. 020/8312-6565, www.nmm.ac.uk).

▲▲**The Royal Observatory Greenwich**—Located on the prime meridian (0 degrees longitude), the observatory is the point from which all time is measured. However, the observatory's early work had nothing to do with coordinating the world's clocks to Greenwich Mean Time (GMT). The observatory was founded in 1675 by Charles II to find a way to determine longitude at sea. Today the Greenwich time signal is linked with the BBC (which broadcasts the "pips" worldwide at the top of the hour).

Look above the observatory to see the orange Time Ball, also visible from the Thames, which drops daily at 13:00. (Nearby, outside the courtyard of the observatory, see how your foot measures up to the foot where the public standards of length are cast in bronze.)

In the courtyard, set your wristwatch to the digital clock showing GMT to a tenth of a second and straddle the prime meridian (called the "Times meridian" at the observatory, in deference to *The Times* of London, which paid for the courtyard sculpture and the inset meridian line that runs banner headlines of today's *Times*—I wish I were kidding).

Inside, check out the historic astronomical instruments and camera obscura. Listen to costumed actors tell stories about astronomers and historical observatory events (shows may require small fee, daily July–Sept).

Cost and Hours: Free entry, daily 10:00–17:00, tel. 020/8858-4422, www.rog.nmm.ac.uk. Planetarium shows twinkle on weekdays at 14:30 and 15:30 and on Saturday and Sunday at 13:30, 14:30, and 15:30 (£4, buy tickets at observatory, a 2-min walk from planetarium).

Before you leave the observatory grounds, enjoy the view from the overlook: the symmetrical royal buildings; the Thames; the square-mile City of London, with its skyscrapers and the dome of St. Paul's Cathedral; the Docklands, with its busy cranes; and the huge Millennium Dome. At night (17:00–24:00), look for the green laser beam the observatory shines in the sky (best viewed in winter), extending along the prime meridian for 15 miles.

Greenwich Town—Save time to browse the town. Covered markets and outdoor stalls make weekends lively. The arts-and-crafts market is an entertaining mini-Covent Garden between College Approach and Nelson Road (Thu–Sun 10:00–17:00, biggest on Sun), and the antique market sells old ends and odds at high prices on Greenwich High Road near the post office. Wander beyond the touristy Church Street and Greenwich High Road to where flower stands spill into the side streets and antique shops sell brass nautical knickknacks. King William Walk, College Approach, Nelson Road, and Turnpin Lane are all worth a look.

TRANSPORTATION CONNECTIONS

Getting to the town of Greenwich is a joy by boat or a snap by Tube.

By boat: From London (50 minutes, 2/hr), cruise down the Thames from central London's piers at Westminster, Embankment, or Tower of London (see "Cruises" under "Tours," page 51).

By Tube: Take the Tube to Bank and change to the Docklands Light Railway (DLR), which takes you right to the *Cutty Sark* station in Greenwich (20-min ride, all in Zone 2, free included with Tube pass).

By train: Mainline trains also go from London (Charing Cross, Waterloo East, and London Bridge stations) several times an hour to the Greenwich station (10-min walk from the sights).

Windsor

The pleasant pedestrians-only shopping zone of Windsor litters the approach to its famous palace with fun temptations. You'll find the **TI** on 24 High Street (April–Sept daily 10:00–17:00, Oct-March daily 10:00–16:00, tel. 01753/743-900, www.windsor.gov.uk).

SIGHTS

▲▲**Windsor Castle**—Windsor Castle, the official home of England's royal family for 900 years, claims to be the largest and oldest occupied castle in the world. The queen considers this sprawling and fortified palace her primary residence. Thankfully, touring it is simple: You'll see immense grounds, lavish staterooms, a crowd-pleasing dollhouse, an art gallery, and the chapel.

Immediately upon entering, you pass through a simple modern building housing a historical overview of the castle. This excellent intro is worth a close look, since you're basically on your own after this. Inside you'll find the motte (artificial mound) and bailey (fortified stockade around it) of William the Conqueror's castle still visible. Dating from 1080, this was his first castle in England.

Follow the signs to the staterooms/gallery/dollhouse. Queen Mary's Dollhouse—a palace in miniature (1/12 scale from 1923) and "the most famous dollhouse in the world"—comes with the longest wait. You can skip that line and go immediately into the lavish staterooms. Strewn with history and the art of a long line of kings and queens, it's the best I've seen in Britain—and well restored after the devastating 1992 fire. The adjacent gallery is a changing exhibit featuring the royal art collection (and some big names, such as Michelangelo and Leonardo). Signs direct you (downhill) to St. George's Chapel. Housing 10 royal tombs, it's a fine example of Perpendicular Gothic, with classic fan vaulting spreading out from each pillar (about 1500). Next door is the sumptuous 13th-century Albert Memorial Chapel, redecorated after the death of Queen Victoria's beloved Prince Albert in 1861 and dedicated to his memory.

Cost and Hours: £11.50, £29 for family (£3 audioguide is better than official guidebook for help throughout). March–Oct daily 9:45–17:15, last entry 16:00, Nov–Feb closes at 16:15 (changing of the guard most days at 11:00, evensong in chapel at 17:15, recorded info tel. 01753/831-118, live info tel. 020/7321-2233, www.royal.gov.uk).

Legoland Windsor—Fun for Legomaniacs under 12, this huge, kid-pleasing park next to Windsor Castle has dozens of tame but fun rides (often with very long lines) scattered throughout its 150 acres. An impressive Mini-Land has 28 million Lego pieces glued together to create 800 tiny buildings and a mini-tour of Europe (£23, children-£20, under 3 free, £10 if you enter during last 2 hrs, April–Oct daily 10:00–17:00, 18:00, or 19:00 depending upon season and day, closed most Tue–Wed in Sept–Oct, closed Nov–March except Dec 21–Jan 5, £2.50 round-trip shuttle bus runs from near Windsor's Parish Church, 2/hr, clearly signposted, easy free parking, tel. 08705-040-404, www.legoland.co.uk).

TRANSPORTATION CONNECTIONS

By train: Windsor has two train stations: Windsor Central (5-min walk to palace and TI) and Windsor & Eton Riverside (10-min walk to palace and TI). Thames Trains run between London's Paddington Station and Windsor Central (2/hr, 40 min, change at Slough, www.thamestrains.co.uk). South West Trains run between London's Waterloo Station and the Windsor & Eton Riverside station (2/hr, 50 min, www.swtrains.co.uk).

By bus: Green Line buses #700 and #702 run hourly between London's Victoria Colonnade (between the Victoria train and coach stations) and Windsor, where the bus stops in front of Legoland and near the castle—the stop is "Parish Church" (1.5 hrs). Bus info: tel. 0870-608-7261.

By car: Windsor, 20 miles from London and just off Heathrow airport's landing path, is well signposted from the M4 motorway. It's a convenient stop for anyone arriving at Heathrow, picking up a car, and not going into London.

Cambridge

Cambridge, 60 miles north of London, is world-famous for its prestigious university. William Wordsworth, Isaac Newton, Lord Alfred

Cambridge

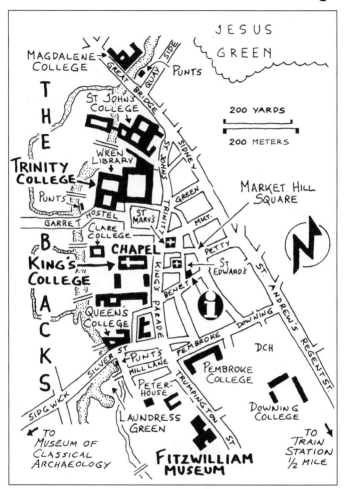

Tennyson, Charles Darwin, and Prince Charles are a few of its illustrious alumni. This historic town of 100,000 people is more pleasant than its rival, Oxford. Cambridge is the epitome of a university town, with busy bikers, stately residence halls, plenty of bookshops, and proud locals who can point out where DNA was modeled, the first atom split, and electrons discovered.

In medieval Europe, higher education was the domain of the Church and was limited to ecclesiastical schools. Scholars lived in "halls" on campus. This scholarly community of residential halls, chapels, and lecture halls connected by peaceful garden courtyards survives today in the colleges that make the universities at Cambridge and Oxford. By 1350 (Oxford is roughly 100 years older), Cambridge had eight colleges, each with a monastic-style courtyard and lodgings. Today, Cambridge has 31 colleges. While a student's life revolves around his or her independent college, the university organizes lectures, presents degrees, and promotes research.

The university dominates—and owns—most of Cambridge. The approximate term schedule is late January to late March (called Lent term), mid-April to mid-June (Easter term), and early October to early December (Michaelmas term). The colleges are closed to visitors during exams, from mid-April until late June, but King's College Chapel and the Trinity Library stay open, and the town is never sleepy.

Planning Your Time

Cambridge is worth most of a day but not an overnight. It's easy and economical as a side trip from London, 50 minutes away by train (cheap £15.60 day-return if you depart London after 9:30 weekdays or anytime Sat–Sun). You can arrive in time for the 11:30 walking tour—an essential part of any visit—and spend the afternoon touring King's College and Fitzwilliam Museum (closed Mon) and simply enjoying the ambience of this stately old college town.

ORIENTATION

Cambridge is small but congested. There are two main streets, separated from the river by the most interesting colleges. The town center, brimming with tearooms, has a TI and a colorful open-air market (daily 9:30–16:00, on Market Hill Square; arts and crafts Sun 10:30–16:30, clothes and produce rest of week). Also on the main square is a Marks & Spencer grocery (Mon–Sat 8:30–20:00, Sun 11:00–17:00). The J. Sainsbury supermarket, with longer hours and a better deli, is three blocks north on Sidney Street. A good picnic spot is Laundress Green, a grassy park on the river, at the end of Mill Lane near the Silver Street punts. Everything is within a pleasant walk.

Tourist Information: At the station, a City Sightseeing office dispenses free city maps and sells fancier ones. The official TI is well signposted and just off Market Hill Square. They book rooms and sell a 50p mini-guide/map (Mon–Fri 10:00–17:30, Sat 10:00–17:00, Sun 11:00–16:00, closed Sun Nov–Easter, toll tel. 0906-586-2526 costs 60p/min).

Arrival in Cambridge: To get to downtown Cambridge from the train station, take a 20-minute walk (the City Sightseeing map is fine for this), a £4 taxi ride, or bus #C1 or #C3 (£1, every 10 min). Drivers can follow signs to any of the handy and central Short Stay Parking Lots.

TOURS

▲▲**Walking Tour of the Colleges**—A walking tour is the best way to understand Cambridge's mix of "town and gown." The walks give a good rundown on the historic and scenic highlights of the university as well as some fun local gossip. From July through August, daily walking tours start at 10:30, 11:30, 13:30, and 14:30 (offered by and leaving from the TI). The rest of the year, they run daily at 13:30 (April–Oct also daily at 11:30). Tours cost £8 and include admission to King's College Chapel. Drop by the TI one hour early to snare a spot. Particularly if you're coming from London, call the day before (tel. 01223/457-574) to reserve a spot with your credit card and confirm departure. Private guides are also available (£40 per hour for the basic tour, £50 for a 2-hour city tour—excellent values, tel. 01223/457-574, www.tourismcambridge.com).

Bus Tours—City Sightseeing hop-on, hop-off bus tours are informative and cover the outskirts, including the American Cemetery (£9, departing every 15 min, can use credit card to buy tickets in their office in train station, tel. 01708-866-000). Walking tours go where the buses can't—right into the center.

SIGHTS

▲▲**King's College Chapel**—Built from 1446 to 1515 by Henrys VI through VIII, England's best example of Perpendicular Gothic is the single most impressive building in town. Stand inside, look up, and marvel, as Christopher Wren did, at what was the largest single span of vaulted roof anywhere—2,000 tons of incredible fan vaulting. Wander through the Old Testament with the 25 16th-century stained-glass windows (the most Renaissance stained glass anywhere in one spot; it was taken out for safety during World War II, then painstakingly replaced). Walk to the altar and admire Rubens' masterful *Adoration of the Magi* (£4, erratic hours depending on school and events, but usually daily 10:00–17:00). During term, you're welcome to enjoy an evensong service (Mon–Sat at 17:30, Sun at 15:30, tel. 01223/331-447).

▲▲**Trinity College**—Half of Cambridge's 63 Nobel Prize winners came from this richest and biggest of the town's colleges, founded in 1546 by Henry VIII. Don't miss the Wren-designed library, with its wonderful carving and fascinating original manuscripts (£2 to enter the library, 10p leaflet, Mon–Fri 12:00–14:00, also Sat 10:30–12:30 during term, always closed Sun; or visit the library for free during the same hours from the riverside entrance by the Garret Hostel Bridge). Just outside the library entrance, Sir Isaac Newton, who spent 30 years at Trinity, clapped his hands and timed the echo to measure the speed of sound as it raced down the side of the cloister and back. In the library's display cases (covered with brown cloth that you flip back), you'll see handwritten works by Newton, John Milton, Byron, Tennyson, and A. E. Housman, alongside A. A. Milne's original *Winnie the Pooh* (the real Christopher Robin attended Trinity College).

▲▲**Fitzwilliam Museum**—Britain's best museum of antiquities and art outside of London is the Fitzwilliam. Enjoy its wonderful paintings (Old Masters and a fine English section featuring Gainsborough, Reynolds, Hogarth, and others, plus works by all the famous Impressionists), old manuscripts, and Greek, Egyptian, and Mesopotamian collections (free, Tue–Sat 10:00–17:00, Sun 14:15–17:00, closed Mon, tel. 01223/332-900, www.fitzmuseum.cam.ac.uk).

Museum of Classical Archaeology—While this museum contains no originals, it offers a unique chance to see accurate copies (19th-century casts) of virtually every famous ancient Greek and Roman statue. More than 450 statues are on display (free, Mon–Fri 10:00–17:00, sometimes also Sat 10:00–13:00 during term, always closed Sun, Sidgwick Avenue, tel. 01223/335-153). The museum is a five-minute walk west of Silver Street Bridge; after crossing the bridge, continue straight until you reach a sign reading *Sidgwick Site* (museum is on your right; the entrance is away from the street).

▲**Punting on the Cam River**—For a little levity and probably more exercise than you really want, try hiring one of the traditional (and inexpensive) flat-bottom punts at the river and pole yourself up and down (around and around, more likely) the lazy Cam. Once you get the hang of it, it's a fine way to enjoy the scenic side of Cambridge. After 17:00, it's less crowded and less embarrassing. Three places rent punts, one at each bridge (£60 deposit required, can use credit card) and offer £12 50-minute punt tours. Trinity Punt, at Garret Hostel Bridge near Trinity College, has the best prices (£10/hr rental, ask for free short lesson). Scudamore's runs two other locations: the central Silver Street Bridge (£12/hr rentals) and the less-convenient Quayside at Great Bridge, at the north end of town (£12/hr, tel. 01223/359-750, www.scudamores.com). Depending on the weather, punting season runs daily March through October, with Silver Street open weekends off-season.

TRANSPORTATION CONNECTIONS

To day trip from London: Catch the train from London's King's Cross Station (2/hr, fast trains leaving at :15 and :45 past each hour run in each direction, 50 min, one-way £15.50, cheap day-return for £15.60).

By train to: York (hourly, 2.5 hrs, transfer in Petersborough, about £62). Train info: tel. 08457-484-950.

By bus to: Heathrow (1/hr, 2.5 hrs). Bus info: tel. 08705-757-747.

BATH

The best city to visit within easy striking distance of London is Bath—just a 90-minute train ride away. Two hundred years ago, this city of 85,000 was the trendsetting Hollywood of Britain. If ever a city enjoyed looking in the mirror, Bath's the one. It has more "government-listed" or protected historic buildings per capita than any other town in England. The entire city, built of the creamy warm-tone limestone called "Bath stone," beams in its cover-girl complexion. An architectural chorus line, it's a triumph of the Georgian style. Proud locals remind visitors that the town is routinely banned from the "Britain in Bloom" contest to give other towns a chance to win. Bath's narcissism is justified. Even with its mobs of tourists (two million per year), it's a joy to visit.

Long before the Romans arrived in the first century, Bath was known for its hot springs. What became the Roman spa town of Aquae Sulis has always been fueled by the healing allure of its 116-degree mineral hot springs. The town's importance carried through Saxon times, when it had a huge church on the site of the present-day Abbey and was considered the religious capital of Britain. Its influence peaked in 973 with King Edgar's sumptuous coronation in the Abbey. Bath prospered as a wool town.

Bath then declined until the mid-1600s, when it was just a huddle of huts around the Abbey and some hot springs, with 3,000 residents oblivious to the Roman ruins 18 feet below their dirt floors. Then, in 1687, Queen Mary, fighting infertility, bathed here. Within 10 months she gave birth to a son...and a new age of popularity for Bath.

The town boomed as a spa resort. Ninety percent of the buildings you'll see today are from the 18th century. Local architect John Wood was inspired by the Italian architect Andrea Palladio to build a "new Rome." The town bloomed in the neoclassical style, and streets were lined not with scrawny sidewalks but with wide "parades," upon which the women in their stylishly wide dresses could spread their fashionable tails.

Beau Nash (1673–1762) was Bath's "master of ceremonies." He organized both the daily regimen of the aristocratic visitors and the city, lighting and improving street security, banning swords, and opening the Pump Room. Under his fashionable baton, Bath became a city of balls, gaming, and concerts and the place to see and be seen in England. This most civilized place became even more so with the great neoclassical building spree that followed.

With the opening of a new spa tapping Bath's soothing hot springs, the town will once again attract visitors in need of a cure or a soak.

Planning Your Time

Bath needs two nights even on a quick trip. On a three-week British trip, spend three nights in Bath, with one day for the city and one for a side trip to Wells, Glastonbury, and Avebury (see next chapter). Bath could easily fill another day. Ideally, use Bath as your jet-lag recovery pillow, and do London at the end of your trip.

Consider starting a three-week British vacation this way:

Day 1: Land at Heathrow. Connect to Bath (either by National Express bus or train—see below). While you don't need or want a car in Bath, and most rental companies have an office there, those who pick up their cars at the airport can visit Windsor Castle (near Heathrow) and/or Stonehenge on their way to Bath on this day.

Day 2: 9:00-Tour the Roman Baths; 10:30-Catch the free city walking tour; 12:30-Picnic on the open deck of a Bath Bus Tour bus; 14:00-Free time in the shopping center of old Bath or spend an hour soaking at the new spa; 15:30-Tour the Costume Museum.

Day 3: Pick up your rental car and tour Avebury, Glastonbury (Abbey and Tower), and Wells (17:15 evensong weekdays at the cathedral, 15:00 on Sun). Without a car, consider a one-day Avebury/ Stonehenge/cute towns minibus tour from Bath ("Mad Max" tours are best; see page 152).

Day 4: 9:00-Leave Bath for South Wales; 10:30-Tour Museum of Welsh Life; 15:00-Stop at Tintern Abbey, then drive to the Cotswolds; 18:00-Set up in your Cotswolds home base.

ORIENTATION

(area code: 01225)

Bath's town square, three blocks in front of the bus and train station, is a bouquet of tourist landmarks, including the Abbey, Roman and medieval baths, and the royal Pump Room.

Tourist Information: The TI is in the Abbey churchyard (Mon–Sat 9:30–18:00, Sun 10:00–16:00, Oct–April Mon–Sat until 17:00, tel. 0870-444-6442, www.visitbath.co.uk, tourism@bathnes.gov.uk). Pick up the 50p Bath mini-guide (includes a map) and the free, info-packed

This Month in Bath. Browse through scads of fliers, books, and maps. Skip their room-finding service (£5) and book direct. If you have a mobile phone and kids along, ask the TI about "Texting Trails," a fun text-message scavenger hunt through Bath.

Arrival in Bath: The Bath **train station** has small-town charm, an international tickets desk, and a privately-run tourism office masquerading as a TI. The **bus station** is immediately in front of the train station. To get to the TI, walk two blocks up Manvers Street from either station and turn left at the triangular "square," by following the small TI arrow on a signpost. My recommended B&Bs are all within a 10- to 15-minute walk or a £3.50 taxi ride from the station.

Helpful Hints

Festivals: The Bath International Music Festival bursts into song from May 21 to June 6 in 2004 (classical, folk, jazz, contemporary; for the line-up, see www.bathmusicfest.org.uk), overlapped by the eclectic Bath Fringe Festival from late May to mid-June (theater, walks, talks, bus trips; www.bathfringe.co.uk). Bath's box office sells tickets for these events and most others, and can tell you exactly what's on tonight (2 Church Street, tel. 01225/463-362, www .bathfestivals.org.uk). Bath's local paper, the *Bath Chronicle,* publishes a "What's On" event listing on Fridays (www.thisisbath.com).

Farmers' Market: It's at Green Park Station on Saturdays (9:00–15:00), with extra days for food stalls in the summer (Wed–Sat 9:00–17:00).

Car Rental: Avis (behind the station and over the river at Unit 4B Riverside Business Park, Lower Bristol Road, tel. 01225/446-680), Enterprise (Lower Bristol Road, tel. 01225/443-311), and Hertz (just outside train station, tel. 01225/442-911) are all trying harder. Sample prices: £39/day, £78/weekend, and £200/week. Most offices are a 10-minute walk from most recommended accommodations. Enterprise will pick you up at your accommodation and bring you down to pick up your car. Most offices close Saturday afternoon and all day Sunday, which complicates weekend pickups. Ideally, pick up your car only on the way out and into the countryside; take the train or bus from London to Bath and rent a car as you leave Bath rather than in London.

Internet Access: The Click Café is across from the train station on Manvers Street (£3/hr, daily 10:00–22:00, tel. 01225/481-008). You can also get wired at St. Chrisopher's Inn (Green Street) and Bath Backpackers Hostel (13 Pierrepont Street; coming from train station, you pass hostel on way to TI).

Laundry: The **Spruce Goose Launderette** is around the corner from Brock's Guest House on the pedestrian lane called Margaret's Buildings (self-service or full-service on same day if dropped off at

8:00, Sun–Fri 8:00–20:00, Sat 8:00–21:00, tel. 01225/483-309). Anywhere in town, **"Speedy Wash"** can pick up your laundry for same-day service (£9/bag, Mon–Fri, most hotels work with them, tel. 01225/427-616). East of Pulteney Bridge, the humble **Lovely Wash** is on Daniel Street (daily 9:00–21:00, self-service only).

TOURS

▲▲▲**Walking Tours**—These free two-hour tours, offered by "The Mayor's Corps of Honorary Guides"—volunteers who want to share their love of Bath with its many visitors—are a chatty, historical, gossip-filled joy, essential for your understanding of this town's amazing Georgian social scene. How else will you learn that the old "chair ho" call for your sedan chair evolved into today's "cheerio" farewell? Tours leave from in front of the Pump Room (year-round daily at 10:30 plus Sun–Fri at 14:00; evening walks offered May–Sept at 19:00 on Tue, Fri, and Sat). For Ghost Walks and Bizarre Bath Comedy Walks, see "Nightlife," page 140. For a private walking tour, call the local guides' bureau (£46/2 hrs, tel. 01225/337-111).

▲▲**City Bus Tours**—The Bath Bus Tour open-top bus (marked "panoramic") makes a 70-minute figure-eight circuit of Bath's main sights with an exhaustingly informative running commentary. For one £8.50 ticket (buy from driver), tourists can stop and go at will for a whole day. The buses cover the city center and the surrounding hills (17 signposted pick-up points, 4/hr spring and fall—runs 9:30–17:00, 6/hr in summer—9:15–18:15, tickets also valid 24 hours on the local First service buses around town and to surrounding areas such as Bradford-on-Avon, Wells, and Glastonbury; tel. 01225/313-222). This is great in sunny weather and a feast for photographers. You can munch a sandwich, work on a tan, and sightsee at the same time. Several competing hop-on, hop-off tour-bus companies, including City Sightseeing, offer similar but less expensive tours that are only 45 minutes and don't include the swing through the countryside. Generally, the Bath Bus Tour guides are better. Note that ticket stubs for any of the bus tours usually get you discounts at some sights. Pick up the various brochures at the TI and see what sights are currently discounted; if you want to see these sights, take the bus tour first.

These tour buses are technically "public service vehicles"—a loophole they use to be able to run the same routes as transit buses. Consequently, tour buses are required to take passengers across town for the normal £1 fare. Nervy tourists have the right to hop on, ask for a "single fare," and pay £1.

Tours from Bath—Bath is a good launchpad for visiting Wells, Avebury, Stonehenge, and more. See the beginning of the next chapter for information on tours.

SIGHTS

▲▲▲**Roman and Medieval Baths**—In ancient Roman times, high society enjoyed the mineral springs at Bath. From Londinium, Romans traveled so often to Aquae Sulis, as the city was called, to "take a bath" that finally it became known simply as Bath. Today a fine museum surrounds the ancient bath. It's a one-way system leading you past well-documented displays, Roman artifacts, mosaics, a temple pediment, and the actual mouth of the spring, piled high with Roman pennies. Enjoy some quality time looking into the eyes of Minerva, goddess of the hot springs. The included self-guided tour audioguide makes the visit easy and plenty informative. For those with a big appetite for Roman history, in-depth 40-minute tours leave from the end of the museum at the edge of the actual bath (included, on the hour, a poolside clock is set for the next departure time). You can revisit the museum after the tour (£8.50, £11.50 combo-ticket includes Costume Museum at a good savings, family combo-£30, combo-tickets good for 1 week; April–Sept daily 9:00–18:00, July–Aug until 22:00—last entry at 21:00, Oct–March until 17:00, tel. 01225/477-784, www.romanbaths.co.uk). After visiting the Roman Baths, drop by the attached Pump Room for a spot of tea.

▲**Pump Room**—For centuries, Bath was forgotten as a spa. Then, in 1687, the previously barren Queen Mary bathed here, became pregnant, and bore a male heir to the throne. Word of its wonder waters spread, and Bath was back on the aristocratic map. High society soon turned the place into one big pleasure palace. The Pump Room, an elegant Georgian hall just above the Roman baths, offers the visitor's best chance to raise a pinky in this Chippendale elegance. Drop by to sip coffee or tea or enjoy a light meal (daily 9:30–12:00 morning coffee, 12:00–14:30 lunch—£10 two-course menu, 14:30–17:30 traditional high tea—£9.75, £7 tea/coffee and pastry available anytime except during lunch, open for dinner July–Aug only, string trio or live pianist plays sporadically between 10:00 and 17:00, tel. 01225/444-477). Above the newspaper table and sedan chairs, a statue of Beau Nash himself sniffles down at you. Now's your chance to have a famous (but forgettable) "Bath bun" and split (and spit) a 50p drink of the awfully curative water. Convenient public WCs are in the entry hallway that connects the Pump Room with the baths.

Thermae Bath Spa—After simmering unused for a quarter-century, Bath's natural thermal springs will once again offer R&R for the masses. The state-of-the-art leisure and curative spa, housed in a complex combining old buildings with controversial new, blocky architecture, is scheduled to open (after numerous delays) in late 2003. The only natural thermal spa in the United Kingdom will include an open-air rooftop thermal pool and all the "pamper thyself" extras—aromatherapy steam rooms, mud wraps, and various healing-type treatments and classes. Swimwear is required (daily 9:00–22:00, £17/2 hrs, £23/4 hrs, £35/full

Bath

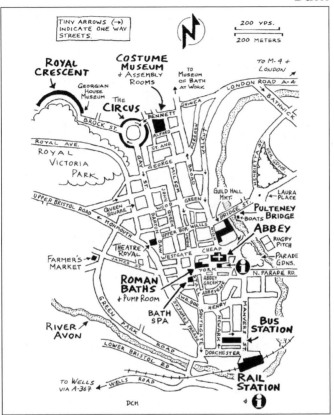

TINY ARROWS (→) INDICATE ONE WAY STREETS.

200 YDS.

200 METERS

ROYAL CRESCENT

COSTUME MUSEUM & ASSEMBLY ROOMS

GEORGIAN HOUSE MUSEUM

TO MUSEUM OF BATH AT WORK

TO M-4 & LONDON

LONDON ROAD A-4

THE CIRCUS

BENNETT

GUINEA

BROCK ST.

ALFRED

ST. AND.

WALCOT

HENRIETTA

BATHWICK

ROYAL AVE.

ROYAL VICTORIA PARK

GEORGE

GAY

MILSOM

BROAD

HENRIETTA GDNS.

LAURA PLACE

UPPER BRISTOL ROAD

QUEEN SQUARE

JOHN

WOOD

GREEN

GUILD HALL MKT.

BRIDGE ST.

BOATS

PULTENEY BRIDGE

MONMOUTH

BARTON

UPPER BOR. WALLS

ABBEY

THEATRE ROYAL

SAW

WESTGATE

CHEAP

RUGBY PITCH

FARMER'S MARKET

JAMES ST.

YORK

ABBEY GREEN &

ABBEYGATE

PARADE GDNS.

N. PARADE RD.

ROMAN BATHS & PUMP ROOM

L.W.B. BOR.

HENRY

BATH SPA

SOUTHGATE

ST. JAMES PARADE

NEWARK

TANVERS

BUS STATION

RIVER AVON

GREEN PARK

ROAD

LOWER BRISTOL RD.

DORCHESTER

TO WELLS VIA A-367

WELLS ROAD

RAIL STATION

DCH

day; prices do not include treatments, massage, or solarium, which range from £26–68, reservations recommended for these extra services; 100 yards from Roman and medieval baths on Beau Street, tel. 01225/331-234, www.thermaebathspa.com).

▲**Abbey**—Bath town wasn't much in the Middle Ages, but an important church has stood on this spot since Anglo-Saxon times. In 973, Edgar was crowned here. Dominating the town center, the present church—the last great medieval church of England—is 500 years old and a fine example of Late Perpendicular Gothic, with breezy fan vaulting and enough stained glass to earn it the nickname "Lantern of the West" (worth the £2.50 donation, Mon–Sat 9:00–18:00, Sun usually 13:00–14:30 & 15:30–17:30, closes at 16:30 in winter, handy flyer narrates a self-guided 19-stop tour, www.bathabbey.org). The schedule for concerts, services, and **evensong** (Sun at 15:30 year-round, plus most Sat in Aug at 17:00) is posted on the door. Take a moment to really appreciate the Abbey's architecture from the Abbey Green square.

A small but interesting exhibit, the Abbey's **Heritage Vaults** tell the story of Christianity in Bath since Roman times (£2.50, Mon–Sat 10:00–16:00, last entry 15:30, closed Sun, entrance just outside church, south side).

▲**Pulteney Bridge, Parade Gardens, and Cruises**—Bath is inclined to compare its shop-lined Pulteney Bridge to Florence's Ponte Vecchio. That's pushing it. But to best enjoy a sunny day, pay £1.30 to enter the Parade Gardens below the bridge (April–Sept daily 10:00–19:00, June–Aug until 20:00, shorter hours off-season, includes deck chairs, ask about concerts held some Sun at 15:00 in summer, tel. 01225/394-041).

Across the bridge at Pulteney Weir, tour boats run cruises from under the bridge (£5, up to 7/day if the weather's good, 50 min to Bathampton and back, WCs on board). Just take whatever boat is running. Avon Cruisers stop in Bathampton if you'd like to walk back; Pulteney Cruisers come with a sundeck ideal for picnics.

▲▲**Royal Crescent and the Circus**—If Bath is an architectural cancan, these are the kickers. These first elegant Georgian "condos" by John Wood (the Elder and the Younger) are well explained in the city walking tours. "Georgian" is British for "neoclassical," or dating from the 1770s. As you cruise the Crescent, pretend you're rich. Pretend you're poor. Notice the "ha ha fence," a drop in the front yard offering a barrier, invisible from the windows, to sheep and peasants. The round Circus is a coliseum turned inside out. Its Doric, Ionic, and Corinthian capital decorations pay homage to its Greco-Roman origin.

▲▲**Georgian House at #1 Royal Crescent**—This museum (on the corner of Brock Street and the Royal Crescent) offers your best look into a period house. It's worth the £4 admission to get behind one of those classy exteriors. The volunteers in each room are determined to fill you in on all the fascinating details of Georgian life...like how high-class women shaved their eyebrows and pasted on carefully trimmed strips of furry mouse skin in their place (Tue–Sun 10:30–17:00, closed Mon, closes at 16:00 in Nov, closed Dec–mid-Feb, "no stiletto heels, please," tel. 01225/428-126, www.bath-preservation-trust.org.uk).

▲▲▲**Costume Museum**—One of Europe's great museums, it displays 400 years of fashion—one frilly decade at a time—and is housed within Bath's Assembly Rooms. Follow the included, excellent audioguide tour (£5.50, £11.50 combo-ticket covers Roman Baths, family combo-£30, daily 10:00–17:00, tel. 01225/477-789, www.museumofcostume.co.uk). The Assembly Rooms, which you'll see en route to the museum, are big, elegant, empty rooms where card games, concerts, tea, and dances were held in the 18th century, before the advent of fancy hotels with grand public spaces made them obsolete. They were gutted by WWII bombs, then restored to their original resplendence.

▲▲▲**Museum of Bath at Work**—This is the official title for Mr. Bowler's Business, a 1900s engineer's shop, brass foundry, and fizzy-drink factory with a Dickensian office. It's just a pile of meaningless old gadgets until a volunteer guide lovingly resurrects Mr. Bowler's creative genius. Also featured are various Bath creations through the years, including the versatile plasticine and a 1914 car. Fascinating hour-long tours go regularly; just join the one in session upon arrival (£3.50, April–Oct daily 10:00–17:00, last entry at 16:00, weekends only in winter, 2 blocks up Russell Street from Assembly Rooms, call to be sure a volunteer is available to give a tour, sporadically open café upstairs, tel. 01225/318-348).

Jane Austen Centre—This exhibition focuses on Jane Austen's five years in Bath (around 1800) and the influence Bath had on her writing. While the exhibit is thoughtfully done and a hit with "Jane-ites," there is little of historic substance here. You'll walk through a Georgian town house that she didn't live in and see mostly enlarged reproductions of things associated with her writing. After a live intro explaining how this romantic but down-to-earth girl dealt with the silly, shallow, and arrogant aristocrat's world where "the doing of nothings all day prevents one from doing anything," you see a 13-minute video and wander through the rest of the exhibit (£4.50, Mon–Sat 10:00–17:30, Sun 10:30–17:30, 40 Gay Street between Queen's Square and the Circus, tel. 01225/443-000, www.janeausten.co.uk). Avid fans gather in mid- to late-September for the annual Bath Jane Austen Festival (readings and lectures, www.janeaustenfestival.co.uk).

The Building of Bath Museum—This offers a fascinating look behind the scenes at how the Georgian city was actually built. It's just a couple rooms of exhibits, but those interested in construction—inside and out—find it worth the £4 (Tue–Sun 10:30–17:00, closed Mon, near the Circus on a street called "The Paragon," tel. 01225/333-895).

Views—For the best views of Bath, try Alexander Park (south of city, 10-min walk from train station), Camden Crescent (10- to 15-min walk north), or Beckfords Tower (steep 45-min walk north up Lansdown Road, www.bath-preservation-trust.org.uk).

▲**American Museum**—I know, you need this in Bath like you need a Big Mac. But this museum offers a fascinating look at colonial and early-American lifestyles. Each of 18 completely furnished rooms (from the 1600s to the 1800s) is hosted by an eager guide waiting to fill you in on the candles, maps, bedpans, and various religious sects that make domestic Yankee history surprisingly interesting. One room is a quilter's nirvana (£6, April–Oct Tue–Sun 14:00–17:00, closed Mon and Nov–March, nice arboretum, at Claverton Manor, tel. 01225/460-503, www.americanmuseum.org). The museum is outside of town and a headache to reach if you don't have a car (10-min walk from bus #18).

ACTIVITIES

Walking—The Bath Skyline Walk is a six-mile wander around the hills surrounding Bath (70p leaflet at TI). Plenty of other scenic paths are described in the TI's literature. For more options, get *Country Walks around Bath,* by Tim Mowls (£4.50 at TI).

To Bathampton by Foot, Cruise, or Bike—Consider the idyllic **walk** up the canal path to Bathampton: From downtown, walk over Pulteney Bridge, through Sydney Gardens, turn left at the canal, and in 30 minutes you'll hit Bathampton.

Sailors enjoy the river **cruise** up to Bathampton; hikers like walking back (see "Pulteney Bridge and Cruises," above). From Bathampton, it's two hours farther along the canal to the fine old town of Bradford-on-Avon, from which you can train back to Bath.

You can **bike** along the canal as well, but you'll have to take an easy bus or train ride out of town to find a rental. Try Dundas Enterprises in the nearby Limpley Stoke Valley (£6/first hr, then £1/per hr, £14/day; daily 9:30–17:30, shorter hours off-season, helmets available, electric boats and canoes also available, 5-min ride on bus #X4 or #X5 from the Bath bus station, tel. 01225/722-292, www.bathcanal.com), or the Lock Inn Café, a short train ride away (£6/first hr, then £1/hr, £10/day; helmets included, daily 9:00–18:00, train to Bradford-on-Avon, then walk 5–10 min down Frome Road/B3109 away from town, tel. 01225/867-187).

Boating—The Bath Boating Station, in an old Victorian boathouse, rents boats and punts (£5/first hour per person, then £1.50/hr, April–Sept 10:00–18:00, Forester Road, a mile northeast of center, tel. 01225/466-407).

Swimming—The Bath Sports and Leisure Centre has a swimming pool—great for laps—and lots of slides and gadgets for kids (£2.75, towels rentable for £1.50 and £5 deposit, daily 8:00–22:00, just across North Parade Bridge, call for open swim times, tel. 01225/462-565).

Shopping—There's great browsing between the Abbey and the Assembly Rooms (Costume Museum). Shops close at 17:30, later on Thursday, and many are open on Sunday (11:00–17:00). Explore the antique shops lining Bartlett Street just below the Assembly Rooms. You'll find the most stalls open on Wednesday. Pick up the local paper (usually out on Fri) and shop with the dealers at estate sales and auctions listed in "What's On" (see "Helpful Hints," page 134).

NIGHTLIFE

Events are listed in *This Month in Bath* (free, available at TI) and "What's On," appearing Fridays in the local newspaper, the *Bath Chronicle* (www.thisisbath.com).

Plays—The Theatre Royal, newly restored and one of England's loveliest, offers a busy schedule of London West End-type plays, including many "pre-London" dress-rehearsal runs (£11–25, cheaper matinees as low as £5, tel. 01225/448-844, www.theatreroyal.org.uk). Forty standby tickets per evening show go on sale, starting at 12:00 on the day of the performance (either pay cash at box office or call and book with credit card, 2 tickets maximum). Or you can buy a £10 last-minute seat 30 minutes before "curtain up."

For a more intimate, small-town experience, take a short trip out to the village of Larkhall to catch a show at the Rondo Theatre, a playhouse that features both amateur and professional productions (£6–8, 5 min on bus #8 or a £3 taxi ride to Larkhall, tel. 01225/463-362, www.rondotheatre.co.uk).

Evening Walks—Take your choice: comedy, ghost, or history. For an immensely entertaining walking comedy act "with absolutely no history or culture," follow J. J. or Noel Britten on their creative and entertaining **Bizarre Bath** walk. This 90-minute tour, which plays off local passersby as well as tour members, is a belly laugh a minute (£5, April–Sept nightly at 20:00, smaller groups Mon–Thu, heavy on magic, careful to insult all minorities and sensitivities, just racy enough but still good family fun; leave from Huntsman pub near the Abbey, confirm at TI or call 01225/335-124, www.bizarrebath.co.uk). **Ghost Walks** are another way to pass the after-dark hours (£5, 20:00, 2 hrs, unreliably Mon–Sat April–Oct; in winter Fri only; leave from Garrick's Head pub near Theatre Royal, tel. 01225/463-618, www.ghostwalksofbath.co.uk). The "Mayors Corps of Honorary Guides" offers **free evening walks** in summer (May–Sept 19:00 on Tue, Fri, and Sat, 2 hrs, leave from Pump Room, confirm at TI); for more information, see "Tours," page 135.

Summer Nights at the Baths—In July and August, you can stretch your sightseeing day at the Roman Baths, open nightly until 22:00 (last admission 21:00), when they're far less crowded and more atmospheric.

SLEEPING

B&Bs near the Royal Crescent

These listings are all a 15-minute uphill walk or an easy £3.50 taxi ride from the train station. Or take the Bath Bus Tour from the station and get off at the stop nearest your B&B (for Brock's—Assembly Rooms; for Marlborough listings—Royal Avenue; confirm with driver), check in, then finish the tour later in the day. All of these B&Bs are non-smoking.

$$$ **Brock's Guest House** will put bubbles in your Bath experience. Marion Dodd has redone her Georgian town house (built by John Wood in 1765) in a way that would make the famous architect proud. It's located between the prestigious Royal Crescent and the elegant Circus (Db-£65–78, 1 deluxe Db-£85, Tb-£90–95, Qb-£105–115,

SLEEP CODE

(£1 = about $1.60, country code: 44, area code: 01225)
Sleep Code: **S** = Single, **D** = Double/Twin, **T** = Triple, **Q** = Quad, **b** = bathroom, **s** = shower only, **no CC** = Credit Cards not accepted. Unless otherwise indicated, you can assume credit cards are accepted.

To help you sort easily through these listings, I've divided the rooms into three categories based on the price for a standard double room with bath:

$$$ **Higher Priced**—Most rooms £80 or more.
$$ **Moderately Priced**—Most rooms between £50–80.
$ **Lower Priced**—Most rooms £50 or less.

Bath is a busy tourist town. To get a good B&B, make a telephone reservation in advance. Competition is stiff, and it's worth asking any of these places for a weekday, three-nights-in-a-row, or off-season deal. Friday and Saturday nights are tightest, especially if you're staying only one night, since B&Bs favor those staying longer. If staying only Saturday night, you're very bad news. At B&Bs (and cheaper hotels), expect lots of stairs and no lifts.

reserve with credit card far in advance, little library on top floor, 32 Brock Street, tel. 01225/338-374, fax 01225/334-245, www.brocksguesthouse.co.uk, marion@brocksguesthouse.co.uk).

$$$ Elgin Villa, also thoughtfully run and a fine value, has five comfy, well-maintained rooms (Ss-£34, Sb-£50, Ds-£50, Db-£80, Tb-£90, Qb-£110, more expensive for 1 night, discounted for 3 nights, continental breakfast served in room, non-smoking, parking, 6 Marlborough Lane, tel. & fax 01225/424-557, www.elginvilla.co.uk, stay@elginvilla.co.uk, Alwyn and Carol Landman).

$$$ Marlborough House Hotel is both Victorian and vegetarian, with seven comfortable rooms—well-furnished with antiques—and organic-veggie dinners available by request (Sb-£45–75, Db-£65–85, Tb-£75–95, price depending on season, varied breakfast menu, room service, 1 Marlborough Lane, tel. 01225/318-175, fax 01225/466-127, www.marlborough-house.net, Americans Laura and Charles).

$$ Parkside Guest House has four Edwardian rooms and a spacious back garden (Db-£67, 11 Marlborough Lane, tel. & fax

01225/429-444, www.parksidebandb.co.uk, Erica and Inge Lynall).

$ Woodville House is run by Anne and Tom Toalster. This grandmotherly little house has three tidy, charming rooms, one shared shower/WC, an extra WC, and a TV lounge. Breakfast is served at a big, family-style table (D-£40, minimum 2 nights, no CC, strictly non-smoking, some parking, below the Royal Crescent at 4 Marlborough Lane, tel. & fax 01225/319-335, toalster@compuserve.com).

$ Prior House B&B, with four well-kept rooms and thoughtful touches such as robes for guests who use the bathroom down the hall, is run by helpful Lynn and Keith Shearn (D-£45, Db-£50, 3 Marlborough Lane, tel. 01225/313-587, fax 01225/443-543, www.greatplaces.co.uk /priorhouse, priorhouse@greatplaces.co.uk).

B&Bs East of the River

These listings are about a 10-minute walk from the city center.

$$$ The Ayrlington, next door to a lawn-bowling green, has attractive rooms that hint of a more genteel time. Though this well-maintained hotel fronts a busy street, it feels tranquil inside, with double-paned windows. Rooms in the back have pleasant views of sports greens and Bath beyond. For the best value, request a standard double with a view of Bath (standard Db-£85–120, superior Db-£110–140, deluxe Db with Jacuzzi-£125–160, high prices on Fri, Sat, and Sun, no Sat night only, access to garden in back, easy parking, 24-25 Pulteney Road, tel. 01225/425-495, fax 01225/469-029, Simon and Mee-Ling).

In Sydney Gardens: The **$$$ Sydney Gardens Hotel** is a classy Casablanca-type place with six tastefully decorated rooms, an elegant breakfast room, garden views, and an entrance to Sydney Gardens park (Sb-£65, Db-£85, Tb-£100, Qb-£115, request garden view, easy parking, located on busy road between park and canal, Sydney Road, tel. 01225/464-818, fax 01225/484-347, www.sydneygardens.co.uk, book@sydneygardens.co.uk, Rory).

Near North Parade Road: The **$$ Holly Villa Guest House,** with a cheery garden, six bright rooms, and a cozy TV lounge, is enthusiastically and thoughtfully run by Jill and Keith McGarrigle (Ds-£50, Db-£50–65, Tb-£75–85, no CC, strictly non-smoking, easy parking, 8-min walk from station and city center: walk over North Parade Bridge, take the first right, and then take the second left, 14 Pulteney Gardens, tel. 01225/310-331, jill@hollyvilla.com).

Near Pulteney Road: **$$ Muriel Guy's B&B** is another good value, mixing Georgian elegance with homey warmth and artistic taste (5 rooms, S-£30, Db-£55, Tb-£65, no CC, serves mostly organic foods, go over bridge on North Parade Road, left on Pulteney Road, cross to church, Raby Place is first row of houses on hill, 14 Raby Place, tel. 01225/465-120, fax 01225/465-283).

East of Pulteney Bridge

These are just a few minutes' walk from the city center.

$$$ **Villa Magdala,** with 18 rooms in a freestanding Victorian town house opposite a park, is formal and hotelesque (Db-£85–140, depending on size and type of bed; in quiet residential area, inviting lounge, parking, Henrietta Road, tel. 01225/466-329, fax 01225/483-207, www.villamagdala.co.uk, office@villamagdala.co.uk, Roy and Lois).

$$ **Edgar Hotel,** with 18 simple rooms and lots of stairs, gives you a budget-hotel option in this elegant neighborhood (Sb-£40–50, Db-£55–75, Tb-£100, Qb-£110, park views from back rooms, smaller rooms on top, avoid #18 on the ground level, pleasant sitting room with old organ and gramophones, 64 Great Pulteney Street, tel. 01225/420-619, fax 01225/466-961, edgar-hotel@pgen.net, Rupert).

The City Center

$$$ **Harington's Hotel,** with 13 newly renovated rooms on a quiet street in the town center, is run by Susan and Desmond Pow (Sb-£78–108, Db-£98–138, prices decrease midweek and increase Fri–Sat, 10 percent discount with this book for 2-night minimum stays Sun–Thu except on public holidays; non-smoking, lots of stairs, attached restaurant-bar serves simple meals and pastries all day, 10 Queen Street, tel. 01225/461-728, fax 01225/444-804, www.haringtonshotel.co.uk).

$$$ **Pratt's Hotel** is as proper and old English as you'll find in Bath. Its creaks and frays are aristocratic. Its public places make you want to sip a brandy, and its 46 rooms are bright, spacious, and come with all the comforts (Sb-£90, Db-£125, advance reservations get highest rate, drop-ins after 16:00 often enjoy substantial discount, dogs-£7.50 but children free, attached restaurant-bar, elevator, 2 blocks immediately in front of the station on South Parade, tel. 01225/460-441, fax 01225/448-807, www.forestdale.com, pratts@forestdale.com).

$$$ **Abbey Hotel** has 60 Best Western-style rooms (some on the ground floor), a super location, and a rare elevator (Sb-£82, standard Db-£128, deluxe Db-£143, attached restaurant, non-smoking rooms, North Parade, tel. 01225/461-603, fax 01225/447-758, www.compasshotels.co.uk, ahres@compasshotels.co.uk).

$$ **Parade Park Hotel,** in a Georgian building, has a central location, helpful owners, and 35 modern, basic rooms (S-£35, D-£50, Db-£60–80, Tb-£90, Qb-£120, non-smoking, *beaucoup* stairs, 10 North Parade, tel. 01225/463-384, fax 01225/442-322, www.paradepark.co.uk, info@paradepark.co.uk).

$$ **Royal York Travelodge**—which offers American-style, characterless, comfortable rooms—worries B&Bs and hotels alike with its reasonable prices (Db-£60, £70 on Fri–Sun, breakfast extra, non-smoking rooms available, 1 York Building, George Street, tel. 0870–191-1718, central reservation tel. 08700-850-950, www.travelodge.co.uk).

Bath Hotels

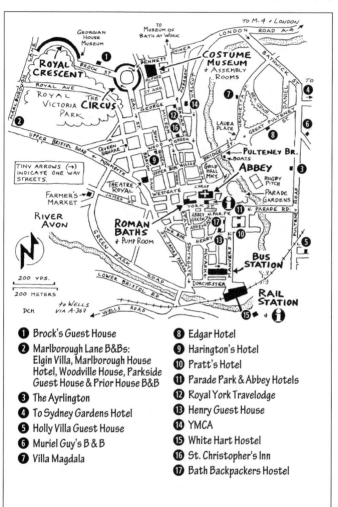

- **1** Brock's Guest House
- **2** Marlborough Lane B&Bs: Elgin Villa, Marlborough House Hotel, Woodville House, Parkside Guest House & Prior House B&B
- **3** The Ayrlington
- **4** To Sydney Gardens Hotel
- **5** Holly Villa Guest House
- **6** Muriel Guy's B & B
- **7** Villa Magdala
- **8** Edgar Hotel
- **9** Harington's Hotel
- **10** Pratt's Hotel
- **11** Parade Park & Abbey Hotels
- **12** Royal York Travelodge
- **13** Henry Guest House
- **14** YMCA
- **15** White Hart Hostel
- **16** St. Christopher's Inn
- **17** Bath Backpackers Hostel

$ Henry Guest House is a plain, clean, old, vertical, eight-room, family-run place two blocks in front of the train station on a quiet side street. Nothing matches—not the curtains, wallpaper, carpeting, throw rugs, or bedspreads—but the rooms are pleasant and affordable, and the newly-renovated, cheerful dining room is now open for healthy lunches (S-£25, D-£50, T-£65, no CC, lots of narrow stairs, 3 showers and 2

WCs for all, café open 10:00–17:00, everything on the menu costs £5 or less, 6 Henry Street, tel. 01225/424-052, fax 01225/316-669, www .thehenry.com, enquiries@thehenry.co.uk, helpful Sue and Derek).

Lower-Priced Dorms

The **YMCA,** central on a leafy square down a tiny alley off Broad Street, has 208 beds in industrial-strength rooms with tired carpeting (S-£20–24, D-£32–36, beds in big dorms-£10–12, higher rates on week-ends, includes meager continental breakfast, cheap lunches, lockers, dorms closed 10:00–16:00, Broad Street Place, tel. 01225/460-471, fax 01225/462-065, reservation@ymcabath.co.uk).

White Hart Hostel is a simple, new place offering adults and fam-ilies good cheap beds in two- to six-bed dorms (£12.50/bed, Db-£50, family rooms, breakfast-£3.50-4.50, smoke-free, kitchen, small café-bar, 5-min walk behind train station at Widcombe—where Widcombe Hill hits Claverton Street, tel. 01225/313-985, www.whitehartbath.co.uk, sue@whitehartinn.freeserve.co.uk, run by Mick and Sue).

St. Christopher's Inn, which opened in 2003 in a prime central Bath location, is part of a chain of low-priced, high-energy hubs for travelers looking for beds and brews (59 beds in 2- to 14-bed rooms-£15–23, deals sometimes available online; lively, affordable restaurant and bar downstairs; Internet access, laundry, lounge with video, 9 Green Street, tel. 020/7407-1856, www.st-christophers.co.uk).

Bath Backpackers Hostel bills itself as a totally fun-packed, mad place to stay. This youthfully run dive/hostel rents bunk beds in 6- to 10-bed rooms (£12/bed, 2 D-£30, T-£45, Internet access for non-guests as well, bar, kitchen, laundry-£2.50/load, a couple of blocks toward city center from train station, 13 Pierrepont Street, tel. 01225/446-787, bath@hostels.co.uk).

EATING

While not a great pub-grub town, Bath is bursting with quaint and styl-ish eateries. There's something for every appetite and budget—just stroll around the center of town. A picnic dinner of deli food or take-out fish 'n' chips in the Royal Crescent Park is ideal for aristocratic hobos.

Between the Abbey and the Station

Three fine and popular places share North Parade Passage, a block south of the Abbey:

Tilley's Bistro, popular with locals, serves healthy French, English, and vegetarian meals with candlelit ambience. Their fun menu lets you build your meal, choosing from an interesting array of £7 starters (Mon–Sat 12:00–14:30 & 18:30–23:00, closed Sun, reservations smart, non-smoking, North Parade Passage, tel. 01225/484-200).

Sally Lunn's House is a cutesy, quasi-historic place for expensive doily meals, tea, pink pillows, and lots of lace (£15–20, nightly, smoke-free, 4 North Parade Passage, tel. 01225/461-634). It's fine for tea and buns (£7–10, served until 18:00), and customers get a free peek at the basement Kitchen Museum (otherwise 30p).

Demuth's Vegetarian Restaurant serves good £12 meals (daily 10:00–22:00, vegan options available, reservations wise, tel. 01225/446-059).

Crystal Palace Pub, with typical pub grub under rustic timbers or in the sunny courtyard, is a handy standby (meals-£7, Mon–Fri 11:00–20:00, Sat 11:00–16:00, Sun 12:00–16:00, children welcome on patio until 16:30 but not indoors, 11 Abbey Green, tel. 01225/482-666).

Evans is decent for fish 'n' chips (Mon–Fri 11:30–15:00, Sat 11:30–17:00, closed Sun, on Abbeygate, near Marks & Spencer). Also greasy is **Seafoods** (daily 12:00–23:00, last seating 22:30, last take-out 23:00; try the mushy peas, cup of tea, and fish 'n' chips special for £4; 27 Kingsmead Street, just off Kingsmead Square).

Between the Abbey and the Circus

George Street is lined with cheery eateries: Thai, Italian, wine bars, and so on.

The hopping **Martini Restaurant** is purely Italian, with class and jovial waiters (entrées-£12, pizzas-£7, daily 12:00–14:30 & 18:00–22:30, reservations smart, smoke-free section, 9 George Street, tel. 01225/460-818, Nunzio, Franco, and Luigi).

Bengal Brasserie, a Bangladeshi place specializing in tandoori and curries, is unpretentious with good food at good prices (daily 12:00–14:00 & 18:00–23:00, 32 Milsom Street, tel. 01225/447-906).

Jamuna makes a mean curry (daily until 23:00, 10 percent discount for take-out, Abbey views, 9-10 High Street, tel. 01225/464-631).

The **Old Green Tree Pub** has good grub, locally brewed real ales, and a non-smoking room (lunch only, served 12:00–14:45, no children, Green Street, tel. 01225/448-259).

Browns, a popular, modern chain, offers affordable—though not great—English food throughout the day (Sun–Fri 12:00–23:00, Sat 11:00–23:00, kid-friendly, nice terrace, half-block east of the Abbey, Orange Grove, tel. 01225/461-199).

The Moon and Sixpence, prized by locals, offers "modern English fusion" cuisine, giving British cooking a needed international flair and flavor (two-course lunch-£7.50, three-course dinner menu-£25, daily 12:00–14:30 & 17:30–22:30, indoor/outdoor seating, 6a Broad Street, tel. 01225/460-962).

Devon Savouries serves greasy-but-delicious take-out pasties, sausage rolls, and vegetable pies (Mon–Sat 9:00–17:30, hours vary on Sun, cheaper if you get it to go, on Burton Street, the main walkway

Bath Restaurants

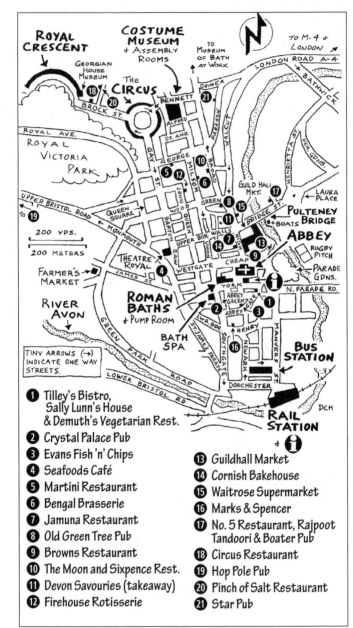

1. Tilley's Bistro, Sally Lunn's House & Demuth's Vegetarian Rest.
2. Crystal Palace Pub
3. Evans Fish 'n' Chips
4. Seafoods Café
5. Martini Restaurant
6. Bengal Brasserie
7. Jamuna Restaurant
8. Old Green Tree Pub
9. Browns Restaurant
10. The Moon and Sixpence Rest.
11. Devon Savouries (takeaway)
12. Firehouse Rotisserie
13. Guildhall Market
14. Cornish Bakehouse
15. Waitrose Supermarket
16. Marks & Spencer
17. No. 5 Restaurant, Rajpoot Tandoori & Boater Pub
18. Circus Restaurant
19. Hop Pole Pub
20. Pinch of Salt Restaurant
21. Star Pub

between New Bond Street and Upper Borough Walls).

If you're missing California, try the popular **Firehouse Rotisserie** (Mon–Sat 12:00–14:30 & 18:00–23:00, Sun 12:00–14:30, make reservations, near Queen Square on John Street, tel. 01225/482-070).

Guildhall Market, across from Pulteney Bridge, is fun for browsing and picnic shopping, with an inexpensive Market Café if you'd like to sip tea surrounded by stacks of used books, bananas on the push list, and honest-to-goodness old-time locals (Mon–Sat 9:00–17:00, closed Sun, a block north of the Abbey, main entrance on High Street).

The **Cornish Bakehouse,** near the Guildhall Market, has good take-away pasties (open until 17:30, 11a The Corridor, off High Street, tel. 01225/426-635).

Supermarkets: **Waitrose,** at the Podium shopping center, is great for picnics with a good salad bar (Mon–Fri 8:30–20:00, Sat 8:30–19:00, Sun 11:00–17:00, just west of Pulteney Bridge and across from post office on High Street). **Marks & Spencer,** near the train station, has a grocery at the back of its department store (Mon–Sat 9:00–10:00, Sun 11:00–17:00, Stall Street).

East of Pulteney Bridge

For a stylish, intimate setting and "new English" cuisine worth the splurge, dine at **No. 5 Restaurant** (main courses with vegetables-£13–16, Mon–Sat 18:30–22:00, closed Sun, Mon–Tue are "bring your own bottle of wine" nights—no corkage fee, smart to reserve, just over Pulteney Bridge at 5 Argyle Street, tel. 01225/444-499).

Rajpoot Tandoori, next door to No. 5, serves good Indian food. You'll hike down deep into a cellar where the classy Indian atmosphere and award-winning cooking makes paying the extra pounds OK (12:00–14:30 & 18:00–23:00, 4 Argyle Street, tel. 01225/466-833).

Down the street, the popular **Boater Pub** offers a good selection of ales and pub grub and a pleasant beer garden overlooking the river (Mon–Sat 11:00–23:00, Sun 12:00–20:30, 9 Argyle Street, tel. 01225/464-211).

Near the Circus and Royal Crescent

Circus Restaurant is intimate and a good value, with Mozartean ambience and candlelit prices: £18 for a three-course dinner special including great vegetables and a selection of fine desserts (Wed–Sun 12:00–14:00 & 18:30–22:00, closed Tue lunch and all day Mon, reservations smart, 34 Brock Street, tel. 01225/318-918).

The Hop Pole pub, across from Victoria Park and popular with locals, serves up Bath ales and affordable creative cuisine (main courses-£9, open daily for ales, lunch and dinner served Tue–Sat, open courtyard in back, Upper Bristol Road, tel. 01225/446-327).

Pinch of Salt is a splurge with a French accent in a trendy space just off Brock Street (main courses-£14–17, closed Sun, 11 Margaret's Buildings, tel. 01225/421-251).

For real ale (but no food), try the **Star Pub** (daily, top of the Paragon street, tel. 01225/444-437).

TRANSPORTATION CONNECTIONS

Bath's train station is called Bath Spa (train info: tel. 08457-484-950). The National Express bus office (Mon–Sat 8:00–17:30, closed Sun, bus info: tel. 08705-808-080), is one block in front of the train station.

To London: You can catch a **train** to London's Paddington Station (2/hr, 90 min, £33–39 one way after 9:30), or save money but not time by taking the National Express **bus** to Victoria Station (nearly 1/hr, a little over 3 hrs, one way-£13, round trip-£21, www.nationalexpress.com).

To get *from* London to Bath and see Stonehenge to boot, consider an all-day organized bus tour from London (see page 116 in the London chapter).

To London's Airports: By National Express bus to **Heathrow** and continuing on to London (10/day, 2.5 hrs, £13, tel. 08705-808-080) and to **Gatwick** (approx 2/hr, 4.5 hrs, £20). Trains are faster but more expensive (1/hr, 2.5 hrs, £29.20).

To the Cotswolds: By train to **Moreton-in-Marsh** (1/hr, 2 hrs, transfer in Didcot). By National Express bus to **Cheltenham** or **Gloucester** (1 direct bus/day, 2.5 hrs, more buses with transfer), **Stratford-upon-Avon** (1/day, 4 hrs, transfer in Bristol or Birmingham), and **Oxford** (1 direct bus/day, 2 hrs, more buses with transfer).

By train: To **Oxford** (1/hr, 1.25 hrs, transfer in Didcot), **Heathrow** (1/hr, 2 hrs, transfer at Reading to bus), **Gatwick** (1/hr, 3 hrs, most transfer in Reading or Clapham Junction), **Birmingham** (1/hr, 2.5 hrs, transfer in Bristol), and **points north** (from Birmingham, a major transportation hub, trains depart for Blackpool, York, Durham, Scotland, and North Wales; use a train/bus combination to reach Ironbridge Gorge and the Lake District).

SIGHTS NEAR BATH:
GLASTONBURY, WELLS, AVEBURY, STONEHENGE, AND SOUTH WALES

Ooooh, mystery, history. Glastonbury is the ancient home of Avalon, King Arthur, and the Holy Grail. Nearby, medieval Wells gathers around its grand cathedral, where you can enjoy an evensong service. Then get neolithic at every Druid's favorite stone circles, Avebury and Stonehenge.

An hour east of Bath, at the Museum of Welsh Life, you'll find South Wales' story vividly told in a park full of restored houses. Relish the romantic ruins and poetic wax of Tintern Abbey, the lush Wye River Valley, and the quirky Forest of Dean.

Planning Your Time

Avebury, Glastonbury, and Wells make a wonderful day out from Bath. Splicing in Stonehenge is possible but stretching it. Everybody needs to see Stonehenge. But I'll tell you now, it looks just like it looks. You'll know what I mean when you pay to get in and rub up against the rope fence that keeps tourists at a distance. Avebury is the connoisseur's circle: more subtle and welcoming. Wells is simply a cute town, much smaller and more medieval than Bath, with a uniquely beautiful cathedral that's best experienced at the 17:15 evensong service. Glastonbury is normally done surgically, in two hours: See the abbey, climb the tor, ponder your hippie past (and where you are now), then scram.

Think of the South Wales sights as a different grouping. Ideally, they fill the day you leave Bath for the Cotswolds. Anyone interested in Welsh culture can spend four hours in the Museum of Welsh Life. Castle lovers and romantics will want to consider the Caerphilly Castle, Chepstow Castle, Tintern Abbey, and Forest of Dean. See the beginning of the Bath chapter for a day-by-day schedule.

Sights near Bath

Getting around near Bath

Wells and Glastonbury are both easily accessible by bus from Bath. **The First bus company** offers a "FirstExplorer" ticket (£6, £12.50-family, good for 1 day, office 1 block from Bath train station, Mon–Sat 8:00–17:30, closed Sun, tel. 0845-606-4446, www.firstbadgerline.co.uk). Glastonbury and Wells are connected with each other by bus and by a 9.5-mile foot/bike path. You can get to South Wales by train via Bristol, connecting by bus from the train station in Wales to the sights.

You can reach Avebury by taking the #X72 bus to Devizes (hrly, 1 hr), then picking up a frequent local bus to Avebury (15 min). Stonehenge is trickier. The most convenient and quickest way to see Avebury and Stonehenge if you don't have a car is to take an all-day bus tour. Of those tours leaving from Bath, "Mad Max" is the liveliest.

"Mad Max" Minibus Tours are thoughtfully organized and informative. Operating daily from Bath, they run with a maximum group size of 16 people and cost £20 per person (cash only). Tours depart from Bath at 8:45 (at the statue on Cheap Street, next to London Camera Exchange) and end at 16:30. They cover 110 miles with stops at

Stonehenge (first off, to beat the crowds), Avebury Stone Circles, and two cute villages—Lacock and Castle Combe. Castle Combe, the southernmost Cotswold village, is as sweet as they come. Book ahead for this popular tour via e-mail (www.madmaxtours.com, maddy@madmax .abel.co.uk) or phone (Bath YMCA tel. 01225/325-900). Please honor or cancel your seat reservation. Mad Max also offers The Cotswold Discovery Tour, a picturesque romp through the countryside with stops in some of the Cotswolds' quaintest villages, including Stow-on-the-Wold, Stanton, Tetbury, and the Coln Valley (£20, £5 discount if you take both Mad Max tours, runs Tue & Thu, departs at 8:45).

If Mad Max is booked up, don't fret. Plenty of companies in Bath offer tours of varying lengths, prices, and destinations. Note that the cost of admission to sites is usually not included with any tour. **Scarper Tours** runs a whirlwind "Top Spots Beyond Bath" minibus tour covering Stonehenge, Glastonbury, and Wells (£19, departs Tue–Sun 9:30, daytime tel. 01225/444-102, evening tel. 07739-644-155, www.scarpertours.com). **Heritage City Guided Tour** runs a Stonehenge Express trip out to the rocks and back (£14, 2.25 hrs, departs Grand Parade daily at 10:00 and 14:00, mobile 07977-792-9486). **Celtic Horizons** runs day tours to a variety of destinations and charges a flat fee for up to six people (Stonehenge-£50, Avebury area-£60, Cotswolds-£100–160, tel. 01373/461-784, www.celtichorizons.com, alan@celtichorizons.com).

Drivers can do a loop from Bath to Avebury (25 miles) to Glastonbury (56 miles) to Wells (6 miles) and back to Bath (20 miles). A loop from Bath to South Wales is 100 miles, mostly on the 70-mph motorway. Each of the Welsh sights is just off the motorway.

Glastonbury

Marked by its hill, or "tor," and located on England's most powerful line of prehistoric sights (called a "ley" line), the town of Glastonbury gurgles with history and mystery.

In A.D. 37, Joseph of Arimathea—one of Jesus' wealthy disciples—brought vessels containing the blood and sweat of Jesus to Glastonbury, and, with them, Christianity came to England. While this story is "proven" by fourth-century writings and accepted by the Church, the Holy Grail legend that sprang from it in the Middle Ages isn't. Many think the grail trail ends at the bottom of the Chalice Well (described below), a natural spring at the base of the Glastonbury Tor.

In the 12th century, England needed a morale-boosting folk hero for inspiration during a war with France. The fifth-century Celtic fort at Glastonbury was considered proof enough of the greatness of the fifth-century warlord Arthur. His supposed remains (along with those of Queen Guinevere) were dug up from the abbey floor, and Glastonbury became woven into the Arthurian legends. Reburied in the abbey choir, their grave site is a shrine today.

The Glastonbury Abbey was England's most powerful in the 10th century. By the year 1500, English monasteries owned one-sixth of all English land and had four times the income of the crown. Henry VIII dissolved the abbeys in 1536. He was particularly harsh on Glastonbury. He not only destroyed the abbey but also hung and quartered the abbot, sending the parts of his body on four different national tours...at the same time.

But Glastonbury rebounded. In an 18th-century tourism campaign, thousands signed affidavits stating that water from the Chalice Well healed them, and once again Glastonbury was on the tourist map. Today Glastonbury and its tor are a center for searchers, too creepy for the mainstream church but just right for those looking for a place to recharge their crystals.

ORIENTATION

(area code: 01458)

Tourist Information: The TI is on High Street—as are many of the dreadlocked folks who walk it (Sun–Thu 10:00–17:00, Fri–Sat 10:00–17:30, until 16:00 in winter, tel. 01458/832-954, www.glastonbury.co.uk). The TI has several booklets about cycling and walking in the area. One 30p brochure outlines a good tor-to-town walk (a brisk, 10-min walk). The TI's Millennium Trail pamphlet (60p) sends visitors on a historical scavenger hunt, following 20 numbered, marble plaques embedded in the pavement throughout the town.

Located in the TI, the Lake Village Museum—featuring tools made of stones, bones, and antlers—is nothing special (£2). Tuesday is market day for crafts, knickknacks, and produce behind the TI (9:00–15:00).

The **Tor Bus** shuttles visitors from the town center and abbey to the base of the tor. If you request it, the bus will stop at the Rural Life Museum and the Chalice Well (£1, 2/hr, 9:30–17:00 throughout the summer, bus does not run during lunchtime, catch bus at St. Dunstan's car park in center).

SIGHTS

▲▲**Glastonbury Abbey**—The evocative ruins of the first Christian sanctuary in the British Isles stand mysteriously alive in a lush, 36-acre park. Start your visit in the good little museum, where a model shows the abbey in its pre-Henry VIII splendor, and exhibits tell the story of a place "grandly constructed to entice even the dullest minds to prayer." Today the abbey attracts people who find God within. Tie-dyed, starry-eyed pilgrims seem to float through the grounds naturally high. Others lie on the grave of King Arthur, whose burial site is marked off in the

Glastonbury

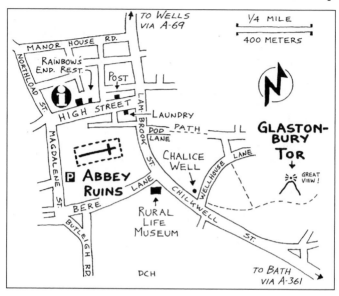

center of the abbey ruins. The only surviving building is the abbot's conical kitchen, which often comes with a cheery, singing monk demonstrating life in the abbey kitchen. If you'd like to see the demo, it's best to phone ahead for the schedule, especially off-season (£3.50, June–Aug daily 9:00–18:00, off-season 9:30 or 10:00 to dusk, closing times vary in the winter—call to check, last entry 30 min before closing, £1 audioguide is informative but can be long-winded, ask at entry for monk's "show" times, tel. 01458/832-267, www.glastonburyabbey.com).

Somerset Rural Life Museum—Exhibits include peat digging, cider making, and cheese making. The Abbey Farmhouse is now a collection of domestic and work mementos that illustrate the life of farmer John Hodges "from the cradle to the grave." The fine 14th-century barn, with its beautifully preserved wooden ceiling, is filled with Victorian farm tools (free, Easter–Oct Tue–Fri 10:00–17:00, Sat–Sun 14:00–18:00, closed Mon, Nov–Easter Tue–Sat 10:00–17:00, closed Sun–Mon, Abbey Farm, Chilkwell Street, Glastonbury, last entry 30 min before closing, admission includes entrance to Taunton Castle, free car park, 8-min walk from abbey, at intersection of Bere Lane and Chilkwell Street, tel. 01458/831-197, fax 01458/834-684).

Chalice Well—The well is surrounded by a peaceful garden. According to tradition, Joseph of Arimathea brought the chalice from the Last Supper to Glastonbury in A.D. 37. Even if the chalice is not in the bottom of the well and the water is red from rust and not Jesus' blood, the tranquil setting is one where nature's harmony is a joy to ponder. The stones of the well shaft date from the 12th century and are believed to have come from the church in Glastonbury Abbey (which was destroyed by fire). During the 18th century, pilgrims flocked to Glastonbury for the well's healing powers and even today, there's a moment of silence at noon for world peace and healing. Have a drink or take some of the precious water home (50-75p bottles available, daily 10:00–18:00, less off-season, 4-min walk from Rural Life Museum, on Chilkwell Street, look for red sign, tel. 01458/831-154, www.chalicewell.org.uk).

Glastonbury Tor—Seen by many as a Mother Goddess symbol, the tor, a natural plug of sandstone on clay, has an undeniable geological charisma. The tower is the remnant of a 14th-century church of St. Michael. A fine Somerset view rewards those who hike to its 520-foot summit.

Back in the 1940s, Catherine Maltwood identified the signs of the zodiac in the ancient rock formations, hedgerows, and waterways surrounding Glastonbury. She saw the tor as the head of the phoenix, another symbol for Aquarius. If this sounds intriguing, you can buy her zodiac map at the TI (£2.50).

Path from Glastonbury Tor to Wells—A 9.5-mile cycling and foot path (a.k.a. Syrens Project) begins at the bottom of Glastonbury Tor and ends in Wells, marked by nine large neolithic-looking sculptures along the way. Designed by local artists, these funky stones are carved with willow leaves, swans, and other images of the journey.

Shopping—If you need spiritual guidance or just an odd rune reading, wander through the **Glastonbury Experience,** a New Age mall at the bottom of High Street.

EATING

Glastonbury, quickly becoming "the windy city," has no shortage of healthy eateries. The vegetarian **Rainbow's End** is one of several fine cafés for beans, salads, herbal teas, and New Age people-watching (daily 10:00–16:00, a few doors up from the TI, 17 High Street, tel. 01458/833-896). If you're looking for a midwife or a male-bonding tribal meeting, check their notice board.

Knights Fish and Chips Restaurant has been in business since 1909 because it serves good food (Mon 17:00–21:30, Tue–Sat 12:00–14:15 & 17:00–21:30, closed Sun, eat in or take away, 5 Northload Street, tel. 01458/831-882).

TRANSPORTATION CONNECTIONS

The nearest train station is in Bath.

By bus to: Wells (1/hr, 20 min, bus #173) and **Bath** (5/day on Sun, 75 min; Mon–Sat no direct connections, transfer in Wells, allow 2 hrs).

Wells

Because this wonderfully preserved little town has a cathedral, it can be called a city. While it's the biggest town in Somerset, it's England's smallest cathedral city (pop. 9,400), with one of its most interesting cathedrals and more medieval buildings still doing what they were originally built to do than in any town you'll visit. Market day fills the town square on Wednesday and Saturday.

Tourist Information: The TI, on the main square, has information about the town's sights and nearby cheese factories (April–Oct daily 9:30–17:30, off-season daily 10:00–16:00, tel. 01749/672-552, wells.tic@ukonline.co.uk).

Ask at the TI about the path from Wells to Glastonbury—ideal for hikers and cyclists, this 9.5-mile path is dotted with nine sculptures that combine ancient and modern motifs. You can rent a bike in Wells (at Bike City, £6.50/half day, £8.50/day, Mon–Sat 9:00–17:30, closed Sun, helmets available, 31 Broad Street, tel. 01749/671-711), but not in Glastonbury.

Local Guide: Edie Westmoreland is a good local guide who offers £2.50 town walks in the summer at 14:30 (tour starts at Penniless Porch on town square, book in advance or tour may not run, tel. 01934/832-350).

SIGHTS

▲▲**Wells Cathedral**—England's first completely Gothic cathedral (dating from about 1200) is the highlight of the city. The newly restored west front displays nearly 300 original 13th-century carvings of the *Last Judgment* and many kings. The bottom row of niches is empty, too easily reached by Cromwell's men, who were hell-bent on destroying "graven images." Stand back and imagine it as a grand Palm Sunday welcome with a cast of hundreds—all gaily painted back then, choristers singing boldly from holes above the doors and trumpets tooting through the holes up by the 12 apostles.

Inside you're immediately struck by the general lightness and the unique "scissors" or hourglass-shaped double arch (added in 1338 to transfer weight from the west—where the foundations were sinking under the tower's weight—to the east, where they were firm). You'll be warmly greeted, reminded how expensive it is to maintain the cathedral, and given a map of its highlights.

Don't miss the fine 14th-century stained glass (the "Golden Window" on the east wall). The medieval clock, which depicts the earth at the center of the universe, does a silly but much-loved joust on the quarter hour (north transept, its face dates from 1390). The outer ring shows hours, second ring shows minutes, and the inner ring shows the lunar dates.

In the choir (the central zone where the daily services are sung), the embroidery work on the cushions is worth a close look. The floral roof painting is based on the original medieval design, discovered under the 17th-century whitewash.

Head over to the south transept. Notice the carvings on the pillars. The figures depict medieval life—a man with a toothache, another man with a thorn in his foot, and, around the top, a ticked-off farmer chasing fruit stealers. Look at the tombstones set in the floor. Notice there is no brass. After the Reformation, the church was short on cash, so they sold the brass to pay for roof repairs.

Walk the well-worn steps up to the grand fan-vaulted chapter house—an intimate place for the theological equivalent of a huddle among church officials. The cathedral library (14:30–16:30 only, 50p), with a few old manuscripts, offers a peek into a real 15th-century library.

The requested £4.50 donation for the cathedral is not intended to keep you out (daily 7:30–19:00 or dusk, 45-min tours Mon–Sat April–Oct at 10:00, 11:00, 13:00, 14:00, and 15:00, pay £2 photography fee at info desk, no flash in choir, good shop and the handy Cathedral Cloister Restaurant, tel. 01749/674-483, www.wellscathedral.org.uk). See "Evensong," below.

Lined with perfectly pickled 14th-century houses, the oldest complete street in Europe is **Vicar's Close** (just a block north of the cathedral). It was built to house the vicar's choir, and it still houses church officials. Go into the chapel at the farthest end of the close and look out of the house on the left, which has been restored to its original state. The mediocre city museum is next door to the cathedral. For a fine cathedral-and-town view from your own leafy hilltop bench, hike 10 minutes up Tor Hill.

▲▲**Cathedral Evensong Service**—Weekdays at 17:15 and Sunday at 15:00, the cathedral choir takes full advantage of heavenly acoustics with a 45-minute evensong service. You will sit right in the old "quire" as you listen to a great pipe organ and boys' and men's voices (generally not sung when school is out in July and Aug unless a visiting choir performs, tel. 01749/674-483 to check). At 17:05 the verger ushers visitors to their seats. There's usually plenty of room.

On weekdays, if you need to catch the last bus to Bath at 17:43, request a seat on the north side of the presbytery, so you can slip out the side door without disturbing the service (10-min walk to station from cathedral).

Cathedral Green—In the Middle Ages the cathedral was enclosed within the "Liberty," an area free from civil jurisdiction until the 1800s. The Liberty included the green on the west side of the cathedral, which, from the 13th to the 17th centuries, was a burial place for common folk, including 17th-century plague victims. During the Edwardian period, a local character known as Boney Foster used to dig up the human bones and sell them to tourists. The green later became a cricket pitch, then a field for grazing animals, and finally the perfect setting for an impressive cathedral.

Bishop's Palace—Next to the cathedral stands the moated Bishop's Palace, built in the 13th century and still in use today as the residence of the Bishop of Bath and Wells. The interior offers a look at elegant furniture and clothing (£3.50, Aug daily 10:30–18:00, April–Oct Mon–Fri 10:30–18:00, Sun 13:00–18:00, closed Sat, closed Nov–March, tel. 01749/678-691).

The palace's spring-fed moat, built in the 14th century to protect the bishop during squabbles with the borough, now serves primarily as a pool for swans, which ring the bell to the left of the drawbridge for food. The bridge was last drawn in 1831. On the grounds (past the old-timers playing a proper game of croquet) is a fine garden with the idyllic springs that gave the city its name.

Cheddar Cheese—If you're in the mood for a picnic, drop by an aromatic cheese shop for a great selection of tasty Somerset cheeses. Real farmhouse cheddar puts "American" cheddar to Velveeta shame. The Cheddar Gorge Cheese Company welcomes and educates guests (tel. 01934/742-810). For all things cheddar in Somerset, check out www .cheddarsomerset.co.uk.

Near Wells

▲**Wookey Hole**—This lowbrow commercial venture, possibly worthwhile as family entertainment, is a real hodgepodge. It starts with a 35-minute wookey-guided tour of some big but mediocre caves complete with history, geology lessons, and witch stories. Then you're free to wander through a traditional paper-making mill, with a demonstration, and into a 19th-century amusements room—a riot of color, funny mirrors, and old penny-arcade machines that visitors can actually play for as long as their pennies last (pennies on sale there). They even have old girlie shows (£8.50 at the gate, £7.50 tickets available at Wells TI, daily 10:00–17:00, last entry 2 hours before closing, closed Dec 17–25, 2 miles east of Wells, tel. 01749/672-243, www.wookey.co.uk).

Scrumpy Farms—Scrumpy is the wonderfully dangerous hard cider brewed in this part of England. You don't find it served in many pubs because of the unruly crowd it attracts. Scrumpy, at 8 percent alcohol, will rot your socks. "Scrumpy Jack," carbonated mass-produced cider, is not real scrumpy. The real stuff is "rough farmhouse cider." This is potent stuff. It's said some farmers throw a side of beef into the vat, and when fermentation is done only the teeth remain. TIs list local cider farms open to the public, such as **Mr. Wilkins Land's End Cider Farm,** a great back-door travel experience (free, Mon–Sat 10:00–20:00, Sun 10:00–13:00, near Wells in Mudgeley a quarter mile off the B3151, 2 miles south of Wedmore—tough to find, get close and ask locals, tel. 01934/712-385). Glastonbury's **Somerset Rural Life Museum** has a cider exhibit (for details, see listing on page 155). Apples are pressed from August through December. Hard cider, while not quite scrumpy, is still typical of the West Country, but more fashionable, decent, and accessible. You can get a pint of hard cider at nearly any pub, drawn straight from the barrel—dry, medium, or sweet.

SLEEPING

$$$ **Swan Hotel,** facing the cathedral, is a big, overpriced hotel (Sb-£70–80, Db-£78–114, often cheaper if you just show up, ask about their weekend deals, breakfast-£9.50, non-smoking rooms, Sadler Street, tel. 01749/836-300, fax 01749/836-301, www.bhere.co.uk, swan@bhere.co.uk).

SLEEP CODE

(£1 = about $1.60, country code: 44, area code: 01749)
Sleep Code: **S** = Single, **D** = Double/Twin, **T** = Triple, **Q** = Quad, **b** = bathroom, **s** = shower only, **no CC** = Credit Cards not accepted. Unless otherwise indicated, you can assume credit cards are accepted.

To help you sort easily through these listings, I've divided the rooms into three categories based on the price for a standard double room with bath:

$$$ **Higher Priced**—Most rooms £80 or more.
$$ **Moderately Priced**—Most rooms between £40–80.
$ **Lower Priced**—Most rooms £40 or less.

Wells is a pleasant overnight stop with a handful of agreeable B&Bs and eateries. The Swan Hotel, Furlong House B&B, and the Fountain Inn are all within a block of each other behind (east of) the cathedral. Coming in on B3139 from Bath, they're just before the cathedral.

$$ **Furlong House B&B,** a grand old house with a huge and peaceful garden, is homey and laid-back (Db-£46–52, reservations recommended, especially on weekends, non-smoking, easy parking, includes breakfast, behind the gate at the end of Lorne Place, a tiny and quiet lane off St. Thomas Street, tel. 01749/674-064, johnhowardwells @aol.com, Lyn and John Howard).

$$ **The Old Farmhouse,** a five-minute walk from the town center, welcomes you with a secluded front garden and tastefully decorated rooms. Upon request, owner Felicity Wilks—a Cordon Bleu chef—can cook up a two-course dinner for £25 per person (Db-£60, secured parking, 62 Chamberlain Street, tel. 01749/675-058, www.plus44.com /oldfarmhouse, oldfarmhouse@talk21.com).

EATING

Fountain Inn is a step above pub grub (£10–15 dinners, Mon–Sat 12:00–14:00 & 18:00–22:00, Sun 12:00–14:00 & 19:00–21:30, creative meals, veggie options, real ales, draft cider, reservations wise on weekends, behind cathedral on St. Thomas Street, tel. 01749/672-317). Their award-winning cheese plate lets you sample cheddar and its local cousins. For a good, traditional local dish, try their founders beef pie.

Anton's Bistro on the main square is pleasant (£8–11, daily 12:00–14:00 & 18:00–21:30, non-smoking section, in Crown Hotel, veggie options, tel. 01749/673-457).

Locals like **Ritcher's**—a little pricey, but good (£17.50 2-course dinner, daily 12:00–14:00 & 19:00–20:00, opposite cathedral near market square, tel. 01749/679-085).

For a heavenly lunch, consider the **Cathedral Cloister Restaurant** (in the cathedral, a lovely stone corridor with leaded windows, £3 lunches, Mon–Sat 10:00–17:00, Sun 12:30–17:00) or the health-conscious **Good Earth** for its quiche, pasta, and salad (Mon–Sat 9:00–17:30, closed Sun, 4 Priory Road at bottom of Broad Street, tel. 01749/678-600).

Carringtons offers a pleasant cream tea break as well as meals (daily 10:00–17:00, 12 Sadler Street, tel. 01749/676-435).

The **City Arms Pub and Restaurant,** run by friendly owner Jim, is a favorite with locals. A city jail in Tudor times and still circled by medieval walls, the restaurant serves a variety of local specialties, including veggie alternatives. The adjacent pub offers six ales on tap (Mon–Sat 9:00–20:00, Sun 12:00–21:00, 69 Arms Street, tel. 01749/673-916).

TRANSPORTATION CONNECTIONS

The nearest train station is in Bath. The bus station in Wells is actually a bus "lot," at the intersection of Priory and Princes roads.

By bus to: To **Bath** (hrly, 75 min), **Glastonbury** (hrly, 20 min),

London's Victoria Coach Station (£17, hrly, 4 hrs, change in Bristol; buses run daily 6:20–17:45, National Express, tel. 08705-808-080, www.nationalexpress.com).

Avebury

The stone circle at Avebury is bigger (16 times the size), less touristy, and, for many, more interesting than Stonehenge. You're free to wander among 100 stones, ditches, mounds, and curious patterns from the past, as well as the village of Avebury, which grew up in the middle of this fascinating, 1,400-foot-wide neolithic circle.

In the 14th century, in a kind of frenzy of religious paranoia, Avebury villagers buried many of these mysterious pagan stones. Their 18th-century descendants broke up the remaining stones and used them for building material. Today the buried stones have been resurrected, and concrete markers show where the broken-down stones once stood.

Take the mile walk around the circle. Visit the archaeology museum, with its new interactive exhibit in a 17th-century barn museum (£4, April–Oct daily 10:00–18:00, Nov–March until 16:00, tel. 01672/539-250). Notice the pyramid-shaped Silbury Hill, a 130-foot-high, yet-to-be-explained mound of chalk just outside of Avebury. Nearly 5,000 years old, this mound is the largest man-made object in prehistoric Europe (with the surface area of London's Trafalgar Square and the height of the Nelson Memorial). It's a reminder that you've just scratched the surface of Britain's mysterious ancient and religious landscape.

The pleasant **Circle Restaurant** serves healthy vegetarian meals and unhealthy cream teas (daily, April–Oct 10:00–18:00, Nov-March until 16:00, next to National Trust store, tel. 01672/539-514). The **Red Lion Pub** has inexpensive pub grub, a creaky, well-worn, dart-throwing ambience, and a medieval well in its dining room (£6–12 meals, cooking daily 12:00–21:00, tel. 01672/539-266).

Sleeping in Avebury makes lots of sense since the stones are lonely and wide open all night. **Mrs. Dixon's B&B,** directly across from Silbury Hill on the main road just beyond the tourist parking lot, rents three small, tidy rooms for a fine price (S-£35, D-£40–45, T-£50, includes breakfast, no CC, non-smoking, 6 Beckhampton Road, Avebury, Wiltshire, SN8 1QT, tel. 01672/539-588).

For transportation connections, see "Getting around near Bath," page 152.

Stonehenge

England's most famous stone circle, with parts older than the oldest pyramid, was built between 2800 and 1500 B.C. Many of these huge stones were rafted and then rolled on logs all the way from Wales to form a remarkably accurate celestial calendar. Even today, every summer solstice (around June 21) the sun sets in just the right slot, and Druids boogie. The monument is roped off, so even if you pay the £5 entry fee (which includes a worthwhile 1-hr audioguide, subject to availability), you're kept at a distance. Cheapskates see it free from the road (June–Aug daily 9:00–19:00, fewer hours off-season, live tel. 01980/625-368, lengthy info tel. 01980/624-715, www.english-heritage.org.uk). A new Visitors Center and shuttle bus to Stonehenge is slated to open in 2005. For transportation connections, see "Getting around near Bath" page 152.

South Wales

▲**Cardiff**—The Welsh capital (pop. 300,000) has a newly renovated waterfront area with shops and entertainment and a pleasant modern center across from its castle (TI tel. 02920/227-281). A castle visit is interesting only if you catch one of the entertaining tours (every 30 min). The interior is a Victorian fantasy (£5.80 with 50-min tour, £2.90 grounds only without tour, daily 9:30–18:00, shorter hours off-season, last entry 1 hour before close, tel. 02920/878-100).

▲▲**Museum of Welsh Life in St. Fagans**—This best look at traditional Welsh folk life displays more than 40 carefully reconstructed old houses from all corners of this little country in a 100-acre park under a castle. Each is fully furnished and comes equipped with a local expert warming herself by a toasty fire and happy to tell you anything you want to know about life in this old cottage. Ask questions!

A highlight is the Rhyd-y-Car 1805 row house, which displays ironworker cottages as they might have looked in 1805, 1855, 1895, 1925, 1955, and 1985, offering a fascinating zip through Welsh domestic life from hearths to microwaves. You'll see traditional crafts in action and a great gallery displaying crude washing machines, the earliest matches, elaborately carved "love spoons," an impressive costume exhibit, and even a case of memorabilia from the local man who pioneered cremation. While everything is well explained, the £2 museum guidebook is a good investment.

The museum has three sections: houses, museum, and castle/garden. A small train trundles among the exhibits from Easter to October (5 stops, 50p per stop, whole circuit takes 45 min). If the sky's dry, see the scattering of houses first. Spend an hour in the large building's fascinating museum. The castle interior is royal enough and surrounded by a fine garden (free, daily 10:00–17:00, tel. 02920/573-500). While the cafeteria near the entrance is handy, you'll eat light lunches better, cheaper, and with more atmosphere in the park at the Gwalia Tea Room. The Plymouth Arms pub just outside the museum serves the best food.

To get from Cardiff to the Welsh Folk Museum in the village of St. Fagans, catch bus #32 (£1.50, £2.50 return, exact change required, departs Cardiff train station Mon–Sat at 10:20, 11:20, 13:20, 15:20, 18:20, and Sun hourly on the half hour between 9:30 and 18:00, tel. 0870-608-2608). Drivers leave the M4 at Junction 33 and follow the signs. Leaving the museum, jog left on the freeway, take the first exit, and circle back, following signs to the M4.

▲**Caerphilly Castle**—The impressive but gutted old castle is the second largest in Europe (after Windsor). English Earl Gilbert de Clare erected this squat behemoth to try to establish a stronghold in Wales. With two concentric walls, it was considered to be a brilliant arrangement of defensive walls and moats. Attackers had to negotiate three drawbridges and four sets of doors and portcullises just to reach the main entrance. Exhibits display clever catapults, castle-dwellers' tricks for harassing intruders, and a good dose of Welsh history. For the record, there were no known successful enemy forays beyond the castle's inner walls (£3, June–Sept daily 9:30–18:00, May and Oct daily 9:30–17:00, Nov–April Mon–Sat 9:30–16:00, Sun 11:00–16:00, last entry 30 min before closing, 45-min audioguide–£1, 9 miles north of Cardiff, 30 min by car from the Museum of Welsh Life in St. Fagans, or take train from Cardiff to Caerphilly—3/hr, 20 min—and walk 5 min, tel. 02920/883-143, www.cadw.wales.gov.uk).

Chepstow Castle—Perched on a hill overlooking the pleasant village of Chepstow on one side and the Wye River on the other, this castle is worth a short stop for drivers heading for Tintern Abbey. The stone-built bastion dating to 1066 was among the first castles the British plunked down to secure their turf in Wales and remained in use through 1690. As you clamber along the battlements, you'll find evidence of military architectural rehabs through the centuries, from Norman to Tudor right up through Cromwellian additions (£3, June–Sept daily 9:30–18:00, Oct–March closes at 16:00, April–May closes at 17:00, last admission 30 min before closing, in Chepstow village a half-mile from train station, tel. 01291/624-065).

▲▲**Tintern Abbey**—Inspiring monks to prayer, William Wordsworth to poetry, J.M.W. Turner to a famous painting, and rushed tourists to a thoughtful moment, this poem-worthy ruined-castle-of-an-abbey is worth a five-mile detour off the motorway. Founded in 1131 on a site chosen by Norman monks for its tranquility, it functioned as an austere Cistercian abbey until its dissolution in 1536. The monks followed a strict schedule. They rose several hours after midnight for the first of eight daily prayer sessions and spent the rest of their days studying and meditating. The daylight that floods through the roofless ruins highlights the Gothic decorated arches—in those days a bold departure from Cistercian simplicity (£2.50, daily 9:30–18:00 in summer, 9:30–17:00 in spring and fall, Mon–Sat 9:30–16:00, Sun 11:00–16:00 in winter, last entry 30 min before closing, 1-hr audioguide-£1 with £5 deposit, summertime concerts in the cloisters, tel. 01291/689-251, www.cadw .wales.gov.uk; from Cardiff catch a 1.5-hr bus or train to Chepstow, then 20-min bus or taxi from Chepstow to abbey). Visit early or late to miss crowds. The abbey's shop sells fine Celtic jewelry and other gifts. Take an easy 15-minute walk up to St. Mary's Church for a view of England just over the River Wye.

If seduced into spending the night, you'll find plenty of B&Bs near the abbey or in the charming castle-crowned town of Chepstow just down the road. The Tintern **TI** is helpful (April–Oct 10:30–17:30, closed Nov–March, tel. 01291/689-566).

▲**Wye River Valley and Forest of Dean**—This land is lush, mellow, and historic. Local tourist brochures explain the Forest of Dean's special dialect, its strange political autonomy, and its oaken ties to Trafalgar and Admiral Nelson.

For a medieval night, check into the **St. Briavels' Castle Youth Hostel** (£11.50 beds in four- to 12-bed dorms, nonmembers-£2 extra, 70 beds, breakfast-£3.50, non-smoking, tel. 01594/530–272, stbriavels @yha.org.uk). The hostel hosts medieval banquets each week in August (£7, for hostel guests only, ask staff for schedule). An 800-year-old Norman castle used by King John in 1215 (the year he signed the Magna Carta), it's comfortable as castles go, friendly, and in the center of the quiet village of St. Briavels just north of Tintern Abbey. For dinner, eat at the hostel or walk "just down the path and up the snyket" to the **Crown Pub** (decent food and local pub atmosphere).

TRANSPORTATION CONNECTIONS

Cardiff
By train to: Caerphilly (3/hr, 20 min), **Bath** (2/hr, 1 hr), **Birmingham** (2/hr, 2 hrs, change in Bristol, once an hour direct), **London** (2/hr, 2 hrs), **Chepstow** (10/day, 30 min, six miles to Tintern by bus). Train info: tel. 08457-484-950.

Route Tips for Drivers
Bath to South Wales: Leave Bath following signs for A4, then M4. It's 10 miles north (on A46 past a village called Pennsylvania) to the M4 superfreeway. Zip westward, crossing a huge suspension bridge into Wales (£4.80 toll westbound only). Stay on the M4 (not M48) past Cardiff, take exit 33, and follow the brown signs south to the Museum of Welsh Life.

To get to Tintern Abbey, take the M4 to exit 21 and get on M48. The abbey is six miles (up A466, signs to Chepstow then Tintern) off M48 at exit 2, right where the northern bridge across the Severn hits Wales.

Cardiff to the Cotswolds via Forest of Dean: On the Welsh side of the big suspension bridge, take the Chepstow exit and follow signs up A466 to Tintern Abbey and the Wye River Valley. Carry on to Monmouth, and follow the A40 and the M50 to the Tewkesbury exit, where small roads lead to the Cotswolds.

THE COTSWOLDS

The Cotswold Hills, a 25-by-50-mile chunk of Gloucestershire, are dotted with villages and graced with England's greatest countryside palace, Blenheim.

As with many fairy-tale regions of Europe, the present-day beauty of the Cotswolds was the result of an economic disaster. Wool was a huge industry in medieval England, and Cotswold sheep grew the best wool. The region prospered. Wool money built fine towns and houses. Local "wool" churches are called "cathedrals" for their scale and wealth. Stained-glass slogans say things like "I thank my God and ever shall, it is the sheep hath paid for all."

With the rise of cotton and the Industrial Revolution, the woolen industry collapsed. Ba-a-a-ad news. The wealthy Cotswold towns fell into a depressed time warp; the homes of an impoverished nobility became gracefully dilapidated. Today visitors enjoy a harmonious blend of man and nature—the most pristine of English countrysides decorated with time-passed villages, rich wool churches, tell-me-a-story stone fences, and kissing gates you wouldn't want to experience alone. Appreciated by hordes of 21st-century romantics, the Cotswolds are enjoying new prosperity.

Planning Your Time

The Cotswolds are an absolute delight by car and, with patience, enjoyable even without a car. On a three-week British trip, I'd spend two nights and a day in the Cotswolds. The Cotswolds' charm has a softening effect on many tight itineraries. You could spend days of enjoyable walking from a home base here.

One-day driver's 100-mile Cotswold blitz, including Blenheim: Use a good map and reshuffle to fit your home base: 9:00-Browse through Chipping Campden; 10:00-Joyride through Snowshill, Stanway, Stanton, Guiting Power, the Slaughters, and Bourton; 13:00-Lunch and explore Stow-on-the-Wold; 15:00-Drive 30 miles to Blenheim Palace, take the hour-long tour (last tour departs at 16:45); 18:00-Drive home for just the right pub dinner.

ORIENTATION

The north Cotswolds are best. Two of the region's coziest towns, Chipping Campden and Stow-on-the-Wold, are eight and four miles, respectively, from Moreton-in-Marsh, the only Cotswold town with a train station. Any of these three towns makes a fine home base for your exploration of the thatch-happiest of Cotswold villages and walks.

Getting Around the Cotswolds

By Bus: The Cotswolds are so well preserved in part because public transport to this area has long been miserable. You can cobble together a trip with buses connecting major towns, but you'll need to be on the ball and flexible (see "Transportation Connections," page 188). Bus service is very limited on Sundays. For bus schedules, consult any local TI or call the Cotswolds bus travel info line at 0870-608-2608.

By Bike: Despite narrow roads and high hedgerows (blocking some views), bikers enjoy the Cotswolds—free from the constraints of bus schedules. You can rent bikes in Moreton-in-Marsh at the **Toy Shop,** which has mountain bikes, route maps, and bike locks, but no helmets (£12/day, Wed–Sat & Mon 9:00–17:00, closed Sun & Tue, can arrange rentals on closed days by calling in advance, High Street, tel. 01608/650-756). In Chipping Campden, try **Cotswold Country Cycles** (£12/day, tandems £25/day, daily 9:30–dusk, includes helmets, route maps, delivery for a fee, tours available, 1.5 miles north of town at Longlands Farm Cottage, tel. 01386/438-706, mobile 077/1500-2972, www.cotswoldcountrycycles.com).

By Foot: Walking guidebooks abound, giving you a world of choices for each of my recommended stops (choose one with clear maps). Villages are generally no more than three miles apart, and most have pubs that would love to feed and water you. For a list of guided walks, ask at any TI for the free AONB (Area of Outstanding Natural Beauty) brochure. The walks are free, range from two to 12 miles, and often involve a stop at a pub or tearoom (April–Sept).

By Car: Robinson's car-rental company, four miles outside Moreton-in-Marsh, offers one-day rentals from £25 including every-thing but gas. Figure a delivery charge of at least £1/mile to just about anywhere in the Cotswolds (Mon–Fri 8:30–17:00, Sat 8:30–12:30, closed Sun, tel. 01608/663-322, www.robgoss.co.uk).

Car hiking is great. Distances are minuscule. In this chapter, I cover the postcard-perfect (but discovered) villages. With a car and the local Ordnance Survey map, you can easily ramble about and find your

COTSWOLD APPRECIATION 101

Much history can be read into the names of the area. *Cotswold* could come from the Saxon phrase meaning "hills of sheep's coats." Or it could mean shelter ("cot" like cottage) on the open upland ("wold").

In the Cotswolds, a town's main street (called High Street) needed to be wide to accommodate the sheep and cattle being marched to market (and today, to park tour buses). Some of the most picturesque cottages were once humble row houses of weavers' cottages, usually located along a stream for their water wheels (Bibury, Castle Combe). The towns run on slow clocks and yellowed calendars. An entire village might not have a phone booth that accepts a telephone card.

Fields of yellow (rapeseed) and pale blue (linseed) separate pastures dotted with black and white sheep. In just about any B&B, when you open your window in the morning you'll hear sheep baaing. The decorative "toadstool" stones dotting front yards throughout the region are medieval staddle stones. Buildings were set upon these to keep the rodents out.

Cotswold walls and roofs are made of limestone. The limestone roof tiles hang by pegs. To make the weight more bearable, smaller, lighter tiles are higher up. An extremely strict building code keeps towns looking what many locals call "overly quaint."

The area is provincial and gossipy. People are ever so polite but commonly catch themselves saying, "It's all very... mmm...yyya." Rich people open their gardens to support their favorite charities, while—until recently—the less couth enjoyed "badger baiting" (a gambling cousin of cockfighting in which a badger, with his teeth and claws taken out, is mangled by right-wing dogs).

This is walking country. The English love their walks and vigorously defend their age-old right to free passage. Once a year the Rambling Society organizes a "Mass Trespass," when each of the country's 50,000 miles of public footpaths is walked. By assuring each path is used at least once a year, they stop landlords from putting up fences. Any paths found blocked are unceremoniously unblocked.

Questions to ask locals: Does badger baiting survive? Do you approve of foxhunting with hounds? Who are the Morris men? What's a kissing gate?

The Cotswolds

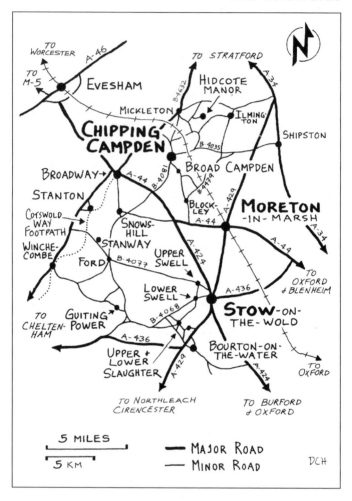

own gems. The problem with having a car is that you are less likely to walk. Try to taxi or bus somewhere so you can walk back to your car and enjoy the scenery.

By Taxi: Two or three taxi trips can make more sense than renting a car. While taking a cab cross-country seems extravagant at about £1.50 per mile, the distances are short (Stow-Moreton is 4 miles, Stow-Chipping Campden is 10), and one-way walks are lovely.

To scare up a taxi in Moreton, call Richard at Four Shires (mobile

077/4780-2555) or Iain's Taxis (tel. 07986/122-690); in Stow, call Iain (above) or Cotswold Safaris (tel. 01451/832-422); and in Chipping Campden, try Marnic Cars & Taxis (tel. 01386/840-014) or Cotswold Private Hire (tel. 07980/857-833).

By Tour: Departing from Bath, "Mad Max" Minibus Tours cover a sampling of the Cotswolds, including Stow-on-the-Wold, Stanton, Tetbury, and the Coln Valley (£20, runs Tue & Thu). Reserve online (www.madmaxtours.com, maddy@madmax.abel.co.uk) or by phone (Bath YMCA tel. 01225/325-900). Please honor or cancel your seat reservation. Also from Bath, Mad Max offers a tour of Stonehenge and Avebury that includes Castle Combe, a charming south Cotswold town (details on page 152).

From Stratford, you can catch the City Sightseeing tour (£17.50, early March–early Oct daily departures at 9:30 & 14:00, off-season one departure at 14:00, drive through 15 villages and stop briefly in Stanton, Chipping Campden, and Stow; buy ticket at and depart from City Sightseeing Tourism Centre on Rother Street, tel. 01789/294-466).

SIGHTS

North Cotswolds

▲▲**Chipping Campden**—Ten miles north of Stow-on-the-Wold and nearly as touristy, Chipping Campden (CAM-den) is a working market town, home of some incredibly beautiful thatched roofs and the richest Cotswold wool merchants. Both the great British historian George Macaulay Trevelyan and I call Chipping Campden's High Street the finest in England.

Walk the full length of High Street; its width is characteristic of market towns. Go around the block on both ends. On one end you'll find impressively thatched homes (out Sheep Street, past the public WC and ugly gas station, and right on Westington Street). Walking north on High Street you'll pass the Market Hall (built in 1627), the wavy roof of the first great wool mansion (the house of William Grevel, from 1380, on left), a fine and free memorial garden (on right), and, finally, the town's famous 15th-century Perpendicular Gothic "wool" church, down Church Street.

Chipping Campden's **TI** is in the Old Police Station on High Street (daily 10:00–17:30, town maps-20p, tel. 01386/841-206, www.chippingcampden.co.uk). For **Internet access,** try the library (High Street, near TI, spotty hours, reservations required, tel. 01386/840-692). For accommodations, see "Sleeping—Chipping Campden," page 178.

Stanton, Snowshill, and Guiting Power—Located between Chipping Campden and Stow, these are my nominations for the cutest Cotswold villages. Like marshmallows in hot chocolate, they nestle side by side,

COTSWOLD MARKET DAYS

Sleepy Cotswold villages wake up on their weekly market days, when stalls fill the sidewalks and everything from socks to bananas are for sale. If you're in town on a market day, take a stroll down High Street and tap into this local ritual. Arrive early for the best pickings and smaller crowds.

Monday: Cirencester (general retail)

Tuesday: Moreton-in-Marsh (general retail); Cirencester and Stratford-upon-Avon (both cattle)

Wednesday: Tetbury (general retail)

Thursday: Stow-on-the-Wold (farmers, 2nd Thu of month)

Friday: Cirencester, Stratford (both general retail), Warwick (farmers, 3rd Fri of month), Tetbury (farmers, 1st Fri of month)

Saturday: Cirencester (farmers, 2nd & 4th Sat of month), Stratford (farmers, 1st & 3rd Sat of month)

Sunday: Bourton (farmers, 4th Sun of month)

awaiting your arrival.

▲▲**Stanway House**—Stanway is notable for its manor house. Lord Neidpath, whose family tree charts relatives back to 1202, occasionally opens his melancholy home to visitors (£4, Aug–Sept Tue and Thu 14:00–17:00, tel. 01386/584-469).

The 14th-century Tithe Barn predates the manor and was originally where monks—in the days before money—would accept one-tenth of whatever the peasants produced. Peek inside—this is a great hall for village hoedowns.

While the Tithe Barn is no longer used to greet motley peasants with their feudal "rents," the lord still collects rents from his vast landholdings. The place feels like a time warp even though the lord has recently remarried.

Ask the ticket taker (inside) to demonstrate the spinning rent-collection table. In the great hall, marvel at the one-piece oak shuffleboard table and the 1780 Chippendale exercise chair (half an hour of bouncing on this was considered good for the liver).

The manor dogs have their own cutely painted "family tree," but Lord Neidpath admits that his current dog, CJ, is "all character and no breeding." The place has a story to tell. And so do the docents stationed in each room—modern-day peasants who, even without family trees, probably have relatives going back just as far in this village. Really. Talk to these people. Probe. Learn what you can about this side of England.

To get to Stanway by car, leave the B4077 at a statue of (the Christian) George slaying the dragon (of pagan superstition); you'll round the corner and see the manor's fine 17th-century Jacobean gatehouse (and the 70-foot-high, 18th-century fountain, if it's on). The only way to get to Stanway by (mostly) public transportation is by train from Moreton to Ashchurch (1.5 hours with transfer at Worcester Shrub Hill), then taxi to Stanway.

From Stanway to Stanton: These towns are separated by a great oak forest and grazing land, with parallel waves echoing the furrows plowed by medieval farmers. Centuries ago, farmers were allotted long strips of land called "furlongs." The idea was to dole out good and bad land equitably. (One square furlong equals an acre.) Over centuries of plowing these furrows were formed. Let someone else drive so you can hang out the window under a canopy of oaks as you pass stone walls and sheep. Leaving Stanway on the road to Stanton, the first building you'll see (on the left, just outside Stanway) is a thatched cricket pavilion overlooking the village cricket green. Dating only from 1930, it's raised up (as medieval buildings were) on rodent-resistant staddle stones. Stanton's just ahead (follow the signs).

▲▲**Stanton**—Pristine Cotswold charm cheers visitors up this village's main street. Stanton's Church of St. Michael betrays a pagan past. It's safe to assume any church dedicated to St. Michael (the archangel who fought the devil) sits upon a sacred pagan site. Stanton is actually at the intersection of two ley lines (lines of prehistoric sights). You'll see St. Michael's well-worn figure (with a sundial) above the door as you enter. Inside, above the capitals in the nave, find the pagan symbols for the sun and the moon. While the church probably dates back to the ninth century, today's building is mostly 15th century with 13th-century transepts. On the north transept, medieval frescoes weakly show through the 17th-century whitewash. (Once upon a time, medieval frescoes were considered too "papist.") Imagine the church interior colorfully decorated throughout. There's original medieval glass behind the altar. The list of rectors (left side wall) goes back to 1269. Finger the grooves in the back pews, worn away by sheepdog leashes. A man's sheepdog accompanied him everywhere.

Sleeping in Stanton: $ Vine B&B, an idyllic hideaway in a classic Cotswold home a block from the Stanton church, is run by Jill Carenza, who also rents horses by the hour (Ds/Db-£58, 4 rooms, most rooms with 4-poster beds, tel. 01386/584-250, fax 01386/584-385, luicarenza @msn.com).

▲**Snowshill Manor**—Another nearly edible little bundle of cuteness, Snowshill (SNOWS-hill) has a photogenic triangular square with a fine pub at its base. The Snowshill Manor is a dark and mysterious old palace filled with the lifetime collection of Charles Paget Wade. It's one big, musty celebration of craftsmanship, from finely carved spinning wheels to frightening samurai armor to tiny elaborate figurines carved by prisoners from the bones of meat served at dinner. Taking seriously his family motto, "Let Nothing Perish," Wade dedicated his life and fortune to preserving things finely crafted. The house (whose management made me promise not to promote it as an eccentric collector's pile of curiosities) really shows off Mr. Wade's ability to recognize and acquire fine examples of craftsmanship. It's all very...ummm...yyya. The manor overlooks the town square, but, ridiculously, it has no direct access from the town square—it aims to stoke business for the overpriced manor shop 300 yards away (£6, April–June and Sept–Oct Wed–Sun 12:00–17:00, closed Mon–Tue; July–Aug Wed–Mon 12:00–17:00, closed Tue; closed Nov–March, car park and shop are a pleasant 500-yard walk from the house—golf-cart-type shuttle available if desired, tel. 01386/852-410, www.nationaltrust.org.uk).

Broadway—With the new road allowing traffic to skirt the town, Broadway is cuter than ever. It's one of the postcard-pretty towns filled with inviting shops and fancy teahouses that visitors enjoy browsing through (a couple of miles west of Chipping Campden).

▲**Hidcote Manor**—If you like gardens, the grounds around this manor house are worth a look. Garden designers here pioneered the notion of creating a series of outdoor "rooms," each with a unique theme and separated by a yew-tree hedge. Follow your nose through a clever series of small gardens that lead delightfully from one to the next. Among the best in England, Hidcote gardens are at their fragrant peak in May, June, and July (£5.90, April–Oct Sat–Wed 10:30–17:00, closed Thu–Fri; closed Nov–March, tearoom, 4 miles northeast of Chipping Campden on B4035, tel. 01386/438-333, www.nationaltrust.org.uk/regions/severn).

Jill Carenza's Riding Centre—Anyone can enjoy the Cotswolds from the saddle. Jill Carenza's Riding Centre is set just outside Stanton village in the most scenic corner of the region. The facility has 50 horses and takes rank beginners on an hour-long scenic "hack" through the village and into the high country (£18/person for 1 hour, lessons available, plus longer rides, rides for experts, and pub tours; well signposted in Stanton, tel. 01386/584-250, www.cotswoldsriding.co.uk). For accommodations, see Jill's recommended Vine B&B in "Sleeping," page 173.

Central Cotswolds

▲▲**Stow-on-the-Wold**—With a name that means "meeting place on the uplands," Stow-on-the-Wold is the highest point of the Cotswolds. Despite its crowds, it retains its charm. Most of the tourists are day-trippers, so even summer nights are peaceful. Stow has no real sights other than itself, some good pubs, antique stores, and cute shops draped seductively around a big town square. Visit the church with its evocative old door guarded by ancient yew trees and the tombs of big shots (who made their money from wool) still boastful in death—find the tombs crowned with the bales of wool. A visit to Stow is not complete until you've locked your partner in the stocks on the green.

At the helpful **TI** on the main square, get the handy little 25p walking-tour brochure called "Town Trail" and the free "Cotswold Events" guide (Easter–Oct Mon–Sat 9:30–17:30, closed Sun, Nov–Easter closes at 16:30, tel. 01451/831-082). The TI also sells National Express Bus tickets, reserves tickets for events (Stratford plays) and rooms for a £2 fee (save money and book direct). **Internet access** is available at the erratically open library across from the TI. You can generally find a parking spot on the main square (free for 2 hrs). For accommodations, see "Sleeping," page 178.

▲**Moreton-in-Marsh**—This workaday town is like Stow or Chipping Campden without the touristic sugar. Rather than gift and antique shops you'll find streets lined with real shops: ironmongers selling cottage nameplates and carpet shops strewn with the remarkable patterns that decorate B&B floors. A traditional market with 260 stalls filling High Street gets the town shin-kicking each Tuesday as it has for the last 400 years (8:00–16:00, handicrafts, farmer produce, clothing, great people-watching, best if you go early). There is an economy outside of tourism in the Cotswolds, and you'll feel it here. Moreton has a tiny, sleepy train station two blocks from High Street, lots of bus connections, and a proficient **TI** (Mon–Fri 8:45–17:00, Thu 8:45–19:30, Sat 9:00–13:00, closed Sun, free "Town Trail" leaflet for self-guided walk, rail and bus schedules, and racks of fliers, tel. 01608/650-881). For accommodations, see "Sleeping," page 178.

For **Internet access,** try the library on High Street (open Tue & Thu, Fri afternoon and Saturday morning) or, if you're desperate, the clunky contraption at The Bell Inn pub across from the TI (daily 11:00–23:00). Public WCs are on Corders Lane, next to the Co-op on High Street (near bus stop).

▲**Bourton-on-the-Water**—I can't figure out if they call this "the Venice of the Cotswolds" because of its quaint canals or its miserable crowds. If you can avoid the midday and weekend crowds, it's worth a drive-through, a few cynical comments, and maybe a short stop. While mobbed with Japanese tour groups during the day, it's pleasantly empty in the early evening and after dark. Parking is predictably tough. Even during the busy business day, rather than park in the "pay and display" car park far from the center, drive right into town and wait for a spot on High Street just past the Green (a long row of 2-hr free spots in front of the Edinburgh Woolen Mills Shop).

Surrounding Bourton's green are sidewalks jammed with disoriented tourists with nametags and three sights worth considering: a Model Railway Exhibition (£2, daily 11:00–17:30, in the back of a hobby shop, with 3 impressive-only-to-train-buffs setups, tel. 01451/820-686, www.bourtonmodelrailway.co.uk); the light but fun

Model Village (£2.75, daily 9:00–16:45, a room full of tiny models showing off various bits of British life, tel. 01451/820-467); and the excellent Motor Museum (described below). Bourton is four miles south of Stow and a mile from the Slaughters.

▲**Motor Museum**—This fine little museum shows off a lifetime's accumulation of vintage cars, old lacquered signs, threadbare toys, and prewar memorabilia. Be sure to peek into the old-time vacation trailers and talk to an elderly Brit touring the place for some personal memories (£2.75, daily 10:00–18:00, closed Nov–Feb, in the mill facing the town center, Bourton-on-the-Water, tel. 01451/821-255).

Upper and Lower Slaughter—Lower Slaughter is a classic village, with ducks, a working water mill, and usually an artist busy at her easel somewhere. Just behind the skippable Old Mill Museum, two kissing gates lead to the path that goes to nearby Upper Slaughter. In Upper Slaughter, walk through the yew trees (sacred in pagan days) down a lane through the raised graveyard (a buildup of centuries of graves) to the peaceful church. In the back of the fine graveyard, the statue of a wistful woman looks over the tomb of an 18th-century rector (sculpted by his son). By the way, "Slaughter" has nothing to do with lamb chops. It comes from the sloe tree (the one used to make sloe gin). These towns are an easy two-hour round-trip walk from Bourton. You could also walk from Bourton through the Slaughters to Stow. The small roads from Upper Slaughter to Ford and Kineton are some of England's most scenic. Roll your window down and take a slow joyride.

South Cotswolds

▲**Cirencester**—Nearly 2,000 years ago, Cirencester (SIGH-ren-ses-ter) was the ancient Roman city of Corinium. It's 20 miles from Stow down A429, which was called Fosse Way in Roman times. In Cirencester, stop by the Corinium Museum to find out why they say, "If you scratch Gloucestershire, you'll find Rome" (opens in summer of 2004 after renovation). Cirencester's church is the largest of the Cotswolds "wool" churches. The cutesy Brewery Art crafts center and workshops entertain visitors with traditional weaving and potting, an interesting gallery, and a good coffee shop. Monday and Friday are general-market days, Tuesday is cattle-market day, Friday features an antique market, and Saturday is a crafts market. The **TI** is in the Cornhill Marketplace (Mon–Sat 9:30–17:30, closed Sun, tel. 01285/654-180).

▲**Northleach**—As one of the "untouched and untouristed" Cotswold villages, Northleach is so untouched, it's interesting only for a short stop. The town's impressive main square and church attest to its position as a major wool center in the Middle Ages. Park on the square to check out the TI (which has walking brochures), the mechanical music museum (described below), and the church. The fine Perpendicular Gothic church of St. Peter and St. Paul has been called the "cathedral of the

Cotswolds." It's one of the Cotswolds' top two "wool" churches (along with Chipping Campden's)—paid for by 15th-century "woolthy" merchants. Find the oldest tombstone. The brass plaques on the floor memorialize big shots, showing sheep and sacks of wool at their long-dead feet and inscriptions mixing Latin and the old English. You're welcome to do some brass rubbing if you get a permit from the post office (£2.50).

▲Keith Harding's World of Mechanical Music—This delightful little one-room place offers a unique opportunity to listen to 300 years of amazing self-playing musical instruments. It's run by well-respected men who are passionate about the restoration work they do on these instruments. The curators delight in demonstrating each one. You'll hear Victorian music boxes and the earliest polyphones (record players) playing cylinders and then discs. The £5 admission fee includes an essential hour-long tour (tours go constantly, join in progress, daily 10:00–18:00, last admission 16:45, guides usually take a break from 12:00–14:00, High Street, Lorthleach, tel. 01451/860-181).

▲Bibury—Six miles northeast of Cirencester, this is an entertaining but money-grubbing and not-very-friendly village with a trout farm, a Cotswolds museum, a stream teeming with fat fish and proud ducks, a row of very old weavers' cottages, and a church surrounded by rose-bushes, each tended by a volunteer of the parish. Don't miss the scenic Coln Valley drive from A429 to Bibury through the enigmatic villages of Coln St. Dennis, Coln Rogers, Coln Powell, and Winson.

▲▲▲Blenheim Palace—Too many palaces can send you into a furniture-wax coma. But everyone should see Blenheim. The Duke of Marlborough's home, the largest in England, is still lived in. And that's wonderfully obvious as you prowl through it. (Note: Americans who pronounce the place "blen-HEIM" are the butt of jokes. It's "BLEN-em.")

John Churchill, first duke of Marlborough, beat the French at the Battle of Blenheim in 1704. So the king built him this nice home, perhaps the finest Baroque building in England. Ten dukes of Marlborough later, it's as impressive as ever. The 2,000-acre yard, well designed by Lancelot "Capability" Brown, is as majestic to some as the palace itself. The view just past the outer gate as you enter is a classic. (The current 11th duke considers the 12th more of an error than an heir, and what to do about him is quite an issue.)

The well-organized palace tour begins with a fine **Churchill exhibit** centered around the bed in which Sir Winston was born in 1874 (prematurely...while his mother was at a Blenheim Palace party). Take your time in the Churchill exhibit. Then catch the guided tours (5/hr, 1 hr, included with ticket, £11.50, family rates, mid-March–Oct 10:30–17:30, last tour at 16:45, the park is open year-round, live tel. 01993/811-091, recorded info tel. 01993/811-325, www.blenheimpalace.com).

For a more extensive visit, follow up the general tour with a 30-minute guided walk through the actual **private apartments** of the duke. Tours leave at the top and bottom of each hour (£4, May–Sept 12:00–16:30, tickets are limited, buy from table in library—last room of main tour, enter in corner of courtyard to left of grand palace entry).

Kids enjoy the pleasure **garden** (a tiny train takes you from the palace parking lot to the garden, but, if you have a car, it's more efficient simply to drive there). A lush and humid greenhouse flutters with butterflies. A kid zone includes a few second-rate games and the "world's largest symbolic hedge maze." The maze is worth a look if you haven't seen one and could use some exercise. Churchill fans can visit his **tomb,** a short walk away, in the Bladon town churchyard.

The train station nearest Blenheim Palace (Hanborough, 1.5 miles away) has no taxi or bus service. Your easiest train connection is to Oxford; then take a bus to Blenheim (from the Oxford train station it's a 5-min walk to Gloucester Green bus station, then catch bus #20a, #20b, or #20c to the palace gate, Mon–Sat 8:55–17:00, Sun 10:00–15:30, 2/hr, 30-40 min; bus tel. 01865/772-250). From Moreton-in-Marsh you can either take the train to Oxford, or take a bus to Chipping Norton (20 min), then transfer to a bus to Woodstock Road (50 min; let bus driver know you are going to Blenheim).

Blenheim Palace sits at the edge of the cute cobbled town of Woodstock. For accommodations, consider the charming $$ **Blenheim Guest House** (Db-from £65, 17 Park Street, in town center, tel. 01993/813-814, fax 01993/813-810, www.theblenheim.com); $$ **The Townhouse,** a refurbished 18th-century stone house with five plush rooms (Sb-£50–55, Db-£65–75, Tb-£90–95, includes breakfast, afternoon tea & snacks on weekends, in town center, 15 High Street, tel. & fax 01993/810-843, www.woodstock-townhouse.com); or the grandmotherly $ **Wishaw House B&B** (one D-£45, 2 Browns Lane, 5-min walk from palace, tel. 01993/811-343, Pat Hillier).

SLEEPING

Chipping Campden
(area code: 01386)

$$$ **Noel Arms Hotel** is the characteristic old hotel on the main square and has welcomed guests for 600 years. Its lobby is decorated with armor, guns, and heraldry; its medieval air is infused with complex, but not unpleasant, odors; and its 26 rooms are well-furnished with antiques (Sb-£90, standard Db-£120, fancier four-poster Db-£135–140, some ground-floor doubles, attached restaurant-bar, High Street, tel. 01386/840-317, fax 01386/841-136, www.cotswold-inns-hotels.co.uk).

$$ **Lygon Arms Hotel** has small public areas and worn carpeting in the hallways, but the recently renovated non-smoking rooms are

SLEEP CODE

(£1 = about $1.60, country code: 44)

Sleep Code: **S** = Single, **D** = Double/Twin, **T** = Triple, **Q** = Quad, **b** = bathroom, **s** = shower only, **no CC** = Credit Cards not accepted. Unless noted otherwise, you can assume credit cards are accepted.

To help you sort easily through these listings, I've divided the rooms into three categories based on the price for a standard double room with bath:

$$$ **Higher Priced**—Most rooms £90 or more.
$$ **Moderately Priced**—Most rooms between £60–90.
$ **Lower Priced**—Most rooms £60 or less.

Chipping Campden is quaint without being overrun. Stow is more touristy but offers the widest range of accommodations. The plain town of Moreton is the only one of the three with a train station. If you have a car, consider grabbing the opportunity to really be away from it all in one of the smaller villages. In any town, B&Bs nearly always offer a better value than hotels.

If you want to take in a play, note that Stow, Chipping Campden, and Moreton are only a 30-minute drive from Stratford and an evening of classy entertainment.

cheerfully decorated, the open-beamed ceilings add charm, and the bathrooms come with all the modern comforts (Sb-£60–70, Ds-£65, Db-£75–90, High Street, tel. 01386/840-318, www.lygonarms.co.uk, Sandra Davenport).

$$ Badgers Hall B&B has three cozy, wood-beamed rooms in its medieval attic (Db-from £70, no CC, non-smoking, serves lunch, personal or traveler's check as deposit, center of High Street, tel. 01386/840-839, www.badgershall.com, badgershall@talk21.com, Karen and Paul Pinfold).

$ Sandalwood House B&B is a big, comfy, modern home with a royal lounge and a sprawling back garden. Just a five-minute walk from the center of town, it's in a quiet, woodsy, pastoral setting. Its two cheery pastel rooms are bright and spacious (D-£60, T-£68, no CC, no kids under age 7, non-smoking, friendly cat, go west on High Street, at church and Volunteer Inn turn right and right again, look for sign in hedge on left, head up long driveway, tel. & fax 01386/840-091, well run by Diana Bendall).

Chipping Campden

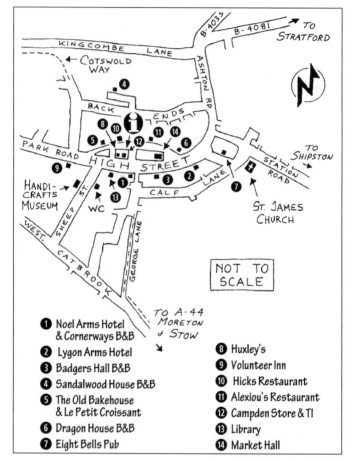

NOT TO SCALE

① Noel Arms Hotel & Cornerways B&B
② Lygon Arms Hotel
③ Badgers Hall B&B
④ Sandalwood House B&B
⑤ The Old Bakehouse & Le Petit Croissant
⑥ Dragon House B&B
⑦ Eight Bells Pub
⑧ Huxley's
⑨ Volunteer Inn
⑩ Hicks Restaurant
⑪ Alexiou's Restaurant
⑫ Campden Store & TI
⑬ Library
⑭ Market Hall

$ **The Old Bakehouse** rents five pleasant rooms, most with beams, in a 600-year-old home (Sb-£35, D/Db-£55, family deals, no CC, fun but dim attic room has beams running through it, small garden, parking, Lower High Street, tel. & fax 01386/840-979, oldbakehouse @chippingcampden-cotswolds.co.uk, Sarah Drinkwater).

$ **Dragon House B&B** rents tidy two-floor suites—with medieval beams—right on the center of High Street, with parking, laundry machines, and a sumptuous stay-awhile garden (Sb-£50, Db-£55, or £50/night if you stay 3 nights, no CC, near market hall, tel. & fax 01386/840-734, www .dragonhouse-chipping-campden.com, valatdragonhouse@btinternet.com,

Valerie and Graeme, the potter).

$ Cornerways is a kid-friendly, family-run B&B with light and airy loft rooms upstairs (Db-£60, Tb-£85, Qb-£105, ask about children's discount, parking, George Lane, just walk through the arch behind Noel Arms Hotel, tel. 01386/841-307, Carole Proctor).

Stow-on-the-Wold
(area code: 01451)

$$$ Stow Lodge Hotel, on the town square in its own sprawling and peaceful garden, offers 21 large, thoughtfully appointed rooms and stately public spaces (Sb-£60-105, Db-£75-130, closed Jan, non-smoking, The Square, tel. 01451/830-485, fax 01451/831-671, www.stowlodge.com, Hartley family).

$$ The Old Stocks Hotel, facing the town square, is a good value, even though the building itself is classier than its 18 big, simply furnished rooms. It's friendly and family-run, yet professional as can be. Beware the man-killer beams (Sb-£37.50, Db-£75–85, Tb-£112.50, family deals, attached bar and restaurant, garden patio, The Square, tel. 01451/830-666, fax 01451/870-014, www.oldstockshotel.co.uk, theoldstockshotel@fsmail.net, Jason & Helen Allen).

$$ Crestow House is a grand manor house dating from the 16th to 19th centuries with four fine rooms run with quiet class by Jorge, Frank, and their old standard poodle. They have also recently completed a tasteful renovation of a light, roomy cottage that sleeps up to six and has a kitchen. With a gracious spaciousness, antique furniture, a pool, and exercise equipment, this place mixes charm and character with modern-day amenities (Db-£75, £65 for 3 nights, cottage-£450–550/week in summer, £279/3 days in winter, children over 12 welcome, non-smoking, sunny-even-in-the-rain conservatory, 2 blocks from square, intersection of A429 and B4068, tel. 01451/830-969, fax 01451/832-129, www.crestow.co.uk, fsimonetti@btinternet.com).

$$ Chipping House B&B is a fine, warm, old place with three rooms and a cozy lounge—it feels like a visit to auntie's house (Db-£52-62, no CC, non-smoking, Park Street, tel. 01451/831-756, chippinghouse @tesco.net, dog-lovers Merv and Carolyne Oliver).

$ Cross Keys Cottage offers three attractive, smallish rooms in a well-maintained 350-year-old beamed cottage (D-from £55, Db-from £58, no CC, Park Street, tel. & fax 01451/831-128, rogxmag@hotmail .com, Margaret and Roger Welton).

$ Number Nine has three large, well-furnished rooms in a 200-year-old home—with watch-your-head beamed ceilings and old wooden doors (Db-£60–70, 9 Park Street, tel. 01451/870-333, numbernine @talk21.com, Trudi Elliott).

$ West Deyne B&B, with two cozy rooms, a peaceful garden, a fountain, and a small conservatory overlooking the countryside, has a

Stow-on-the-Wold

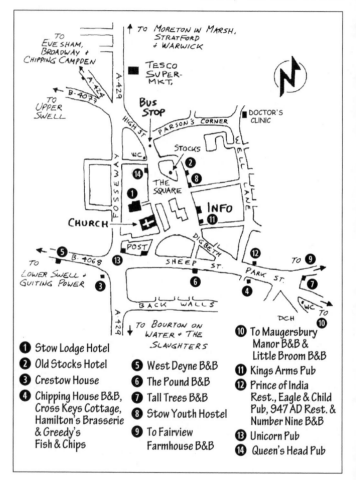

① Stow Lodge Hotel
② Old Stocks Hotel
③ Crestow House
④ Chipping House B&B,
   Cross Keys Cottage,
   Hamilton's Brasserie
   & Greedy's
   Fish & Chips

⑤ West Deyne B&B
⑥ The Pound B&B
⑦ Tall Trees B&B
⑧ Stow Youth Hostel
⑨ To Fairview
   Farmhouse B&B

⑩ To Maugersbury
   Manor B&B &
   Little Broom B&B
⑪ Kings Arms Pub
⑫ Prince of India
   Rest., Eagle & Child
   Pub, 947 AD Rest. &
   Number Nine B&B
⑬ Unicorn Pub
⑭ Queen's Head Pub

comforting grandmotherly charm (D-£40, no CC, evening tea and biscuits, parking, Lower Swell Road, tel. 01451/831-011, run by thoughtful Joan Cave).

$ **The Pound** is the quaint, 500-year-old yet fresh, heavy-beamed home of Patricia Whitehead. She offers two bright, inviting twin-bedded rooms and a classic old fireplace lounge (D-£40, no CC, non-smoking, downtown on Sheep Street, tel. & fax 01451/830-229, brent.ford@zoom.co.uk).

$ **Tall Trees B&B,** on the Oddington Road at the edge of Stow, rents six modern rooms in an old-style building overlooking a farm (Db-£50–60, family room-£60–80, no CC, 2 ground floor rooms, parking, tel. 01451/831-296, fax 01451/870-049, talltreestow@aol.com, run by Jennifer).

Hostel: The **Stow-on-the-Wold Youth Hostel,** on Stow's main square, has a friendly atmosphere, good hot meals, and a members' kitchen (dorm bed-£13, includes sheets, nonmembers-£2 extra, 48 beds in 9 rooms, some family rooms with private bathrooms, closed 10:00–17:00, laundry, lockers, reserve long in advance, tel. 01451/830-497, fax 01451/870-102, stow@yha.org.uk).

Near Stow-on-the-Wold

$ **Fairview Farmhouse B&B** feels more like a countryside mansion than a farmhouse. It's regally situated a mile outside Stow, and its six rooms come with all the thoughtful touches (Db-£50, deluxe Db-£60, no CC, non-smoking, just down Bledington Road, tel. & fax 01451/830-279, sdavis0145@aol.com, Susan and Andrew Davis).

$ **Holmleigh B&B,** in a working farmhouse in the nearby hamlet of Donnington, rents two rooms, the cheapest around (D-£32, no CC, open April–Oct, tel. 01451/830-792, the Garbetts).

In Maugersbury: The last two listings are in the hamlet of Maugersbury, an easy 10-minute walk from Stow. Here you'll find the peace Stow once had. To get to Maugersbury, drive (or walk) east on Park Street, taking the right fork to Maugersbury, then turn right on the road marked "No Through Road."

$ The ivy-covered **Maugersbury Manor** rents three huge rooms, one with countryside views, another a sprawling ground-floor suite with a kitchen. Although it could use some spiffing up, it's grand staying in what could be a haunted house (Db-£45–50, no CC, family deals, open March–Nov, non-smoking, tel. 01451/830-581, karen@manorholidays .co.uk, Mrs. Martin has lived here more than 40 years).

$ **Little Broom B&B,** a few doors down, has five cozy rooms to rent, a larger family room, and an open-air pool (S-£30, Db-£50–60, apartment Db-£60 for 2 plus £10 for each extra person, no CC, non-smoking, tel. 01451/830-510, fax 01451/830-313, www.completely-cotswold.com).

Moreton-in-Marsh
(area code: 01608)

A handy **launderette** is a block in front of the train station on New Road (Laundercentre, daily 7:30–20:00, £4.50 self-service, or drop off Mon-Fri 9:00–10:30 for £1 extra and same-day service, tel. 01608/650-888).

$$$ **Manor House Hotel** is Moreton's big old hotel, dating from 1545 but sporting such modern amenities as toilets, electricity, and a swimming pool. Its 38 classy-for-the-Cotswolds rooms and garden

Moreton-in-Marsh

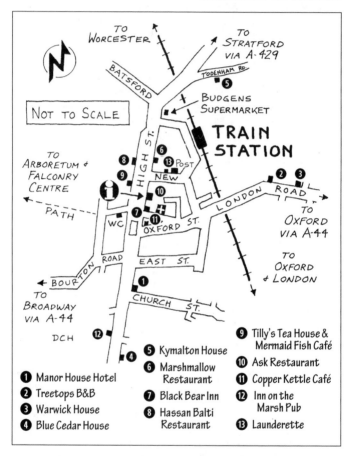

TO WORCESTER

TO STRATFORD VIA A·429

TODENHAM RD.

NOT TO SCALE

BATSFORD

BUDGENS SUPERMARKET

TRAIN STATION

HIGH ST.

TO ARBORETUM & FALCONRY CENTRE

POST

NEW

LONDON ROAD

TO OXFORD VIA A·44

PATH

WC

OXFORD ST.

TO OXFORD & LONDON

ROAD

EAST ST.

BOURTON

BOURTON

TO BROADWAY VIA A·44

DCH

CHURCH ST.

- 9 Tilly's Tea House & Mermaid Fish Café
- 5 Kymalton House
- 10 Ask Restaurant
- 6 Marshmallow Restaurant
- 11 Copper Kettle Café
- 1 Manor House Hotel
- 7 Black Bear Inn
- 12 Inn on the Marsh Pub
- 2 Treetops B&B
- 8 Hassan Balti Restaurant
- 13 Launderette
- 3 Warwick House
- 4 Blue Cedar House

invite relaxation (Sb-£115–155, Db-£135–200, family suite-£170–210, elevator, parking, log fire in winter, attached restaurant, on far end of High Street, away from train station, tel. 01608/650-501, fax 01608/651-481, www.cotswold-inns-hotels.co.uk).

$ Treetops B&B is plush, with six spacious, attractive rooms, a sun lounge, and a three-quarter-acre backyard. Liz and the family cat and dog will make you feel right at home (large Db-£45, gigantic Db-£50, ground-floor rooms have patios, easy parking, set far back from the busy road, London Road, tel. & fax 01608/651-036, www.treetopscotswolds.co.uk, treetops1@talk21.com, Liz and Brian Dean). It's an eight-minute walk from town and the railway station (exit station, keep left, go left on bridge over train tracks, look for sign, then long driveway).

$ **Warwick House,** just down the road, rents three rooms (Db-£42, no CC, will pick up from train station, access to nearby Fire Service College Leisure Club swimming pool, London Road, tel. 01608/650-773, www.snoozeandsizzle.com).

$ **Blue Cedar House** has four comfortable rooms and two bungalow apartments with an airy breakfast room full of plants. It's on a busy road but has double-paned windows and a pleasing setting, surrounded by a large garden (S-£24, D/Db-£48, apartment-£70, no CC, smoke-free, easy parking, 5-min walk from center, Stow Road, tel. 01608/650-299, gandsib@dialstart.net, Sandra and Graham Billinger).

$ **Kymalton House** has two recently-refurbished, bright rooms in a gracious house with a pleasant garden set back off a busy street just outside the town center (Db-£50, no CC, non-smoking, closed Dec–Jan, tel. 01608/650-487, mobile 0781-070-4952, Sylvia and Douglas Gould). It's a 10-minute walk from town (walk past Budgens supermarket, turn right on Todenham Road, look for house on the right).

Near Moreton-in-Marsh

For weeklong stays: Hope Cottage, a 250-year-old cottage nestled in the quaint village of Longborough a couple miles from Moreton, has three double bedrooms, two baths, a kitchen, conservatory, beamed ceilings, Cotswold stone flooring, and a cozy fireplace (£475-750 weekly, 3-day rentals may be available off-season, VCR, microwave, dishwasher, washer/dryer, between Moreton and Stow, U.S. tel. 949/494-4370, British tel. 01451/830-343, British fax 01451/832-043, www.hopecottage.com, cby25@aol.com, Cindy Young and Elizabeth Langton).

EATING

Chipping Campden

Locals like **Eight Bells,** a charming 14th-century inn on Leysbourne (daily, reservations recommended, tel. 01386/840-371); **Huxley's,** which is pricey but a good value (closed Mon–Tue, in town center on High Street); and **Bantam Tea Rooms** (daily until 17:00, High Street, opposite Market Hall).

Volunteer Inn serves decent pub grub (daily, grassy courtyard in back, Park Road) and so does the **Lygon Pub** (daily).

The chic brasserie **Hicks,** in the Cotswolds House Hotel, serves up specialties such as saffron risotto (£11–15 meals, daily 9:30–22:00, reservations recommended).

Alexiou's, a fun Greek restaurant on High Street, breaks plates at closing every Saturday night (closed Sun to clean up, tel. 01386/840-826).

Badgers Hall B&B makes a healthful lunch and afternoon tea (£7–8, Wed–Mon 10:30–16:30, closed Tue, High Street). **Le Petit**

Croissant, a great little French deli with a cozy tearoom in the back, serves pastries, quiche, cheese, and wine (closed Sun–Mon and from 14:00–14:30, Lower High Street, tel. 0386/841-870).

The small **Campden Store,** on High Street, is the town's main grocery (Mon–Sat 7:00–22:00, Sun 8:00–22:00).

Stow-on-the-Wold

These places are all within a five-minute walk of each other either on the main square or downhill on Queen and Park Streets.

The formal but friendly bar in **Stow Lodge** serves fine £7 lunches and a popular £19.50 three-course dinner (daily 12:00–14:00 & 19:00–20:45, smoke-free, veggie options, good wines; also have pricier restaurant; just off main square).

The Kings Arms, across the square, dishes up fresh local fare with a Mediterranean flavor in a pubby wood-beamed ambience complete with fireplace (daily 12:30–14:30 & 6:00–9:30, tel. 01451/830-364).

The Prince of India serves good Indian food in a delightful atmosphere (nightly 18:00–23:30, Park Street, tel. 01451/870-821).

The Eagle and Child Pub serves delicious food at good prices in a stripped-down pub (food Mon–Sat 12:00–14:00 & 18:00–22:00, Sun 12:00–15:00 & 18:00–21:00, non-smoking section, Park Street, tel. 01451/830-670). To go upscale, step up to their new adjoining restaurant, **947 A.D.** (named for the building's original construction date), where the old beams got a major makeover and the food looks like sculpture (two-course dinner-£18, three-course dinner-£22, less for lunch, Tue–Sat, brunch Sun, closed Mon, tel. 01451/830-670).

Locals also like **The Unicorn** pub (daily 12:00–14:00 & 18:00-21:30, Sheep Street).

For fancy and expensive high Brit/Euro cuisine in sleek ambience, consider **Hamilton's Brasserie** (£20 dinners, Mon–Sat, Sun lunch only, last orders at 14:30 and 21:30, Park Street, tel. 01451/831-700).

Greedy's Fish and Chips on Park Street is a favorite with locals (Mon–Sat 12:00–14:00 & 16:30–21:00).

The **Queen's Head,** next door to the Stow Lodge—with a classic pub ambience—doesn't serve food, but it's a great place to bring your dog, smoke a cigarette, and drink the local Cotswold brew, Donnington Ale (closed Sun).

Fine Cuisine in Great Country Pubs near Stow-on-the-Wold

These three places are known for their great £10 meals and fine settings. All are very popular, so arrive early or call in a reservation. These pubs allow "well-behaved children," and are practical only for those with a car. The first two (in Oddington, 2 miles from Stow) are more trendy and fresh, yet still in a traditional pub setting. The Plough (in Ford, a few miles farther away) is your jolly-old dark pub.

The Horse and Groom Village Inn in Upper Oddington is a smart place with a sea-grass-green carpet in a 16th-century inn, serving modern English food with a good wine list (daily 12:00–14:00 & 19:00–21:30, non-smoking section, tel. 01451/830-584).

The Fox Inn in Lower Oddington is old but fresh and famous among locals for its quality cooking (Mon–Sat 12:00–14:00 & 18:30–22:00, Sun 19:00–21:30, also rents 3 good doubles—£58–85, tel. 01451/870-555).

The Plough Inn fills a fascinating old building—once an old coaching inn and later a courthouse. Ask the bar staff for some fun history—like what "you're barred" means. It takes no reservations, so arrive early (Mon–Sun 12:00–14:00 & 18:30–21:00, 4 miles from Stow on Tewkesbury Road in hamlet of Ford, tel. 01386/584-215).

Moreton-in-Marsh

A stroll up and down High Street lets you survey your small-town options. Consider the upscale but affordable **Marshmallow** with a menu including traditional English dishes as well as lasagna and cannelloni (£8–11 entrées, 15 different teas, Tue–Sun 10:00–20:00, closed Mon, reservations advised, back garden for summer dining, tel. 01608/651-536).

The **Black Bear Inn** offers traditional English food (£5–8 meals, daily specials, daily 12:00–14:00 & 18:30–21:00, after entering, head to dining room on the left, pub on the right, tel. 01608/652-992).

The friendly **Hassan Balti,** with tasty Bangladeshi food, is a fine value for sit-down or takeout (daily 12:00–14:00 & 18:00–23:30, tel. 01608/650-798).

Tilly's tea house serves fresh soups, salads, sandwiches, and pastries for lunch in a cheerful spot on High Street across from the TI (£3–5 light meals, daily 9:00-17:00, tel. 01608/650-000).

Ask, a chain restaurant across the street, has decent pastas, pizzas, salads, and a breezy, family-friendly atmosphere (£7 pizzas, daily, takeout available, tel. 01608/651-119).

Mermaid Fish is popular for its take-out fish and tasty selection of traditional pies (closed Sun), and the **Budgens** supermarket is indeed super (Mon–Sat 8:00–22:00, Sun 10:00–16:00, far end of High Street). There are picnic tables across the busy street in pleasant Victoria Park.

For a light bite or sandwiches to go, consider **Copper Kettle** on Oxford Street (Mon–Sat 10:00–16:30, closed Sun).

The **Inn on the Marsh** pub offers good pub grub; a great selection of ales and wine; a separate, cozy non-smoking dining area; and a cute back garden (Mon–Sat 12:00–14:00 & 19:00–21:00, Sun 19:00–20:30, 2-min walk from center, directly across street from library on road to Stow, tel. 01608/650-709).

TRANSPORTATION CONNECTIONS

Moreton, the only Cotswolds town with a train station, also has good bus connections.

Moreton by bus to: Chipping Campden and **Stratford** (9/day, same bus connects all 3 towns, Moreton-Chipping Campden 25 min, Moreton-Stratford 1 hr, First Midland Red buses, tel. 01905/763-888), **Blenheim** (involves a transfer: catch bus to Chipping Norton, 2/day, 20 min; then catch bus to Woodstock Road, tell driver you want to stop at Blenheim, nearly hrly, 50-min trip), **Cirencester** via **Stow** and **Burton** (13/day, Moreton-Cirencester 1 hr, Moreton-Stow 10 min, Beaumont buses, tel. 01452/390-770), **Cheltenham** (8/day, Moreton-Cheltenham 1 hr, with stops at a few nontouristy towns, Pulham buses, tel. 01451/820-369). Ask for specific schedules at a local TI. Generally, buy tickets from the driver.

Moreton by train to: London's Paddington Station (one way-£23, round trip after 8:00-£21, 10/day, 1.75 hrs; One-Day Travelcard for £23.70 includes round-trip and London tube travel), **Heathrow** (10/day, 2.5 hrs, train to Reading, then RailAir Link shuttle bus to airport), **Bath** (10/day, 1.5 hrs, transfers at Oxford and Didcot Parkway), **Oxford** (10/day, 40 min), **Ironbridge Gorge** (1/hr, 3.5 hrs, with transfers at Worcester Shrub Hill and Birmingham New Street, arrive Telford, then catch bus or cab 7 miles to Ironbridge Gorge). Train info: tel. 08457-484-950.

Drivers' Tips: Distances are wonderfully short (but only if you invest in the Ordnance Survey map of the Cotswolds—sold locally at TIs and newsstands). **Moreton** to: **Broadway** (10 miles), **Chipping Campden** (8 miles), **Stratford** (17 miles), **Warwick** (23 miles), **Stow** (4 miles).

Near the Cotswolds: Stratford, Warwick, and Coventry

Stratford is Shakespeare's hometown. To see or not to see? A walking tour with a play is the thing to bring the Bard to life in this touristy town. Explore Warwick, England's finest medieval castle; and stop by Coventry, a blue-collar town with a spirit that Nazi bombs couldn't destroy.

Planning Your Time

Stratford, Warwick, and Coventry are a made-to-order day for drivers connecting the Cotswolds with Ironbridge Gorge (IBG) or North Wales. While connections from the Cotswolds to IBG are tough, Stratford, Warwick, and Coventry are well served by public transportation.

Stratford is a classic tourist trap. But since you're passing through, it's worth a half-day (and an overnight if you take in a play). Warwick is

From the Cotswolds to North Wales

England's single most spectacular castle. It's very touristy but historic and fun for three hours. Have lunch in Warwick town. Coventry, the least-important stop on a quick trip, is most interesting as a chance to see a real, struggling, north-English industrial city (with some decent sightseeing).

If you're speedy, hit all three sights on a one-day drive-through. If you're more relaxed, see a play and stay in Stratford, then stop by Warwick and Coventry the following morning en route to your next destination.

Stratford-upon-Avon

Stratford is the most overrated tourist magnet in England, but nobody back home would understand if you skipped Shakespeare's house. The old town is compact, with the TI and theater along the riverbank and Shakespeare's birthplace a few blocks off the river; you can walk easily to everything except Anne Hathaway's and Mary Arden's places. The river has an idyllic yet playful feel, with a park along the opposite bank, paddleboats, and an old, one-man, crank-powered ferry just beyond the theater.

Tourist Information: Pick up a free Attractions map at the TI (April–Oct Mon–Sat 9:30–17:30, Sun 10:30–16:30; Nov–March Mon–Sat 9:00–17:00, Sun 10:00–15:00, room-finding service-£3, Bridgefoot, tel. 01789/293-127, www.shakespeare-country.co.uk).

Helpful Hints

Internet Access: The Cyber Junction is across from the Teddy Bear Museum (Mon–Fri 10:00-18:00, closes at 17:30 Sat and 17:00 Sun, 28 Greenhill Street, tel. 01789/263-400) or the library on Henley Street just below Shakespeare's Birthplace (daily, tel. 01789/292-209).

Taxis: Try 007 Taxis (tel. 01789/414-007) or Platinum Cars (tel. 01789/264-626).

Launderette: Sparklean is a 10-minute walk from the city center and near the Grove Road and Broad Walk B&Bs (daily 8:00–21:00, self-serve wash-£3.20, 4-hour drop off service for laundry delivered before noon, 74 Bull Street, tel. 01789/269-075).

TOURS

Stratford and Beyond

City Sightseeing Bus Tours' open-top buses constantly make the rounds, allowing visitors to hop on and hop off at every sight in town. The full circuit takes about an hour and comes with a steady and informative commentary (£7.50, buses leave from Pen & Parchment Inn by the TI every 15 min 9:00–17:40, live guide on the hour and half-hour, otherwise taped commentary, buses generally run every 30 min in winter, buy tickets on bus or at TI, tel. 01789/294-466).

City Sightseeing offers longer tours of the **Cotswolds** (£17.50, late March–early Oct daily departures at 9:30 & 14:00, off-season one departure at 14:00, drive through 15 villages with brief stops in Stanton—15 min, Chipping Campden—20 min, and Stow—30 min, buy ticket at and depart from City Sightseeing Tourism Centre on Rother Street, tel. 01789/294-466).

If you've got a king-sized appetite for **castles,** consider City Sightseeing's guided hop-on, hop-off castle tours offering various combinations of Warwick and two other nearby spreads, Kenilworth and Charlecote (£12.50–27.50 depending on the combination, includes entry, £8 for bus ride only, daily departures May–Sept every 2 hours starting at 10:00 from Civic Hall on Rother Street, tel. 01789/294-466, 24-hr line 01708/866-000).

SIGHTS

▲**Shakespeare's Birthplace**—This half-timbered Elizabethan building is furnished as it was when young William was growing up and is filled with bits about his life and work. It was restored in the 1800s after serving variously as a pub and a butcher's shop after Shakespeare's kin vacated. This sight is most worthwhile if you get the attendants in each room talking. Ask questions. The attached Shakespeare exhibition gives a fine historical background.

While William Shakespeare (1564–1616) was born in this house, he spent most of his career in London, where he taught his play-going public about human nature with plots that entertained the both the highest and the lowest minds. His tool was an unrivaled mastery of the English language. He retired—rich and famous—back in Stratford, spending his last five years at a house called New Place.

Little is known about Shakespeare the man. The scope of his brilliant work, his humble beginnings, and the fact that no original Shakespeare manuscripts survive raise a few scholarly eyebrows. While some wonder who penned all these plays, most scholars accept his authorship (£6.50, June–Aug Mon–Sat 9:00–17:00, Sun 9:30–17:00; April–May and Sept–Oct Mon–Sat 10:00–17:00, Sun 10:30–17:00; Nov–March Mon–Sat 10:00–16:00, Sun 10:30–16:00, last admission 60 min before closing, in town center, tel. 01789/204-016, www.shakespeare.org.uk).

▲**Other Shakespeare Properties**—Shakespeare's hometown is blanketed with opportunities for Bardolatry. There are four other Shakespearean properties, all run by the Shakespeare Birthplace Trust, in and near Stratford. Each has a garden and helpful docents who love to tell a story.

Anne Hathaway's Cottage, a mile out of town in Shottery, is a picturesque thatched 12-room farmhouse where the bard's wife grew up. It has little to do with Shakespeare but offers an intimate peek at lifestyles in Shakespeare's day. Guides in each room do their best to lecture to the stampeding hordes (£5, June–Aug Mon–Sat 9:00–17:00, Sun 9:30–17:00; opens a half-hour later April–May and Sept–Oct; Nov–March Mon–Sun 10:00–16:00).

Mary Arden's House, the girlhood home of William's mom, is in Wilmcote, about three miles from town. This 16th-century farmhouse sees far fewer tourists, so the guides in each room have a chance to do a little better guiding (£5.50, June–Aug Mon–Sat 9:30–17:00, Sun 10:00–17:00; opens a half-hour later April–May and Sept–Oct; Nov–March Mon–Sat 10:00–16:00, Sun 10:30–16:00). A 19th-century farming exhibit and a falconry demonstration are on the grounds.

Hall's Croft, the home of Shakespeare's daughter, who married a doctor, is in the town. This fine old Tudor house, the richest house of the group, is interesting only if you're into 16th-century medicine

Stratford-upon-Avon

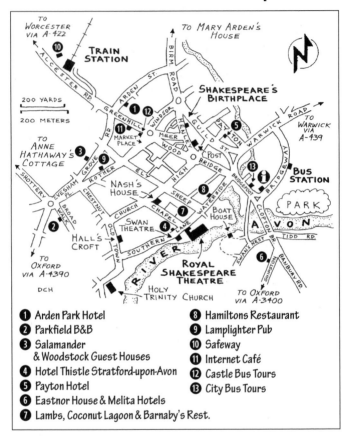

1 Arden Park Hotel
2 Parkfield B&B
3 Salamander & Woodstock Guest Houses
4 Hotel Thistle Stratford-upon-Avon
5 Payton Hotel
6 Eastnor House & Melita Hotels
7 Lambs, Coconut Lagoon & Barnaby's Rest.
8 Hamiltons Restaurant
9 Lamplighter Pub
10 Safeway
11 Internet Café
12 Castle Bus Tours
13 City Bus Tours

(£3.50, June–Aug Mon–Sat 9:30–17:00, Sun 10:00–17:00; opens at 10:00 April–May and Sept–Oct; Nov–March opens at 11:00).

Nash's House, built beside New Place, the house where Shakespeare retired, is the least impressive of the properties. (Nash was the first husband of Shakespeare's granddaughter.) While Shakespeare's New Place is long gone, Nash's house has survived. It has the town's only general-history exhibit—fascinating if you like chips of Roman pottery (£3.50, same hours as Hall's Croft). Pilgrims save money buying combo-tickets: £9 for three sights, or £13 for all.

Shakespeare's grave is in the riverside Holy Trinity Church (a 10-min walk past the theater).

Avon Riverfront—The River Avon is a playground with swans and canal boats. These canal boats, which saw their workhorse days during a short window of time between the start of the Industrial Revolution and the establishment of the railways, are now mostly pleasure boats. They are long and narrow, so two can pass in the narrow canals. There are 2,000 miles of canals here in the Midlands. These were built to connect centers of industry with seaports and provided vital transport during the early days of the Industrial Revolution.

▲▲**Royal Shakespeare Company**—The RSC, undoubtedly the best Shakespeare company on earth, performs year-round in Stratford and London (see page 91). If you're a Shakespeare fan, see if the RSC schedule fits into your itinerary either here or in London. Tickets in Stratford range from £5 (standing) to £42 (Mon–Sat at 19:30, Thu and Sat matinees at 13:30, no shows Sun, standing tickets available in advance at the White Swan theater and the day of performance only at the Royal Shakespeare Theatre). You'll probably need to buy your tickets ahead of time, although 50 restricted-view and standing-room places are saved to be sold each morning in person at the box office (from 9:30, £5–14) and returned tickets can sometimes be picked up with cash the evening of an otherwise-sold-out show (box office window open Mon–Sat 9:30–20:00, closed Sun, tel. 01789/403-403, ticket hotline open Mon–Sat from 9:00, tel. 0870-609-1110, www.rsc.org.uk). If you're feeling bold, buy a £5 standing ticket and then slip into an open seat as the lights dim—if there's not something available right away, chances are there will be plenty of seats after intermission. (Before the show, theater-goers pack the adjoining restaurant, Quarto's, which overlooks the Avon but has mediocre food; you'll eat better at the recommended eateries listed below.)

Theater **tours** are given most days (£4, 13:30 and 17:30 if no matinee; at 11:30 and 17:30 on matinee days and Sat; Sun on the hour from noon-15:00; tours also given after performances, schedule subject to change—call to check, good idea to book in advance, but sometimes available on the spot, booking Mon–Sat 9:30–17:30, Sun 11:30–16:00, tel. 01789/403-405).

The theater also sponsors "Shakespeare's Life in Stratford" **walks** (£6, Sat at 10:30 plus July–Sept Thu at 10:30, 2 hrs).

SLEEPING

(£1 = about $1.60, country code: 44, area code: 01789)
If you want to spend the night after you catch a show, options abound. Ye olde timbered hotels are scattered through the city center. Most B&Bs are on busy streets on the fringes of town. Unless otherwise noted, breakfast is included and the rooms are all non-smoking.

West of the City Center

$$ **Arden Park Hotel,** just around the corner from Shakespeare's birthplace, has nine attractive rooms, a garden, and a lounge with free Internet access (Db-£62, 6 Arden Street, tel. 01789/262-126).

$ **Parkfield** B&B has seven colorful rooms, a garden and parking out back, and clippings of theater reviews in the lounge. Some rooms have shower and toilet; the others have private facilities in the hall—the price is the same for either (Sb-£26, Db-£46, special breakfast menu available upon request, can book theater tickets, 3 Broad Walk, tel. & fax 01789/293-313, www.parkfieldbandb.co.uk, parkfield@btinternet.com).

$ **Salamander Guest House,** run by gregarious Frenchman Pascal and his wife Anna, rents seven well-priced, simple rooms on a busy street across from a small garden on the edge of town (S-£18–30, Db-£36–60, Tb-£54–90, Qb-£75–100, 40 Grove Road, tel. & fax 01789/205-728, www.salamanderguesthouse.co.uk, p.delin@btinternet.com, Pascal & Anna).

$ **Woodstock Guest House,** just down the block, is a friendly, frilly, pink, place with comfortable rooms (D/Db-£60, family room-£72-80, 30 Grove Road, tel. 01789/299-881, www.woodstock-house.co.uk).

The City Center

$$$ **Thistle Stratford-upon-Avon,** with 63 smallish, hotelesque rooms, sits right across from the theaters. There's a clubby lounge upstairs, a terrace off the dining room, and sandwiches available after the show (Db-£130–180, attached restaurant, theater packages available, some non-smoking rooms, Waterside, tel. 0870-333-9146, fax 0870-333-9246, www.stratfordthistle.co.uk).

$$ **The Payton,** tucked away on John Street, has a central but quiet location and five tight but pleasant rooms (Sb-£42, Db-£68, discounts available during the week, 6 John Street, tel. & fax 01789/266-442, www.thepayton.com).

Southeast of the River

A handful of attractive B&Bs line Shipston Road, with racing traffic in the front and peaceful gardens and a pathway to the theater in the back.

$$ **Eastnor House Hotel** has 10 appealing rooms, wide stairways, and a comfortable lounge with an Internet connection (Sb-£45–49, Db-£69–79, Tb-£105, 33 Shipston Road, 01789/268-115, www.eastnorhouse.com, enquiries@eastnorhouse.com, Derek & Barbara Janes).

$$ **Melita Hotel** welcomes the after-theater crowd with a relaxing lounge and honor bar. The dozen rooms are tastefully decorated and the back garden is a welcome refuge (S-£39, Sb-£49, Db-£54–82, family rooms-£92–115, 37 Shipston Road, tel. 01789/292-432, fax 01789/204-876, www.melitahotel.co.uk, info@melitahotel.co.uk, Patricia & Russell Andrews).

Hostel: **Hemmingford House** is a 10-minute bus ride from town (132 beds in 2- to 10-bed rooms, from £16.50/bed, take bus #X18, #18, or #77 to Alveston, tel. 01789/297-093, stratford@yha.org.uk).

EATING

Stratford's numerous eateries vie for your pre- and post-theater business with special hours and meal deals. Most offer light two- and three-course menus from 17:30–19:00. You'll find them lined up along Sheep Street and Waterside. Here are several good options.

The Coconut Lagoon serves tasty, spicy nouveau South Indian cuisine (pre-theater two-course menu-£10, three-course-£13, daily, 21 Sheep Street, tel. 01789/293-546).

Lambs assembles meat, fish and veggie dishes with panache (pre-theater two-course menu-£11.50, three-course menu-£14, daily, 12 Sheep Street, tel. 01789/292-554).

Hamiltons has creative light bites for lunch on weekdays and a daily evening menu with starters that work as small meals (£5–7 starters, £11–15 entrées, daily 10:30-23:00, 8 Waterside, tel. 01789/209-109).

Barnaby's is a decent fish and chips joint near the theater (daily, at Sheep Street and Waterside).

The **Lamplighter** is a friendly pub that serves dinner only on weekdays (Mon–Thu 18:00–21:00, 42 Rother Street, tel. 01789/293-071).

For groceries, try **Somerfield** in the Town Centre mall (daily) or the huge **Safeway** next to the train station (Mon–Sat 8:00–20:00, Sun 10:00–16:00, pharmacy, tel. 01789/267-106).

TRANSPORTATION CONNECTIONS

To: London (4 trains/day, 2.5 hrs, direct to Paddington Station), **Chipping Campden** (9 buses/day, 1 hr, on First Midland Red bus, tel. 01905/763-888), **Warwick** (hrly, 15 min, by train or Stagecoach bus, tel. 01926/422-462), **Coventry** (1 bus/hr, 1 hr, tel. 01788/535-555). Train info: tel. 08457-484-950.

Driving is easy: Stow to Stratford (20 miles), Warwick (8 miles), and Coventry (10 miles).

Warwick and Coventry

▲▲**Warwick Castle**—England's finest medieval castle is almost too groomed and organized, giving its hordes of visitors a decent value for the steep £13.50 entry fee (includes gardens and all the castle attractions). This cash-poor but enterprising lord hired the folks at Madame Tussaud's to wring maximum tourist dollars out of the castle. The latest marketing strategy is to build up the "kingmaker" reputation of the Earl of Warwick (WAR-ick).

With a lush, green, grassy moat and fairy-tale fortifications, Warwick will entertain you from dungeon to lookout. Standing inside the castle gate, you can see the mound where the original Norman castle of 1068 stood. Under this "motte," the wooden stockade, or "bailey," defined the courtyard as the castle walls do today. The castle is a 14th- and 15th-century fortified shell holding an 18th- and 19th-century royal residence surrounded by another dandy "Capability" Brown landscape job.

There's something for every taste—a fine and educational armory, a terrible torture chamber, a recently restored mill and engine house, a knight in shining armor on a horse that rotates with a merry band of musical jesters, a Madame Tussaud re-creation of a royal weekend party with an 1898 game of statue-maker, a grand garden, and a peacock-patrolled, picnic-perfect park. The Great Hall and Staterooms are the sumptuous highlights. The "King Maker" exhibit (It's 1471, and the townsfolk are getting ready for battle...) is highly promoted but not quite as good as a Disney ride. Be warned: The tower is a one-way, no-return, 250-step climb offering a view not worth a heart attack. The £3 audio-guide provides 60 easy-listening minutes of number-coded descriptions of the individual rooms (rent from kiosk on lane after turnstile). The £3.95 guidebook gives you nearly the same script in souvenir-booklet form. Either is worthwhile if you want to understand the various rooms. If you tour without help, pick the brains of the earnest and talkative docents (£13.50, April–Oct daily 10:00–18:00, Nov–March daily 10:00–17:00, 10-min walk from Warwick train station, tel. 0870-442-2000, 24-hr recorded message, www.warwick-castle.co.uk). The Stables self-service restaurant upstairs is much nicer than the cafeteria near the turnstiles. From the castle, a lane leads into the old-town center, a block away, where you'll find the TI (daily 9:30–16:30, tel. 01926/492-212), doll museum, county museum, and several pubs serving fine lunches.

Sleeping in Warwick: Friendly **Forth House** rents two suites in a restored 16th-century house and stable in the center of Warwick a short walk from the castle (suites for 2-3 people-£68-75, non-smoking, 44 High Street, tel. 01926/401-512, www.forthhouseuk.co.uk, Elizabeth Draisey).

▲**Coventry**—The Germans bombed Coventry to smithereens in 1940. From that point on, the German phrase for "to really blast the heck out of a place" was "to coventrate" it. But Coventry rose from its ashes, and its message to our world is one of forgiveness and reconciliation. The symbol of Coventry is the bombed-out hulk of its old cathedral with the huge new one adjoining it. The inspirational complex welcomes visitors. Climb the tower (£1.50, 180 steps, daily 9:00–16:30, tel. 02476/267-070).

Coventry's most famous hometown girl, Lady Godiva, rode bare-back through the town in the 11th century to help lower taxes. You'll see her bronze statue a block from the cathedral (near Broadgate). Just beyond that is the Coventry Transport Museum—the first, fastest, and most famous cars and motorcycles came from this British "Detroit" (free, daily 10:00–17:00). Other sights include the Herbert Art Gallery and Museum, which cover the city's history (free, Mon–Sat 10:00–17:30, Sun 12:00–17:00), and St. Mary's Guildhall, with 14th-century tapestries, stained glass, and an ornate ceiling (free, Easter–Sept Sun–Thu 10:00–16:00, closed Fri–Sat, during events, and off-season).

Browse through Coventry, the closest thing to normal, everyday, urban England you'll see. Get a map at the TI (Mon–Fri 9:30–16:30, Sat–Sun 10:00–16:30, Bayley Lane, tel. 02476/227-264).

TRANSPORTATION CONNECTIONS

Route Tips for Drivers

Stratford to Ironbridge Gorge via Warwick and Coventry: Entering Stratford from the Cotswolds, you cross a bridge. Veer right (following *Through Traffic, P,* and *Wark* signs), go around the block—turning right and right and right over the speed bumps—then enter the multistory garage (60p/hr, £6/day, you'll find no place easier or cheaper). The TI and City Sightseeing/Guide Friday bus stop are a block away. Leaving the garage, circle to the right around the same block but stay on "the Wark" (Warwick Road, A439). Warwick is eight miles away. The castle is just south of town on the right. If the free castle lot is full, you'll be directed to a city lot. You might lurk across the street until someone leaves. After touring the castle, carry on through the center of Warwick and follow signs to Coventry (still A439, then A46). If stopping in Coventry, follow signs painted on the road into the "city centre" and then to cathedral parking. Grab a place in the high-rise car park. Leaving Coventry, follow signs to Nuneaton and M6 North through lots of sprawl, and you're on your way. If you're skirting Coventry, take the M69 (Leicester) to M6. M6 threads through giant Birmingham. Try to avoid the 14:00–20:00 rush hour (see Ironbridge Gorge chapter for tips). From M6 (northwest), take M54 to the Telford/Ironbridge exit. Follow the *Ironbridge* signs and do-si-do through a long series of roundabouts until you're there.

IRONBRIDGE GORGE

The Industrial Revolution was born in the Severn River Valley. In its glory days, this valley (blessed with abundant deposits of iron ore and coal and a river for transport) gave the world its first iron wheels, steam-powered locomotive, and cast-iron bridge. The museums in Ironbridge Gorge (IBG) take you back into the days when Britain was racing into the modern age and pulling the rest of the West with her.

Planning Your Time

Without a car, IBG isn't worth the headache. Drivers can slip it in between the Cotswolds/Stratford/Warwick and North Wales. Speed demons zip in for a midday tour of Blists Hill, look at the bridge, and speed out. For an overnight visit, arrive in the early evening to browse the town and spend the morning and early afternoon touring the sights before driving on to North Wales (10:00-Museum of the Gorge, 11:00-Blists Hill Victorian Town for lunch and sightseeing, 15:30-Drive to Wales).

With a month in Britain, I'd spend two nights and a leisurely day: 9:30-Iron Bridge and the town, 10:30-Museum of the Gorge, 11:30-Coalbrookdale Museum of Iron, 14:30-Blists Hill, dinner at Coalbrookdale Inn.

ORIENTATION

(area code: 01952)

The town is just a few blocks gathered around the Iron Bridge, which spans the peaceful, tree-lined Severn River. While the smoke-belching bustle is long gone, knowing that this wooded, sleepy river valley was the Silicon Valley of the 19th century makes wandering its brick streets almost a pilgrimage. The actual museum sites are scattered over three miles. The modern cooling towers (for coal, not nuclear energy) that loom ominously over these red-brick remnants seem strangely appropriate.

Tourist Information: The TI is in the tollhouse on the Iron Bridge (Mon–Fri 9:00–17:00, Sat–Sun 10:00–17:00, room-finding service, tel. 01952/432-166). The TI has lots of booklets for sale; hikers like the homegrown *Walks in the Severn Gorge* (11 walks, £4) or the further-ranging *Ten Walks That Changed the World* (£6). If you're here on the weekend, ask the TI for the schedule of the steam train that runs for fun most Sundays in Ironbridge Gorge.

Getting around IBG: On weekends, the Gorge Connect bus service runs among the museum sites (all-day Rover ticket-£3, 1–2/hr, Sat–Sun 9:00–18:00 year-round, a couple mid-morning runs go all the way to the Telford rail station, tel. 01952/200-005).

SIGHTS

Ironbridge Gorge

▲▲**Iron Bridge**—While England was at war with her American colonies, this first iron bridge was built in 1779 to show off a wonderful new building material. Lacking experience with iron, the builders erred on the side of sturdiness and constructed it as if it were made out of wood. Notice that the original construction used traditional timber-jointing techniques rather than rivets. (Any rivets are from later repairs.) The valley's centerpiece is free, open all the time, and thought-provoking. Walk across the bridge to the tollhouse/TI/gift shop/museum (free, daily 10:00–17:00). Read the fee schedule and notice the subtle slam against royalty (England was not immune to the revolutionary sentiment brewing in the colonies at this time). Pedestrians paid half a penny to cross; poor people crossed cheaper by coracle—a crude tublike wood-and-canvas shuttle ferry (you'll see old photos of these upstairs). Cross back to the town and enjoy a pleasant walk downstream along the towpath. Where horses once dragged boats laden with Industrial Age cargo, today locals walk their dogs.

▲▲▲**Ironbridge Gorge Industrial Revolution Museums**—This group of widely scattered sites has varied admission charges (usually £2–5.15; Blists Hill is £8.25). The £12.95 Passport ticket (families-£40) gets you into all the sights, which all have the same hours (April–Oct daily 10:00–17:00; from Nov–March, a few Coalbrookdale sights close, Blists Hill's hours are Sat–Wed 10:00–16:00, closed Thu–Fri; tel. 01952/432-166, www.ironbridge.org.uk). Even though several of the sights may not be worth your time, seeing Blists Hill Victorian Town, Museum of the Gorge, and the Coalbrookdale Museum of Iron costs £15.50 without the £12.95 Passport ticket.

Museum of the Gorge: Orient yourself to the valley here in the Severn Warehouse (£2.10, daily 10:00–17:00, 500 yards upstream from the bridge, parking-£1). See the eight-minute introductory movie, check out the exhibit and the model of the gorge in its heyday, and buy a Blists

Ironbridge Gorge

Hill guidebook and Passport ticket. From the parking lot, a tiny tour boat sometimes does a 45-minute round-trip Severn River tour (£4.50, look for sign near WC, slow-moving taped commentary, peaceful photo opportunity for bridge and lazy fishermen along riverbanks, tel. 01952/418-844, mobile 07790-367-263). Further upstream is the fine riverside Dale End Park, with picnic areas and a playground.

Blists Hill Victorian Town: Save most of your time and energy for this wonderful town. You'll wander through 50 acres of Victorian industry, factories, and a re-created community from the 1890s, complete with carriage rides, chemists, a candy shop, an ancient dentist's chair, candle makers, a working pub, a greengrocer's shop, a fascinating squatter's cottage, and a snorty, slippery pigsty. Don't miss the explanation of the winding machine at the Blists Hill Mine (demos throughout the day, call for times). Walk along the canal to the "inclined plane." Grab lunch in the Victorian Pub or in the cafeteria near the squatter's cottage and children's old-time rides. The board by the entry lists which exhibits are staffed and lively (with docents in Victorian dress). The £2 Blists Hill guidebook gives a good step-by-step rundown (£8.25, tel. 01952/583-003).

Coalbrookdale Museum of Iron: This does a fine job of explaining the original iron-smelting process (£5.15, opposite Darby's furnace—see below). The Coalbrookdale neighborhood is the birthplace of the Industrial Revolution. Abraham Darby's blast furnace sits like a shrine inside a big glass pyramid (free), surrounded by the evocative Industrial Age ruins. It was here that, in 1709, Darby first smelted iron, using coke as fuel. If you're like me, "coke" is a drink, and "smelt" is the past tense of smell...nevertheless, this event kicked off the modern Industrial Age.

All the ingredients of the recipe for big industry were here in abundance—iron ore, top-grade coal, and water for power and shipping. Wander around Abraham Darby's furnace. Before this furnace was built, iron ore was laboriously melted by charcoal. With a huge waterwheel-powered bellows, Darby burned top-grade coal super hot (burning off the impurities to make "coke"). Local iron ore was dumped into the furnace and melted. Impurities floated to the top, while the pure iron sank to the bottom of a clay tub in the bottom of the furnace. Twice a day the plugs were knocked off, allowing the "slag" to drain away on the top and the molten iron to drain out on the bottom. The low-grade slag was used locally on walls and paths. The high-grade iron trickled into molds formed in the sand below the furnace. It cooled into pig iron (named because the molds look like piglets suckling their mother). The pig iron "planks" were broken off by sledgehammers and shipped away. The Severn River became one of Europe's busiest, shipping pig iron to distant foundries, where it was remelted and made into cast iron (for projects such as the Iron Bridge), or to forges, where it was worked like toffee into wrought iron.

Enginuity, recently opened next door, is a hands-on funfest for kids. Riffing on Ironbridge's engineering roots, this converted 1709 foundry is full of mesmerizing water contraptions, pumps, magnets, and laser games. Build a dam, try your hand at earthquake-proof construction, navigate a water maze, operate a remote-controlled robot, or power a turbine with your own steam (£5.15, kids 5–18-£3.60, family-£15.50, daily 10:00–17:00).

Rosehill House, just up the hill, is the 18th-century Darby mansion furnished as a Quaker ironmaster's home would have been in 1850 (£3, April–Sept daily 10:00–17:00, closed Oct–March). The adjacent Dale House from the 1780s is less interesting.

Coalport China Museum, Jackfield Tile Museum, and Broseley Pipeworks: Housed in their original factories, these showcase the region's porcelain, decorated tiles, and clay tobacco pipes. These industries were developed to pick up the slack when the iron industry shifted away from Severn Valley. Each museum features finely decorated pieces, and the china and tile museums offer low-energy workshops. The Jackfield Tile Museum re-opens in summer 2004 after renovation.

Ironbridge Open Air Museum of Steel Sculpture—This park is an arresting tribute to the region's industrial heritage. Stroll the 10-acre grounds and spot works by Roy Kitchin and other sculptors stashed in the forest and perched in rolling grasslands (£2, March–Nov Tue–Sun 10:00-17:00, usually closed Mon but open Mon bank holidays, closed Dec–Feb, 2 miles from Iron Bridge, Moss House, Cherry Tree Hill, Coalbrookdale, Telford, tel. 01952/433-152, www.go2.co.uk/steelsculpture).

Near Ironbridge Gorge

Skiing, Swimming, and Fishing—There's a small, brush-covered ski slope with two Poma lifts at Telford Ski Centre in Madeley, two miles from Ironbridge Gorge; you'll see the signs for it as you drive into IBG (£9.10/hr including gear, less for kids, unreliably open Mon and Thu 10:00–20:00, Tue–Wed 10:00–22:00, Fri 12:00–22:00, Sat 12:00–14:00 & 16:00–18:00, Sun 10:00–16:00, tel. 01952/586-862). A public swimming pool is next door. The Woodlands Farm, on Beech Road, runs a private fishing business where only barbless hooks are used and locals toss their catch back to hook again (kind of a fish hell).

Royal Air Force Museum Cosford—This Red Baron magnet displays more than 80 aircraft, from warplanes to rockets. Get the background on ejection seats and a primer on the principles of propulsion (free, daily 10:00–18:00, last admission 16:00, closed Dec 24–26 and Jan 1, Shifnal, Shropshire, on A41 near junction with M54, tel. 01902/376-200, fax 01902/376-211, www.rafmuseum.com).

More Sights—If you're looking for reasons to linger in IBG, these sights are all within a short drive: the RAF Museum (listed above), medieval town of Shrewsbury, abbey village of Much Wenlock, scenic Long Mynd gorge at Church Stretton, castle at Ludlow, and the steam railway at the river town of Bridgnorth. Shoppers like Chester (en route to North Wales).

SLEEPING

The Town Center

$$$ **Library House** is Better-Homes-and-Gardens elegant. In the town center, a half block downhill from the bridge, it's classy, friendly, and a fine value. Helpful Chris and George Maddocks run this smoke-free place, and their breakfast won a "healthy heartbeat" award. The complimentary drink upon arrival is a welcome touch (Sb-£55, Db-£65, Tb-£85, family room-£80, no CC, video library, free parking, 11 Severn Bank, Ironbridge Gorge, tel. 01952/432-299, fax 01952/433-967, www.libraryhouse.com, info@libraryhouse.com). George will pick you up from the Telford train station if you request it in advance.

$$$ **Severn Lodge B&B** is an elegant, Georgian "captain of industry" house offering three fine, newly refurbished rooms (Sb-£49–55,

SLEEP CODE

(£1 = about $1.60, country code: 44, area code: 09152)
Sleep Code: **S** = Single, **D** = Double/Twin, **T** = Triple, **Q** = Quad, **b** = bathroom, **s** = shower only, **no CC** = Credit Cards not accepted. You can assume credit cards are accepted unless noted otherwise.

To help you sort easily through these listings, I've divided the rooms into three categories based on the price for a standard double room with bath during high season:

$$$ **Higher Priced**—Most rooms £60 or more.
$$ **Moderately Priced**—Most rooms between £35–60.
$ **Lower Priced**—Most rooms £35 or less.

Db-£64–74, no CC, non-smoking, walled garden, easy parking, 200 yards above river, a block above town center on New Road, tel. 01952/432-147, fax 01952/432-148, www.severnlodge.com, Julia).

Three lesser places right in the town center overlook the bridge:

$$ Eley's Bridge View B&B rents five rooms (Db-£45–55, at bridge find 13 Tontine Hill and climb the metal stairway, tel. 01952/432-541, www.ironbridgeview.co.uk, Rich).

$$ Post Office House B&B is literally above the post office, where the postmaster's wife, Janet Hunter, rents three rooms (Db-£52, discount for 2 nights or more, family rooms available, no CC, 6 The Square, tel. 01952/433-201, fax 01952/433-582, hunter@pohouse -ironbridge.fsnet.co.uk).

$$ Tontine Hotel is the town's big, 12-room, musty, smoky, Industrial Age hotel (S-£22, D-£40, Db-£56, 10 percent discount with this book, The Square, tel. 01952/432-127, fax 01952/432-094, tontine @netscapeonline.co.uk). Check out the historic photos in the bar.

Outside of Town

$$ Bridge House rents four rooms in a 17th-century residence on the banks of the Severn River a few miles from the town center (Sb-£45, Db-£60–65, family room-from £80–95, non-smoking rooms available, Buildwas Road, Telford, tel. & fax 01952/432-105).

$ Coalport Youth Hostel, plush for a hostel, fills an old factory at the China Museum in Coalport (most beds are in quads, but they have plenty of bunk-bed Ds-£31, Db-£31). The **Coakbrookdale Hostel,** built in 1859 as the grand Coalbrookdale Institute, is another fine hostel (a 20-min walk from the Iron Bridge down A4169 toward Wellington,

4- to 6-bed rooms, no CC). Each hostel charges £11.25 per bed with sheets, serves meals, has a self-service laundry, closes from 10:00 to 17:00, requires that you have a hostel membership (available for £13), and uses the same telephone number and e-mail address (tel. 01952/ 588-755, ironbridge@yha.org).

$ **Wilderhope Manor Youth Hostel,** a beautifully remote and haunted 400-year-old manor house, is one of Europe's best hostels. On Saturdays, tourists actually pay to see what hostelers sleep in for £11.50 (under 18-£8.25, dinner served at 19:00, unreliable hours throughout year, reservations recommended, tel. 01694/771-363, wilderhope @yha.org.uk). It's six miles from Much Wenlock down B4371 toward Church Stretton.

EATING

Oliver's is a smoke-free vegetarian place with prices and meals that make you want to turn—or stay—vegetarian (£9 main course, using CC adds 5 percent, reserved seating Tue–Sat 19:00–23:00, also Sat 11:00–15:00 and Sun 11:00–17:00, reservations essential, not kid-friendly, High Street, tel. 01952/433-086).

Ironbridge Bar & Brasserie is an inviting bistro with an imaginative menu and a focus on fish, good wine, and real ale (£16 meals, Tue–Sun 18:30–22:00, also Sat–Sun lunch, closed Mon, plenty of indoor/outdoor seating, non-smoking, veggie options, reservations smart, on High Street half a block uphill from Oliver's, tel. 01952/432-716). Its cool wine bar is a fun place for a drink.

Da Vinci's serves good, though pricey, Italian food in a dressy ambience (£15 main course, Mon–Sat 19:00–22:00, closed Sun, 26 High Street, tel. 01952/432-250).

Aftab is the place for Indian food—eat in or take out (daily 17:30–24:00, 25 High Street, tel. 01952/432-055).

The Malt House, located in an 18th-century beer house, offers an English menu with a European accent. This is a very popular scene with the local twenty-something gang—and consequently smoky (£12 main course, bar menu at the Jazz Bar, daily 12:00–14:30 & 18:30–21:30, near Museum of the Gorge, 5-min walk from center, The Wharfage, tel. 01952/433-712). The Malt House is *the* vibrant nightspot in town, with live music and a fun crowd generally from Wednesday through Sunday.

For a local scene, fine spit-and-sawdust ambience, excellent ales, and surprisingly good food, try **Coalbrookdale Inn** (lunches 12:00–14:00, dinner from 18:00, last order 20:00, no food Sun, no reservations, folk music on third Sun every month, lively ladies' loo, across street from Coalbrookdale Museum of Iron, 1 mile from IBG, tel. 01952/433-953, run by Corrine and Mike, who are on the quest for the perfect pint). This former "best pub in Britain" has a tradition of offering free samples from a lineup of featured beers. Each is listed on a blackboard with its price and alcohol content. Ask a local to explain...or ask if he's ever tried a brew called the Prior's Piddle.

Lawrence Welk would prefer eating at the **Meadow Inn,** a local favorite that serves prize-winning pub grub (£8 meals, daily 18:00–21:00, weekends until 21:45, can get crowded, no reservations, a pleasant 15-min walk from the center, head upstream, at Dale End Park take the path along the river, the inn is just after railway bridge, tel. 01952/433-193).

TRANSPORTATION CONNECTIONS

IBG is seven miles from Telford, which has the nearest train station. To get between IBG and Telford, take a bus (£1, hrly, 20 min, none on Sun) or taxi (£7.50). Although Telford's train and bus stations are an annoying 15-minute walk apart, you can connect on bus #44 (every 10 min, 35p) or #55 (every 20 min) or with a £2 cab ride. The Telford bus station is part of a large modern mall, an easy place to wait for the hourly bus to IBG. The Gorge Connect bus service, which runs among Ironbridge Gorge sights on weekends, makes a couple runs between IBG and the Telford train station. For schedule information on the Gorge Connect and other bus routes, call Telford Travelink at 01952/200-005. If you need a **taxi** while in Ironbridge Gorge, call 01952/501-050.

By train from Telford to: Birmingham (2/hr, 40 min), **Conwy** in North Wales (9/day, 3 hrs, 1–2 changes usually include Crewe), **Blackpool** (1–2/hr, 3.5 hrs, usually 2 changes), **Keswick** and the **Lake District** (every 2 hrs, 3.5 hrs to Penrith with 2 changes, then catch a bus to Keswick, hrly except Sun 6/day, 40 min), **Edinburgh** (hrly, 5–6.5 hrs, 1–2 transfers). Train info: tel. 08457-484-950.

By car to Telford: Driving in from the **Cotswolds** and **Stratford,** take M6 through Birmingham then M54 to the Telford/Ironbridge exit. Follow the brown *Ironbridge* signs through lots of roundabouts to Ironbridge Gorge. The traffic north through Birmingham is miserable from 14:00 to 20:00, especially on Fridays. From **Warwick,** consider the M40, M42, Kidderminster alternative, coming into IBG on the A442 via Bridgnorth to avoid the Birmingham traffic. Driving from IBG to North Wales takes two hours to Ruthin or 2.5 hours to Conwy.

NORTH WALES

Wales' top historical, cultural, and natural wonders are found in the north. From towering Mount Snowdon to lush forests to desolate moor country, North Wales is a poem written in landscape. For sightseeing thrills and diversity, North Wales is Britain's most interesting slice of the Celtic crescent. But be careful not to be waylaid by the many gimmicky sights and bogus "best of" lists. The region's economy is poor, and they're wringing every possible pound out of the tourist trade. Sort carefully through your options.

ORIENTATION

Welsh

Language: The Welsh language, Cymraeg, has been a written language since about A.D. 600 and was spoken 300 years before French or German. It remains alive and well. Although English imperialism tried to kill it, today Welsh and those who speak it are protected by law. In northwest Wales, well over half the population is fluent in Welsh. It's either the first or the required second language in the public schools. Tourists hardly notice that the locals chatter away in Welsh and, as they turn to you, switch seamlessly to English. Listen in.

Welsh is a Celtic language (like Irish) and most closely related to the Breton language in western France. The common "ll" is pronounced as if you were ready to make an "l" sound and then blew it out (a bit like the tl in antler). The language is phonetic but comes with a few tricks: the Welsh "dd" sounds like the English "th," f = v, ff = f, w = oo, and y = i. In a pub, impress your friends (or make some) by toasting the guy who just bought your drink. Say "Yeach-hid dah" (YECH-id dah "Good health to you") and "Dee olch" ("Thank you") or "Dee olch un vowr" (dee olch un vawr "Thanks very much"). If the beer's bad, just make something up.

North Wales

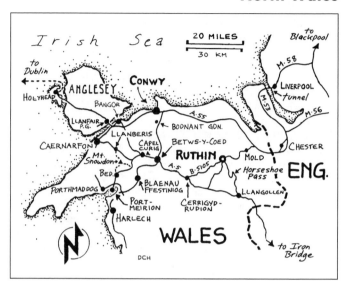

Choirs: Every town has a choir (men's or mixed) that practices weekly. Visitors are usually welcome to observe and very often follow the choir down to the pub afterwards for a good, old-fashioned, beer-lubricated singsong. Choirs practice weekly in the towns of **Ruthin** (mixed choir at Tabernacle Church, Thu 20:00–21:30 except Aug), **Llangollen** (men's choir Fri at 19:30 at Hand Hotel, 21:00 pub singsong afterward, tel. 01978/860-303), **Denbigh** (men's choir Mon at 19:00 except in Aug), **Llandudno** (Sun 19:30–21:00, near Conwy), and **Caernarfon** (Tue 19:45–21:30 at Conservative Club on Castle Street, except Aug). Confirm choir schedules with your B&B hostess or a local TI.

Planning Your Time

On a three-week Britain trip, give North Wales two nights and a day, and it'll give you mighty castles, a giant slate mine, and some of Britain's most beautiful scenery. Many visitors are charmed and find an extra day.

Drivers interested in a medieval banquet should set up in Ruthin and do this loop:

9:00-Drive over Llanberis mountain pass to Caernarfon (with possible short stops in Trefriw Woolen Mills, Betws-y-Coed, Pen Y Gwryd Hotel Pub, and Llanberis), 12:00-Caernarfon Castle. Catch noon tour and 13:00 movie in Eagle Tower. See Prince Charles (of Wales) exhibit. Climb to the top for the view. Browse through Caernarfon town and have lunch. 14:30-Drive the scenic road (A4085) to Blaenau Ffestiniog,

15:30-Tour Llechwedd Slate Mine, 17:30-Drive home to Ruthin, 19:00-Arrive at home, 19:45-Medieval banquet at castle (if not last night).

With a car and no interest in a banquet, skip Ruthin and shorten your drive time by spending two nights in Conwy. Without a car, skip Ruthin. From Conwy, you can tour Snowdonia and Caernarfon by bus and train.

With a second day, add the train up Mount Snowdon (or take a hike) and visit Conwy. With more time and a desire to hike, consider using the mountain village of Beddgelert as a base.

Getting around North Wales

North Wales (except Ruthin) is well covered by a combination of buses and trains. A main train line zips along the north coast from Chester to Holyhead via Llandudno Junction, Conwy, and Bangor (1/hr). From Llandudno Junction, the Conwy Valley line goes scenically south to Betws-y-Coed and Blaenau Ffestiniog (5/day, 1 hr). Without a car you'll manage fine if you use these two train lines; public buses (get the Gwynedd Public Transport Guide at any local TI); and Arriva buses, which circle Snowdonia National Park with the needs of hikers in mind (£5 day pass available, buy on bus, tel. 01286/870-765).

For day trips from Conwy, consider Ian Shaw's "Celtic Routes" driving tours, handy for those without wheels (see page 213).

Ruthin

Ruthin (RITH-in) is a low-key, market town whose charm is in its ordinary Welshness. The people are the sights. Admission is free if you start the conversation. The market square, castle, TI, bus station, and in-town accommodations are all within five blocks of each other. Ruthin is Welsh as can be, makes a handy base for drivers doing North Wales, and serves up a medieval banquet. You'll find the **TI** in the busy crafts center (June–Sept daily 10:00–17:30, Oct–May Mon–Sat 10:00–17:00, Sun 12:00–17:00, tel. 01824/703-992).

SIGHTS

▲▲**Ruthin Castle Welsh Medieval Banquet**—English, Scottish, Irish, and Welsh medieval banquets are all variations on the same touristy theme. This one, while growing more tired and tacky each year, remains fun and more culturally justifiable (if that's necessary) than most. You'll be greeted with a chunk of bread dipped in salt, which, the maiden explains, will "guarantee your safety." Your medieval master of ceremonies then seats you, and the candlelit evening of food, drink, and music rolls gaily on. You'll enjoy harp music, angelic singing, and lots of

Ruthin

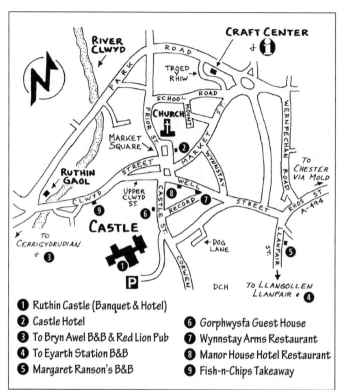

① Ruthin Castle (Banquet & Hotel)
② Castle Hotel
③ To Bryn Awel B&B & Red Lion Pub
④ To Eyarth Station B&B
⑤ Margaret Ranson's B&B
⑥ Gorphwysfa Guest House
⑦ Wynnstay Arms Restaurant
⑧ Manor House Hotel Restaurant
⑨ Fish-n-Chips Takeaway

entertainment, including insults slung at the Irish, Scots, English, and even us brash colonists. With fanfare (and historic explanation), wenches serve mead, spiced wine, and four hearty traditional courses. Drink from a pewter goblet, wear a bib, and eat with your fingers and a dagger. Food and mead are unlimited—just ask for more (£32, starts at 19:45, 2–5 nights per week year-round, depending upon demand; vegetarian options, non-smoking, call for reservations, easy doorstep parking, down Castle Street from town square, tel. 01824/703-435 or, after hours, the hotel at 01824/702-664). Ask to be seated with other readers of this book to avoid being stuck in a dreary tour group.

Ruthin Gaol—Get a glimpse into crime and punishment in 17th- to early 20th-century Wales in this 100-cell prison. Explore the "dark" and condemned cells, give the dreaded hand-crank a whirl, and learn about the men, women, and children who did time here before the prison closed in 1916 (£3, family-£8, daily 10:00–17:00, Thu until 19:00,

Nov–March closed Mon, last entry 60 min before closing, Clwyd Street, tel. 01824/708-281, www.ruthingaol.co.uk).

Walks—For a scenic and interesting one-hour walk, try the Offa's Dyke Path to Moel Famau (the "Jubilee Tower," a 200-year-old war memorial on a peak overlooking stark moorlands). The trailhead is a 10-minute drive from Ruthin.

▲▲**Welsh Choir**—The mixed choir performs at the Tabernacle Church on Thursday 20:00–21:30 (except Aug, tel. 01824/703-757).

SLEEPING

$$$ Ruthin Castle, the ultimate in creaky, faded, Old World elegance for North Wales, is actually not a castle, but a hotel near castle ruins (Sb-from £69, standard Db-£112, tel. 01824/702-664, fax 01824/705-978, www.ruthincastle.co.uk). Enjoy lavish public places, armor, antlers, ghosts, and your private snooker table (giant billiards, £1/hr). Explore the fascinating grounds, complete with a drowning pool and 40 peacocks. You'll wake up to their cry thinking it's a Looney Tunes damsel in distress.

$$$ The **Castle Hotel,** not to be confused with the Ruthin Castle hotel, is a more modern 19-room hotel on the town square (Sb-£43, Db-£70, family suites-£80, front rooms are larger and overlook the town square, non-smoking rooms, St. Peter's Square, tel. 01824/702-479, fax 01824/703-488).

$$ Bryn Awel, a traditional and charming farmhouse B&B with a paradise garden, is run by Beryl and John Jones in the hamlet of Bontuchel just outside of Ruthin. Beryl, a prizewinning quilter, is helpful with travel tips and key Welsh words (Db-£46, £4 less per night for

SLEEP CODE

(£1 = about $1.60, country code: 44, area code: 01824)
Sleep Code: **S** = Single, **D** = Double/Twin, **T** = Triple, **Q** = Quad, **b** = bathroom, **s** = shower only, **no CC** = Credit Cards not accepted. You can assume credit cards are accepted unless otherwise noted.

To help you sort easily through these listings, I've divided the rooms into three categories based on the price for a standard double room with bath:

$$$ **Higher Priced**—Most rooms £65 or more.
$$ **Moderately Priced**—Most rooms between £45–65.
$ **Lower Priced**—Most rooms £45 or less.

2 nights or more, no CC, non-smoking, Bontuchel, tel. 01824/702-481, www.accomodata.co.uk/010797.htm, beryljjones@msn.com). From Ruthin, take Bala road #494, then B5105/Cerrigydrudion road. Turn right after the church, at the *Bontuchel/Cyffylliog* sign. Look for the B&B sign on the right, 1.8 fragrant miles down a narrow road.

$$ Eyarth Station, an old railway station converted to a country guest house, rents six rooms in the scenic Vale of Clwyd about a mile outside Ruthin (Sb-£30, Db-£50, country supper-£12.50, non-smoking rooms, closed Nov–Feb, Llanfair D.C., tel. 01824/703-643, fax 01824/707-464, www.eyarthstation.com, stay@eyarthstation.com).

$ Margaret Ranson's B&B is friendly and comfortable, with three rooms (Db-£42, no CC, strictly non-smoking, Rhianfa, Ffordd Llanrhydd, Ruthin, Clwyd, a 10-min walk from castle; from Anchor Pub drive 100 yards toward hospital—it's the first big red-brick house on right, *Rhianfa* sign on stone wall, tel. & fax 01824/702-971). Margaret's husband, John, a natural tour guide, will lend you an excellent North Wales road map. Or you can just play croquet in their sprawling backyard.

$ Gorphwysfa Guest House, in a cozy 16th-century Tudor home between the castle and the town square, has a library, a grand piano, and three huge, comfortable rooms (Db-£44, Tb-£56, Qb-£68, no CC, 8a Castle Street, tel. & fax 01824/707-529, marg@gorphwysfa.fsnet.co.uk, Margaret O'Riain).

For cheap beds, go to the **Llangollen Youth Hostel** (15 miles from Ruthin in Llangollen, see next page).

EATING

For pub grub, try **Wynnstay Arms,** the classier **Manor House Hotel Restaurant** (a tad expensive), or the **Red Lion** pub (a mile out of town in Cyffylliog). For fish and chips, locals paddle over to the bottom of Clwyd Street (take-away only).

TRANSPORTATION CONNECTIONS

Ruthin to: Llangollen (15 miles, 7 buses/day but never on Sun, 1 hr), **Betws-y-Coed** (30 miles, 3–4 hrs, bus to Rhyl, train to Llandudno Junction, train to Betws-y-Coed), **Conwy** (3 hrs by bus, with transfer at Rhyl or Llanrwst), **Chester** (5 buses/day, 30 min, or a £20 taxi).

Llangollen

Worth a stop if you have a car, Llangollen is famous for its **International Musical Eisteddfod** (July 6-11 in 2004, www.international -eisteddfod.co.uk), a very popular and very crowded festival of folk songs and dance. Men's choir practice is held on Friday nights throughout the year (19:30 at the Hand Hotel, 21:00 pub singsong afterward, tel. 01978/860-303).

Walk or ride a horse-drawn boat down the old canal (£4, March–Oct, 45 min, 3-mile round trip, tel. 01978/860-702) toward the lovely 13th-century **Cistercian Vale Crucis Abbey** (£2, daily 10:00–17:00) near the even older cross, **Eliseg's Pillar.** The same cruise company offers relaxing and scenic narrow-boat canal trips (£7.50, 2 hrs).

Llangollen has a handful of other amusements and attractions, including scenic steam-train trips (daily Easter–Dec), the world's largest permanent exhibition of model railways, and the biggest *Doctor Who* exhibition anywhere. (**TI:** daily 9:30–17:30, tel. 01978/860-828.)

Sleeping in Llangollen: Glasgwm B&B rents spacious rooms in a Victorian townhouse (£Sb-27.50, Db-£45, Abbey Road, tel. 01978/86975). The **Llangollen Youth Hostel** is cheap (£12.25/bed in 2- to 20-bed rooms, £2 less for members, tel. 01978/860-330, llangollen @yha.org.uk).

Llangollen is a 30-minute drive from Ruthin. Llangollen is connected by bus with Ruthin (4/day, none on Sun, 60 min, year-round) and train stations at Chirk (hrly), Ruabon (hrly), and Wrexham (hrly).

Conwy

This garrison town was built with the Conwy castle in the 1280s to give Edward I an English toehold in Wales (see page 214). What's left today are the best medieval walls in Britain surrounding a humble town and crowned by the bleak and barren hulk of a castle that was awesome in its day. Conwy's charming High Street leads from Lancaster Square (with the bus stop, unmanned train station, and a column honoring the town's founder, Welsh prince Llywelyn the Great) down to a fishy harbor that permitted Edward to safely restock his castle. Since the highway was tunneled under the town, a strolling ambience has returned to Conwy. Beyond the castle, the mighty Telford suspension bridge is a 19th-century slice of English imperialism, built in 1826 to better connect (and control) the route to Ireland.

Tourist Information: The TI is near the castle (daily April–May and Sept–Oct 9:30–17:00, June–Aug until 18:00; Nov–March until 16:00 and opens at 11:00 on Sun, tel. 01492/592-248). Ask about train or bus schedules for your departure (Conwy doesn't have a staffed train or bus station—only a lonely train platform and bus stop). The TI sells books and maps on the area, such as *Footprints' Walks around Snowdonia* (£3.50, 16 walks with maps) and the "cartoon" illustrated Lap Map (£1.20, includes sight descriptions and mileage chart). The TI also books rooms for a £1 fee and does theater bookings. Don't confuse the TI with the tacky "Conwy Visitors Centre"—with its goofy little 80p video show—near the station.

Helpful Hints

Every Monday night: The gritty Malt Loaf pub hosts the Conwy Folk Music Club (across from train station) from 20:30 on. **Every Tuesday,** a small market hums in the train station's parking lot (year-round, canceled if rainy).

Trains: Train schedules are posted outside the unstaffed station. Trains do drop off and pick up in Conwy (if your train is listed with an "x," you'll need to flag it down). The nearest "real" train station is in Llandudno Junction, a mile away.

Car Rental: A dozen car-rental agencies in the city of Llandudno (1.5 miles away) offer cars for about £40 per day and can deliver to you in Conwy (get list of car-rental agencies from Conwy TI). The closest is Avis, a 10-minute walk from Conwy (tel. 01492/585-101).

Bike Rental: Conwy Outdoor rents bikes for £12.50 per day, including helmets (daily 9:00–18:00, packed lunches available, 9 Castle Street, tel. 01492/593-390).

Internet Access: Try the library at the bottom of High Street (free, Mon & Thu–Fri 10:00–17:30, Tue 10:00–19:00, Wed & Sat 10:00–13:00, closed Sun, tel. 01492/596-242) or Llys Llywelyn B&B (starting at £2, see "Sleeping," page 218).

TOURS

North Wales

"Celtic Routes" Driving Tours—Keen guide Ian Shaw, who grew up in North Wales, offers a made-to-order route based on your interests (up to 4 people, from half day-£55, full day-£95, evening-£35, can also arrange climbing, hiking, horseback riding, and canoeing, book well in advance, tel. 01492/592-449, www.exploringwales.net). Ian and his wife Janet own the recommended Bryn B&B.

"Back Wales" Minibus Tours—BusyBus runs an all-day circuit departing from Conwy and covering Snowdonia, Betws-y-Coed, Chester, Llandudno, and the smallish mountain called Great Orme (£19.75/person, pick-up from bus shelter near TI or from your B&B, tel. 0870-874-1800).

SIGHTS

▲**Conwy Castle**—Built dramatically on a rock overlooking the sea with eight linebacker towers, this castle has an interesting story to tell. Built in four years, the castle had a water gate that allowed safe entry for

KING EDWARD'S CASTLES

In the 13th century, the Welsh, under two great princes named Llywelyn, created a united and independent Wales. The English king Edward I fought hard to end this Welsh sovereignty. In 1282, Llywelyn was killed (and went where everyone speaks Welsh). King Edward spent the next 20 years building or rebuilding 17 great castles to consolidate his English foothold in troublesome North Wales. The greatest of these (such as Conwy Castle) were masterpieces of medieval engineering, with round towers (tough to undermine by tunneling), a castle-within-a-castle defense (giving defenders a place to retreat and wreak havoc on the advancing enemy...or just wait for reinforcements), and sea access (safe to stock from England). These were English islands in the middle of angry Wales. Most were built with a fortified grid-plan town attached and were filled with English settlers. (With this blatant abuse of Wales, you have to wonder, where was Greenpeace 700 years ago?) Edward I was arguably England's best monarch. By establishing and consolidating the United Kingdom (adding Wales and Scotland to England), he made his kingdom big enough to compete with the rising European powers.

Castle-lovers will want to tour each of Edward's five greatest castles. With a car and two days, this makes one of Europe's best castle tours. I'd rate them in this order: **Caernarfon** is most entertaining and best presented (described below); **Conwy** is attached to the cutest medieval town and the best public transport (described below); **Harlech** is the most dramatic (£3, early April–late Oct daily 9:30–17:00 or 18:00, late Oct–early April Mon–Sat 9:30–16:00, Sun 11:00–16:00, tel. 01766/780-552, TI is open Easter–Oct, tel. 01766/780-658); **Beaumaris,** surrounded by a swan-filled moat, was the last, largest, and most romantic (£3, April–June & Oct daily 9:30–17:30, June–Sept until 18:00, Nov–March Mon–Sat 9:30–16:00, Sun 11:00-16:00, tel. 01248/810-361); and **Criccieth** (KRICK-ith), built in 1230 by Llywelyn, is also dramatic and remote (£2.50, daily early April–late Oct 10:00–17:00 or 18:00, closed off-season, tel. 01766/522-227). For photos and more information on the castles, as well as information on Welsh historic monuments in general, check www.cadw.wales.gov.uk.

English boats in a land of hostile Welsh (£3.50, or £6.50 Joint Ticket with Plas Mawr, April–May and Sept–Oct daily 9:30–17:00, June–Aug until 18:00, Nov–March until 16:00 and opens at 11:00 on Sun, tel. 01492/592-358). Guides wait inside to take you on a 60-minute, £1 tour. If the booth is empty, look for the group and join it. The guides also do inexpensive city walking tours in the evening; consider enthusiastic Neville Hortop (£1–2.50 depending on number of people on tour, tel. 01492/878-209.)

▲**City Wall**—Much of the wall, with its 22 towers and castle and harbor views, can be walked for free. Start at Upper Gate (the highest point) or Berry Street (the lowest), or do the small section at the castle entrance.

▲**Plas Mawr**—A rare Elizabethan house from 1580, this was built after the reign of Henry VIII. It was the first Welsh home to be built within Conwy's walls. (The Tudor family was Welsh—and therefore relations between Wales and England warmed.) Billed as the oldest house in Wales, Plas Mawr offers a delightful look 16th-century domestic life to anyone patient enough to spend an hour following the excellent included audioguide (£4.50, or £6.50 Joint Ticket with Conwy Castle, Tue–Sun 9:30–18:00, closed Mon, shorter hours Sept–Oct, closed Nov–March, tel. 01492/580-167).

St. Mary's Parish Church—Sitting lonely in the center of town, Conwy's church was the centerpiece of a Cistercian abbey that stood here a hundred years before the town. The Cistercians were French monks who built their abbeys in lonely places, "far from the haunts of man." Popular with the locals because they were French and *not* English, the Cistercians taught locals farming and mussel-gathering techniques. Edward moved the monks 12 miles upstream but kept the church for his town. Notice the tombstone of a victim of the Battle of Trafalgar just left of the north transept. On the other side of the church, a tomb containing seven brothers and sisters is marked "We Are Seven." It inspired William Wordsworth to write his poem of the same name. The slate tombstones look new even though many are hundreds of years old. Pure slate weathers better than marble (cemetery always open, church may be staffed June–Aug Mon–Fri 10:00–12:00 & 14:00–16:00).

High Street—Lancaster Square marks the top of Conwy's charming High Street. Its centerpiece is a column honoring the town's founder, the Welsh prince Llywelyn the Great. Find the cute pointed arch built into the medieval wall so the train could get through. Side-trip up York Place (past Alfredo's restaurant) to a wall of slate memorials from the 1937 coronation of King George (his wife, the Queen Consort Elizabeth, is the late Queen Mum). Notice the Welsh lesson here: the counties (shires), months (only "mai" is recognizable), days, numbers, and alphabet with its different letters.

Conwy

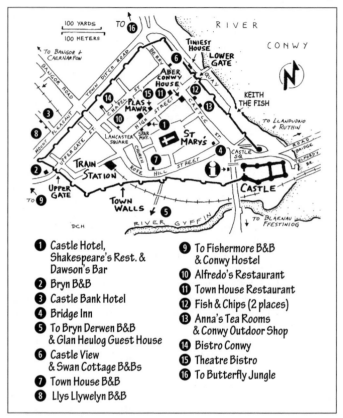

Conwy

① Castle Hotel,
Shakespeare's Rest. &
Dawson's Bar
② Bryn B&B
③ Castle Bank Hotel
④ Bridge Inn
⑤ To Bryn Derwen B&B
& Glan Heulog Guest House
⑥ Castle View
& Swan Cottage B&Bs
⑦ Town House B&B
⑧ Llys Llywelyn B&B
⑨ To Fishermore B&B
& Conwy Hostel
⑩ Alfredo's Restaurant
⑪ Town House Restaurant
⑫ Fish & Chips (2 places)
⑬ Anna's Tea Rooms
& Conwy Outdoor Shop
⑭ Bistro Conwy
⑮ Theatre Bistro
⑯ To Butterfly Jungle

High Street leads down to the harborfront. Wander downhill, enjoying the slice-of-Welsh-life scene: bakery, butcher, newsstand, old timers, and maybe even suds in the fountain. Plas Mawr (on the left), the first Welsh house built within the town walls, dates from the time of Henry VIII (well worth touring, described above). Opposite the Castle Hotel, a lane leads to the Carmel Church. This is a fine example of stark Methodist "statement architecture": stern, with no frills, and typical of these churches built in the early 20th century.

Aberconwy House marks the bottom of High Street. One of the oldest houses in town, it's a museum (not worth touring). Imagine this garrison town filled with half-timbered buildings like this. From here, Barry Street leads left. Originally "burial street," it was a big ditch for mass burials during a 17th-century plague. Continue downhill, crossing under the wall to the harborfront.

▲**Harborfront**—Still called the King's Quay, the stones date from the 13th century, when the harbor served Edward's castle and town. Conwy was once a busy slate port. Slate, barged downstream to here, was loaded onto big three-masters and shipped off to Europe. Back when much of Europe was roofed with Welsh slate, Conwy was a boomtown. In 1900, it had 48 pubs. All the mud is new, as the modern bridge caused this part of the river to silt up.

Strolling along the harbor from the castle end, you'll find plenty of interest. The harbormaster house fills the former customs building. The lifeboat house welcomes visitors. Each coastal town has a similar house, outfitted with a rescue boat suited to the area—in the shallow waters around Conwy, inflatable boats work best. Mussels, historically a big "crop" for Conwy, are processed "in the months with an *r*" by the **Mussels Center.** In the other months, it's open to visitors (free). **Keith the Fish** provides locals with fresh fish and strollers with tasty treats (daily 8:00–18:00). Drop by his shack for a tasty 10p crab stick. Keith, Conwy's honorary secretary of lifeboats, loves to chat. The benches are great for a picnic (two fish-and-chips shops are just around the corner, see "Eating," page 219) or a visit with the noisy gulls. The **Queen Victoria tour boat** departs from here (£3.50, lazy 30-min cruise, nearly hourly, pay on boat, tel. 01492/592-830).

The **Liverpool Arms pub** was built by a captain who ran a ferry service to Liverpool in the 19th century, when the North Wales coast was discovered by English holiday-goers. Today it's a fisherman's hangout. It's easy to miss **The Tiniest House in Britain,** but don't. It's red, 72 inches wide, 122 inches high, and worth 50p to pop in and listen to the short audio-tour. (No WC—but it did have a bedpan.)

From the quay, it's a peaceful half-mile shoreline stroll along the harbor promenade (from smallest house, walk through wall gate and keep going).

Butterfly Jungle—Butterflies flutter in a steamy, lush greenhouse with tropical forest sounds. It's sweet, small, and too humid to linger long (£3.50, families-£9, ticket valid all day—OK to return, 50p identification chart not necessary because charts posted inside, April–Aug daily 10:00–17:30, Sept–Oct daily 10:00–15:30, closed Nov–March, follow signs from harbor, pleasant 5-min walk north, tel. 01492/593-149). If it's not busy, ask the owner why he started a butterfly house.

Pony Riding—Cowpokes mosey on down to Pinewood Riding Stables, a mile from Conwy (£14/hr for scenic rides to Conwy Mount, longer rides possible, Sychnant Pass Road, past hostel, tel. 01492/592-256).

▲**Bodnant Garden**—This sumptuous 80-acre display of floral color is six miles south of Conwy. Set in the lush green of Snowdonia, this garden is one of Britain's best. It's famous for its magnolias, rhododendrons, camellias, and floral arch (£5.20, mid-March–Oct daily

10:00–17:00, closed Nov–mid-March, café, best in spring, phone message tells what's blooming, tel. 01492/650-460).

Hill Climb—For lovely views across the bay to Llandudno, take a pleasant walk (40 min one way) along the footpath up Conwy Mount (follow Sychnant Pass Road past the Bryn B&B, look for fields on the right and a sign with a stick-figure of a walker).

SLEEPING

(£1 = about $1.60, country code: 44, area code: 01492)

Conwy has decent budget B&Bs, each located within a five-minute walk from the bus and train station. There's no launderette in town.

$$$ **Castle Hotel** in the town center rents 29 elegant rooms where Old World antique furnishings mingle with modern amenities. Owners Peter and Bobbi Lavin are eager to make your stay comfortable (Sb-£65–69, superior Sb-£75–79, Db-£75–105, superior Db-£90–125, posh new suites-£120–200 rates vary with season, 10 percent discount promised with this book, show book when checking in, non-smoking rooms, High Street, tel. 01492/582-800, fax 01492/582-300, www.castlewales.co.uk, mail@castlewales.co.uk). Award-winning chef Graham Tinsley helps Peter run Shakespeare's Restaurant, a hit with locals and worth the splurge. For a lighter meal, try the hotel bar's bistro menu.

$$ **Bryn B&B** offers five large, clutter-free rooms in a big 19th-century house with the city wall right in the backyard (Sb-£25, Db-£46, no CC, non-smoking, 1 ground-floor room, parking, immediately outside upper gate of wall, Sychnant Pass Road, tel. 01492/592-449, www.bryn.org.uk, Janet and Ian Shaw). Ian Shaw runs the "Celtic Routes" driving tours, mentioned on page 213 in "Tours."

$$ **Castle Bank Hotel** is a small hotel with nine spacious rooms (Sb-from £45, Db-from £60, non-smoking, easy parking, just outside town wall at Mount Pleasant, tel. 01492/593-888, fax 01492/596-466).

$$ **The Bridge Inn** rents six brightly decorated rooms above its pub. The floor just above the pub is noisy, particularly on weekend nights; the top floor is quieter (Db-from £50 weeknights, from £60 Fri–Sat, discount for 2-night stay, some views, non-smoking, separate entrance from pub, tel. 01492/573-482, www.bridge-conwy.co.uk).

$$ **Bryn Derwen,** an eight-minute walk from town, is in a near-mansion atop a hill, set back from a busy road. Most of its six rooms are pink and frilly without being sugary (Db-£45, no CC, antlered breakfast room with medieval-type table; exit train station from its furthest and lowest corner, go through gate in city wall to busy road—Woodlands—and turn right, look for sign and climb to hotel, Woodlands, tel. 01492/596-134, Alan and Wendy, www.conwy-wales.com/brynderwen).

$$ Glan Heulog Guest House, next door in the other half of the mansion, is also good, with fresh, bright rooms and a pleasant enclosed sun porch (Db-£46, non-smoking, ask about healthy breakfast option, will pick up from train station, tel. 01492/593-845, www.walesbandb .com, glanheulog@no1guesthouse.freeserve.co.uk, Stanley and Vivien Watson-Jones, speak Welsh with Stan).

$ Castle View B&B, near the waterfront, rents two cozy, pleasant rooms decorated with warm wood furnishings (D-£34, T-£45, no CC, non-smoking, 3 Berry Street, tel. 01492/596-888, elainepritchard156 @hotmail.com, Elaine Pritchard).

$ Swan Cottage B&B, across the street, is a homey place with three compact rooms (D/Db-£36, both D rooms have harbor view, no CC, 18 Berry Street, tel. 01492/596-840, Mr. and Mrs. Roberts, swancottage@btopenworld.com).

$ Town House B&B rents six tidy, bright rooms—some with views—near the entrance of the castle (S-£25, D-£40, Db-£45, no CC, non-smoking, parking, 18 Rosehill Street, tel. 01492/596-454, mobile 0797/465-0609, www.thetownhousebb.co.uk, thetownhousebb@aol.com, Alan and Elaine Naughton).

$ Llys Llywelyn B&B has nine faded rooms, but Alan Hughes' pleasant nature helps compensate (Sb-£22–30, Db-£44, 10 percent discount with this book, Internet access starting at £2, easy parking, ramp from parking lot allows access to first floor rooms, next to Castle Bank Hotel—see previous page, Mount Pleasant, tel. 01492/593-257).

$ Fishermore B&B, a family-run B&B, is a 10-minute walk from downtown Conwy. The large house has a sprawling yard, sweet garden patio, and three tidy rooms with flowery bedspreads (Db-£40, no CC, off-road parking available, non-smoking rooms, half-mile south of Conwy, tel. 01492/592-891, www.northwalesbandb.co.uk/fishermore, dyers@tesco.net, Catherine and Peter Dyer).

$ The Conwy Hostel, welcoming travelers of any age, has super views from all its rooms (including four bunk-bed doubles) and a spacious garden. Each room is equipped with either two or four bunk beds and a shower; WCs are down the hall. The airy dining hall and glorious rooftop deck make you feel like you're in the majestic midst of Wales (Db-£32, bed in quad-£13, book in advance for doubles, Internet access, laundry, lockers, dinners, elevator, parking, no lock-out times, 10-min uphill walk from upper gate of Conwy's wall, Larkhill, Sychnant Pass Road, tel. 01492/593-571, fax 01492/593-580, conwy@yha.org.uk).

EATING

For dinner, stroll down High Street, comparing the cute teahouses and smoky pubs. At the top, on Lancaster Square, is **Alfredo's Restaurant,** a family-friendly place serving good and reasonable Italian food (nightly from 18:00, last orders at 21:30, lunch Fri–Sun, reservations recommended, tel. 01492/592-381, Christine).

For a splurge, try **Shakespeare's Restaurant** (£20 meals, daily for dinner, also Sun for lunch, reservations smart, at recommended Castle Hotel on High Street, tel. 01492/582-800). For lighter bistro-style meals, try the adjoining hotel bar, **Dawson's** (daily 11:00–21:30).

Town House Restaurant serves modern English cuisine in a romantic candlelit setting (£17 dinners, Tue–Sun 10:00–15:00 & 18:00–21:00, closed Mon, High Street, reservations wise, tel. 01492/596-436).

At the bottom of High Street, two fish-and-chips joints—**Galleon's** (daily) and **Fisherman's** (daily, closed Mon off-season)—brag that they're the best (Fisherman's probably is). Consider taking your fish and chips down to the harbor and sharing it with the noisy seagulls.

Locals like **Anna's Tea Rooms,** located upstairs in the **Conwy Outdoor Shop** (daily 10:00–17:00, near Fisherman's fish-and-chips, 9 Castle Street, tel. 01492/580-908).

The recently-opened **Bistro Conwy,** tucked away on Chapel Street, serves freshly prepared modern and traditional Welsh cuisine in a cozy wood-floor and candlelight setting (£12–14 entrees with vegetables, potato, and salad, Tue–Sat 11:30–14:00 & 19:00–21:00, Sun 11:30–14:30, closed Sun night and Mon, dinner reservations a must, tel. 01492/596-326, www.bistroconwy.com).

Theatre Bistro, also new to the scene, dishes up continental cuisine with an up-to-date twist in a relaxed loft space off High Street (daily 12:00–14:30, 18:00–21:00, tel. 01492/581-942, www.theatrebistro.net).

The smoky **Bridge Inn,** at the intersection of Rosehill and Castle Streets, serves decent grub (daily 12:00–14:30 & 18:30–20:30).

For picnic fixings, try the **Spar** grocery (daily 8:00–22:00, top of High Street).

TRANSPORTATION CONNECTIONS

Be proactive whether taking the bus or train; let the driver or conductor know you want to stop at Conwy. Consider getting train times and connections for your onward journey at a bigger station before you get to Conwy. For train information in town, ask at the TI or call 08457/484-950. If you want to depart Conwy by train, flag down the train. For a quick pick of more frequent trains, catch a bus—or walk a mile to Llandudno Junction.

Conwy to: Llandudno Junction (2 buses/hr, 5 min; 4 trains/day, 5 min), **Caernarfon** (2 buses/hr, 1 hr), **Trefriw-Betws-y-Coed-Penygwryd-Llanberis** (bus #19, 1/hr in summer).

Llandudno Junction by train to: Chester (2/hr, 1 hr), **Birmingham** (2/hr, 2.5 hrs, some with change in Crewe), **London's Euston Station** (1/hr, 3.5 hrs, most with 1 change).

Caernarfon

The small and lively little town of Caernarfon (kah-NAR-von) is famous for its striking castle—the place where the Prince of Wales is "invested." Like Conwy, it was an Edward I garrison town marching out from the castle. It still follows the original medieval grid plan laid within its well-preserved ramparts.

But Caernarfon is mostly a 19th-century town. At that time, the most important thing in town wasn't the castle but the area—now a parking lot—that sprawls below the castle. This was once a booming slate port, shipping tidy bundles of slate from North Wales mining towns to roofs all over Europe.

The statue of local boy David Lloyd George looks over the town square. A member of parliament from 1890 to 1945, he was the most important politician Wales ever sent to London and ultimately became Britain's prime minister. Boy George began his career as a noisy non-conformist liberal advocating Welsh rights. He ended up an eloquent spokesperson for the notion of Great Britain, convincing his slate-mining constituents that only as part of the Union would their slate industry boom.

Caernarfon bustles with shops, cafés, and people. Market-day activities fill its main square on Saturdays year-round; a smaller, sleepy market yawns on Monday from late May to September. The charming grid-plan medieval town is worth a wander.

Tourist Information: The TI, across from the castle entrance, has a wonderful free town map/guide (with a good self-guided town walk) and train and bus schedules. They sell hiking books, and book rooms here and elsewhere for a £1 fee (April–Oct daily 9:30–17:30, Nov–March daily 10:00–16:30 with a 13:00–14:00 lunch break, tel. 01286/672-232). Donna "Caernarfon is more than a castle" Goodman leads historic walks almost nightly through the season as well as day trips of the area (£3.50, 1.5 hrs; for private hire-£180/full day—book a few days in advance, tel. 01286/677-059 for her schedule, mobile 07946-163-906, info@turnstonetours.co.uk).

Arrival in Caernarfon: If you arrive by bus, walk a few steps to Bridge Street, then go left on Bridge Street until you hit the main square and the castle. The TI faces the castle entrance. Public WCs are off the main square, on the road down to the harbor parking lot. Drivers pay £2.50 to park below the castle.

Helpful Hints

Within a couple of blocks of the bus stop, you'll find the **Dimensiwm 4** Internet café (Mon–Sat 9:30–17:30, closed Sun, Turf Square), the post office (main square), and **Pete's Laundromat** (same-day full-service-

£5/load, self-service-£4/load, Mon–Sat 9:00–17:30, Sun 11:00–17:30, Skinner Street, tel. 01286/678-395).

Two shops rent **bikes:** Cycle Hire (£13/day, long-term rental discounts, on the harbor, tel. 01286/676-804) and Green's Bike Shop (£14/day, tandem-£25, includes helmets and locks, call ahead if you're renting more than a couple bikes, closed Sun–Mon, High Street, tel. 01286/677-400).

SIGHTS

▲▲**Caernarfon Castle**—Edward I built this impressive castle 700 years ago to establish English rule over North Wales. Modeled after the striped and angular walls of ancient Constantinople, the castle—while impressive—was never finished and never really used. From the inner courtyard, you can see the notched walls ready for more walls that were never built. Its fame is due to its physical grandeur and from its association with the Prince of Wales. The English king got the angry Welsh to agree that if he presented them with "a prince, born in Wales, who spoke not a word of English," they would submit to the crown. In time, Edward had a son born in Wales, who spoke not a word of English, Welsh, or any other language—as an infant. In modern times, as another political maneuver, the Prince of Wales has been "invested" (given his title) here. This "tradition" actually dates only from the 20th century, and only two of 21 Princes of Wales have taken part.

In spite of its disappointing history, it's a great castle to tour. An essential part of any visit is the guided tour (50-min tours for £1.50 leave on the hour—and occasionally on the half-hour—from the courtyard steps just beyond the ticket booth; if you're late, ask to join one in progress). In the huge Eagle Tower (on the seaward side), see the *Chieftains and Princes* history exhibit (ground floor), watch the 20-minute movie (a broad mix of Welsh legend and history, shown on the hour and half-hour, upstairs, comfortable theater seats), and climb the tower for a great view. In the nearby Queen's Tower, you'll find several semi-interesting videos of various British battles, firearms, and military strategies. The northeast tower, at the opposite end of the castle, has an exhibit about the investiture of Prince Charles in 1969 (£4.50, June–Sept daily 9:30–18:00, April–May and Oct daily 9:30–17:00, Nov–March Mon–Sat 9:30–16:00, Sun 11:00–16:00, CC, tel. 01286/677-617). Martin de Lewandowicz gives mind-bending tours of the castle (tel. 01286/674-369).

Distractions—A Welsh Highland **steam train** billows through the countryside to, Rhyd Ddu, and back (£8 round-trip to Waunfawr, 1.5 hrs; £12 round trip to Rhyd Ddu, 2 hrs, March–Oct daily, 4/day, tel. 01766/512-340, www.festrail.co.uk). Narrated **harbor cruises** on the *Queen of the Sea* run daily in summer (June–Sept 11:00–18:00 or 19:00, depending on weather, tides, and demand, 40 min, castle views, tel. 01286/672-772). The **Segontium Roman Fort,** dating from A.D. 77, is the westernmost Roman fort. It was manned for more than 300 years to keep the Welsh and the coast quiet. Little is left but foundations (free, Tue–Sun 12:30–16:00, closed Mon, tel. 01286/675-625). For **pony riding,** try Snowdonia Riding Stables (£14/1 hr, longer and shorter time available, 3 miles from Caernarfon, off the road to Beddgelert, bus #89 or #95 from Caernarfon, tel. 01286/650-342).

Men's Choir—If spending a Tuesday night, drop by the local men's choir practice (Tue 19:45–21:30 at Conservative Club on Castle Street, except Aug).

SLEEPING

(£1 = about $1.60, country code: 44, area code: 01286)

$$$ **Celtic Royal Hotel** rents 110 comfortable rooms with a gym, pool, Jacuzzi, and sauna. Its grand, old-fashioned look comes with modern-day conveniences—but it's still overpriced (Db-£100, non-smoking rooms, bar, restaurant; from bus stop, go right on Bridge Street, which turns into Bangor Street; 5-min walk; Bangor Street, tel. 01286/674-477, fax 01286/674-139, www.celtic-royal.co.uk).

$$ **Isfryn B&B,** just down the street from the castle, has four pleasant rooms (S-from £22.50, Db-from £50, family room, no CC, 11 Church Street, tel. & fax 01286/675-628, graham.bailey2@btinternet .co.uk, Graham).

$$ **Caer Menai B&B** rents seven bright, attractive rooms and pre-pares evening meals as well as breakfast (Sb-£30–35, Db-£50, family room-£60–70, ask for harbor view room, three-course dinner-£12, á la carte also available, no CC, non-smoking, 15 Church Street, tel. 01286/672-612, caer.menai@btopenworld.com).

$ **Totters Hostel** is a creative little hostel well run by Bob and Henriette (28 beds in 5 dorm rooms, £11/bed with sheets, includes continental breakfast, no CC, couples can have their own room when available-£28, open all day, lockers, welcoming game room/lounge, free kitchen, a block from castle at 2 High Street, tel. 01286/672-963, mobile 07979-830-470, www.applemaps.co.uk/totters, bob@totters.free-online .co.uk).

EATING

You'll find charming cafés and bistros lining "Hole in the Wall Street" (between Castle Square and TI), and plenty of cheap and cheery sandwich shops and tearooms on nearby High Street. **J&C's,** a fish-and-chips joint, is one block from the main square on Pool Street. The most convenient supermarket is **Farm Foods** (Mon–Sat 9:00–18:00, until

19:00 Thu–Fri, Sun 10:00–16:00, Pool Street). Kwik Save and a larger Safeway are a five-minute walk from the city center on Bangor Street.

TRANSPORTATION CONNECTIONS

Caernarfon by bus to: Conwy (2/hr, hrly on Sun, 1.25 hrs, buy ticket on bus), **Llanberis** (2/hr, 30 min), **Beddgelert** (1/hr, 30 min), **Blaenau Ffestiniog** (1/hr, 1.5 hrs), **Beddgelert-Penygwryd-Llanberis** (bus #95, every 2 hrs, 1.5 hrs, June–Sept only). Buy tickets from the driver.

Snowdonia National Park

This is Britain's second-largest national park, and its centerpiece—the tallest mountain in England and Wales—is Mount Snowdon. Each year half a million people ascend one of seven different paths to the top of 3,560-foot Snowdon (the small book *The Ascent of Snowdon*, by E. G. Bowland, describes the routes, £2, sold by local TIs). Hikes take from five to seven hours. If you're fit and the weather's good, it's an exciting day. Trail info abounds. As you explore, notice the slate roofs—the local specialty.

SIGHTS

Betws-y-Coed—The resort center of Snowdonia National Park, Betws-y-Coed (BET-oos-uh-coyd) bursts with tour buses and souvenir shops. Its good national park office, TI, and guided walks are the only reasons to stop here (April–Oct daily 10:00–18:00, Nov–March daily 9:30–12:30 & 13:30–16:30, tel. 01690/710-426). Consider a long but not strenuous guided walk in the hills (£3.50, April–early Sept Thu–Sun, depart TI at 10:00, 6- to 8-mile hike, call Robin Hamlett to book: Mon–Wed call tel. 0151/488-0052, Thu–Sat 17:00-19:00 call mobile 07790-851-333).

If you drive west out of town on A5, after two miles you'll see the car park for scenic Swallow Falls, a pleasant five-minute walk from the road. A half-mile past the falls on the right, you'll see "The Ugly House," built overnight to take advantage of a 15th-century law that let any quickie building avoid fees and taxes. Buses connect Conwy and Betws-y-Coed (with a change, 1/hr June–Aug, 50 min). Trains run from Llandudno Junction near Conwy through Betws-y-Coed to Blaenau Ffestiniog (6/day).

▲**Trefriw Woolen Mills**—The mill in Trefriw (TREV-roo), five miles north of Betws-y-Coed, is free and surprisingly interesting if the machines are running (April–Oct Mon–Fri 9:30–17:30, Sat 10:00-17:00, closed Sun, Nov–March closes Mon–Fri at 17:00, off-season only weaving is demonstrated, tel. 01492/640-462). Follow the 11 stages of

THE LEGEND OF HOW BEDDGELERT GOT ITS NAME

Prince Llywelyn, who had a dog named Gelert, went hunting one day, leaving his baby son with his dog. When the prince came home, he found the crib overturned and blood everywhere. The prince immediately drew his sword and killed the dog. In that instant, he heard a baby crying from under the crib. He turned the crib over and found the baby. Nearby, a dead wolf lay in the corner. The prince realized that his faithful dog Gelert had killed the preying wolf to protect the baby. He buried Gelert in a grave (*bedd* in Welsh).

Actually, the town is named for a sixth-century saint. Years ago, some clever entrepreneur invented the canine legend and set up a fake grave to attract visitors. To this day, local kids love to spy on gullible tourists mourning at the grave.

wool transformation: warping, weaving, carding, hanking, spanking, spinning, and so on. The hand-spinning house (next to the WC) has a charming spinster and a petting cupboard filled with all the various kinds of raw wool that can be spun into cloth (June–Sept only, Mon-Fri 10:00–17:00). Silkworms are also at work (and on display) here. Be sure to enjoy the fine woolen shop, the pleasant town, and the coffee shop. The grade school next door is rambunctious with Welsh-speaking kids—fun to listen to at recess. The woolen mill at Penmachno (also near Betws-y-Coed) is smaller and much less interesting.

▲Beddgelert—This is the quintessential Snowdon village, packing a scenic mountain punch without the tourist crowds (17 miles from Betws-y-Coed). Set on a river in the shadow of Snowdon and her sisters, with a fine variety of hikes from its doorstep and pretty good bus service, Beddgelert (BETH-geh-let) makes a good stop for those wanting to experience the peace of Snowdonia. The Glaslyn Homemade Ice Cream shop offers surprising quality and selection for this altitude. (**TI**: April–Oct daily 10:00–18:00, closed 13:00–14:00 for lunch Sept–Oct, closed Nov–March, tel. 01766/890-615.)

Locals can recommend walks. You can follow the lane along the river (3 miles round trip), walk down the river and around the hill (3 hrs, 6 miles, 900-foot gain, via Cwm Bycham), hike along (or around) Llyn Gwynant Lake and four miles back to Beddgelert (ride the bus to the lake), or try the dramatic ridge walks on Moel Hebog (Hawk Hill).

Sleeping in Beddgelert: $$ Plas Tan Y Graig Guest House, at the village bridge, is a good value (Db-£36–55, family room, fine lounge, tea garden, tel. 01766/890-310, fax 01766/890-329, www.plastanygraig.co.uk). Also just over the bridge, Brian Wheatley rents six rooms at **$ Plas Gwyn,** a 19th-century town house (S-£22, Db-£44, discount with this book, family deals, no CC, non-smoking, tel. 01766/890-215, www.plas-gwyn .com, bandb@beddgelert.fsbusiness.co.uk). **$$ Plas Colwyn Guesthouse** is a bigger place just next door (D-£40, Db-£46, bed only–from £12/person, tel. 01766/890-458). **$$$** The **Royal Goat Hotel** offers well-worn, chandeliered, woody elegance in a grand hotel built for the rugged 19th-century aristocrat (Sb-£47, Db-£82, 10 percent off with this book through 2004, cheaper for 2-night stays, tel. 01766/890-224, fax 01766/890-422, www.royalgoathotel.co.uk).

Mountaineers note that this area was used by Sir Edmund Hillary and his men as they practiced for the first ascent of Mount Everest. **$$** The **Pen Y Gwryd Hotel Pub** (at the top of the pass north of Beddgelert) is strewn with fascinating memorabilia from Hillary's 1953 climb (D-£54, Db-£64, no CC, saggy beds, smoky, old-time-elegant public rooms, those in D rooms get to use museum-piece Victorian tubs and showers, grand five-course dinners-£20, tel. 01286/870-211, www .pyg.co.uk). With its crampon ambience, it's ideal for well-bred hikers.

Llanberis—A town of 2,000 people with as many tourists on a sunny day, Llanberis is a popular base for Snowdon activities. Along with the station for the Snowdon train, there is a good information center, a few touristy museums, pony trekking, and good bus connections (1 bus/hr to Beddgelert, 45 min). To explore an old slate mine frozen in time, stop by the free Welsh Slate Museum to catch the giant water wheel and the slate-splitting demo (Easter–Oct daily 10:00–17:00, Nov–Easter Sun–Fri 10:00–16:00, closed Sat, last admission 1 hr before closing).

Sleeping in Llanberis: Consider **$$ Dolafon Hotel,** an 1860s Victorian building with seven traditionally furnished rooms (D-£40, Db-£48, large Db-£55–65, non-smoking, garden, High Street, tel. & fax 01286/870-993, www.dolafon.com).

▲▲**Mount Snowdon and the Mountain Railway**—The easiest and most popular ascent of Mount Snowdon is by the Snowdon Mountain Railway, a rack-and-pinion railway from 1896 that climbs 3,500 feet over 4.5 miles from Llanberis to the summit (£18 round-trip, 2.5 hrs, includes 30-min stop at the top, tel. 01286/870-223, www.snowdonrailway.co.uk). The 9:00 departures—scheduled only in July and August—are half-price.

The first departure is often at 9:30. While the schedule flexes with weather and demand, they try to run several trips each day mid-March through October (2/hr in peak season). On sunny summer days, trains fill up (office opens at 9:00, waits are longer in the afternoon; arrive by lunchtime and get a departure appointment time—usually a wait of 1–2 hrs, reservations possible a day in advance). Off-season trains often stop short of the summit (due to snow and high winds).

Blaenau Ffestiniog

This quintessential Welsh slate-mining town is notable for its slate-mine tour and its old steam train. The town—a dark, poor place—seems to struggle on, oblivious to the tourists who nip in and out. Take a walk. The shops are right out of the 1950s. Long rows of humble "two-up and two-down" houses (4 rooms) feel pretty grim. There are some buses from the town to the slate mines; the road isn't pedestrian friendly. (**TI:** daily 10:00–13:00 & 14:00–18:00, July–Aug does not close for lunch, closed Nov–Easter, tel. 01766/830-360.)

SIGHTS

▲▲**Llechwedd Slate-Mine Tour**—Slate mining played a blockbuster role in Welsh heritage, and this mine on the northern edge of the bleak town of Blaenau Ffestiniog (BLIGH-nigh FES-tin-yog) does a fine job of explaining the mining culture of Victorian Wales. The Welsh mined and split most of the slate roofs of Europe. For every ton of usable slate found, 10 tons were mined. The exhibit has three parts: a tiny Victorian mining town (with a miners' pub and a view from "The Top of the Tip," free and worthwhile) and two 30-minute tours (3/hr). Do the "tramway" tour first—a level train ride with three stops, no walking, and a live guide. It focuses on working life and traditional mining techniques. Then descend into the "deep mine" for a tour featuring an audiovisual dramatization of social life and a half-mile of walking. Both are different and, considering the cheap combo-ticket, worthwhile. Don't miss the slate-splitting demonstration at the end of the tramway tour (£7.75 for 1 tour, £11.95 for both tours, March–Sept daily 10:00–18:00, Oct–Feb 10:00–17:00, last tour starts 45 min before closing, tel. 01766/830-306, www.llechwedd.co.uk). Dress warmly—I mean it. You'll freeze underground without a sweater. Lines are longer when rain drives in the hikers.

▲**Ffestiniog Railway**—This 13-mile narrow-gauge train line was built in 1836 for small horse-drawn wagons to transport the slate from the Ffestiniog mines to the port of Porthmadog. In the 1860s, horses gave way to steam trains. Today hikers and tourists enjoy these tiny titans (£14 round trip, 1/hr in peak season, 2.5 hrs round trip; first trains of the day are £3 cheaper, first-class observation cars are £5 extra, tel. 01766/512-340). This is a novel steam-train experience, but the full-size Llandudno-Blaenau Ffestiniog train is more scenic and works better for hikers.

Near Blaenau Ffestiniog
Portmeirion—Ten miles southwest of Blaenau Ffestiniog, this "Italian Village" was the lifework of a rich local architect who began building it

in 1925. Set idyllically on the coast just beyond the poverty of the slate-mine towns, this flower-filled fantasy is extravagant. Surrounded by lush Welsh greenery and a windswept mudflat at low tide, the village is an artistic glob of palazzo arches, fountains, gardens, and promenades filled with cafés, tacky shops, a hotel, and local tourists who always wanted to go to Italy (or who are fans of the cultish British 1960s TV series *The Prisoner*). The architect explains his purpose in a videotaped slide presentation (not worth the £5.50 admission, daily 9:30–17:30, 2 miles from Porthmadog, tel. 01766/770-000).

TRANSPORTATION CONNECTIONS

North Wales
Two major transfer points out of (or into) North Wales are Chester and Crewe.

Chester by train to: London (1/hr, 3.5 hrs), **Liverpool** (2/hr, 50 min), **Birmingham** (1/hr, 2 hrs), points in **North Wales** (2/hr).

Crewe by train to: London (2/hr, 2 hrs), **Bristol,** near Bath (1/hr, 2.5 hrs), **Cardiff** (1/hr, 2.5 hrs), **Holyhead** (nearly 1/hr, 2 hrs), **Blackpool** (4/day, 2.5 hrs, more frequent with transfer in Preston), **Keswick,** the **Lake District** (1/hr, 1.75 hrs to Penrith, then catch a bus to Keswick, 1/hr except Sun 6/day, 40 min), **Glasgow** (nearly 1/hr, 3.5 hrs).

Ferry Connections—North Wales and Ireland
Holyhead and Dun Laoghaire: Stena Line sails between Holyhead (North Wales) and Dun Laoghaire near Dublin (3/day, 2 hrs on HSS *Catamaran,* one-way walk-on fare-£30, reserve by phone—they book up long in advance on summer weekends, Dun Laoghaire tel. 01/204-7777, Holyhead tel. 01407/606-606, general reservations number for Stena Line in Britain tel. 08705-707-070, can book online at www.stenaline.com).

Holyhead and Dublin: Irish Ferries sail between Holyhead (North Wales) and Dublin (5/day—2 slow, 3 fast; slow boats 3.25 hrs, one-way walk-on fare-£22–24, price depends on month; fast boats 2 hrs, £28-30, price depends on month; car fares prohibitively expensive, Holyhead tel. 08705-329-129, Dublin tel. 01/638-3333, www.irishferries.co.uk).

Sleeping near Holyhead dock: The fine $ **Monravon B&B** has seven smoke-free rooms (Db-£40–45, family deals, 15-min uphill walk from dock, Porth-Y-Felin Road, tel. & fax 01407/762-944, len@monravon .co.uk). Another option is the family-run **Orotavia B&B** with three rooms (Db-£35, 66 Walthew Avenue, 15-min uphill walk to dock, tel. 01407/760-259, www.orotavia.co.uk, shirley@orotavia.fsnet.co.uk, Shirley & Martin Williams).

Route Tips for Drivers

Ironbridge Gorge to Ruthin: Drive for an hour to Wales via A5 through Shrewsbury, crossing into Wales and following the A5 to Llangollen. Cross the bridge in Llangollen, turn left, and follow A542 and A525 past the romantic Valle Crucis abbey, over the scenic Horseshoe Pass, and into Ruthin. Driving to Conwy is faster via Wrexham and then the A55, but more scenic if you stay on the A5 from Llangollen to Betws-y-Coed and then zip north to Conwy from there.

Ruthin to Caernarfon (56 miles) to Blaenau Ffestiniog (34 miles) to Ruthin (35 miles): This route connects the top sights with the most scenic routes. From Ruthin, take B5105 (steepest road off main square) and follow signs to Cerrigydrudion. Then follow A5 into Betws-y-Coed, with a possible quick detour to the Trefriw Woolen Mills (5 miles north on B5106, well signposted). Climb west on A5 through Capel Curig, then take A4086 over the rugged Pass of Llanberis, under the summit of Mount Snowdon (to the south, behind those clouds), and on to Caernarfon. Park under the castle in the harborside car park (£2.50).

Leaving Caernarfon, take the lovely A4085 southeast through Beddgelert to Penrhyndeudraeth. (Make things even more beautiful by taking the little B4410 road from Garreg through Rhyd.) Then take A487 toward What Maentwrog and A496 to Blaenau Ffestiniog. Go through the dark and depressing mining town of Blaenau Ffestiniog on A470, continue over hills of slate, and turn right into the Llechwedd Slate Mine.

After the mine, continue uphill on A470, snapping photos north through Dolwyddelan (passing a fine old Welsh castle ruin) and back to A5. For a high and desolate detour, return to Ruthin via the curvy A543 road. Go over the stark moors to the Sportsman's Arms Pub (the highest pub in Wales, good food), continue through Denbigh, and then go home.

BLACKPOOL

This is Britain's fun puddle. It's one of England's most-visited attractions, the private domain of its working class, a faded and sticky mix of Coney Island, Las Vegas, and Woolworth's. Juveniles of any age love it. My kids declared it better than Disneyland.

Blackpool grew up with the Industrial Revolution. In the mid-1800s, entire mill towns would close down and take a two-week break here. They came to drink in the fresh air (much needed after a hard year in the mills) and—literally—the seawater. Back then they figured this was healthy.

Blackpool's heydays are past now, as more and more working people can afford the cheap charter flights to sunny Spain. Recently, the resort has become popular for "stag" and "hen" (bachelor and bachelorette) parties—basically a cheap drunk weekend for the twenty-something crowd. Consequently, the late-night ambience can suffer on weekends. Within a couple of years, Blackpool will probably add a few casinos and draw more crowds. No matter what, the town remains an accessible and affordable fun zone for the Flo and Andy Capps of northern England. People come year after year. They stay for a week, and they love it.

Most Americans don't even consider a stop in Blackpool. Many won't like it. It's an ears-pierced-while-you-wait, tipsy-toupee kind of place. Tacky, yes. Lowbrow, OK. But it's as English as can be, and that's what you're here for. An itinerary should feature as many facets of a culture as possible. Blackpool is as English as the queen—and considerably more fun.

Spend the day "muckin' about" the beach promenade of fortune-tellers, fish-and-chips joints, amusement piers, warped mirrors, and Englanders wearing hats with built-in ponytails. A million greedy doors try every trick to get you inside. Huge arcade halls advertise free toilets and broadcast bingo numbers into the streets; the wind machine under a wax Marilyn Monroe blows at a steady gale; and the smell of fries, tobacco, and sugar is everywhere. Milk comes in raspberry or banana in this land where people under incredibly bad wigs look normal. If you're bored in Blackpool, you're just too classy.

Planning Your Time

Ideally, get to Blackpool around lunchtime for a free afternoon and evening of making bubbles in this cultural mud puddle. For full effect, it's best to visit during peak season: June through early November.

Blackpool's Illuminations, when much of the waterfront is decorated with lights, draws crowds in fall, particularly on weekends (Sept 3–Nov 7 in 2004). The early evening light is great with the sun setting over the sea. Walk out along the peaceful North Pier at twilight.

Blackpool is easy by car or train. Speed demons with a car can treat it as a midday break (it's just off the M6 on M55) and continue north. If you have kids, they'll want more time here (hey, it's cheaper than Disneyland). If you're into nightlife, this town delivers. If you're before or beyond kids and not into kitsch and greasy spoons, skip it. If the weather's great and you love nature, the lakes are just a few hours north. A visit to Blackpool does sharpen the wonders of Windermere.

ORIENTATION

(area code: 01253)

Everything clusters along the six-mile beachfront promenade, a tacky, glittering good-time strip mall punctuated by three fun-filled piers reaching out into the sea. The Pleasure Beach rides are near the South Pier. Jutting up near the North Pier is Blackpool's stubby Eiffel-type tower. The most interesting shops, eateries, and theaters are inland from the North Pier. For a break from glitz, you can hike north along the waterfront path for 20 miles or so.

Tourist Information: There are two TIs near the tower. The main one is on Clifton Street (April–early Nov Mon–Sat 9:00–17:00; early Nov–March Mon–Sat 9:00–16:30, closed Sun, £1.50 fee to book shows, tel. 01253/478-222, the same number gives recorded entertainment info after hours). The other TI is on the Promenade (June–early Nov daily 9:00–17:00, closed off-season). Get the city map (£1), pick up brochures on the amusement centers, and ask about special shows. The *What's On* booklet listing local events costs £1.25. Both TIs do same-day room bookings for one-night stays for a £3 fee (room-finding service closes at 16:30).

For a history fix, get the TI's *Heritage Trail* booklet, which takes you on an hour's walk through downtown Blackpool. Saying much about little, it's endearing (60p).

Arrival in Blackpool: The train station is three blocks from the town center (no maps given but one is posted, no ATM in station but

Blackpool

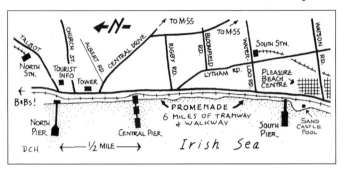

many in town). While the station has no luggage lockers, nearby hotels offer the service. The motorway funnels you down Yeadon Way into a giant parking zone (formerly the central station).

Helpful Hints

Internet Access: Try the public library in the big domed building on Queen Street (24 computers, Mon–Sat 9:00–17:00, Tue and Thu until 19:00, closes Sun at noon, tel. 01253/478-111).

Post Office: The main PO is on Abingdon Street, a block inland from the TI (Mon–Sat 9:00–17:30, closed Sun).

Markets: At the Abingdon Market, vendors sell fruit, bras, jewelry, eggs, and more (Mon–Sat 9:00–17:30, on Abingdon Street next to PO). The Fleetwood Market, eight miles north, is huge, with two buildings full of produce, clothes, and crafts spilling out into the street (May–Oct daily 9:00–17:00 except Wed and Sun, Nov–April Tue, Fri, Sat only; catch tram marked Fleetwood, 30 min, £1.80 one-way).

Car Rental: In case you decide to tour the Lake District by car, you'll find plenty of rental agencies in Blackpool (closed Sat afternoon and Sun), including Avis (292 Waterloo Road, tel. 01253/408-003) and Budget (242 Waterloo Road, tel. 01253/691-632).

Getting around Blackpool

Vintage tram cars run 13 miles up and down the waterfront, connecting all the sights. This first electric tramway in Europe dates from 1885 (90p–£2, depending on length of trip, £4.95 for all-day pass, pay conductor, trams come every 5 min or so, Nov–May every 10–20 min, runs 6:00–24:00).

A hop-on, hop-off bus tour with a recorded commentary and 16 stops leaves the Block Tower every 15–30 minutes (June–early Nov from 9:30, last departure at 20:00, no runs off-season, www.city-sightseeing.com).

Taxis are easy to snare in Blackpool and three to five people travel cheaper by cab than by tram. Hotels can get a taxi by phone within three minutes (no extra charge).

SIGHTS

▲▲**The Piers**—Blackpool's famous piers were originally built for Victorian landlubbers who wanted to go to sea but were afraid of getting seasick. Each of the three amusement piers has a personality and is a joy to wander. The sedate North Pier is most traditional and refreshingly uncluttered. Dance down its empty planks at twilight to the early English rock on its speakers. Its Carousel Bar at the end is great for families—with a free kids' DJ nightly from 20:30 to 23:00 (parents drink good beer while the kids bunny-hop and boogie). The something-for-everyone Central Pier is lots of fun. Ride its great Ferris wheel for the best view in Blackpool (rich photography at twilight, get the operator to spin you as you bottom out). And check out the masochist running the adjacent Waltzer ride—just watch the miserably ecstatic people spinning. The rollicking South Pier is all rides. From the far end of any pier you can see the natural gas drilling platforms lining the horizon.

▲**Blackpool Tower**—This mini-Eiffel Tower is a vertical fun center 100 years old. You pay £11.50 to get in; after that, the fun is free. Work your way up from the bottom through layer after layer of noisy entertainment: a circus (2–3 acts/day generally at 15:00 and 19:00), Out of This World, a dinosaur ride, an aquarium, and a wonderful old ballroom with barely live music and golden oldies dancing to golden oldies all day. Enjoy a break at the dance-floor-level pub or on a balcony perch. Kids love this place. With a little marijuana, adults would, too. Ride the glass elevator to the tip of the 500-foot-tall symbol of Blackpool for a smashing view, especially at sunset (Easter–May daily 10:00–18:00, June–early Nov daily 10:00–23:00, early Nov–Easter 10:00–18:00 weekends only, top of tower closed when windy, tel. 01253/622-242, www.theblackpooltower.co.uk). If you want to leave and return, request a hand stamp.

▲**Pleasure Beach**—These 42 acres, littered with over 100 rides (including "the best selection of white-knuckle rides in Europe"), ice-skating, circus and illusion shows, and amusements, attract seven million people a year. The top two rides are The Pepsi Max Big One (one of the world's fastest and highest roller coasters at 235 feet, 85 mph) and Ice Blast (which rockets you straight up before letting you bungee down). Also memorable are the Pasaje del Terror and the Steeple Chase—carousel horses stampeding down a roller-coaster track. The Valhalla ride zips you on a Viking boat in watery darkness past scary Nordic things like lutefisk. With two 80-foot drops and lots of hype, first you're scared, then you're soaked, and—finally—you're just glad you survived. Most of the rides are variations on the roller-coaster theme. Pleasure

Beach medics advise brittle senior travelers to avoid the old wooden-framed rides, which are much jerkier. Only the admission is free. You can pay individually for rides with your £1 tickets (most are a few tickets each), or get unlimited rides with a £26 armband (March–early Nov daily, opens at around 10:30 and closes as early as 17:00 or as late as 24:00, depending on season, weather, and demand, tel. 0870-444-5566, www.blackpoolpleasurebeach.co.uk).

There are several other major amusement centers, including a popular water park called **Sand Castle**—with a big pool, long slides, and a wave machine—across the street from Pleasure Beach (£6.25, kids 6-15-£5.40, after 14:00 £5.25, kids-£4.40, July–Aug daily 10:00–17:30, Tue–Thu until 18:30, last admission 1 hour before closing, shorter hours off-season, tel. 01253/343-602, www.blackpool-sandcastle.co.uk).

▲▲▲**People-Watching**—Blackpool's top sight is its people. You'll see England here as nowhere else. Grab someone's hand and a big stick of rock (candy), and stroll. Grown men walk around with huge teddy bears looking for places to play "bowlingo," a short-lane version of bowling. Ponder the thought of actually retiring here and spending your last years, day after day, surrounded by Blackpool and wearing a hat with a built-in ponytail. Blackpool puts people in a talkative mood. Ask someone to explain the difference between tea and supper. Back at your B&B, join in the lounge chat sessions.

▲**Showtime**—Blackpool always has a few razzle-dazzle music, dancing-girl, racy-humor, magic, and tumbling shows. Box offices around town can give you a rundown on what's available (tickets £7–15). Your B&B has the latest. For something more highbrow, try the Opera House for musicals (tel. 01253/292-029) and the Grand Theatre for drama and ballet (£15–25, tel. 01253/290-190). Both are on Church Street, a couple of blocks behind the tower. For the latest in evening entertainment, see the window display at the tourist office on Clifton Street.

▲▲**Funny Girls**—Blackpool's current hot bar is in a dazzling location a couple blocks from the train station. Most nights from 20:15 to 23:30 Funny Girls puts on a "glam bam thank you ma'am" burlesque-in-drag show that delights footballers and grannies alike. Cover is only £3 (£5.50 on weekends, dinner before show-£12.95, dinner reservations required). Get your drinks at the bar unless the transvestites are dancing on it. The show, while racy, is not raunchy. The music is very loud. The crowd is young, old, straight, gay, very down-to-earth, and fun-loving. Go on a weeknight; Friday and Saturday are too jammed. While the area up front can be a mosh pit, there are more sedate tables in back where service comes with a vampish smile. You can pay £10 for VIP seats on Sun and Tue–Thu to avoid lines and look down on the show and crowded floor from a mezzanine level (Tue–Sun, closed Mon, must be 18 to enter, 5 Dickson Street, to reserve in advance call 01253/624-901).

Blackpool's **clubs and discos** are cheap, with live bands and an interesting crowd (nightly 22:00–2:00). With all the stag and hen parties, the late-night streets can be clotted with rude rowdies.

The pubs of Blackpool have a unique tradition of "and your own, luv." Say that here and your barmaid will add 20p to your bill and drop it into her tip jar. (Say it anywhere else and they won't know what you mean.)

▲Illuminations—Blackpool was the first town in England to "go electric" in 1879. Now, every fall (Sept 3–Nov 7 in 2004), Blackpool stretches its tourist season by illuminating its six miles of waterfront with countless lights, all blinking and twinkling. The American in me kept saying, "I've seen bigger, and I've seen better," but I filled his mouth with cotton candy and just had some simple fun like everyone else on my specially decorated tram. Look for the animated tableaux on North Shore.

SLEEPING

North of the Tower

These listings are on or near the waterfront in the quiet area they call "the posh end," a mile or two north of the tower, with easy parking and easy access to the center by tram.

$$$ I know, staying at the **Hilton Hotel** in Blackpool is like wearing a tux to eat a falafel. But if you need a splurge, this is a grand place with lots of views, a pool, sauna, kids' playground, gym and comfortable rooms (Db-£100–116, "club deal Db"-£20 more—with lots of extras, ask if there are any "special rates" being advertised, request room with view—no extra charge, includes breakfast, non-smoking rooms, tram stop: Warley Road, North Promenade, tel. 01253/623-434, fax 01253/627-864, www.hilton.com).

$$$ The **Best Western Carlton Hotel** rents business-class rooms (Sb-£60–70, Db-£90–105, a long block closer to town from the Hilton, tram stop: Pleasant Street, North Promenade, tel. 01253/628-966, fax 01253/752-587, www.carltonhotelblackpool.co.uk).

$$ **Robin Hood Hotel** is a cheery place with a big, welcoming living room and 10 tastefully refurbished, spacious rooms with big beds and sea views (especially rooms 1, 5, and 9). Run by nutritionist and therapist Kathy, it also serves as a diet retreat center (Sb-£22–27, Db-£44–54, entirely non-smoking, various facial and massage treatments available, tram stop: St. Stephen's Avenue and walk 1 block north; 1.5 miles north of tower across from a peaceful stretch of beach, 100 Queens Promenade, North Shore, tel. 01253/351-599, www.robinhoodhotel.co.uk, rhhblackpool@hotmail.com).

$ **Beechcliffe Private Hotel** is clean, smoke-free, and family-run, with more charm than average and cute but tight rooms (Sb-£19.50-22.50, Db-£39–45, cocktail bar, tram stop: Uncle Tom's, walk a block

SLEEP CODE

(£1 = about $1.60, country code: 44, area code: 01253)

Sleep Code: **S** = Single, **D** = Double/Twin, **T** = Triple, **Q** = Quad, **b** = bathroom, **s** = shower only, **no CC** = Credit Cards not accepted. You can assume credit cards are accepted unless otherwise noted.

To help you sort easily through these listings, I've divided the rooms into three categories based on the price for a standard double room with bath:

$$$ **Higher Priced**—Most rooms £90 or more.
$$ **Moderately Priced**—Most rooms between £45–90.
$ **Lower Priced**—Most rooms £45 or less.

Blackpool's 140,000 people provide 120,000 beds in 3,500 mostly dumpy, cheap, nondescript hotels and B&Bs. Remember, the town's in the business of accommodating the people who can't afford to go to Spain. Most have the same design—minimal character, maximum number of springy beds—and charge £15–20 per person. Empty beds abound except from September through November and summer weekends. It's only really tight on Illumination weekends. I've listed regular high-season prices. With the huge number of hotels in town, prices get really soft in the off-season. And everyone bumps things up during the Illuminations. There's usually a launderette within a five-minute walk of your B&B; ask your host or hostess.

away from beach, 16 Shaftesbury Avenue, North Shore, tel. 01253/353-075, www.thebeechcliffehotel.co.uk, Harry and Lesley).

Near the Train Station

$ Valentine Private Hotel is a handy and friendly 13-room place. Smoking is allowed, but the breakfast room is smoke-free. Owners Denise and Garry are avid collectors; check out their bar and breakfast-room niches (Db-from £34, bunky family deals, 1 kid sleeps free, 3 blocks from station, with back to tracks, exit station far right, go up Springfield 3 blocks to Dickson, 35 Dickson Road, tel. 01253/622-775, fax 01253/293-953, Denise and Garry Hinchliffe). The Funny Girls bar is a block away.

Blackpool Center

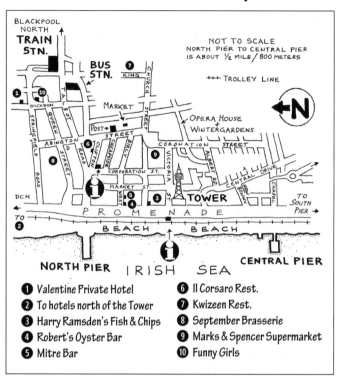

1 Valentine Private Hotel
2 To hotels north of the Tower
3 Harry Ramsden's Fish & Chips
4 Robert's Oyster Bar
5 Mitre Bar
6 Il Corsaro Rest.
7 Kwizeen Rest.
8 September Brasserie
9 Marks & Spencer Supermarket
10 Funny Girls

EATING

Your hotel may serve a cheap, early-evening meal. Generally, food in the tower and along the promenade is terrible. The following places are all between the tower and the North Pier.

"World Famous" **Harry Ramsden's** is *the* place for mushy peas, good fish and chips, and a chance to get goofy with waiters—call the place *Henry* Ramsden's and see what happens (£4–8, order a side of mushy peas, daily 11:30–22:00, off-season until 20:00, 60 The Promenade, tel. 01253/294-386).

Robert's Oyster Bar is a fixture that actually predates the resort—as do some of its employees. Read the plaque on the outside wall. You can take out or eat in—just point to what looks good (daily 9:30–22:00, until 17:00 off-season or during bad weather, at the corner of West Street and the Promenade, 1 block south of North Pier, tel. 01253/621-226).

The **Mitre Bar** serves light lunches and beers in a truly rare old-time Blackpool ambience. Drop in anytime to survey the fun photos of old Blackpool and for the great people scene (daily 11:00–23:00, around corner from Oyster Bar on West Street, tel. 01253/623-718).

Clifton Street is lined with decent eateries: Indian, Chinese, and Italian. **Il Corsaro** takes its Italian cooking seriously (Mon–Sat 18:00–23:00, Sun until 22:00, 36 Clifton Street, tel. 01253/627-440).

When pressed to recommend the best places in town, locals like **Kwizeen**, a bistro that serves good Mediterranean and modern English "kwizeen" in a—refreshing for Blackpool—plain atmosphere (£10 main courses, Mon–Sat from 18:00, closed Sun, 47 King Street, tel. 01253/290-045) and **September Brasserie,** which requires reservations and serves traditional and modern English in a dressy second-floor location (£22.50 3-course dinners, Tue–Sat 12:00–14:00 & 19:00–21:30, closed Sun–Mon, 15 Queen Street, tel. 01253/623-282).

Marks & Spencer has a big supermarket in its basement (Mon–Sat 9:00–18:00, Sun 10:30–16:30, near recommended eateries, on Coronation Street and Church Street). Picnic at the beach.

TRANSPORTATION CONNECTIONS

If you're heading to (or from) Blackpool by train, you'll usually need to transfer at **Preston** (3/hr, 30 min). Train info: tel. 08457-484-950.

Preston to: Keswick, the Lake District (hrly trains, 1.5 hrs to Penrith, then catch a bus to Keswick, 1/hr except Sun 6/day, 40 min), **Edinburgh** (8/day, 3 hrs).

Points south: To **Moreton-in-Marsh** in the Cotswolds (every 2 hrs, 5 hrs, 2 transfers), **Bath** (1/hr, 5 hrs, 2 transfers), **Conwy** in North Wales (nearly hrly, 3 hrs, 2 transfers). **London** (nearly hrly, 4 hrs, usually 2–3 transfers). Although you'll usually have transfers, sometimes you'll find fast and frequent trains. Some trains go direct from Blackpool to: **Liverpool** (every 2 hrs, 1.5 hrs), **York** (1/hr, 3.25 hrs).

Drivers entering and leaving Blackpool: As you approach Blackpool, the motorway dumps you right onto Yeadon Way, which funnels you into a huge city parking lot. Day-trippers need to park here. Leaving, to go anywhere, follow signs to M55, which starts at Blackpool and zips you to the M6 (for points north or south).

Near Blackpool: Liverpool

Liverpool, a gritty but surprisingly enjoyable city, is a fascinating stop for Beatles fans and those who would like to look urban England straight in its eyes.

Tourist Information: One of Liverpool's TIs is in the midst of most of the sights—on the huge, tidy Albert Dock (daily 10:00–17:30, tel. 0151/708-8854). Get a free, small map (also available at station for £1). In summer, guided hour-long city walking tours leave from another TI on Queen Square (£3, May–Aug Sun at 14:00, sometimes depart from other locations, call 0151/709-5111; TI open Mon–Sat 9:00–17:30, opens at 10:00 Thu, Sun 10:30–16:30).

Arrival in Liverpool: From the train station to the dock, it's a 20-minute walk or short ride on a bus (#1), taxi (£3), or Metro (get off at James Street). When returning to the center from the dock, it's best to walk or take the bus (since the Metro makes a long loop before returning to the station). Luggage storage at the station costs £2 (daily 7:00–22:00) For public transportation information, call Merseytravel (tel. 0151/236-7676).

Sunday Market: Heritage Market transforms Stanley Dock into a commotion of clothes, produce, and sweets (8:30–16:00).

Planning Your Time

Here's an easy day plan: From the station, take the Metro to Albert Dock. At the dock, choose among museums, shops, cafés, The Beatles Story, and the Lennon and McCartney Homes tour (departs from Albert Dock, reserve in advance). Consider a 50-minute ferry cruise on the river (departs Mersey Ferry dock, a 5-min walk from Albert Dock). Then walk back to the station, stopping at Mathew Street if you're a Beatles fan (to see the famous Cavern Club, the new Cavern Club nearby, a statue of the young John Lennon, and the Beatles Shop at #31) and browsing the central pedestrian core (Church Street, Williamson Square, and more) on the way. You'll have seen the art and the heart of the city.

TOURS

▲**Lennon and McCartney Homes**—John and Paul's boyhood homes are now both restored circa 1950s and open for visits, but if you want to go inside, you have to take a National Trust Tour (£10).

It's a worthwhile pilgrimage for the faithful. A minibus shuttles up to 16 people at a time from Albert Dock out to the 'burbs, first to 20 Forthlin Road, the tidy, tiny postwar council house where Paul invited John over to play. There, a guide answers questions; you hear an audio tour with reminiscences from Paul, his family, and friends; and have 40 minutes to wander. Stand in the humble front parlor where Paul and John spent their afternoons bent over their guitars strumming up "I Saw You Standing There" and more. Then wander into the dining room and check out the Beatles tchotchkes on display in the glass cabinet.

Next, the bus takes you to the posher part of town and Mendips, where John moved in with his aunt and uncle in 1945 at age five and lived until he, his wife Cynthia, and son Julian moved to London. After a brief introduction, you're armed with a brochure and set free for 20 minutes to explore the peaceful, spacious 1930s home where John wrote poetry, painted, and learned to play the guitar. Along with photographs of John as a boy, the house features a desk and china cupboard that belonged to his Aunt Mimi and period furniture designed to recapture the feel of the place during the Beatles' early years (April–Oct Wed–Sun, 4–6 tours/day, departing from either Albert Dock—tel. 0151/708-8574, or Speke Hall outside of town—tel. 0151/427-7231, 2 hrs, reservations recommended; photos, mobile phones, and large bags prohibited inside the homes).

Beatles Tours—Beatles fans may want to invest a couple of hours taking the "Magical Mystery" bus tour, which hits the lads' homes (from the outside), Penny Lane, and so on (£11, 2 hrs, generally departing the Albert Dock TI 12:00 and 14:30). The TI has specifics on the big bus that goes daily.

For something more extensive, fun, and intimate, consider a three-hour minibus Beatles tour from Phil Hughes. It's longer because it includes information on historic Liverpool as well as the Beatles stuff (£11.50/person, minimum £65/group, includes free beverages and Beatles Story discount, can coordinate times with National Trust tour of Lennon and McCartney homes, 8-seat minibus, tel. & fax 0151/228-4565, mobile 07961/511-223, www.tourliverpool.co.uk).

Jackie Spencer also hits the highlights and does private tours—just say when and where you want to go (5 people in minivan-£130, 4 people in private taxi-£100, 2.5 hrs, will pick you up at hotel or train station, tel. 0151/330-0844, mobile 0799/076-1478, www.liveapool.com).

The "sights" each tour covers are basically houses where the Fab Four grew up (outside only), places they performed, and spots made famous by the lyrics of their hits ("Penny Lane," "Strawberry Fields," the Eleanor Rigby graveyard, etc.). While boring to anyone not into the Beatles, fans will enjoy the commentary and seeing the shelter on the roundabout, the fire station with the clean machine, and the barber who shaves another customer.

Ferry Cruise—Mersey Ferries offer narrated cruises departing from Mersey Dock, an easy five-minute walk from Albert Dock. The cruise makes two brief stops on the other side of the river; you can hop off and catch the next boat back (£4.50, year-round, Mon–Fri 10:00–15:00, Sat–Sun 10:00–18:00, leaves at top of hour, café, WCs on board, tel. 0151/639-0609, www.merseyferries.co.uk).

Harbor and City Tour—The Yellow Duckmarine runs wacky tours of Liverpool's waterfront, city, and docks by land and by sea in its amphibious tourist assault vehicles (£10, buy tickets at the Gower Street bus stop or office on Albert Dock near the Beatles Story, mid-Feb–Dec daily every 75 min from 11:00 until dusk, be prepared to quack, tel. 0151/708-7799, www.theyellowduckmarine.co.uk).

SIGHTS

Liverpool's Albert Dock—Opened in 1852 by Prince Albert and enclosing seven acres of water, Albert Dock is surrounded by five-story brick warehouses. In its day, Liverpool was England's greatest seaport. It prospered as one corner of the triangular commerce of the 18th-century slave trade. As England's economy boomed, so did the port of Liverpool. From 1830 to 1930, nine million emigrants sailed from Liverpool to find their dreams in the New World. But the port was not deep enough for the big new ships; trade declined after 1890, and by 1972 it was closed entirely. Like Liverpool itself, the docks have enjoyed a renaissance, and today they are the featured attraction of the city. The city's main attractions and a half-dozen trendy eateries are lined up here out of the rain and padded by lots of shopping mall-type distractions. There's plenty of parking.

▲**Merseyside Maritime Museum**—This museum, which tells the story of this once-prosperous shipping center, gets an A for effort but feels designed for visiting school groups. While the ships section is pretty dull, the slavery, smuggling, customs, and emigration sections are interesting (tel. 0151/478-4499). The associated **Museum of Liverpool Life** offers a good look at the town's story (both free, daily 10:00–17:00, check events board upon arrival, tel. 0151/478-4080).

Tate Gallery Liverpool—This prestigious gallery of modern art is next to the Maritime Museum. It won't entertain you as well as its London sister, Tate Modern, but if you're into modern art, any Tate's great (free, special exhibits-£4, Tue–Sun 10:00–18:00, closed Mon, tel. 0151/702-7400, www.tate.org.uk/liverpool, liverpoolinfo@tate.org.uk).

▲**The Beatles Story**—It's sad to think the Beatles are stuck in a museum (and Ringo's in reruns of *Shining Time Station*). Still, while overpriced and not very creative, the story's a fascinating one, and even an avid fan will pick up some new information (£8, daily 10:00–18:00, until 17:00 in winter, sometimes open until 20:00 Sat in July–Aug, last admission 1 hour before closing but if you arrive later, ask if they'll let you in for a discount, tel. 0151/709-1963). The shop is an impressive pile of Beatles buyables.

SLEEPING

(£1 = about $1.60, country code: 44, area code: 0151)
$$ Holiday Inn Express, which has 135 comfortable, American-style rooms, many with great harbor views, is right on Albert Dock (Db-£67, £70 Fri–Sat, includes breakfast, best to book at least a week ahead, next to Beatles Story, Albert Dock, tel. 0151/709-1133, fax 0151/709-1144, expressbyholidayinn@cidc.co.uk).

$$ **Henry's Premier Lodge,** older and more central, is a budget hotel with 39 decent rooms that could use sprucing up (Db-£50, up to 2 adults and 2 kids OK, breakfast-£4.25–6.25, parallel to Mathew Street, 5-min walk from station, 45 Victoria Street, tel. 0151/236-1366, fax 0870/990-6585).

$ **International Inn** hostel, run by the daughter of the Beatles' first manager, is located in a former Victorian warehouse and has 100 budget beds (Db-£36, bed in 4- to 10-bed room-£15, bedding provided, all rooms en suite, free toast, tea & coffee, Internet access, laundry room-£2/load, games in lobby, TV lounge, video library, café, 4 South Hunter Street, if you're taking a taxi, mention that it's the Hunter Street near Hardman Street, tel. 0151/709-8135, www.internationalinn.co.uk, info@internationalinn.co.uk).

TRANSPORTATION CONNECTIONS

By Train to: Blackpool (every 2 hrs, 1.5 hrs, more frequent with transfer at Preston), **York** (1/hr, 2.5 hrs), **Edinburgh** (7/day, 4 hrs, can involve transfer), **London** (1/hr, 2.5 hrs), **Crewe** (18/day, 45 min), **Chester** (2/hr, 45 min). Train info: tel. 08457-484-950.

By ferry to Belfast, Nothern Ireland: Merchant Ferries sails most mornings (Tue–Thu & Sat–Sun) and every evening year-round (9 hrs, £30 one-way day crossing, £40 one-way overnight, cabins-£50 extra, can carry cars, tel. 0870-600-4321).

Route Tips for Drivers
Ruthin to Blackpool via Liverpool: From Ruthin, follow signs to the town of Mold, then Queensferry, then Manchester M56, then Liverpool M53, which tunnels under the Mersey River (£1). In Liverpool, follow signs to City Center and Albert Dock, where you'll find a huge car park at the dock. Leaving Liverpool, drive north along the waterfront, following signs to M58 (Preston). Once on M58 (and not before), follow signs to M6, and then M55 into Blackpool.

Ruthin to Blackpool (100 miles): From Ruthin, take A494 through the town of Mold and follow the blue signs to the motorway. M56 zips you to M6, where you'll turn north toward Preston and Lancaster. Don't miss your turnoff. A few minutes after Preston, take the not-very-clearly signed next exit (#32, M55) into Blackpool and drive as close as you can to the stubby Eiffel-type tower in the town center. Downtown parking is terrible. If you're just spending the day, head for one of the huge £6/day garages. If you're spending the night, drive to the waterfront and head north. My top B&Bs are north on the promenade (easy parking).

LAKE DISTRICT

In the pristine Lake District, Wordsworth's poems still shiver in trees and ripple on ponds. This is a land where nature rules and man keeps a wide-eyed but low profile. Relax, recharge, take a cruise or a hike, and maybe even write a poem. Renew your poetic license at Wordsworth's famous Dove Cottage.

The Lake District, about 30 miles long and 30 miles wide, is nature's lush, green playground. Explore it by foot, bike, bus, or car. While not impressive in sheer height (Scafell Pike, the tallest peak in England, is only 3,206 feet), there's a walking-stick charm about the way nature and the local culture mix. Walking along a windblown ridge or climbing over a rock fence to look into the eyes of a ragamuffin sheep, even tenderfeet get a chance to feel very outdoorsy.

You'll probably have rain mixed with brilliant bright spells. Drizzly days can be followed by delightful evenings. Pubs offer atmospheric shelter at every turn. As the locals are fond of saying, "There's no such thing as bad weather, only unsuitable clothing."

While the south lakes (Windermere, Bowness, Beatrix Potter's cottage) get the promotion and tour crowds and are closer to London, the north lakes (Ullswater, Derwentwater, Buttermere) are less touristy and at least as scenic.

The town of Keswick, the lake called Derwentwater, and the vast time-passed Newlands Valley will be our focus. The area works great by car or by train or bus. And Wordsworth and Potter fans can easily side-trip south to see the authors' homes.

Planning Your Time
On a three-week trip in Britain, I'd spend two days and two nights in the area. The quickest way in is to leave the motorway or train line at Penrith.

Those without a car will use Keswick as a springboard. Cruise the lake and take one of the many hikes in the Cat Bells area. Non-hikers can take a minibus tour.

Here's the most exciting way for drivers to pack their day of arrival: Get an early start from Blackpool or North Wales, leave the motorway at Kendal by 10:30, drive along Windermere and through Ambleside, 11:30-Tour Dove Cottage, 12:30-Backtrack to Ambleside, where a small road leads up and over the dramatic Kirkstone Pass (far more scenic northbound than southbound, get out and bite the wind) and down to Glenridding on Ullswater. You could catch the 15:00 boat. Hike six miles (15:30–18:45) from Howtown back to Glenridding. Drive to your farmhouse B&B near Keswick, with a stop as the sun sets at Castlerigg Stone Circle.

On your second day, explore Buttermere Lake, drive over Honister Pass, explore Derwentwater, and do the Cat Bells High Ridge walk. Spend the evening at the same B&B.

If great scenery is commonplace in your life, the Lake District can be more soothing (and rainy) than exciting. If you're rushed, you could make this area a one-night stand—or even a quick drive-through.

Getting around the Lake District

Those based in Keswick without a car can manage fine. Be sure to pick up the excellent *Lakeland Explorer* magazine (free from TIs and some hotels), which explains all the local bus and boat schedules and outlines some great walks for the first-time visitor.

By Foot: Piles of hiking information are available everywhere you turn. Consider buying a detailed map (such as the various Ordnance Survey maps, £7–11, sold at Keswick TI). For easy hikes, the fliers at TIs and B&Bs describing particular routes are helpful. The best ridge walk is immediately outside of town (see "Cat Bells High Ridge Hike," page 250). The Lake District's TIs advise hikers to check the weather before setting out (for an up-to-date weather report, ask at TI or tel. 017687/75757), wear suitable clothing, and bring a map.

By Boat: A circular boat service glides you around Derwentwater (for a sail/hike option, see "Derwentwater Area," page 249).

By Bus: Local buses take you quickly and easily (if not always frequently) to all nearby points of interest. Stop by the TI for a free, 30-page *Lakeland Explorer* bus brochure for schedules and suggested bus/hike outings. Lakeland Explorer bus passes (£17/4 days) are sold at the TI and the Keswick post office (April–Sept Mon–Fri 8:30–17:30, Sat 9:00–13:00, closed Sun, just off main square at corner of Main and Bank Streets). Purchase £7.50 one-day passes on the bus (bus and rail info Web site: www.traveline.org.uk).

By Bike: Several shops rent bikes in Keswick; Keswick Mountain Bikes has the largest selection (£14/day, daily 9:00–17:30, Oct–March

Lake District

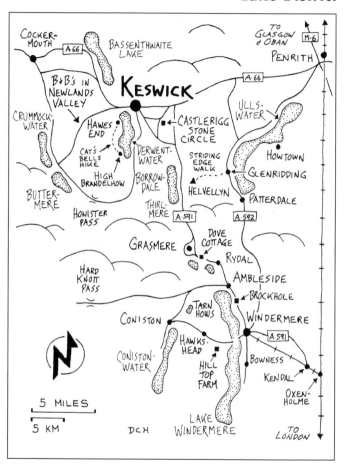

closed Tue, includes helmet, tandems available, guided bike tours by request, Southey Hill Trading Estate past Pencil Museum, tel. 017687/75202, www.keswickbikes.co.uk). Keswick Mountain Bikes and the TI sell cycling maps (£2–6).

By Car: Nothing is very far from Keswick and Derwentwater. Get a good map, get off the big roads, and leave the car, at least occasionally, for some walking. In summer, the Keswick-Ambleside-Windermere-Bowness corridor (A591) suffers from congestion. If you want to rent a car in Keswick, Fiat is your only choice (from £32/day, Mon–Sat 8:30–17:30, closed Sun, only ages 25–70, must have U.S.

license and passport, Lake Road in town center, tel. 017687/72064, aftersales.keswickmotorcompany.53807@fiatuk.net).

Bus Tours from Keswick

Bus tours are great for people with bucks who'd like to see the area without hiking or messing with public transport.

The National Trust runs a variety of full- and half-day tours from Keswick, covering Ullswater sights, Beatrix Potter territory, and more. Their half-day "North Lake Tourer" features the area around Keswick: Borrowdale, Brandelhow, Buttermere, and Honister Pass (£12/half day, £20–27/full day, April–Oct Mon–Sat, none Sun, some offered year-round, book at TI or NT office between town theater and Keswick boat dock, Mon–Tue 9:15–16:00, Wed–Sun 9:15–19:00, tel. 017687/73780, www.nationaltrust.org.uk).

Mountain Goat Tours runs a few minibus tours from Keswick (£14/half day, £27/full-day tour, tours offered Easter-Oct but run only if there are sufficient sign-ups, book in advance with Keswick TI or by calling tel. 017687/73962, same company also runs tours from Windermere, see "Sights—Windermere Area" page 252, www.mountain-goat.com).

As a super-cheap **alternative to tours,** take a round-trip on bus #77 from Keswick to Buttermere and back; it loops around Honister Pass (£5.50, May–Oct, 4/day clockwise, 4/day "anti-clockwise," 1.5 hrs, bus info: tel. 0870-608-2608, www.traveline.org.uk).

Keswick

As far as touristy Lake District centers go, Keswick (KEZ-ick, pop. 5,000) is far more enjoyable than Windermere, Bowness, or Ambleside. An important mining center (slate, copper, lead) through the Middle Ages, Keswick became a resort in the 19th century. Its fine Victorian buildings recall those romantic days when city slickers first learned about "communing with nature." Today the compact town is lined with tearooms, pubs, gift shops, and hiking-gear shops. The lake is a pleasant five-minute walk from the town center.

Keswick is the ideal home base: plenty of good B&Bs (see "Sleeping," page 255), an easy bus connection to the nearest train station at Penrith, and a prime location near the best lake in the area, Derwentwater. In Keswick everything is within a five-minute walk of everything else: the pedestrian market square, the TI, recommended B&Bs, a grocery store, the municipal pitch-and-putt golf course, the bus stop, a lakeside boat dock, the post office (with Internet access), and a central car park. Saturday is market day, and the town square is packed and lively.

Keswick hosts an annual convention in July that books up a lot of rooms. Reserve well in advance if you plan to visit in July.

Tourist Information: The helpful TI is in Moot Hall right in the middle of the main square (Easter–Oct daily 9:30–17:30, sometimes until 18:00, Nov–Easter daily 9:30–16:30, tel. 017687/72645, www.lake-district.gov.uk). The staff books rooms (free) and are pros at advising you about hiking routes and helping figure out public transportation to outlying sights. The bookstore has fine books and maps for hikers, cyclists, and drivers. The TI also sells great brochures and maps outlining nearby hikes (60p-£1, including a 50p Keswick Town Trail for history buffs, and a user-friendly £1.30 Lap Map featuring sights, walks, and a mileage chart); tickets to the town theater and Mountain Goat and National Trust minibus tours; Lakeland Explorer bus passes (see "Getting around the Lake District," above); and discounted Derwentwater Launch tickets (£4.40; £5.40 at the lake). Check the "What's On" boards (inside TI's foyer and on outside wall at post-office end) for information about walks, talks, and entertainment. The TI posts a daily weather forecast just outside the front door. Pop upstairs for a series of short videos (free) about the history of Keswick and the Lake District.

Internet Access: U-Compute, a computer store above the post office, provides Internet access (£3/hr, July–Sept Mon–Sat 9:00–17:30, Sun 9:30–16:30; don't wait in PO queue, use staircase midway through building on the right, just off main square at corner of Main and Bank Streets, tel. 017687/75127). The library also has six terminals (50p minimum charge, £2/hr, Mon–Wed & Fri 9:30–19:00, Thu & Sat 9:30–12:30, closed Sun, tel. 017687/72656).

SIGHTS

Keswick
▲▲**Daily Walks**—Walks of varying levels of difficulty led by local guides depart from the Keswick TI daily at 10:15, regardless of the weather (£5, Easter–Oct, meet at TI 10 min before departure, bring a lunch and plenty of water; sometimes taxi, bus, or boat fare required; return by 17:00, TI tel. 017687/72645 or 017687/71292, www.keswickrambles.co.uk).

For a list of free daily guided walks offered throughout the Lake District by "Voluntary Wardens," check the *Events 2004* booklet at any local TI. Many of the hikes start at Brockhole National Park Visitors Centre, which is an easy bus ride or a short drive from Keswick, but usually two hikes a week originate in Keswick (on Sun and Wed afternoons, July–Sept).

▲**Pencil Museum**—Graphite was first discovered centuries ago in Keswick. A hunk of the stuff proved great for marking sheep in the 15th century, and the rest is history (which you can learn all about here).

Keswick

TO NEWLANDS VALLEY B&B's
TO A-66 & PHEASANT INN
CROSSTHWAITE
PATH
BIKE RENTAL
FITZ PARK
POOL
ART MUSEUM
HIGH HILL
PENCIL MUSEUM
GRETA
RIVER
MAIN
LAUNDRY
STANGER
TO PENRITH
HOSTEL
STATION
BUS STOP
& SUPERMARKET
HEADS
HEADLANDS
BANK
VICTORIA
POST
MARKET
PENRITH ROAD
CAMPING
THE HEADS
ROAD
PL.
ST. JOHNS
LAKE RD
BORROWDALE
SOUTHEY
TO CASTLERIGG STONE CIRCLE
AMBLESIDE
PITCH+PUTT GOLF
PARKS
LAKE ROAD
HEADS ROAD
TO WINDERMERE VIA A-591
TO BUTTERMERE VIA B-5289
P – PARKING
¼ MILE
400 METERS
DOCK
DERWENT WATER
DCH
PATH TO FRIAR'S CRAG

6 Morrel's Restaurant
7 Sigi's Restaurant
8 Pack Horse Inn
9 Lakeland Pedlar Café
10 Maysons Restaurant
11 Bryson's Bakery
12 Coffee Lounge
13 Library
14 Theatre by the Lake
15 National Trust Tours
16 Keswick Launch Cruises

1 Howe Keld Lakeland Hotel, Parkfield B&B & West View Guest House
2 Berkeley Guest House
3 Stanger Street B&Bs
4 Dog and Gun Pub
5 The Four in Hand Restaurant

While you can't tour the 150-year-old factory where the famous Derwent pencils are made, the charming museum on the edge of Keswick is a good way to pass a rainy hour. Take a look at the "war pencils" made for WWII bomber crews (and filled with tiny maps and compasses) and the 25-foot pencil that took a crew of 15 four weeks to create (£2.50, daily 9:30–16:00, July–Aug until 17:30, free 10-min film is worthwhile, cheap brass rubbing in shop, tel. 017687/73626, www.pencils.co.uk).

▲**Plays**—Locals are proud of their Theatre by the Lake, which offers events year-round and plays comedy, drama, music, and dance almost nightly in the summer. This is a fine opportunity to do something completely local (£10–18, discounts for old and young, 20:00 shows in summer, 19:30 in winter, smart to book ahead July–Aug, parking £1.35/2 hrs but free after 19:00, tel. 017687/74411, www.theatrebythelake.com).

▲**Golf**—A lush nine-hole pitch 'n' putt golf course separates the town from the lake and offers a classy, cheap, and convenient chance to golf near the birthplace of the sport (£2.60 for 9 holes, £1.40 for 18 tame holes of "obstacle golf," Easter–Oct daily 9:30–20:00, closed Nov-Easter, tel. 017687/73445).

Swimming—The Leisure Center has an indoor pool kids love, with a huge water slide and wave machine (pool: adults-£3.70, kids ages 3–16-£2.90, cheaper in winter, Mon–Fri 11:00–19:00, Thu closes at 18:00, Sat–Sun 10:00–18:00, call to confirm hours, shorter hours off-season, no towels or suits for rent, lockers-50p deposit, a 10-min walk from town center, follow Station Road past Fitz Park and veer left, tel. 017687/72760). The Leisure Centre's Fitness Centre offers a "Quick Holiday Day Pass" for £10 (includes mandatory first-time orientation to gym, each subsequent visit-£4.20).

Fitz Park—A pleasant grassy park stretches alongside Keswick's tree-lined, duck-filled River Greta. There's plenty of room for kids to burn off energy. Consider an after-dinner stroll on the footpath. You may catch men in white playing a game of cricket or lawn bowling.

Derwentwater Area

Derwentwater—This is one of the region's most photographed and popular lakes. With four islands, good circular boat service, plenty of trails, and the pleasant town of Keswick at its north end, Derwentwater entertains.

The roadside views aren't much, so walk or cruise. You can walk around the lake (fine trail, floods in heavy rains, 9 miles, 3 hrs), cruise it (50 min), or do a hike/sail mix. I suggest the hike/sail combo. From mid-March to October, boats run from Keswick about every 30 minutes—alternating clockwise and "anticlockwise"—from 10:00 to 20:00 (at start and end of season until 16:30; in winter 5/day on weekends), making seven stops on each 50-minute round-trip. The boat trip costs £5.40 per circle (£4.40 if you book through TI), with free stopovers, or

85p per segment. Stand on the pier or the boat may not stop. The Keswick Launch also offers a 60-minute cruise every evening mid-June through September (£6, free glass of wine or soft drink, 20:30 May–mid-Aug, 19:30 mid-Aug–mid-Sept) and rents rowboats for two (£4/30 min, £6.50/hr, located at town dock at the end of Lake Road, tel. 017687/72263).

The best hour-long lakeside walk is the 1.5-mile path between the docks at High Brandelhow and Hawes End. You could continue on foot along the lake back into Keswick.

Lodore is an easy stop for its Lodore Falls, a 10-minute walk from the dock (falls behind Lodore Hotel, which serves lunch). For a better eatery, try the tiny High Lodore Farm Café, run by a sheep farmer, Martin, who serves breakfast, cakes, and drinks to hikers and day-trippers (daily 9:00–18:30, shorter hours in bad weather, from the dock, walk up the road, turn right over bridge uphill to café, tel. 017687/77221).

▲▲Cat Bells High Ridge Hike—For a great (and fairly easy) "king of the mountain" feeling, sweeping views, and a close-up look at the weather blowing over the ridge, hike about two hours from Hawes End up along the ridge to Cat Bells (1,480 feet) and down to High Brandelhow. From there, you can catch the boat or take the easy path along the shore of Derwentwater to your Hawes End starting point. This is probably the most dramatic family walk in the area (but wear sturdy shoes, bring a raincoat, and watch your footing). From Keswick, the lake, or your farmhouse B&B, you can see silhouetted stick figures hiking along this ridge. Drivers can park free at Hawes End or at the Littletown Farm on the Newlands Valley side of Cat Bells (tel. 017687/78353). The Keswick TI sells a *Skiddaw & Cat Bells* brochure about the hike (60p).

Cat Bells is just the first of a series of peaks all connected by a fine ridge trail. Hardier hikers continue up to nine miles along this same ridge, enjoying valley and lake views as they arc around the Newlands Valley toward (and even down to) Buttermere. After High Spy, you can descend an easy path into Newlands Valley. An ultimate day plan would be to bus to Buttermere, climb Robinson, and follow the ridge around to Cat Bells and back to Keswick.

▲▲Car Hiking from Keswick—Distances are short, roads are narrow and have turnouts, and views are rewarding. Ask your B&B host for advice. Particularly scenic drives include Latrigg (from a car park just north of Keswick, walk a few minutes to the top of the hill for a commanding view of the town and lake). Two miles south of Keswick on the lakeside B5289 Borrowdale Valley Road, take the small road left (signposted *Watendlath*) for a half mile to the Ashness packhorse bridge (a quintessential Lake District scene) and, a half mile farther, to a car park and the "surprise view" of Derwentwater. It's wisest to turn around here because if you continue, the road gets extremely narrow en route to the hamlet of Watendlath, which has a tiny lake and lazy farm animals. (On summer Sundays, free Rambler shuttle buses—offered to minimize traffic congestion—run hourly between Keswick and Watendlath. Ride to the end and hike home.) Return down to B5289 and back to Keswick or farther south to scenic Borrowdale and over the dramatic pass to Buttermere.

▲▲**Buttermere**—This ideal little lake with a lovely, encircling four-mile stroll offers nonstop, no-sweat Lake District beauty. If you're not a hiker but kind of wish you were, take this walk. If you're very short on time, at least stop here and get your shoes dirty. (Parking and pubs are in Buttermere village.) Buttermere is connected with Borrowdale and Derwentwater by a great road over the rugged Honister Pass, strewn with glacial debris and curious shaggy Swaledale sheep (looking more like goats with their curly horns). In the other direction, you can explore the cruel Newlands Valley or carry on through gentler scenery along Crummock Water and through the forested Whinlatter Pass (fine Visitors Centre with a café the flying squirrels love) and back to Keswick. From May through October, bus #77 makes a round-trip loop between Keswick and Buttermere over Honister Pass (£5.50, 4/day in both directions, 1.5 hrs).

▲▲**Castlerigg Stone Circle**—These 38 stones, 90 feet across and 3,000 years old, are mysteriously laid out on a line between the two tallest peaks on the horizon. For maximum goose pimples (as they say here), show up at sunset (free, open all the time, 3 miles east of Keswick, follow brown signs, 3 min off A66, easy parking).

▲▲**More Hikes**—The area is riddled with wonderful hikes. B&Bs all have fine advice. From downtown Keswick you can walk the seven-mile Latrigg trail, which includes the Castlerigg Stone Circle (pick up 60p map/guide from TI). From the car park at Newlands Pass, at the top of Newlands Valley, an easy one-mile walk to Knottrigg probably offers more thrills per calorie burned than any walk in the region.

Derwent Bay Bears—You'll see the Derwent Bay Bears' shop, featuring wooden chainsaw sculptures of bears, on the main square in downtown Keswick, across from the TI. For a free demo showing how these life-sized, totem-pole bears are made, you can visit the workshop outside of town (April–Oct daily 10:00–18:00, Nov–March Tue–Sun 10:00–16:00, closed Mon, demos daily 10:00–17:00, call ahead for times, 1 mile from Keswick to Portinscale village, then go 2 more miles and look for sign, tel. 017687/74788, www.derwentbaybears.co.uk).

Penrith

If you're using public transportation, chances are you'll transfer at Penrith, which has one decent sight.

Rheged—This mountaineering-themed exhibition center—named for a Celtic Cumbrian kingdom—is a good rainy-day retreat. The National Mountaineering Exhibition displays artifacts from expeditions to Everest and other climbs: diaries, scrapbooks, breathing equipment, and other climbing paraphernalia. The IMAX-style "giant movie" theater shows eye-popping movies (including the 1-hour "Rheged—The Movie: The Lost Kingdom," featuring this region's original Celtic warriors and other historical residents). The center also has shops, restaurants, and a good TI (mountaineering exhibition-£5.50, any 1 movie-£5.50, combo-ticket for any 2 attractions-£9.45, any 3 attractions-£13.40, daily 10:00–17:30, in Penrith, call ahead or check Web site for specific movie times, tel. 01768/868-000, www.rheged.com). Buses X4 and X5, which run between Keswick and the Penrith train station, stop at the Rheged main entrance (see "Transportation Connections," page 260), or hop on X50 (direction Workington) at the Penrith train station.

Windermere Area

▲**Brockhole National Park Visitors Centre**—Check the events board as you enter. The center offers a free 15-minute life-in-the-Lake District slide show (played upon request), an information desk, organized walks, exhibits, a bookshop, a good cafeteria, gardens, nature walks, and a large car park. It's in a stately old lakeside mansion between Ambleside and the town of Windermere on A591 (April–Oct daily 10:00–17:00, grounds open until dusk, free entry but £3 to park, tel. 015394/46601, www.lake-district.gov.uk). The bookshop has an excellent selection of maps and guidebooks.

▲▲**Dove Cottage**—William Wordsworth, the poet whose appreciation of nature and back-to-basics lifestyle put this area on the map, spent his most productive years (1799-1808) in this well-preserved old cottage on the edge of Grasmere. Today it's the obligatory sight for any Lake District visit. Even if you're not a fan, Wordsworth's "plain living and high thinking," his appreciation of nature, his romanticism, and the ways his friends unleashed their creative talents are appealing. The 30-minute cottage tour (departures on the hour and half-hour) and adjoining museum are excellent. In dry weather, the garden where the poet was much inspired is worth a wander (open weather permitting). Even a speedy, jaded museum-goer will want at least an hour here (£5.80, includes voucher for 15 percent off Rydal Mount, below, and Cockermouth, Wordsworth's birthplace, daily 9:30–17:30, last entry at 17:00, closed mid-Jan to mid-Feb, tel. 015394/35544, www.wordsworth.org.uk). The modern-art gallery next to Dove Cottage, 3°W @ Island View, has rotating exhibits dedicated to "contemporary meditations on Romantic themes."

On Tuesday evenings in summer, poetry readings are held at Thistle Hotel (across from Dove Cottage) at 18:30, followed by an optional dinner in the Dove Cottage Restaurant at 20:45 (readings-£5 at the door or £4 prebooked, dinner with wine-£13.50, you may even get to eat with the writer, book ahead at tel. 015394/35544).

Rydal Mount—Wordsworth's final, higher-class home, with a lovely garden and view, lacks the charm of Dove Cottage. He lived here 37 years. Just down the road from Dove Cottage, it's worthwhile only for Wordsworth fans (£4, includes voucher for 15 percent off Dove Cottage and Cockermouth, March–Oct daily 9:30–17:00; Nov–Feb Wed–Mon 10:00–16:00, closed Tue; 1.5 miles north of Ambleside, tel. 015394/33002).

Hayes Garden World—This extensive gardening center—a popular weekend excursion for locals—offers garden supplies, a bookstore, and gorgeous grounds. Gardeners could wander this place all afternoon. Upstairs is a fine cafeteria-style restaurant called The Four Seasons (daily 11:00–18:00, in Ambleside near Grasmere/Dove Cottage, tel. 0113/273-1949, www.hayesgardenworld.co.uk).

▲**Hill Top Farm and Other Beatrix Potter Sights**—Many come to the lakes on a Beatrix Potter pilgrimage. Sensing this, entrepreneurial locals have dreamed up a number of BP sights. This can be confusing—and disappointing if you visit on Thursday, Friday, or winter, when the two best sights, Hill Top Farm and the Beatrix Potter Gallery, are closed.

The most important (and least advertised) is **Hill Top Farm,** the 17th-century cottage where Potter wrote many of her Peter Rabbit books (£4.50, £7 combo-ticket with Beatrix Potter Gallery saves only 50p, April–Oct Sat–Wed 10:30–16:30, Thu–Fri cottage closed but gardens open 11:00–16:00 and free, closed Nov–March, last entry 30 min before closing, in Near Sawrey village, 2 miles south of Hawkshead, tel. 015394/36269, hilltop@nationaltrust.org.uk). Small, dark, and crowded, it gives a good look at her life and work. In summer, hourly buses connect Hill Top Farm and Hawkshead Square, where you'll find...

The **Beatrix Potter Gallery** (in the neighboring, likeable town of Hawkshead) shows off BP's original drawings and watercolor illustrations used in her children's books and tells more about her life and work (£3, £7 combo-ticket with Hill Top Farm, same hours as Hill Top, closed Thu–Fri and Nov–March, Main Street, tel. 015394/36355, beatrixpottergallery@nationaltrust.org.uk).

The gimmicky **World of Beatrix Potter** tour—a hit with children—features a five-minute video trip into the world of Mrs. Tiggywinkle and company, a series of Lake District tableaux starring the same imaginary gang, and a 15-minute video biography of BP (not worth £3.75, Easter–Sept daily 10:00–17:30, Oct–Easter daily 10:00–16:30, closed Jan, in Bowness near Windermere town, tel. 015394/88444, www.hop-skip-jump.com).

Mountain Goat's "Beatrix Potter's Boat & Goat" five-hour **minibus tour** covers the World of Beatrix Potter and a cruise across

Lake Windermere. It also stops for lunch at Hawkshead, providing an opportunity to visit the Beatrix Potter Gallery (admission not included) and rolls through Langdales and Grasmere (£20.50, includes admission to World of Beatrix Potter and boat ride, runs Tue–Thu, leaves Windermere at 10:30 and returns at 15:30, tel. 015394/45161, www.mountain-goat.com).

Hard Knott Pass—Only 1,300 feet above sea level, this pass is a thriller, with a narrow, winding, steeply graded road. Just over the pass are the scant but evocative remains of the Hard Knott Roman fortress. There are great views but miserable rainstorms, and it can be very slow and frustrating when the one-lane road with turnouts is clogged by traffic. Avoid it in summer.

Ullswater Area

▲▲**Ullswater Hike and Boat Ride**—Long, narrow Ullswater offers eight miles of diverse and grand Lake District scenery. While you can drive it or cruise it, I'd ride the boat from the south tip halfway up and hike back. Boats leave Glenridding regularly—from four to nine per day, depending on the season (£3.90 one-way, £6.40 round-trip, daily 10:00–16:15, less off-season, 35-min ride to Howtown; safe "pay and display" parking lot-£2/2 hrs, £4/12 hrs, parking not included with boat tickets; café, free timetable shows walking route, tel. 017684/82229 for schedule, arrive 20 min before departure in summer especially for departures around lunch, www.ullswater-steamers.co.uk). Ride to the first stop, Howtown, halfway up the lake. Then spend four hours hiking and dawdling along the well-marked path by the lake south to Patterdale and then along the road back to Glenridding. This is a serious seven-mile walk with good views, varied terrain, and a few bridges and farms along the way. Wear good shoes and be prepared for rain. For a shorter hike from Howtown Pier, consider a three-mile loop around Hallin Fell.

Several steamer trips chug daily up and down Ullswater. A good rainy-day plan is to ride the covered boat up and down the lake (to the furthest point—Pooley Bridge, £8.80 round-trip, 2 hrs) or to Howtown and back (£6.40 round-trip, 1 hr). To reach Glenridding by bus from Keswick, allow two hours with a transfer at Penrith (direct buses in summer, 5/day, 40 min).

Helvellyn—Often considered the best high-mountain hike in the Lake District, this breathtaking, round-trip route from Glenridding includes the spectacular Striding Edge ridge walk. Be careful; do this six-hour hike only in good weather and get advice from the Glenridding TI (summer daily 9:00–18:00; winter Fri–Sun 9:30–15:30, maybe closed Mon–Thu; tel. 017684/82414). While there are shorter routes, the Glenridding ascent is best. The Keswick TI has a helpful *Helvellyn from Glenridding* leaflet on the hike (60p).

SLEEPING

Keswick

The Lake District abounds with attractive B&Bs, guest houses, and hostels. It needs them all when summer hordes threaten the serenity of this romantic mecca. Alert: Book well in advance if you plan to visit during Keswick's annual convention in July.

Outside of summer, if you have a car, you should have no trouble finding a room. But to get a particular place (especially on Sat), call ahead. Those using public transportation should stay in Keswick. With a car, drive into a remote farmhouse experience. Lakeland hostels are cheaper and filled with an interesting crowd. The Keswick TI can give you phone numbers of places with vacancies if you call, or book you a room if you drop in.

In Keswick, I've featured two streets, each within three blocks of the bus station and town square. "The Heads" is a classier area lined with proud Victorian houses, close to the lake and new theater, overlooking a golf course. Stanger Street, a bit humbler but also quiet and handy, has smaller homes. All of my Keswick listings are strictly smoke-free.

The **launderette** is around the corner from the bus station on Main Street (daily 7:30–19:00, £4.40/load wash and dry, change machine and coin-op flake dispenser, about £1 extra for full service by 10:00 or earlier; if you drop off before 9:00 just leave clothes and a note inside by the office door closest to the front, tel. 017687/75448).

The Heads

$$$ **Howe Keld Lakeland Hotel** offers more of a guest-house feel, with 15 fine rooms, a wide variety of breakfast selections, and optional £14.75 evening meals (Sb-£33, Db-£60, prices listed are for 2-night stays, more for 1-night stays, CC but prefer cash, 2 ground-floor rooms, family deals, vegetarian options, 5-7 The Heads, tel. & fax 017687/72417, www.howekeld.co.uk, run with care by David and Valerie Fisher).

$$ **Berkeley Guest House,** a big slate mansion enthusiastically run by Barbara Crompton, has a pleasant lounge, narrow hallways, and carefully appointed, comfortable rooms. The chirpy, skylight-bright £40 bathless double in the attic is a fine value if you don't mind the stairs (D-£38-40, Db-£52-54, family deals, great family room, no CC, The Heads, tel. 017687/74222, www.berkeley-keswick.com, berkeley@tesco.net).

$$ **Parkfield B&B** is thoughtfully run and decorated by John and Susan Berry. This big Victorian house is bright and pastel, offering a wonderful view from its lounge and sincere warmth from its hosts (Db-£54–56 with this book through 2004, 2-night minimum stay, 8 rooms, 1 on the ground floor, car park, no kids under 16, vegetarian options, plenty of fruit at breakfast, The Heads, tel. 017687/72328, www .parkfieldkeswick.com, enquiries@parkfieldkeswick.com).

SLEEP CODE

(£1 = about $1.60, country code: 44, area code: 017687)
Sleep Code: **S** = Single, **D** = Double/Twin, **T** = Triple, **Q** = Quad, **b** = bathroom, **s** = shower only, **no CC** = Credit Cards not accepted. You can assume credit cards are accepted unless otherwise noted.

To help you sort easily through these listings, I've divided the rooms into three categories based on the price for a double room with bath:

$$$ **Higher Priced**—Most rooms £60 or more.
$$ **Moderately Priced**—Most rooms between £30–60.
$ **Lower Priced**—Most rooms £30 or less.

$$ **West View Guest House,** next door to Parkfield, is run by friendly Carole and John Fullagar. The tasteful doily lounge and seven flowery rooms are pleasant and a decent value. John, an avid walker, helps guests map out hiking routes (Db-£52–54, 2-night min, no CC, The Heads, tel. 017687/73638).

Stanger Street

$$ **Dunsford Guest House** is an old Victorian slate town house run by an energetic couple who get their exercise "fellrunning"—running the mountain trails. The four color-coordinated rooms are a fine value. Stained glass and wooden pews give the blue-and-white breakfast room a country-chapel feel (Db-£48, veggie breakfast options, no CC, parking available in back lot, no kids under 16, can book theater tickets, 16 Stanger Street, tel. 017687/75059, www.dunsford.net, enquiries@dunsford.net, Pat and Peter Richards).

$$ **Fell House B&B,** with six charming rooms, is run by Barbara Hossack, who sets out cakes each afternoon (S-£20, D-£40, Db-£50, no CC, lots of rules, parking, 28 Stanger Street, tel. & fax 017687/72669, www.fellhouse.co.uk, info@fellhouse.co.uk).

$$ **Abacourt House,** with a daisy-fresh breakfast room, has five pleasant doubles with firm beds, TVs, and shiny, modern bathrooms. Ask about the "rocking horse" room (Db-£50, no CC, no children, veg-etarian options, parking, 26 Stanger Street, Keswick, tel. 017687/72967, www.abacourt.co.uk, Judith and David Lewis).

$$ **Badgers Wood B&B,** at the top of the street, has six bright, pastel, stocking-feet-comfortable view rooms (Sb-£26, Db-£50, no CC,

30 Stanger Street, tel. 017687/72621, www.badgers-wood.co.uk, info @badgers-wood.co.uk, Irene and David).

$$ Ellergill Guest House has three spick-and-span rooms, one with a super view (D-£46, Db-£50 with this book, 2-night min, large showers, no CC, can book theater tickets, 22 Stanger Street, tel. 017687/73347, www.ellergill.uk.com, stay@ellergill.uk.com, run by Keith Taylor, a lively one-man show).

$$ Lincoln House, across the street, has a colorful carpeted hallway that leads to seven basic, tidy rooms (S-£20, D-£40, Ds-£50, family rooms, 23 Stanger Street, CA12 5JU, tel.017687/72597, fax 017687/73014, www.lincolnguesthouse.com, info@lincolnguesthouse .com, Joan and Mike).

Hostels in and near Keswick

The Lake District's inexpensive hostels, usually located in great old buildings, are handy sources of information and social fun. Local TIs have lists. The Lake District's free booking service (Easter–Oct daily 9:00–18:00, tel. 015394/31117) will tell you which of the area's 30 hostels have available beds and can even book a place on your credit card (no more than 7 days in advance). Since most hostels don't answer their phones during the day and many are full, this is a helpful service. Hostelers need to be members or buy a £13 membership. More hostels are listed under "Buttermere," next page.

Two former hotels in and near Keswick now operate as hostels offering £11.50 dorm beds.

$ Keswick Youth Hostel, with 90 beds, has a great riverside balcony lined with church pews (3- to 10-bed rooms, Internet access, laundry machines, 23:30 curfew, 3 cheap meals served daily, center of town just off Station Road before river, tel. 017687/72484, keswick @yha.org.uk).

$ The Derwentwater hostel, two miles south of Keswick, has 88 dorm beds (£11.50, family rooms from £25, 4- to 22-bed rooms, Internet access, laundry machines, 23:00 curfew, 3 cheap meals served daily, follow B5289 from Keswick, look for sign 100 yards after Ashness exit, tel. 017687/77246, derwentwater@yha.org.uk).

Newlands Valley

With a car, I'd drive 10 minutes past Keswick down the majestic Newlands Valley. Hiking opportunities are wonderful. If the place had a lake it would be packed with tourists. But it doesn't—and it isn't. The valley is studded with 500-year-old farms that have been in the same family for centuries. Shearing day is reason to rush home from school. Sons get school out of the way ASAP and follow their dads. Neighbor girls marry sons and move in. Grandparents retire to the cottage next door. With the price of wool depressed, most of the wives supplement the family income by running B&Bs. The rooms are much plainer than in town. Traditionally, farmhouses lacked central heating, and, while they are now heated, you can still request a hot-water bottle to warm up your bed.

Newlands Valley is just over the Cat Bells ridge from Derwentwater between Keswick and Buttermere. Leave Keswick heading west on the Cockermouth Road (A66). Take the second Newlands Valley exit through Braithwaite and follow signs through Newlands Valley (drive toward Buttermere). You'll pass Ellas Crag first, then a curious purple house, then Birkrigg Farm B&B, and finally Keskadale Farm (about 4 miles before Buttermere). The road is one lane with passing turnouts.

$$ **Ellas Crag B&B,** with a glorious view of Cat Bells, is more a comfortable stone house than a farm. This homey place, with a good mix of modern and traditional, is enthusiastically run by Tony, Jean, and Catherine Hartley, who cook up great gourmet-type breakfasts with an emphasis on freshness (Db-£53-57, no CC, 4 rooms, 1 with a spectacular valley view, non-smoking, veggie options, packed lunches, laundry possible, Stair, Newlands Valley, CA12 5TT, tel. 017687/78217, http://ellascrag.co.uk, ellascrag@talk21.com).

$$ **Birkrigg Farm** is a fine farmhouse B&B. Mrs. Margaret Beaty offers visitors a comfy lounge, evening tea (good for socializing with her other guests), a classy breakfast, and a territorial view. Take your toast and last cup of tea out to the front-yard bench (£22 per person in S, D, T, or Q, discounts for kids and 1-week stays, no CC, 1 shower, 1 tub, and 3 WCs for 6 rooms, parking, closed Dec–March, Newlands Pass Road, tel. 017687/78278).

$$ **Keskadale Farm B&B** is another good farmhouse experience, with valley views and ponderosa hospitality. This working farm has lots of curly horned sheep and three rooms to rent (Db-£52, apartment with kitchen also available, no CC, non-smoking, closed Dec–Feb, 1 min farther down Newlands Pass Road to Buttermere Road on a hairpin turn, Keskadale Farm, Newlands, tel. 017687/78544, fax 017687/78150, keskadale.b.b@kencomp.net, Margaret Harryman). One of the valley's oldest, the house is made from 500-year-old ship beams.

Buttermere

$$ The **Bridge Hotel,** just beyond Newlands Valley at Buttermere, offers a classic, Old World, countryside-hotel experience (£63–76 per person with a 5-course dinner, cheaper for 4 nights or more, £15-per person less B&B only upon request, 21 rooms, non-smoking rooms, Buttermere, tel. 017687/70252, fax 017687/70215, www.bridge-hotel.com, enquiries@bridge-hotel.com). There are no shops within 10 miles—only peace and quiet a stone's throw from one of the region's most beautiful lakes.

Hostels in Buttermere and Borrowdale

$ The **Buttermere King George VI Memorial Hostel,** a quarter-mile south of Buttermere village on Honister Pass Road, has good food, family rooms, and a royal setting (£11.50/bed in 4- to 6-bed rooms, 70 beds, 3 cheap meals served daily, office open 7:00–10:00 & 17:00–23:00, 23:00 curfew, tel. 017687/70245, buttermere@yha.org.uk).

$The well-run **Borrowdale Hostel** is secluded in Borrowdale Valley just south of Rosthwaite (£11.50/bed, 88 beds, Internet access, laundry machines, 23:00 curfew, 3 cheap meals served daily, tel. 017687/77257, borrowdale@yha.org.uk).

EATING

Keswick

Most restaurants stop serving by 21:00.

The bus station faces a fine **supermarket** (Mon–Sat 9:00–20:00, Sun 10:00–16:00, The Headslands) and the smoke-free **Tithe Barn Coffee Shop and Restaurant,** which is popular with locals. It features daily regional specialties and a menu that's healthy for your body and your pocketbook (Mon–Sat 8:00–17:00, Sun 10:00–16:00).

The Dog and Gun serves good pub food, but mind your head—low ceilings and wooden beams (£7, daily 12:00–23:00, meals until 21:00, Thu until 20:00, lamb curry and goulash, no chips and proud of it, can get smoky, 2 Lake Road, tel. 017687/73463, warmly run by Ede family). On Thursday nights at 21:30, Papa Ede hosts Quiz Night (£1 entry/table); proceeds go to Keswick's Mountain Rescue team (also the recipients of the coin contributions wedged in the stone fireplace).

The Four in Hand is another good bet, with hefty portions and fine trout. Despite the American colonial interior, the place used to be a stopover for stagecoach drivers who pulled up with their team of four horses and four (reins) in hand (£7–9, Sun–Fri 12:00–15:00 & 17:00–20:30, Sat 12:00–21:00, off-season generally closed for dinner Mon–Thu, Lake Road, tel. 017687/72069).

The town splurge, **Morrel's,** is simple yet elegant, with a creative menu, wood floors, and gauzy yellow drapes (£15–20, daily 18:00–21:00, reservations recommended, don't expect a fast dinner, all meals cooked to order, 34 Lake Road, tel. 017687/72666).

Sigi's serves tasty roasts, fish, and vegetarian dishes in a relaxed, colorful café atmosphere (3-course dinner-£12.50, Tue–Sun, 21 Station Street, tel. 017687/75159).

Pack Horse Inn offers a great pub atmosphere, low exposed-beam ceilings, and a fireplace (£9 meals, daily 12:00–14:30 & 18:00–21:30, sometimes stops serving after 20:00, smoky but better upstairs, find peek-a-boo alley off of Market Street leading to Pack Horse courtyard, tel. 017687/71389).

The **Lakeland Pedlar,** a wholesome, pleasant café (with a bike shop upstairs) serves freshly-baked vegan and vegetarian fare, including soups, organic bread, and daily specials (£5, daily 9:00–17:00, closes at 16:00 off-season, Hendersons Yard, find the narrow walkway off Market Street between the pink Johnson's sweet shop and Ye Olde Golden Lion Inn, tel. 017687/74492).

Maysons Whole Food Restaurant, with Californian ambience, offers curry, Cajun, and vegetarian options, but most everything is microwaved (£7, June–Oct daily 10:00–20:45, Nov–May daily 10:30–16:30, family-friendly, also take-out, 33 Lake Road, tel. 017687/74104).

The **Pheasant Inn,** on the outskirts of town, is known for its pub-simple country fare. It's decorated with photos and memorabilia from the area's well-known Blencathra foxhunting club (£6, daily 12:00–14:00 & 17:30–20:00, Crosthwaite Road, tel. 017687/72219). The inn is a pleasant 10-minute walk from the Stanger Street B&Bs. (At top of Stanger Street, turn right at gravel alley, walk 100 yards, and make a sharp left toward river. Across river, turn left along riverside path, turn right at Crosthwaite Road, then continue straight, passing hospital.)

It's easy to find ready-made sandwiches for your hike: Try the supermarket at the bus station; the popular, aromatic **Bryson's Bakery** on the main square (Mon–Sat 8:30–17:30, Sun 9:30–17:00, Jan–Feb closed Sun, meaty pasties and gooey pastries, 42 Main Street, tel. 017687/72257); or the **Coffee Lounge** (£3, daily 9:00–16:30, less off-season, behind TI, squeeze down narrow alley between Pattinson Shoes and Rock Shop to 5 Lupton Court, tel. 017687/73075).

Newlands Valley

Since most farmhouses don't serve dinner to their guests, take the lovely 10-minute drive to Buttermere for your evening meal at the **Fish Hotel** pub (£8, daily 12:00–14:00 & 18:00–21:00, family-friendly, limited menu, good fish, beaucoup chips, no vegetables) or the more expensive but much cozier and tastier **Bridge Hotel** pub (£6–7, daily 12:00–21:30, more interesting menu, crunchy veggies).

TRANSPORTATION CONNECTIONS

The nearest train station to Keswick is in Penrith. For train and bus info, check at a local TI, visit www.traveline.org.uk, or call 08457-484-950 (train), or either tel. 0870-608-2608 or 01604/676-060 (bus).

Keswick by bus to: Penrith (2/hr 7:00–21:50, only 6 on Sun, 40 min, £3.55, pay driver, Stagecoach X4, X5, and X50 buses), **Buttermere** (8/day via Whinlatter Forestry Centre and Lorton, 40 min), **Borrowdale** (11/day, only 6 on Sun, to the scenic valley south of Derwentwater, Grange, and Seatoller, 30 min), **Grasmere/Ambleside/Windermere**

(1/hr, 1 hr). The Keswick bus stop is at the supermarket on The Headlands (schedules are posted on poles).

Penrith by bus to: Keswick (1/hr 7:15–22:30, only 6 on Sun, 40 min, £3.55, pay driver, Stagecoach X4, X5, and X50 buses), Ullswater and Glenridding (6/day, 1 hr, direction: Patterdale). The Penrith bus stop is in the train station's parking lot (bus schedules posted inside and outside station).

Penrith by train to: Oban (1/hr to Glasgow, 2 hrs; then to Oban, 2/day, 3 hrs), Edinburgh (8/day, 2 hrs), Blackpool (1/hr to Preston, 1 hr; then to Blackpool, 3/hr, 20 min), Liverpool (1/day, 2.5 hrs), Birmingham's New Street Station (2/hr, 2 hrs), London's Euston Station (1/hr, 4 hrs). Penrith's small train station has a ticket window (Mon–Sat 5:30–21:00, Sun 11:30–21:00) but no lockers.

Route Tips for Drivers

North Wales or Blackpool to the Lake District: The direct, easy way to Keswick is to leave the M6 at Penrith and take the A66 highway 16 miles to Keswick. For the scenic sightseeing drive through the south lakes to Keswick, exit the M6 on A590/A591 through the towns of Kendal and Windermere to reach Brockhole National Park Visitors Centre. From Brockhole, the A road to Keswick is fastest, but the high road—the tiny road over Kirkstone Pass to Glenridding and lovely Ullswater—is much more dramatic.

For the drive north to Oban, see the Oban chapter.

YORK

Historic York is loaded with world-class sights. Marvel at the York Minster, England's finest Gothic church. Ramble through the Shambles, York's wonderfully preserved medieval quarter. Enjoy a walking tour led by an old Yorker. Hop a train at Europe's greatest railway museum, travel to the 1800s in the York Castle Museum, and head back a thousand years to Viking York at the Jorvik exhibit.

York has a rich history. In A.D. 71 it was Eboracum, a Roman provincial capital. Constantine was actually proclaimed emperor here in A.D. 306. In the fifth century, as Rome was toppling, a Roman emperor sent a letter telling England it was on its own, and York became Eoforwic, the capital of the Anglo-Saxon kingdom of Northumbria. A church was built here in 627, and the town became an early Christian center of learning. The Vikings later took the town, and from about 860 to 950 it was a Danish trading center called Jorvik. The invading and conquering Normans destroyed then rebuilt the city, giving it a castle and the walls you see today. Medieval York, with 9,000 inhabitants, grew rich on the wool trade and became England's second city. Henry VIII spared the city's fine minster in order to use York as his Anglican Church's northern capital. The Archbishop of York is second only to the Archbishop of Canterbury in the Anglican Church. In the Industrial Age, York was the railway hub of North England. When it was built, York's train station was the world's largest. Today, York's leading industry is tourism. Its leading drug? Starbucks and Costa are doing their best to turn high tea into high coffee.

Planning Your Time

York rivals Edinburgh as the best sightseeing city in Britain after London. On even a 10-day trip through Britain, it deserves two nights and a day. For the best 36 hours, follow this plan: Catch the 19:00 city

York

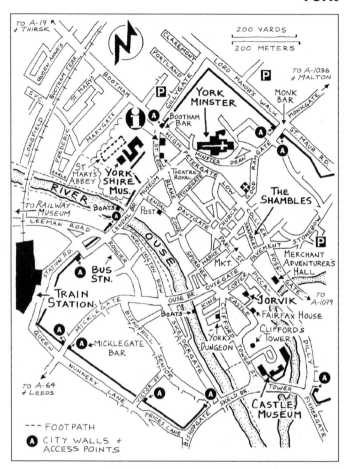

TO A-19 & THIRSK

200 YARDS
200 METERS

TO A-1036 & MALTON

QUEEN ANNE'S
BOOTHAM TERR.
ST. MARY'S
CLAREMONT
PORTLAND
GILLYGATE
LORD MAYOR'S WALK
MONK BAR
MONKGATE

SYC.
LONGFIELD
FREDERIC
MARYGATE
BOOTHAM
ST. LEONARDS
HIGH PETERGATE
BOOTHAM BAR

YORK MINSTER

ST. MAUR RD.

EARLES
ST. MARY'S ABBEY
YORKSHIRE MUS.

THEATRE ROYAL
MUSEUM
BLAKE
STONEGATE
LOW PETERGATE
DEAN GATE
MINSTER YD
GOODRAMGATE

THE SHAMBLES

RIVER
TO RAILWAY MUSEUM
BOATS
LEEMAN ROAD
LENDAL BR.
Post
CONEY
DAVYGATE
CHURCH
COLLIER
STONEBOW
PAVEMENT
FOSS
MERCHANT ADVENTURER'S HALL

OUSE
ROUGIER
WELLINGTON ROW
SPURRIERGATE
MARKET ST.
MKT.
SHAMBLES
PICCA-DILLY
JORVIK

TO A-1079

STATION RD.
BUS STN.

TRAIN STATION

MICKLEGATE
BISHOPHILL
OUSE BR.
BOATS
OUSEGATE
COPPERGATE
KING
CASTLEGATE
CLIFFORD ST.

FAIRFAX HOUSE
CLIFFORD'S TOWER

QUEEN
MICKLEGATE BAR

SKELDERGATE
YORK'S DUNGEON

TOWER ST.

TO A-64 & LEEDS
NUNNERY LANE
VICTOR ST.
SENIOR
PRICES LANE
BISHOPGATE
SKELD. BR.
TOWER
DILLY

CASTLE MUSEUM
FISHERGATE

- - - FOOTPATH

ⓐ CITY WALLS & ACCESS POINTS

---

walking tour on the evening of your arrival. The next morning, be at the Castle Museum at 9:30 when it opens—it's worth a good two hours. Then browse and sightsee through the day. Train buffs love the National Railway Museum, and scholars give the Yorkshire Museum three stars. Tour the minster at 16:00 before catching the 17:00 evensong service (at 16:00 Sun). Finish your day with an early evening stroll along the wall and perhaps through the abbey gardens. This schedule assumes you're there in the summer (evening orientation walk) and that there's an evensong on. Confirm your plans with the TI.

ORIENTATION

(area code: 01904)

The sightseer's York is small. Virtually everything is within a few minutes' walk: the sights, train station, TI, and B&Bs. The longest walk a visitor might take (from a B&B across the old town to the Castle Museum) is 15 minutes.

Bootham Bar, a gate in the medieval town wall, is the hub of your York visit. At Bootham Bar (and on Exhibition Square facing it) you'll find the TI, the starting points for most walking tours and bus tours, handy access to the medieval town wall, and Bootham street, which leads to the recommended B&Bs. (In York, a "bar" is a gate and a "gate" is a street. Go ahead, blame the Vikings.) When finding your way, navigate by sighting the tower of the minster or the strategically placed green signposts pointing out all places of interest to tourists.

Tourist Information: The TI at Bootham Bar sells a 90p *York Map and Guide.* Ask for the free monthly *What's On* guide and the *York MiniGuide,* which includes a map and some discounts (April–Oct Mon–Sat 9:00–18:00, Sun 10:00–17:00, likely 10:00–16:00 off-season, WCs next door, tel. 01904/621-756). The TI books rooms for a £4 fee. The train-station TI is smaller but provides all the same information and services (same hours as main TI).

Arrival in York: The train station, which stores luggage for day-trippers (£3, Mon–Sat 8:00–20:30, Sun 9:00–20:30, platform 1), is a five-minute walk from town; turn left down Station Road and follow the crowd toward the Gothic towers of the minster. After the bridge, a block before the minster, signs to the TI send you left on St. Leonard's Place. Recommended B&Bs are a five-minute walk from there. (For a shortcut to B&B area from station, walk 1 block toward the minster, cut through parks to riverside, cross railway bridge/pedestrian walkway, cross parking lot for B&Bs on St. Mary's Street, or duck through pedestrian walkway under tracks to B&Bs on Sycamore and Queen Anne's Road.) **Taxis** zip new arrivals to their B&B for £3.

Helpful Hints

Study Ahead: York has a great Web site: www.visityork.org.

Internet Access: Get online at Internet Exchange (Mon–Sat 9:00–19:00, Sun 11:00–18:00, 13 Stonegate, tel. 01904/638-808) or Gateway (Mon–Wed 10:00–20:00, Thu–Sat until 23:00, Sun 12:00–16:00, 26 Swinegate, tel. 01904/646-446, fax 01904/670-386).

Festivals: The Viking Festival in late February features lur-blowing, warrior drills, and re-created battles. The Early Music Festival zings its strings in mid-July. And the York Festival of Food and Drink takes a 10-day bite out of the middle of September. Book a room well in advance during festival times and weekends any time of year.

Bike Rental: Trotters, just outside Monk Bar, has free cycling maps. The riverside path is pleasant (£10/day, tandem-£30/day, helmets-£2, Mon–Sat 9:00–17:30, Sun 10:00–16:00, tel. 01904/622-868). Europcar at the train station also rents bikes (£10/day, platform 1, tel. 01904/658-161).

Car Rental: If you're nearing the end of your trip, consider dropping your car upon arrival in York. The money saved by turning it in early nearly pays for the train ticket that whisks you effortlessly to Edinburgh or London. Here are some car-rental agencies in York: Avis (Mon–Sat, closed Sat afternoon and Sun, 3 Layerthorpe, tel. 01904/610-460), Hertz (April–Sept daily, Sat–Sun until 13:00, at train station, tel. 01904/612-586), Sixt (Mon–Sat, closed Sun, inconveniently 3 miles out of town at Clifton Moor Industrial Estate, tel. 01904/479-715), Budget (daily, Sat & Sun until 11:00, 1 mile past recommended B&Bs at Clifton 82, tel. 01904/644-919), and Europcar (Mon–Fri 8:00–18:00, Sat–Sun until 12:00, train station platform 1, tel. 01904/658-161). Beware, car-rental agencies close Saturday afternoon and some close all day Sunday—when drop-offs are OK, but picking up is impossible.

TOURS

▲▲▲**Walking Tours**—Charming local volunteer guides give energetic, entertaining, and free two-hour walks through York (daily 10:15 all year, plus 14:15 April–Oct, plus 18:45 July–Aug, from Exhibition Square across from TI). There are many other commercial York walking tours. YorkWalk Tours, for example, has reliable guides and many themes from which to choose, such as Roman York, City Walls, or Snickleways—small alleys (£5, tel. 01904/622-303, TI has schedule). The ghost tours, all offered after nightfall, are more fun than informative. Haunted Walk relies a bit more on storytelling and history than on masks and surprises (£3, April–Nov nightly at 20:00, 90 min, just show up, depart from Exhibition Square, across street from TI, end in the Shambles, tel. 01904/621-003).

▲**Hop-on, Hop-off Bus Tours**—With one £7.50 ticket, you can jump on or off either of the two tours circling York. The tours, run by the same company, generally follow the same route. The main difference is that the Guide Friday York Tour (green bus, 45 min loop) is shorter and has live guides, and the City Sightseeing tour (red bus, 1 hr) has recorded narration and a few extra stops, including the York Racecourse and Rowntree Park. Both tours cover secondary York sights that the city walking tours skip—the mundane perimeter of town (pay driver cash, can also buy from TI with CC, departures every 10 min or more from

9:00 until around 17:00, less frequent off-season, red tours don't run Nov–March, tel. 01904/655-585). While you can hop on and off all day, the tours are of no real value from a transportation-to-the-sights point of view because York is so compact. I'd catch the tour at the Bootham Bar TI and ride it for an orientation all the way around or get off at the Railway Museum, skipping the last five minutes.

Boat Cruise—The York Boat does a lazy 60-minute lap along the River Ouse (£6, Feb–Nov daily from 10:30 on, narrated cruise, leaves from Lendal Bridge and King's Staith landing) and also offers themed evening cruises—ghost, dinner, floodlit, and so on (boat rentals possible, tel. 01904/628-324, www.yorkboat.co.uk).

SIGHTS

York Minster

▲▲▲**Minster**—The pride of York, this largest Gothic church north of the Alps (540 feet long, 200 feet tall) brilliantly shows that the High Middle Ages were far from dark. The word "minster" means a place from which people go out to minister or spread the word of God.

Cost, Hours, and Tours: The cathedral opens daily for worship at 7:00 and for sightseeing Mon–Sat from 9:00 and Sunday from 12:30, when they begin charging £4.50 admission. The closing time flexes with the season (roughly May–Oct at 18:30, earlier off-season—call for details, tel. 01904/557-216). The tower (£2.50) and undercroft (£2.50, or £6 combo-ticket with cathedral entry) have shorter hours, typically opening a half-hour later and closing a half-hour earlier.

When you enter go directly to the welcome desk, pick up the worth-while "Welcome to the York Minster" flier, and ask when the next free guided **tour** departs (tours go about every half-hour until 15:00, even with just one or two people; you can join one in progress). The helpful minster guides, wearing blue armbands, are happy to answer your questions.

Self-Guided Tour: Your first impression might be the spacious-ness and brightness of the nave (built 1280–1350). The nave—from the middle period of Gothic, called "Decorated Gothic"—is one of the widest Gothic naves in Europe. Notice the Great West Window (1338) above the entry. The heart in the tracery is called "the heart of Yorkshire."

Look down the nave. The mysterious gold-and-red dragon's head (in the middle of the nave, sticking out of the side) was probably used as a crane to lift a font cover.

The north and south transepts are the oldest parts of today's church (1220–1270). The oldest complete window in the minster is the entire wall of glass in the north transept (1260). Known as the Five Sisters Window, these 50-foot-high panels were made of modern-looking grisaille (gray-silver) glass. Off the north transept is the **chapter house,** with an elaborately decorated 13th-century Gothic dome—the largest in England without a central supporting pillar—featuring playful details carved in the stonework (pointed out in the flier at the north transept entrance). The south transept has access to the tower and undercroft (see below).

The fanciful choir and the east end (high altar) is from the last stage of Gothic, Perpendicular (1360–1470). The Great East Window (1405), the largest medieval glass window in existence, shows the beginning and the end of the world, with scenes from Genesis and the book of Revelation. A chart (on the right, with a tiny, more helpful chart within) highlights the core Old Testament scenes in this hard-to-read masterpiece. Enjoy the art close up on the chart and then step back and find the real thing.

There are two extra visits to consider, both in the south transept. You can scale the 275-step **tower** for the panoramic view (£2.50). The **undercroft** consists of the crypt, treasury, and foundations (£2.50, or £6 combo-ticket, includes informative audioguide). The crypt is an actual bit of the Romanesque church, featuring 12th-century Romanesque art, excavated in modern times. The foundations give you a chance to climb down—archaeologically and physically—through the centuries to see the roots of the much smaller, but still huge, Norman church (Romanesque, 1100) that stood on this spot and, below that, the Roman excavations. Constantine was proclaimed Roman emperor here in A.D. 306. Peek also at the modern concrete save-the-church foundations.

Evensong and Church Bells: To experience the cathedral in musical and spiritual action, attend an evensong (Mon–Fri 17:00, Sat–Sun 16:00, 45 min). When the choir is off on school break (mid-July–Aug), visiting choirs usually fill in. Arrive 10 minutes early and wait just outside the choir in the center of the church, from where you'll be ushered in and can sit in one of the big wooden stalls. If you're a fan of church bells, Sunday morning (around 10:00) and the Tuesday-evening practice (19:30–21:30) are heavenly.

More Sights

▲**City Walls**—The historic walls of York provide a fine two-mile walk. Walk from Bootham Bar (gate) to Monk Bar for outstanding cathedral views. They're free and open from dawn until dusk (barring attacks).

▲**The Shambles**—This is the most colorful old York street in the half-timbered, traffic-free core of town. Ye olde downtown York, while very touristy, is made for window-shopping, street musicians, and people-watching. The frumpy Newgate Market is fun. For a cheap lunch, consider the cute, tiny **St. Crux Parish Hall.** This medieval church is now used by a medley of charities selling tea, homemade cakes, and light meals. They each book the church for a day, often a year in advance. Chat up the volunteers (Mon–Sat 10:00–16:00, closed Sun, at bottom end of the Shambles, at intersection with Pavement).

▲▲▲**Castle Museum**—Truly one of Europe's top museums, this is a Victorian home show, the closest thing to a time-tunnel experience England has to offer. It includes the 19th-century Kirkgate (a collection of old shops well stocked exactly as they were 150 years ago), a "From Cradle to Grave" clothing exhibit, and a fine costume collection. The one-way plan allows you to see everything: a working water mill (April–Oct), prison cells, WWII fashions, and old toys. Bring 20p coins to jolt a mechanical Al Jolson into song. The museum's £3 guidebook isn't necessary but makes a fine souvenir (£6, April–Oct daily 9:30–17:00, Nov–March until 16:30, gift shop, parking, cafeteria midway through museum, tel. 01904/687-652).

Clifford's Tower, across from the Castle Museum, is all that's left of York's 13th-century castle, the site of a 1190 massacre of local Jews (read about this at base of hill). If you do climb inside, there are fine city views from the top of the ramparts (not worth the £2.50, April–Sept daily 10:00–18:00, Oct–March until 16:00).

▲**Jorvik**—Sail the "Pirates of the Caribbean" north and back 800 years and you get Jorvik—more a ride than a museum. Innovative 10 years ago, the commercial success of Jorvik (YOR-vik) inspired copycat ride/museums all over England. You'll ride a little Disney-type train car for 13 minutes through the re-created Viking street of Coppergate. It's the year 975, and you're in the village of Jorvik. Next, your little train takes you through the actual excavation site that inspired this. Finally you'll browse through a small gallery of Viking shoes, combs, locks, and other intimate glimpses of that redheaded culture (£7.20, April–Sept opens at 9:30 with last entry at 17:30, Oct–March opens at 10:00, closing varies from 15:30 to 16:30, tel. 01904/643-211, www.vikingjorvik.com).

Midday lines can be an hour long. Avoid the line by going very early or very late in the day or by prebooking (call 01904/543-403, you're given a time slot, booking fee-£1). Some love this "ride," others call it a gimmicky rip-off. If you're looking for a grown-up museum, the Viking exhibit at the Yorkshire Museum is far better. If you're thinking Disneyland with a splash of history, Jorvik's fun. To me, Jorvik is a commercial venture designed for kids with nearly as much square footage devoted to its shop as to the museum.

▲▲**National Railway Museum**—If you like model railways, this is train-car heaven. The thunderous museum shows 150 fascinating years of British railroad history. Fanning out from a grand roundhouse is an array of historic cars and engines, including Queen Victoria's lavish royal car and the very first "stagecoaches on rails." There's much more, including exhibits on dining cars, post cars, sleeping cars, train posters, and videos. At the "Works" section you can see live train switchboards. And don't miss the English Channel Tunnel video (showing the first handshake at breakthrough). Red-shirted "explainers" are everywhere, eager to talk trains. This biggest and best railroad museum anywhere is interesting even to people who think "Pullman" means "don't push" (free, £3 audio-guide with 60 bits of railroad lore—punch in exhibit numbers as you go, daily 10:00–18:00, tel. 01904/621-261).

Cute little "street trains" shuttle you between the minster and the Railway Museum (£1.50 each way, runs Easter–Oct, leaves Railway Museum every 30 min from 12:00 to 17:00 at the top and bottom of the hour; leaves minster—from Duncombe Place—every 30 min, :15 and :45 min after the hour, no trains Nov-Easter).

▲▲Yorkshire Museum—Located in a lush, picnic-perfect park next to the stately ruins of St. Mary's Abbey, Yorkshire Museum is the city's forgotten, serious "archaeology of York" museum. While the hordes line up at Jorvik, the best Viking artifacts are here—with no crowds and a better historical context. A stroll around this museum takes you through Roman (wonderfully described battle-bashed skull in first case), Saxon (great Anglo-Saxon helmet from A.D. 750), Viking, Norman, and Gothic York. Its prize piece is the delicately etched 15th-century pendant called the Middleham Jewel—for which the museum raised $4 million to buy. The 20-minute video about the creation of the abbey is worth a look (£4, various exhibitions can increase price, daily 10:00–17:00, tel. 01904/687-687).

Theatre Royal—A full variety of dramas, comedies, and works by Shakespeare is put on to entertain the locals (£10–17, 19:30 almost nightly, tickets easy to get, closes several weeks during the summer, on St. Leonard's Place next to TI and a 5-min walk from recommended B&Bs, booking tel. 01904/623-568).

Honorable Mention

York has a number of other sights and activities (described in TI material) that, while interesting, pale in comparison to the biggies.

Fairfax House—This well-furnished building is perfectly Georgian inside, with docents happy to talk with you (£4.50, Mon–Thu and Sat 11:00–17:00, Sun 13:30–17:00, Fri by tour only at 11:00 and 14:00—the tours are worthwhile, on Castlegate, near Jorvik, tel. 01904/655-543).

Hall of the Merchant Adventurers—Claiming to be the finest medieval guildhall in Europe (from 1361), it's basically a vast half-timbered building with marvelous exposed beams and 15 minutes worth of interesting displays about life and commerce back in the days when York was England's second city (£2, Mon–Sat 9:00–17:00, Fri–Sat opens at 9:30, Sun 12:00–16:00, early Nov–mid-March Mon–Sat 9:30–15:30, closed Sun, below the Shambles off Piccadilly, tel. 01904/654-818).

Richard III Museum—This is interesting only for Richard III enthusiasts (£2, daily March–Aug 9:00–20:00, Sept–Oct 9:30–18:00, Nov–Feb until 16:00, Monk Bar, tel. 01904/634-191).

York Dungeon—It's gimmicky, but, if you insist on papier-mâché gore, it's better than the London Dungeon (£8.95, daily 10:00–17:30, less off-season, 12 Clifford Street, tel. 01904/632-599).

Lawn Bowling Green—Visitors are welcome to watch the action—best in the evenings—at the green on Sycamore Place; you can buy a pint of beer (near recommended B&Bs, tell them which B&B you're staying at). Another green is in front of the Coach House Hotel Pub on Marygate.

Shopping—With its medieval lanes lined with classy as well as tacky little shops, York is a hit with shoppers. I find the **antique malls** interesting. Three places within a few blocks of each other are filled with stalls and cases owned by antique dealers from the countryside. The malls sell the dealers' bygones on commission. Serious shoppers do better heading for the countryside, but York's shops are a fun browse: The Antiques Centre York (daily 9:00–18:00, 41 Stonegate, tel. 01904/635-888), the antique mall at 2 Lendal (Mon–Sat 10:00–17:00, closed Sun, tel. 01904/641-582), and the Red House Antiques Centre (daily 9:30–17:30, as late as 19:00 in summer, a block from the minster at Duncombe Place, tel. 01904/637-000).

Near York

Eden Camp—Once an internment camp for German and Italian POWs during World War II, this is now a theme museum on Britain's war experience. Various barracks detail the rise of Hitler and the fury of the Blitz (with the sound of bombs, the acrid smell of burning, and quotes such as "Hitler will send no warning—so always carry your gas mask.") This award-winning museum energetically conveys the spirit of a country Hitler couldn't conquer. Don't miss hut #10, which details the actual purpose of the camp—a prison for captured Nazis during World War II. Consider the relative delight of being in the care of the gentlemanly English rather than in a Nazi camp. It's no wonder the Germans settled right in (£4, daily 10:00–17:00, closed late-Dec–mid-Jan, mess-kitchen cafeteria, in Malton, 18 miles northeast of York, tel. 01653/697-777, www.edencamp.co.uk). To get to the camp from York, catch the Coastliner bus at the York Railway Station (leaves from front of station, on station side of road). Buses are marked with the destination "Whitby" or "Pickering" and are numbered #840, #842, or #X40, depending on the time of day (£4 round-trip, Mon–Sat 11/day, fewer on Sun, 50 min). From York, drivers take A169 toward Scarborough, then follow signs to the camp.

SLEEPING

B&Bs near Bootham

These recommendations are in the handiest B&B neighborhood, a quiet residential area just outside the old-town wall's Bootham gate, along the road called Bootham. All are within a five-minute walk of the minster and TI and a 10-minute walk or taxi ride (£3) from the station. If driving, head for the cathedral and follow the medieval wall to the gate called Bootham Bar. Bootham "street" leads away from Bootham Bar.

These B&Bs are all small, non-smoking, and family run. They come with plenty of steep stairs but no traffic noise. For a good selection, call well in advance. B&B owners will generally hold a room with a phone call and work hard to help their guests sightsee and eat smartly. Most have permits for street parking. And most don't take credit cards.

Laundry: Regency Dry Cleaning does small loads (£3.50/kilogram—about 2 lbs, Mon–Fri 8:30–18:00, Sat 9:00–17:00, closed Sun, drop off by 9:30 for same-day service, 75 Bootham, at intersection with Queen Anne's Road, tel. 01904/613-311). The next-nearest place is a long 15-minute walk away (Washeteria Launderette, 124 Haxby Road, tel. 01904/623-379).

$$$ The Hazelwood, my most hotelesque listing in this neighborhood, is plush, but lacks the intimacy of a B&B. This spacious house has 13 beautifully decorated rooms with modern furnishings and lots of thoughtful touches (Db-£80/90/100 depending on room size, 2 ground-floor rooms, classy breakfast, quiet for being so central, laundry service-£5; a fridge, ice, and great travel library in the pleasant basement lounge; 24 Portland Street, tel. 01904/626-548, fax 01904/628-032, www.thehazelwoodyork.com, reservations@thehazelwoodyork.com).

$$ 23 St. Mary's is extravagantly decorated. Chris and Julie Simpson have done everything super-correctly and offer nine comfy rooms, a classy lounge, and all the doily touches (Sb-£34–40, Db-£64–80 depending on season and size, DVD library and some rooms with DVD players, 23 St. Mary's, tel. 01904/622-738, fax 01904/628-802,www.23stmarys.co.uk).

$$ Crook Lodge B&B, with seven charming, tight rooms, is elegant for a B&B (Db-£64–72, parking, quiet, 26 St. Mary's, tel. 01904/ 655-614, fax 01904/625-915, www.crooklodge.co.uk, crooklodge @hotmail.com, Brian and Louise Aiken).

$$ The Coach House Hotel is a labyrinthine, funky old place—a little musty, but well-located facing a bowling green and the abbey walls. It offers 12 comfortable old-time rooms and a crackerjack lounge (S-£31, Sb-£34, Db-£68, free parking, 20 Marygate, Bootham, tel. 01904/652-780, fax 01904/679-943, www.coachhousehotel-york.com, info@coachhousehotel-york.com).

$$ Arnot House, run by a hardworking daughter-and-mother team, is homey and lushly decorated with early-1900s memorabilia. The four well-furnished rooms have little libraries and VCRs (Db-£58–62, minimum 2-night stay, video library, 17 Grosvenor Terrace, tel. & fax 01904/641-966, www.arnothouseyork.co.uk, kim.robbins@virgin.net, Kim and Ann Robbins).

$ Airden House, the most central of my Bootham-area listings, has eight spacious rooms, a cozy TV lounge, and brightness and warmth

SLEEP CODE

(£1 = about $1.60, country code: 44, area code: 01904)
Sleep Code: **S** = Single, **D** = Double/Twin, **T** = Triple, **Q** = Quad, **b** = bathroom, **s** = shower only, **No CC** = Credit Cards not accepted. You can assume credit cards are accepted unless otherwise noted.

To help you sort easily through these listings, I've divided the rooms into three categories based on the price for a standard double room with bath (during high season):

$$$ **Higher Priced**—Most rooms £90 or more.
$$ **Moderately Priced**—Most rooms between £60–90.
$ **Lower Priced**—Most rooms £60 or less.

I've listed peak-season, book-direct prices. Don't use the TI. Outside of July and August, some prices go soft. B&Bs will sometimes turn away one-night bookings, particularly for peak-season Saturdays. (York is worth 2 nights anyway.) Remember to book ahead during festival times (late Feb, mid-July, middle of Sept) and weekends year-round.

throughout. It's simple, clean, comfortable, and friendly (D-£44–46, Db-£54–56, no CC, 1 St. Mary's, tel. 01904/638-915, www.airdenhouse.co.uk, info@airdenhouse.co.uk, Graham and Lynda Scarisbrick).

$ The Sycamore is a fine value, with seven homey, flowery rooms. It's at the end of a dead end opposite a bowling green that is fun to watch (D-£46, Db-£50–60, family room-£60–69, no CC, 19 Sycamore Place off Bootham Terrace, tel. 01904/624-712, www.thesycamore.co.uk, run by Elizabeth).

$ Abbeyfields Guest House has eight cozy, bright rooms and a quiet lounge. This doily-free place, which lacks the usual clutter, has been designed with care (Sb-£37, Db-£60, no CC, 19 Bootham Terrace, tel. & fax 01904/636-471, www.abbeyfields.co.uk, Richard and Gwen Martin).

$ Queen Anne's Guest House has seven clean, cheery rooms (May–Sept D-£42, Db-£44, Oct–April D-£32, Db-£34, prices good through 2004 with this book, 1 family room, lounge, 24 Queen Anne's Road, tel. 01904/629-389, fax 01904/619-529, www.queen-annes-guesthouse.co.uk, queen.annes@btopenworld.com, Judy and David).

$ Alcuin Lodge has five flowery rooms and solid-wood furnishings (Db-£45–55, 1 small top-floor D-£40, 15 Sycamore Place, tel.

01904/632-222, fax 01904/626-630, alcuinlodg@aol.com, Zoe Collinson and Lea Thomlinson).

B&Bs along the Riverside

Three smoke-free places front the River Ouse midway between the train station and the minster. The Water's Edge B&B is best; the other two places are simpler, a bit worn, and a lesser value. Each faces the same pleasant pedestrian path and comes with a delightful front garden and no traffic noise. Front rooms overlook the river; back rooms watch a sprawling car park.

$ **Water's Edge B&B,** a pastel place with five comfy rooms a teddy bear would like, is well-run by Julie Mett (Db-£55, four-poster riverview Db-£60, 2-room family room, prices through 2004 with this book, CC for 3.5 percent extra, 5 Earlsborough Terrace, tel. 01904/644-625, www .watersedgeyork.co.uk, julie@watersedgeyork.co.uk).

$ **Abbey Guest House** has seven basic rooms (S-£28, Sb-£35, D-£50, Db-£60, Qb-£80, CC for 2.5 percent extra, free parking, Internet access, laundry-£5/load, 14 Earlsborough Terrace, tel. 01904/627-782, fax 01904/671-743, www.bedandbreakfastyork.co.uk, abbey@rsummers .cix.co.uk, Hilary Summers).

$ **Riverside Walk B&B** has 12 small rooms, steep stairs, and narrow hallways (Db-£52–62, CC for 2.5 percent extra, free parking, 8 Earlsborough Terrace, tel. 01904/620-769, fax 01904/671-743, www .bedandbreakfastyork.co.uk, Mr. Summers).

Hotels in the Center

$$$ **Dean Court Hotel,** facing the minster, is a big, stately Best Western hotel with classy lounges and 40 comfortable rooms (small Db-£115, standard Db-£140, superior Db-£155, spacious deluxe Db-£170, some non-smoking rooms, tearoom, restaurant, elevator to most rooms, Duncombe Place, tel. 01904/625-082, fax 01904/620-305, www.deancourt-york.co.uk).

$$ **Galtres Lodge Hotel,** a block from the minster, offers comfy, recently refurbished rooms above a restaurant in the old-town center (S-£30-35, Sb-£35–45, Db-£70–80, non-smoking, Internet access, 54 Low Petergate, tel. 01904/622-478, fax 01904/627-804).

$ **Travelodge** offers 90 identical, affordable rooms near the Castle Museum (Db-£60, kids' bed free, some smoke-free rooms, 90 Piccadilly, central reservations tel. 0870-085-0950, www.travelodge.co.uk).

$ **York Youth Hotel** is a well-run hostel, with a kitchen, laun-derette, game room, and 120 beds (S-£22, bunk bed D-£32, beds in 4-to 6-bed dorms-£14, beds in larger dorms-£12, less for multi-night stays, family rates, same-sex or coed possible, no breakfast, 10-min walk from station at 11 Bishophill Senior Road, tel. 01904/625-904, fax 01904/612-494, www.yorkyouthhotel.com).

York Hotels and Restaurants

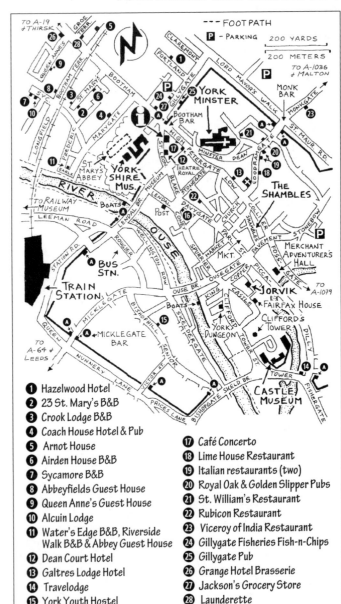

1 Hazelwood Hotel
2 23 St. Mary's B&B
3 Crook Lodge B&B
4 Coach House Hotel & Pub
5 Arnot House
6 Airden House B&B
7 Sycamore B&B
8 Abbeyfields Guest House
9 Queen Anne's Guest House
10 Alcuin Lodge
11 Water's Edge B&B, Riverside Walk B&B & Abbey Guest House
12 Dean Court Hotel
13 Galtres Lodge Hotel
14 Travelodge
15 York Youth Hostel
16 Betty's Teahouse

17 Café Concerto
18 Lime House Restaurant
19 Italian restaurants (two)
20 Royal Oak & Golden Slipper Pubs
21 St. William's Restaurant
22 Rubicon Restaurant
23 Viceroy of India Restaurant
24 Gillygate Fisheries Fish-n-Chips
25 Gillygate Pub
26 Grange Hotel Brasserie
27 Jackson's Grocery Store
28 Launderette
A City walls & access points

EATING

Traditional Tea

York is famous for its elegant teahouses. Drop into one around 16:00 for tea and cakes. Ladies love **Betty's Teahouse** where you pay £5.65 for a cream tea (tea and scones) or £10 for a full traditional English afternoon tea (tea, elegant sandwich, scones, and sweets). Your table is so full of doily niceties that the food is served on a little three-tray tower. While Betty's food is nothing special, the ambience and people-watching are hard to beat (daily 9:00–21:00, piano music nightly 18:00–21:00, mostly non-smoking, St. Helen's Square; fine view of street scene from a window seat on the main floor, downstairs near WC is a mirror signed by WWII bomber pilots—read the story). If there's a line, it moves quickly. I'd wait for a seat by the windows on the ground level rather than sit in the much bigger basement.

Near the Minster

Of these listings, the first listing faces the minster, the last two are behind the minster, and the rest are on Goodramgate near the minster.

Café Concerto, a French-style bistro with a fun menu, has an understandably loyal following. Their food is the best I've had in York (great lunch-£8, dinner-£15, daily 10:00–22:00, serves meals all day, smoke-free, smart to reserve for dinner, facing the minster, High Petergate 21, tel. 01904/610-478).

The **Lime House Restaurant** is a small, modern, candlelit place enthusiastically run by chef Adam Fisher. His menu features European dishes revolving with the seasons and always includes a good vegetarian plate. Adam offers a free glass of house wine to anyone with this book (plates-£12, 10 percent off on orders before 19:15, Tue–Sat 12:00–14:00 & 18:00–21:30, closed Sun–Mon, lunch specials, 55 Goodramgate, tel. 01904/632-734).

For Italian food, you'll find a couple popular places along Goodramgate: **Little Italy** (#12, closed Mon, tel. 01904/623-539) and **Caesars** (#27, nightly, tel. 01904/670-914).

There's a pub serving grub on every block. Eat where you see lots of food. The **Royal Oak** offers £5 pub grub throughout the day, a small non-smoking room, and hand-pulled ale (daily 11:00–20:00, Sun opens at noon, heavy meat dishes, fat fries, but don't look in their kitchen, Goodramgate, a block from Monk Bar, a block east of the minster, tel. 01904/653-856). The **Golden Slipper,** next door, is also a classic for basic pub grub and darts (open daily).

St. Williams Restaurant, just behind the great east window of the minster in a wonderful half-timbered, 15th-century building (read the history), serves quick and tasty lunches and elegant candlelit dinners (£15 plates, daily 10:00–17:00 & 18:00–22:00, Oct–March closed Sun–Mon nights, English and Mediterranean, College Street, tel. 01904/634-830).

For vegetarian, try **Rubicon**, a pastel café with dinner specials until 18:30 (£8.50/2 courses, daily, 5 Little Stonegate, tel. 01904/676-076).

The Viceroy of India—just outside Monk Bar and therefore outside the tourist zone—serves great Indian food at good prices to mostly locals. If you've yet to eat Indian on your trip, do it here (plates-£8, Mon–Fri 18:00–24:00, Sat–Sun 12:00–24:00, friendly staff, continue straight through Monk Bar to 26 Monkgate, tel. 01904/622-370).

Near Bootham Bar and Your B&B

Gillygate Fisheries is a wonderfully traditional little fish-and-chips joint where tattooed people eat in and housebound mothers take out (Mel serves £4–5 meals, "eat your mushy peas," Mon–Fri 11:30–13:30 & 17:00–23:30, Sat 11:30–23:30, closed Sun, smoke-free seating, two blocks from the TI at 59 Gillygate).

The **Gillygate** pub has local color and serves decent pub food in a cozy smoke-free room or with the smoking beer drinkers (daily 11:00–19:30, beer garden out back, across from Wackers at 48 Gillygate, tel. 01904/654-103).

The well-worn **Coach House** serves good-quality food with fresh vegetables but can be smoky (£8–11, nightly 18:30–21:00, 20 Marygate, tel. 01904/652-780).

The **Grange Hotel Brasserie,** a couple of blocks from the B&Bs, is classier than a pub and serves a smattering of traditional European dishes. Go downstairs—avoid the pricey main-floor restaurant (£9–13 main dishes, Mon–Sat 12:00–14:00 & 18:00–22:00, Sun 19:00–22:00, 1 Clifton, tel. 01904/644-744).

Jackson's grocery store is open every day 7:00–23:00 (near B&Bs, outside Bootham Bar, on Bootham). For an atmospheric **picnic spot,** try the Museum Gardens (near Bootham Bar) at the evocative 12th-century ruins of St. Mary's Abbey.

TRANSPORTATION CONNECTIONS

By train to: Durham (hrly, 45 min), **Edinburgh** (2/hr, 2.5 hrs), **London** (2/hr, 2 hrs), **Bath** (hrly, 5 hrs, change in Bristol), **Cambridge** (nearly hrly, 2 hrs, change in Peterborough), **Birmingham** (2/hr, 2.5 hrs), **Keswick** (with transfers to Penrith then bus, 4.5 hrs). Train info: tel. 08457-484-950.

Connections with London's Airports: Heathrow (hrly, allow 2.5–3 hrs, take Heathrow Express train to London's Paddington Station, tube to King's Cross, train to York—2/hr, 2 hrs), **Gatwick** (from Gatwick catch low-profile Thameslink train to King's Cross-Thameslink station in London; from there, walk 100 yards to King's Cross Station, train to York—2/hr, 2 hrs).

Buses: The **York Bus Information Centre** is at 20 Hudson Street, near the train station (Mon–Fri 8:30–17:00, tel. 01904/551-400, phone answered Mon–Sat 8:00–20:00, Sun 8:00–14:00).

Route Tips for Drivers

As you near York (and your B&B), you'll hit the A1237 ring road. Follow this to the A19/Thirsk roundabout (next to river on northeast side of town). From roundabout, follow signs for York City, traveling through Clifton into Bootham. All recommended B&Bs are four or five blocks before you hit the medieval city gate (see neighborhood map, page 274). If you're approaching York from the south, take M1 until it ends. Then follow A64 for 10 miles until you reach York's ring road (A1237), which allows you to avoid driving through the city center.

North York Moors

The North York Moors are a vacant lot compared with the Cumbrian Lake District. But that's unfair competition. In the lonesome North York Moors, you can wander through the stark beauty of its time-passed villages, bored sheep, and powerful landscapes.

If you're driving, get a map. Without wheels, you have several choices: Take a bus/steam-train combination (below); choose one of several guided bus tours from York (focusing on Herriot or Brontë country, moors, Lake District, or Holy Island, different tour every day, offered by various companies for roughly £10/half day or £16/full day); or hire a private guide. John Smith, a licensed guide and driver, can take up to three people on one of his Yorkshire Tours—such as Herriot Country, a Castle Howard/steam train/Whitby combination, or a tour tailored to your interests (£15/hr, admissions extra, tel. 01904/636-653, mobile 07850-260-511).

▲**The Moors**—Car hike across the moors on any small road. You'll come upon tidy villages, old Roman roads, and maybe even a fox hunt. The Moors Visitors Centre provides the best orientation for exploring the moors. It's a grand old lodge that offers exhibits, shows, nature walks, an information desk with plenty of books and maps, brass rubbing, a cheery cafeteria, and brochures on several good walks that start right there (free but £1.50 parking fee, April–Oct daily 10:00–17:00, Nov–Dec and March daily 11:00–16:00, Jan–Feb weekends only 11:00–16:00, a half mile from train station, tel. 01439/772-737, www.moors.uk.net).

▲**North Yorkshire Moors Railway**—This 18-mile, one-hour steam-engine ride between Pickering and Grosmont (GROW-mont) goes through some of the best parts of the moors almost hourly. Even with the windows small and dirty (wipe off the outside of yours before you roll) and the track mostly in a scenic gully, it's a good ride. You can stop

North York Moors

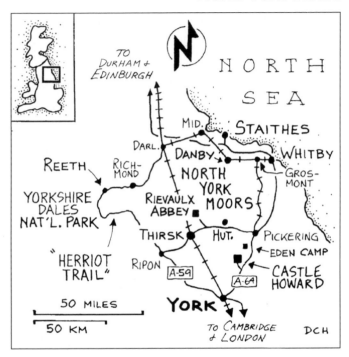

along the way for a walk in the moors and then catch the next train (£12 round-trip, April–Oct, first train departs Pickering about 10:20, last train departs Grosmont about 16:50, allow 3.5 hrs round-trip due to scheduling, tel. 01751/472-508, talking timetable tel. 01751/473-535). It's not possible to leave luggage at any stop on the steam-train line—pack lightly if you decide to hike.

Pickering—With its rural-life museum, castle, and Monday market (produce, knickknacks), this town is worth a stop. You could catch an early York-Pickering bus (Mon–Sat 1/hr, only one bus on Sun, 65 min, leaves from train station), see Pickering, and carry on to Grosmont on the North Yorkshire Moors Railway (above). Grosmont is on a regular train line with limited connections to Whitby (see next page) and points north and south (TI tel. 01751/473-791).

▲**Hutton-le-Hole**—This postcard-pretty town is home of the fine Ryedale Folk Museum, which illustrates "farm life in the moors" through reconstructed and furnished 18th-century local buildings (£3.50, mid-March–Oct daily 10:00–17:30, last entry at 16:30, tel. 01751/417-367).

Castle Howard—Especially popular since the filming of *Brideshead Revisited,* this fine, palatial 300-year-old home is about half as interesting as Blenheim Palace in the Cotswolds (£9, daily 11:00–17:00, last entry 1 hour before closing, closed early Nov–mid-Feb, 1 bus/day from York, 40 min, tel. 01653/648-333).

Rievaulx Abbey—Rievaulx (ree-VOH) is a highlight of the North York Moors and beautifully situated, but if you've seen other fine old abbeys, this is a rerun (£3.80, April–Sept daily 10:00–18:00, Oct daily 10:00–17:00, Nov–March daily 10:00–16:00, tel. 01439/798-228).

World of James Herriot—Devotees of the *All Creatures* books can visit the folksy veterinarian's digs in Thirsk. Built in the original surgery room of the author/veterinarian Alf Wright, this museum recreates the '40s Skeldale House featured in the Herriot novels and explores the development of veterinary science. Try out the interactive exhibit on horse dentistry and find out if you're strong enough to calve a cow (£4.70, April–Sept daily 10:00–18:00, Oct–April 11:00–16:00, last admission 1 hour before closing, 23 Kirkgate, tel. 01845/524-234).

Herriot fans will find the Yorkshire Dales more interesting than the neighboring moors. Local booklets at the TI lay out the *All Creatures Great and Small* pilgrimage route for drivers, or you could consider a tour from York (see leaflets at TI).

Whitby and Staithes

These towns are seaside escapes worth a stop for the seagulls, surf, and Captain Cook lore. Whitby is accessible by train, but Staithes makes sense only with a car.

▲**Whitby**—An important port since the 12th century, Whitby is now a fun coastal resort town with a busy harbor and steep and salty old streets. It's a carousel of Coney Island-type amusements overseen by the stately ruins of its seventh-century abbey. The **Captain Cook Memorial Museum** offers an interesting look at the famous hometown sailor and his exotic voyages (£3, daily 9:45–17:00, closed Nov–March, down Grape Lane in the old town just over the bridge). Two of Captain Cook's boats (*Resolution* and *Endeavour*) were built in the Whitby shipyards. The **TI** is on the harbor next to the train and bus stations (May–Sept daily 9:30–18:00, Oct–April daily 10:00–16:30, tel. 01947/602-674).

If driving, upon arrival park across from the TI at the pay-and-display supermarket lot near the train and bus station. Wander along the harbor out along Pier Road and Fish Quay past all the Coney Island-type distractions. The **Magpie Restaurant** is famous for its fish and chips (generally a line of hungry pilgrims waiting to get in). The small Dracula exhibit is a reminder that some of that story was set here. As you return to your car, cross the bridge where you'll find a warren of touristy lanes filled with hard candy, knickknack shops, and the small Captain Cook Memorial Museum.

▲Staithes—A ragamuffin village where the boy who became Captain James Cook got his first taste of the sea, Staithes (just north of Whitby) is a salty tumble of cottages bunny-hopping down a ravine into a tiny harbor. While tranquil today, in 1816 it was home to 70 boats and the busiest fishing station in north England. Ten years ago the town supported 20 fishing boats—today, only three. But fishermen (who pronounce their town "steers") still outnumber tourists in undiscovered Staithes. The town has changed little since Captain Cook's days. Little is done to woo tourism here. Lots of flies and seagulls seem to have picked the barren cliffs raw. There's nothing to do but drop by the lifeboat house (a big deal in England; page through the history book, read the not-quite-stirring accounts of the boats being called to duty; drop a coin in the box), stroll the beach, and nurse a harborside beer or ice cream. Just an easy drive north of Whitby, Staithes is worthwhile by car—probably not by bus (hourly Whitby-Staithes buses, 30 min; 10-min walk from bus stop into town).

SLEEPING

Whitby

Whitby has plenty of rooms. August is the only tight month. The **Crescent House** rents six good rooms just south of the harbor with some sea views (Db-£48, family deals, no CC, non-smoking, on the bluff at the top of Khyber Pass at 6 East Crescent, tel. & fax 01947/600-091, janet@whitby.fsbusiness.co.uk, Janet and Mike Paget). **Dolphin Hotel,** in the old-town center at the bridge overlooking the harbor, is a colorful old pub with five salty rooms upstairs (Db-£55, pub closes at 23:30, 3 blocks from train station, Bridge Street, tel. 01947/602-197). The **hostel** is next to the abbey above the town (£10.25/bed, 58 beds in 8 rooms, office closed 10:00–17:00, tel. 01947/602-878).

Staithes

There are no fancy rooms. It's a cash-only town with no ATMs. Parking is tough—generally you can drive in only to unload. Service trucks clog the windy main (and only) lane much of the day. There's a pay-and-display lot at the top of the town (when paying the night before, time spills over past 9:00 the next morning). Each of these three- or four-bedroom places is cramped, with tangled floor plans that make you feel like a stowaway. The **Endeavour Restaurant B&B** is a tidy little place and the only one in town that offers parking (Db-£60–70, serves great food—see below, 1 High Street, tel. 01947/840-825, www.endeavour -restaurant.co.uk, Brian Kay & Charlotte Willoughby). **Harborside Guest House** is the roughest place, but the only place actually on the harbor. It provides rumpled old beds, three seaview rooms, breakfast on linoleum, and the sound of waves to lull you to sleep (D-£45, no CC, tel. 01947/841-296).

EATING

Staithes

The **Endeavour Restaurant** is oddly classy for this town, and it offers excellent £25 dinners (Tue–Sat 18:45–21:30, closed Sun–Mon, seafood, vegetarian, reservations wise, tel. 01947/840-825). Two pubs serve dinner (generally 19:00–21:00): the **Black Lion** and the **Royal George.** For a scenic brew, stop by the **Cod and Lobster,** overlooking the harbor, with outdoor benches and a cozy living room warmed by a coal fire. Drop in to see its old-time Staithes photos. For fish and chips or a coffee on the harbor, try the friendly **Sea Drift Sweet Shop** or **Harborside Guest House.**

TRANSPORTATION CONNECTIONS

Buses connect **Whitby** and **York** (4–6/day depending on season, 2 hrs, tel. 01653/692-556). Trains connect **Durham** with **Middlesbrough** (5/day, 50 min, more frequent with transfer in Darlington); the **Middlesbrough-Whitby** train (4/day, 90 min) stops at **Grosmont** (where you can catch the Moors steam train) and **Danby** (a half mile from the Moors info center).

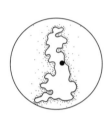

DURHAM AND NORTHEAST ENGLAND

Some of England's best history is harbored in the northeast. Hadrian's Wall reminds us that Britain was an important Roman colony 2,000 years ago. After a Roman ramble, you can make a pilgrimage to Holy Island, where Christianity gained its first toehold in Britain. At Durham, marvel at England's greatest Norman church and enjoy an evensong service. And, at the Beamish open-air folk museum, you can travel back in time to the year 1913.

Planning Your Time

For train travelers, Durham is the most convenient overnight stop in this region. If you like Roman ruins, visit Hadrian's Wall en route between Edinburgh and Durham (doable with transfers, easiest late May–late Sept). The Beamish folk museum is an easy day trip from Durham (hrly bus, 20 min).

By car it's easy. On a one-month driving trip, connect Edinburgh and Durham with this string of sights—Holy Island, Bamburgh Castle, Hadrian's Wall, and Beamish folk museum. Spend a night near Hadrian's Wall and a night in Durham.

For drivers or train travelers with 36 hours between Edinburgh and York, leave Edinburgh early, hike a bit of Hadrian's Wall and tour Housesteads Fort, and get to Durham in time to tour the cathedral and enjoy the evensong service (Tue–Sat 17:15, Sun 15:30). Sleep in Durham. Tour Beamish (15 min north of Durham by car or bus) the next morning. Drivers can then tour the North York Moors, arriving in York by late afternoon.

Durham

Without its cathedral it would hardly be noticed. But this magnificently situated cathedral is hard not to notice (even if you're zooming by on the train). Durham sits, seemingly happy to go nowhere, along its river and below its castle and famous cathedral. It has a medieval, cobbled atmosphere and a scraggly peasant's indoor market just off the main square (closed Sun). While Durham is the home of England's third-oldest university, the town feels working class, surrounded by recently closed coal mines and filled with tattooed and pierced people in search of job security. Yet Durham has a youthful vibrancy and a smalltown warmth that shines especially on sunny days, when most everyone is licking an ice-cream cone or is planning to.

ORIENTATION

(area code: 0191)

Tidy little Durham clusters everything safely under its castle within the protective hairpin bend of its river. The longest walk you'd make would be a 15-minute jaunt from the train station to the cathedral.

Tourist Information: The TI, located one block north of the town square, past St. Nicholas church, in the Gala Theatre building, books rooms and local theater tickets, and provides train times (Mon–Sat 9:30–17:30, Sun 11:00–16:00, WC, café, tel. 0191/384-3720). They also offer city walking tours in summer (£3, June–Sept, 90 min, Wed and Fri–Sun at 14:00, confirm schedule with TI). To go further afield, consult the TI's brochure *Guided Walks in County Durham*, which lists themed walks led by local experts (£3, several times weekly, some hikes start in Durham).

Arrival in Durham: From the train station, follow the road downhill and take the second pedestrian turnoff (within sight of railway bridge), which leads almost immediately over a bridge above busy Alexander Crescent road. Then take North Road into town or to the first couple of B&Bs (take Alexander Crescent to the other B&Bs). Day-trippers can store luggage at the station (£1.50, daily 7:00–20:00, ask at platform 1, bags may be searched by security). Drivers simply surrender to the wonderful Prince Bishop's car park (at the roundabout at the base of the old town). It's perfectly safe, inexpensive, and an elevator deposits you right in the heart of Durham (a short block from the town square).

Internet Access: The library, just across from the TI, has about 40 terminals and offers free Internet access (Mon–Fri 9:30–19:00, Sat 9:30–17:00, closed Sun, need to show ID, tel. 0191/384-7641).

Durham

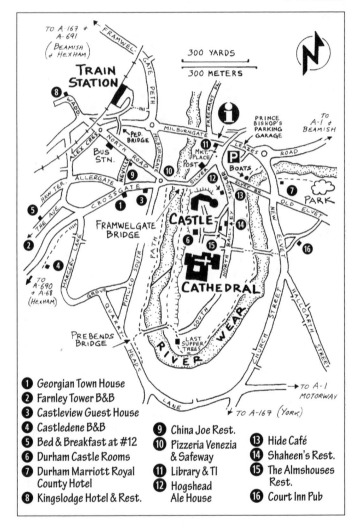

TO A·167 &
A·691
(BEAMISH
& HEXHAM)

TRAIN
STATION

300 YARDS
300 METERS

PRINCE
BISHOP'S
PARKING
GARAGE

TO
A·1 &
BEAMISH

PED.
BRIDGE

BUS
STN.

MILBURNGATE

MKT.
PLACE

LEASES
ROAD

POST

BOATS

ROAD

ALLERGATE

CROSSGATE

NORTH
ROAD

NEVILLE
ST.

REX CRES.

YARD

THIRBURNGATE

SILVER

SADDLER

NEW
ELVET

ELVET
BR.

OLD
ELVET

PARK

TO
A·1 &
BEAMISH

HAWTHORN TER.

THE AVE.

FRAMWELGATE
BRIDGE

CASTLE

NORTH
BAILEY

TO
A·690
& A·68
(HEXHAM)

MARGERY LANE

GROVE

QUARRY
HEADS

PATH

PIMLICO SOUTH

SOUTH
BAILEY

CATHEDRAL

PREBENDS
BRIDGE

LANE

RIVER WEAR

LAST
SUPPER
TREES

CHURCH
STREET

HALLGARTH
STREET

TO A·1
MOTORWAY

TO A·167 (YORK)

1 Georgian Town House
2 Farnley Tower B&B
3 Castleview Guest House
4 Castledene B&B
5 Bed & Breakfast at #12
6 Durham Castle Rooms
7 Durham Marriott Royal
County Hotel
8 Kingslodge Hotel & Rest.

9 China Joe Rest.
10 Pizzeria Venezia
& Safeway
11 Library & TI
12 Hogshead
Ale House

13 Hide Café
14 Shaheen's Rest.
15 The Almshouses
Rest.
16 Court Inn Pub

Getting around Durham

While all listed hotels, eateries, and sights are easily walkable in
Durham, taxis are available to zip tired tourists to their B&Bs (£2, wait
on Market Place or on west side of Framwelgate Bridge).

SIGHTS

Durham

▲▲▲**Cathedral**—Built to house the much-venerated bones of St. Cuthbert from Lindisfarne, the cathedral offers the best look at Norman architecture in England. (Norman is British for Romanesque.) The cathedral is free but a £4 donation is requested (Mon–Sat 9:30–18:15, mid-June–Aug until 20:00, Sun 12:30–17:00, April–Sept until 18:00, open at 7:30 for worship and prayer). For various fees, you can also climb the tower, ogle the treasury, and tour the Monk's Dormitory. I'd skip the AV show on St. Cuthbert. Try to fit in some music (see "Evensong," page 287). No photos or videos are allowed. A bookshop, cafeteria, and WC are tucked away in the cloisters.

A Tour Plan: From the cathedral green, notice how this fortress of God stands boldly across from the Norman keep of Durham's fortress of man. (The castle, now part of the university, is not worth touring.)

At the cathedral door, notice the big, bronze, lion-faced knocker, a replica of the 12th-century original (now in the treasury), which was used by criminals seeking sanctuary (read the explanation).

Immediately inside you'll see the **information desk.** Church attendants happily answer questions. Ideally, follow a church tour (£3.50 donation, mid-July–Aug Mon–Fri at 11:00 and 14:30, Sat 18:15, Sun 18:00, if one's in session you're welcome to join). The pamphlet, *A Walk Round Durham Cathedral,* is informative but dull (60p).

Notice the modern window with the novel depiction of the Last Supper (above and to the left of the entry door). It was given to the church by a local department store in 1984. The shapes of the apostles represent worlds and persons of every kind from the shadowy Judas to the brightness of Jesus. This window is a good reminder that the cathedral remains a living part of the community.

Near the entrance, the black marble strip on the floor was as close to the altar as women were allowed in the days when this was a Benedictine church (until 1540). Sit down (ignoring the black line) and let the fine proportions of England's best Norman (and arguably Europe's best Romanesque) nave stir you. Any frilly woodwork and stonework were added in later centuries.

The architecture of the **nave** is particularly harmonious because it was built in a mere 40 years (1093–1133). Few additions were made, and the bulk of what you see today—especially the round arches and zigzag carved decorations—are textbook Norman. The church was also proto-Gothic, built by well-traveled French masons and architects who knew the latest innovations from Europe. Its stone and ribbed roof, Britain's first pointed arches, and first flying buttresses were revolutionary in this country. Notice the clean lines and simplicity. It's not as cluttered as other churches for several reasons: Out of respect for St. Cuthbert, for

Durham Cathedral

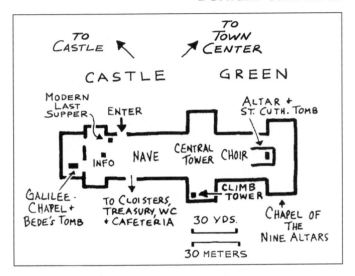

centuries no one else was buried here. During Reformation times, sumptuous Catholic decor was cleaned out. And subsequent fires and wars destroyed what Protestants didn't.

Enter the **Galilee Chapel** (late Norman, from 1175) in the back of the nave. The paintings of St. Cuthbert and St. Oswald (seventh-century king of Northumbria) on the side walls of the side altar niche are rare examples of Romanesque or Norman paintings. Facing this altar, look above to your right to see more faint paintings on the upper walls above the columns. Near the center of the chapel, the upraised tomb topped with a black slab contains the remains of the Venerable Bede, an eighth-century Christian scholar who wrote the first history of England. The Latin reads: *In this tomb are the bones of the Venerable Bede.*

Back in the main church, stroll down the nave to the center, under the highest bell tower in Europe (218 feet). Gaze up. The ropes pull hammers that ring the bells. If you're stirred by the cheery ringing of **church bells,** tune into the cathedral on Sunday (9:30–10:00 & 14:30–15:00) or Thursday (19:30 practice) when the resounding notes tumble merrily through the entire town.

Continuing east (all medieval churches faced east), you enter the **choir.** Monks worshiped many times a day, and the choir in the center of the church provided a cozier place to gather in this vast, dark, and cold building. Here in the heart of the cathedral, Mass has been said daily for 900 years. The fancy wooden chairs are from the 17th century. Behind the altar is the delicately carved stone Neville Screen from 1380 (made of Normandy stone in London, shipped to Newcastle by sea, then brought here by wagon); until the Reformation the niches contained statues of 107 saints. Exit the choir from the far right side (south). Look for the stained-glass window (to your right) commemorating the church's 1,000th anniversary in 1995. The colorful scenes depict England's history from coal miners to cows to computers.

Step down into the **apse,** the Gothic east end of the church. Climb a few stairs to the tomb of St. Cuthbert. An inspirational leader of the early Christian Church in North England, St. Cuthbert lived in the Lindisfarne monastery on Holy Island (100 miles north of Durham). He died in 687. Eleven years later his body was exhumed and found to be miraculously preserved. This stoked the popularity of his shrine, and pilgrims came in growing numbers. When Vikings raided Lindisfarne in 875, the monks fled with his body (and the famous illuminated *Lindisfarne Gospels,* now in the British Library in London). In 995, after 120 years of roaming, the monks settled in Durham on an easy-to-defend tight bend in the River Wear. The cathedral was built over Cuthbert's tomb. Throughout the Middle Ages a shrine stood here— and was visited by countless pilgrims. In 1539, during the Reformation—whose proponents advocated focusing on God rather than saints—the shrine was destroyed. Cuthbert's tomb is part of the larger 13th-century Gothic Chapel of the Nine Altars—taller, lighter, and relatively more extravagant than the Norman nave.

Consider the cathedral's other sights. The entry to the **tower** is in the south transept; the view from the tower will cost you 325 steps and £2 (April–Oct Mon–Sat 10:00–16:00, Nov–March Mon–Sat 10:00–15:00, closed Sun). The following sights are within the cloisters: The **treasury,** filled with medieval bits and holy pieces (including Cuthbert's coffin, vestments, and cross), fleshes out this otherwise stark building. The actual relics from St. Cuthbert's tomb are at the far end (treasury well worth the £2 admission, Mon–Sat 10:00–16:30, Sun 14:00–16:30). The **Monks' Dormitory,** now a library with an original 14th-century timber roof filled with Anglo-Saxon stones, is worth 80p (Mon–Sat 10:00–15:30, Sun 12:30–15:15). The unexceptional AV show in the unexceptional undercroft tells about St. Cuthbert (Mon–Sat 10:00–15:00, no showings Sun, off-season also no showings Fri, not worth 80p). The fine cafeteria (Mon–Sat 10:00–17:00, lunch 12:00-14:00, Sun 10:30–17:00, mid-Oct–late May, closes at 16:30, non-smoking), bookshop (in the old kitchen), and WCs are near the treasury.

Evensong: For a thousand years this cradle of English Christianity has been praising God. To really experience the cathedral, go for an evensong service. Arrive early and ask to be seated in the choir. It's a spiritual Oz, as 40 boys sing psalms—a red-and-white-robed pillow of praise, raised up by the powerful pipe organ. If you're lucky and the service went well, the organist runs a spiritual musical victory lap as the congregation breaks up (Tue–Sat 17:15, Sun at 15:30, 1 hr, normally not sung on Mon; when choir is off on school break during mid-July–Aug visiting choirs often fill in; tel. 0191/386-2367).

Riverside Walk—For a 20-minute woodsy escape, walk Durham's riverside path from busy Framwelgate Bridge to sleepy Prebends Bridge. Just beyond the Prebends Bridge on the old-town side of the river, you'll find the Upper Room, a cluster of trees carved to show the Last Supper when viewed from a tree-trunk throne. Where are the apostles? Count the tree trunks.

Boat Cruise and Rental—For a relaxing 60-minute narrated cruise of the river, hop on the *Prince Bishop* (£4.50, for schedule call 0191/386-9525, check at TI, or go down to the dock at **Brown's Boat House** at Elvet Bridge, just east of old town). For some exercise with the same scenery, you can rent a rowboat at the same pier (£3/hr per person, £5 deposit, Easter–Sept daily 10:00–18:00, last boat rental 1 hr before dusk, tel. 0191/386-3779).

Near Durham: Beamish Open-Air Museum

This huge museum, which re-creates the year 1913 in northeast England, takes at least three hours to explore. A vintage tram shuttles visitors to the four stations: Coal Mine Village, Home Farm, The Town, and an 1820s manor house and steam train. This isn't wax. If you touch the exhibits, they may smack you. Attendants at each stop happily explain everything. In fact, the place is only really interesting if you talk to these attendants.

Start with the **Coal Mine Village** (company village around a coal mine), with a school, church, miners' homes, and a fascinating—if claustrophobic—20-minute tour into a real "drift" mine.

The Town is a bustling street featuring a 1913 candy shop, a dentist's office, a garage, a working pub (fun for a smoky beer), and a modern, smoke-free cafeteria (Dainty Dinah's Tea Room, upstairs). The old train station isn't much.

The Pockerley Manor is an 1820s manor house whose attendants have plenty to explain. Adjacent is the re-created first-ever passenger train from 1825, which takes modern-day visitors for a spin on 1825 tracks—a hit with railway buffs. The **Home Farm** is the least interesting section (£12, April–Oct daily 10:00–17:00; from Nov–March only The Town is open, 10:00–16:00, closed Mon and Fri; check events schedule as you enter, last tickets sold 2 hrs before closing, tel. 0191/370-4000, www.beamish.org.uk).

The museum is five minutes off the A1/M1 motorway (one exit north of Durham at Chester-le-Street, well sign-posted). To get to Beamish from Durham, catch a #720 bus (marked "Stanley via Beamish," 1/hr, 30 min, stops 500 yards from museum).

SLEEPING

The only **launderette** in town is at Dunelm House, the Student Union building—a 10- to 15-minute walk east of the B&B neighborhood (open to public, daily 8:00–21:00 during school term, otherwise 9:00–15:00, self-service only, east end of Kingsgate Bridge, tel. 0191/344-777).

B&Bs

$$ Georgian Town House, near Framwelgate Bridge, has a cheery bossa nova ambience with a breezy garden, plush sitting room, new pancake café and tearoom, and eight bright rooms decorated with care and flair. The hearty breakfast is served in the conservatory (Sb-£55–60, Db-£70–75, first night discount with this book, no CC, non-smoking, tubs lack showers, some rooms with castle views, drivers must ask for parking permit, 10 Crossgate, tel. & fax 0191/386-8070, www.thegeorgiantownhouse.co.uk, enquiries@georgian-townhouse.fsnet.co.uk, Charlotte and Lucy Weil).

$$ Farnley Tower is a luxurious B&B. Opened in mid-1999, it still feels like it just came out of the box. Its 10 spacious rooms have all the comforts, and some have views. The hotel is on a quiet dead end at the top of a hill, a 10-minute uphill hike from the town center (one Sb-£50, Db-£68, superior Db-£78, family rooms available, CC for 2 percent extra, non-smoking, phones in rooms, easy parking, inviting yard, The Avenue, tel. 0191/375-0011, fax 0191/383-9694, www.farnley-tower.co.uk, enquiries@farnley-tower.co.uk, John and Gail Khan).

$$ Castleview Guest House, a few doors down the street from the Georgian Town House, rents six airy, comfortable rooms in a classy well-located house (Sb-£45, Db-£65, no CC, prices promised with book through 2004, non-smoking, drivers must ask for parking permit, 4 Crossgate, tel. & fax 0191/386-8852, castle_view@hotmail.com, Mike and Anne Williams).

$ Castledene B&B is tidy, simple, and friendly, with two twin-bedded rooms and double-glazed windows to keep the house quiet and warm (S-£25, D-£40, no CC, at intersection of Crossgate and Margery Lane, go up stairway to pedestrian-only walkway—running parallel to Crossgate Peth—to last house, 37 Nevilledale Terrace; drivers go a few yards past Crossgate intersection and turn right on Summerville, tel. & fax 0191/384-8386, Lorna and Brian Byrne).

$ The low-key **Bed & Breakfast at #12** has two simple rooms on a quiet dead-end street (small S-£21, D-£42, no CC, non-smoking, no sign on door, 12 The Avenue, tel. 0191/384-1020, jan.hanim@aol.com, run by kindly Jan Metcalfe).

$ Student Housing—Open to Anyone: Durham Castle, a student residence actually on the castle grounds facing the cathedral, rents 100 singles and 30 doubles during the summer break (July–Sept

SLEEP CODE

(£1 = about $1.60, country code: 44, area code: 0191)

Sleep Code: **S** = Single, **D** = Double/Twin, **T** = Triple, **Q** = Quad, **b** = bathroom, **s** = shower only, **no CC** = Credit Cards not accepted. You can assume credit cards are accepted unless otherwise noted.

To help you sort easily through these listings, I've divided the rooms into three categories based on the price for a standard double room with bath (during high season):

$$$ **Higher Priced**—Most rooms £80 or more.
$$ **Moderately Priced**—Most rooms between £50–80.
$ **Lower Priced**—Most rooms £50 or less.

The B&Bs are a five- or 10-minute walk from the station and the town center. Durham hosts a rowing regatta the second weekend in June; book ahead.

only, £20.50/person, £32 with private facilities, can reserve long in advance, elegant breakfast hall, parking-£2 on the cathedral green, University College, The Castle, Palace Green, tel. 0191/334-4106, fax 0191/374-7470, Julie Marshall). Request a room in the classy old main building or you may get one of the few bomb-shelter-style modern dorm rooms.

Hotels

$$$ **Durham Marriott Royal County Hotel,** a four-star hotel, scatters its 150 posh rooms among several buildings sprawling along the river near the city center. The Leisure Club has a pool, sauna, Jacuzzi, and fitness equipment (Db-£145, £25 less on weekends, breakfast extra, 2 restaurants, bar, parking, Old Elvet, tel. 0191/386-6821, fax 0191/386-0704, www.marriotthotels.co.uk).

$$$ **Kingslodge Hotel & Restaurant,** a renovated lodge with charming terraces, an attached restaurant, and a champagne and oyster bar, is a cush option convenient to the train station (Sb-£78, Db-£98, includes breakfast, rooms non-smoking, parking, Waddington Street, Flass Vale, tel. 0191/370-9977, run by the same people who own recommended Castleview Guest House).

EATING

Durham is a university town with plenty of lively, inexpensive eateries. Stroll down North Road, across Framwelgate Bridge, through Market Place, and up Saddler Street, and consider the places listed here (in walking order) as you do so.

China Joe is a cheap and modern Chinese buffet a couple blocks from the west end of Framwelgate Bridge (daily 12:00–20:30, specials until 19:00, 50 North Road, tel. 0191/370-9180).

Pizzeria Venezia, at the west end of the bridge, serves good, affordable Italian food (Mon–Fri 12:00–13:45 & 18:00–21:45, early-bird specials 18:00–19:00, closed Sun–Mon, no CC, go through Millburngate Shopping Centre archway, tel. 0191/384-6777).

Bimbi's, on Market Place, is a standby for fish and chips (daily 9:30–23:30).

Saddler Street, leading from Market Place up to the cathedral, is lined with eateries. After the pasta place and the pizza place, consider the **Hogshead Ale House** for pub grub (£4–5, serving food daily 12:00–21:00, more drinking than eating in evening, smoky, tel. 0191/386-9550).

The hip **Hide Café,** across the street, serves the best modern continental cuisine in the old town (£8–10, Mon–Sat 9:30–22:30, Sun 9:30-15:00, fun, jazz-filled ambience, 39 Saddler Street, tel. 0191/384-1999).

Shaheen's is the place for good Indian cuisine (Tue–Sun 18:00–23:30, closed Mon, 48 Saddler Street, just past turnoff to cathedral, tel. 0191/386-0960).

The Almshouses on the cathedral green, serves tasty, light meals (daily 9:00–20:00, Oct–Easter until 17:00, tel. 0191/386-1054).

Court Inn, on the outskirts of town, is a local favorite for traditional pub grub (bar meals-£7–10, daily 11:00–22:30, 5-min walk east of old town, take Elvet or Kingsgate Bridge, Court Lane, tel. 0191/384-7350).

Drivers looking for a nontouristy splurge can eat modern French/English at **Bistro 21** (£25 meals, Mon–Sat 12:00–14:00 & 19:00–22:00, closed Sun, Aykley Heads, 3 miles north of town, tel. 0191/384-4354).

Supermarkets: Of Durham's two supermarkets, **Safeway** has longer hours and is closer to the recommended B&Bs (Mon–Fri 8:30–20:00, Sat 8:00–18:00, Sun 10:00–17:00, in Millburngate Shopping Center, west end of Framwelgate Bridge). In the old town, try **Marks & Spencer,** just off the main square (Mon–Sat 9:00–18:00, Sun 11:00–17:00, on Silver Street; across from PO, which has same hours as M&S). You can **picnic** on the benches and grass outside the cathedral entrance (but not on the Palace Green, unless the park police have gone home).

TRANSPORTATION CONNECTIONS

By train to: Edinburgh (nearly hrly, 2 hrs), **York** (1–3/hr, 1 hr), **London** (hrly, 3 hrs), **Hadrian's Wall** (take train to Newcastle—1–4/hr, 15 min; then a train/bus combination to Hadrian's Wall, see "Hadrian's Wall," below), **Bristol** (near Bath, 9/day, 5 hrs). From September to May only about half of the London-Edinburgh trains stop in little Durham; frequency drops to about six trains daily in winter (but you don't need to wait; from Durham, catch a milk-run train to busier Newcastle—1–4/hr, 15 min—where all the trains stop). Train info: tel. 08457-484-950.

Hadrian's Wall

This is one of England's most thought-provoking sights. Around A.D. 130, during the reign of Emperor Hadrian, the Romans built this great stone wall. Its actual purpose is still debated. While Rome ruled Britain for 400 years, it never quite ruled its people. The wall may have been used to define the northern edge of the empire, protect Roman Britain from invading Scottish clans (or at least cut down on pesky border raids), monitor the movement of people, or simply give an otherwise bored army something to do. (Nothing's more dangerous than a bored army.) Stretching 75 miles coast to coast across the narrowest stretch of northern England, it was built and defended by nearly 20,000 troops. The wall was flanked by ditches, and a military road lies on the south side. At every mile of the wall a castle guards a gate, and two turrets stand between each castle. The mile castles are numbered. (Eighty of them cover the 75 miles because a Roman mile was slightly shorter than our mile.)

Today, several chunks of the wall, ruined forts, and museums thrill history buffs. About a dozen Roman sites cling along the wall's route; the best are Housesteads Fort and Vindolanda. Housesteads shows you where the Romans lived; Vindolanda's museum shows you how they lived (tel. 01434/322-002, www.hadrians-wall.org).

The new Hadrian's Wall National Trail, completed in spring 2003, follows the wall's route from coast to coast (for details, see www .countryside.gov.uk).

SIGHTS

▲▲**Housesteads Fort**—With its tiny museum, powerful scenery, and the best-preserved segment of the wall, this is your best single stop. All Roman forts were the same rectangular shape and design and contained a commander's headquarters, barracks, and latrines (lower end); this fort

Durham and Northeast England

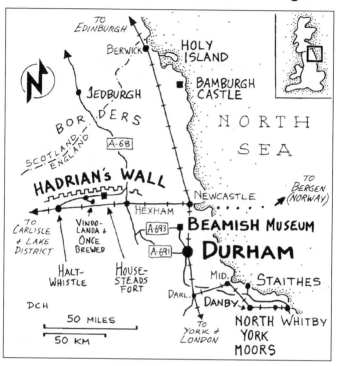

TO EDINBURGH

BERWICK

HOLY ISLAND

BAMBURGH CASTLE

JEDBURGH

BOR DERS

SCOTLAND ENGLAND

A-68

NORTH SEA

HADRIAN'S WALL

NEWCASTLE

TO BERGEN (NORWAY)

HEXHAM

TO CARLISLE & LAKE DISTRICT

VINDO-LANDA & ONCE BREWED

A-693

A-691

BEAMISH MUSEUM

DURHAM

HALT-WHISTLE

HOUSE-STEADS FORT

MID.

STAITHES

Darl.

DANBY

DCH

50 MILES

50 KM

TO YORK & LONDON

NORTH YORK MOORS

WHITBY

even has a hospital. The fort is built right up to the wall, which is on the far side (£3.10 for site and museum, April–Sept daily 10:00–18:00, Oct closes at 17:00, Nov–May closes at 16:00 or dusk, parking-£1, tel. 01434/344-363). At the car park are WCs, a snack bar, and a gift shop. You can leave your baggage at the gift shop, but confirm its closing hours. From the car park, it's a half-mile, mostly uphill walk to the entrance of the minuscule museum and sprawling fort.

▲▲**Hiking the Wall**—From Housesteads, hike west along the wall speaking Latin. For a good, craggy, three-mile walk along the wall, hike between Housesteads and Steel Rigg. You'll pass a castle sitting in a nick in a crag (castle #39, called Castle Nick). There's a car park near Steel Rigg (take the little road up from Twice Brewed Pub).

▲**Vindolanda**—This larger Roman fort (which actually predates the wall by 40 years) and museum are just south of the wall. Although Housesteads has better ruins and the wall, Vindolanda has the better museum, revealing intimate details of Roman life. Eight forts were built on this spot. The Romans, by carefully sealing the foundations from each successive fort, left modern-day archaeologists seven yards of remarkably well-preserved artifacts to excavate: keys, coins, brooches, scales, pottery, glass, tools, leather shoes, bits of cloth, and even a wig. Impressive examples of early Roman writing were recently discovered here. While the actual letters, written on thin pieces of wood, are in London's British Museum, see the interesting video here and read the translations—the first known example of a woman writing to a woman is an invitation to a birthday party. These varied letters, about parties held, money owed, and sympathy shared, bring Romans to life in a way that stones alone can't.

From the car park you'll walk through 500 yards of grassy parkland decorated by the foundation stones of the Roman fort and a full-size replica chunk of the wall. At the far side of the site is the museum, gift shop, and cafeteria (£4.10, £6 combo-ticket includes Roman Army Museum, daily 10:00–17:00 or 18:00 depending on the season, closed mid-Nov–early Feb, can leave baggage at entrance, tel. 01434/344-277). The **Roman Army Museum,** a few miles farther west at Greenhead, is redundant if you've seen Vindolanda (£3.30, or buy combo-ticket, see above, same hours, tel. 016977/47485).

SLEEPING AND EATING

(£1 = about $1.60, country code: 44, area code: 01434)
Near Hexham

$ **Crow's Nest B&B** offers three rooms in a remodeled farmhouse a quarter mile from the wall (D-£40, no CC, on B6318 road 500 yards from Once Brewed TI, Bardon Mill, Hexham, tel. 01434/344-348, Claire Watson). The nearby **Mile Castle Pub** cooks up all sorts of exotic game and offers the best dinner around, according to hungry national park rangers (daily 12:00–20:30).

$ **Montcoffer,** a restored country home in Bardon Mill, is decorated with statues, old enamel advertising signs, and other artifacts collected by John McGrellis, who runs the B&B with his wife Dehlia (Sb-£29–32, Db-£56–64, includes hearty breakfasts, 2 miles from Vindolanda, Bardon Mill, Hexham, tel. 01434/344-138, fax 01434/344-730, www.montcoffer.co.uk, john-dehlia@talk21.com).

$ **West Wharmley Farm** rents two rooms in a friendly farmhouse about seven miles from the wall in Hexham (Sb-£30, Db-£48, no CC, family deals, non-smoking, lounge, off A69 between Hexham and Haydon Bridge, follow signs, tel. 01434/674-227, Ros Johnson).

$ **High Reins** offers three rooms in a stone house built by a shipping tycoon in the 1920s (Db-£52, no CC, non-smoking, ground-floor bedrooms, lounge, one mile west of Hexham and train station, 15 miles from Vinolanda, tel. 01434/603-590, www.highreins.co.uk, walton45@hotmail.com, Jan Walton).

In and near Haltwhistle

$$ Ashcroft Guest House, a former vicarage, is 400 yards from the Haltwhistle train station. The family-run B&B has seven rooms and pleasant gardens (Sb-£45, Db-£56, four-poster Db-£60, non-smoking, 1.5 miles from the Wall, Lanty's Lonnen, tel. 01434/320-213, fax 01434/321-641, www.ashcroftguesthouse.co.uk, enquiries@ashcroftguesthouse.freeserve.co.uk, Geoff & Christine).

$$ Twice Brewed Pub and Hotel, two miles west of Housesteads, serves decent pub grub nightly to a local darts-and-pool crowd (D-£39-55, Db-£56, tel. 01434/344-534).

$ Once Brewed Youth Hostel is a comfortable place next door to the Twice Brewed Pub (£11.50/bed with sheets, £2 extra for nonmembers, 4–8 beds/room, no CC, breakfast-£3.50, cheap lunches and dinners, Military Road, Bardon Mill, tel. 01434/344-360, fax 01434/344-045, oncebrewed@yha.org.uk).

$ Doors Cottage B&B rents a couple of rooms just across the street from a section of the Roman wall and five miles from Housesteads Fort (S-£20, D-£40, includes good English breakfast, non-smoking, Shield Hill, Haltwhistle, tel. 01434/322-556, doors-cottage@supanet.com).

TRANSPORTATION CONNECTIONS

By car: Take B6318; it parallels the wall and passes several viewpoints, minor sights, and "severe dips." (If there's a certified nerd or bozo in the car, these road signs add a lot to a photo portrait.)

By train and bus: A train/bus combination (which operates with greatest frequency late May–late Sept) delivers you to the wall. From England's east coast, Newcastle is the gateway to the Newcastle-Carlisle train that parallels the wall (Mon–Sat 8:30–16:30 every 30 min to Hexham, every hr to Haltwistle, Sun hrly 9:00–18:30, from Newcastle it's 30 min to Hexham, 20 more min to Haltwistle). But the train only gets you near the wall. During peak season (end of May through Sept), take Hadrian's Wall bus #122AD to get to the wall and all the Roman sights. Get off the train at either Hexham or Haltwhistle to catch this bus (5 buses/day in each direction, late May–late Sept; Hexham-Housesteads 30 min, Housesteads-Vindolanda 10 min, Vindolanda-Haltwhistle 20 min).

At Newcastle's train station, pick up a Hadrian's Wall bus schedule at the TI (Mon–Sat 9:30–17:00, Sat opens at 9:00, closed Sun, call for schedule, tel. 0191/232-7021; no luggage storage at station). Or call Haltwhistle's helpful TI for schedule information (Mon–Sat 9:30–13:00 & 14:00–17:30, Sun 13:00–17:00; Nov–Easter Mon–Tue and Thu–Sat 10:00–12:30 & 13:00–15:30, closed Wed and Sun, tel. 01434/322-002, www.hadrians-wall.org). If you start from Newcastle by at least 11:00 (earlier is better), you can fit in both Housesteads and Vindolanda.

To visit Housesteads off-season (late Sept–late May), take a train to Haltwhistle and catch a taxi (taxi services: Sprouls tel. 01434/321-064, Turnbulls tel. 01434/320-105, one way-£8; arrange for return pickup or have museum staff call a taxi). If you're staying on the wall, your B&B host can arrange a taxi.

Holy Island and Bamburgh Castle

▲**Holy Island**—Twelve hundred years ago, this "Holy Island" was Christianity's toehold on England. It was the home of St. Cuthbert. We know it today for the *Lindisfarne Gospels,* decorated by monks in the seventh century with some of the finest art from Europe's "Dark Ages" (now in the British Museum). It's a pleasant visit, a quiet town with a striking castle (not worth touring) and an evocative priory. The Priory Exhibit is a tiny but instructive museum (£3) adjacent to the ruined abbey (tel. 01289/389-200). You can wander the abbey grounds and graveyard and pop into the church without paying. Holy Island is reached by a two-mile causeway that's cut off daily by high tides. Tidal charts are posted, warning you when this holy place becomes Holy Island and you become stranded. For TI and tide information, call the **Berwick TI** at tel. 01289/330-733 (May–Sept Mon–Sat 10:00–18:00, Sun 11:00–15:00; Oct–April Mon–Sat 10:00–16:00, closed Sun). Park at the pay-and-display lot and walk five minutes into the village. For a peaceful overnight in the center, try **Britannia Guest House** (D-£40, Db-£44, no CC, tel. 01289/389-218, Mrs. Patterson).

▲▲**Bamburgh Castle**—About 10 miles south of Holy Island, this grand castle dominates the Northumbrian countryside and overlooks Britain's loveliest beach. The place was bought and passionately refurbished by Lord Armstrong, a Ted Turner-like industrialist and engineer in the 1890s. Its interior, lined with well-described history, feels lived in because it still is—with Armstrong family portraits and aristocratic-yet-homey knickknacks hanging everywhere. The included **Armstrong Museum** features the inventions of the industrialist family that has owned the castle through modern times (£5, daily 11:00–17:00, last entry 16:30, closed Nov–March, tel. 01668/214-515, www.bamburghcastle.com). Rolling dunes crisscrossed by walking paths lead to a vast sandy beach and lots of local families on holiday. This area is only worthwhile for those with a car.

EDINBURGH

Edinburgh, the colorful city of Robert Louis Stevenson, Sir Walter Scott, and Robert Burns, is Scotland's showpiece and one of Europe's most entertaining cities. Historical, monumental, fun, and well organized, it's a tourist's delight.

Promenade down the Royal Mile through Old Town. Historic buildings pack the Royal Mile between the castle (on the top) and Holyrood Palace (on the bottom). Medieval skyscrapers stand shoulder to shoulder, hiding peaceful courtyards connected to High Street by narrow lanes or even tunnels. This colorful jumble is the tourist's Edinburgh.

Edinburgh (ED'n-burah) was once the most crowded city in Europe—famed for its skyscrapers and filth. The rich and poor lived atop one another. In the Age of Enlightenment, a magnificent Georgian city, today's New Town, was laid out to the north, giving the town's upper class a respectable place to promenade. Georgian Edinburgh, like the city of Bath, shines with broad boulevards, straight streets, square squares, circular circuses, and elegant mansions decked out in colonnades, pediments, and sphinxes in the proud, neoclassical style of 200 years ago.

While the Georgian city celebrated the union of Scotland and England (with streets and squares named after English kings and emblems), "devolution" is the latest trend. In a 1998 election, the Scots voted to gain more autonomy and bring their parliament home. Though Edinburgh has been the historic capital of Scotland for centuries, parliament had not met there since 1707. In 2000, Edinburgh resumed its position as home to the Scottish Parliament (although London still calls the strategic shots). A strikingly modern new parliament building, slated to open in 2004, will be one more jewel in Edinburgh's crown.

Planning Your Time
While the major sights can be seen in a day, on a three-week tour of Britain I'd give Edinburgh two days and three nights.

Day 1: Tour the castle. Then consider catching one of the city bus tours (from a block below the castle at The Hub/Tolbooth church) for a 60-minute loop, returning to the castle. Explore the Royal Mile, going downhill-having lunch, going to museums, shopping, and taking a walking tour (one leaves at 14:00 from Mercat Cross). If you tour Holyrood Palace, do it near the end of the day since it's at the bottom of the Mile. In the evening, take in live music at a pub, a literary pub crawl, or a haunted walk.

Day 2: Tour the Museum of Scotland. After lunch, stroll through the Princes Street Gardens and the National Gallery of Scotland. Then tour the good ship *Britannia*.

ORIENTATION

(area code: 0131)

The center of Edinburgh holds the Princes Street Gardens park and Waverley Bridge, where you'll find the TI, Princes Mall, train station, bus info office (starting point for most city bus tours), National Gallery, and a covered dance-and-music pavilion. Weather blows in and out—bring your sweater.

Tourist Information

The crowded TI is as central as can be atop the Princes Mall and train station (May–June and Sept Mon–Sat 9:00–19:00, Sun 10:00–19:00; July–Aug daily 9:00–20:00; April and Oct Mon–Wed 9:00–17:00, Thu–Sat until 18:00, Sun 10:00–17:00; ATM outside entrance, tel. 0845-225-5121). Unfortunately, all their information—their assessment of museums and even which car-rental companies "exist"—is skewed by tourism payola. Buy a map (£1 if in stock, or the excellent £4 Collins Illustrated Edinburgh map, which comes with opinionated commentary and locates virtually every major shop and sight), and ask for the free monthly entertainment *Gig Guide* if you're interested in late-night music. The *Essential Guide to Edinburgh* (£1), while not essential, lists additional sights and services. Book your room direct without the TI's help (B&Bs charge more for rooms booked through the TI, and you pay the TI a £3 finder's fee). Browse the racks (tucked away in hallway at back of TI) for brochures on the various Scottish folk shows, walking tours, and regional bus tours. Connect@edinburgh, a small Internet café, is beyond the brochure racks (see "Helpful Hints," next page). The best monthly entertainment listing, *The List*, sells for £2.20 at newsstands.

Arrival in Edinburgh

Arriving by train at Waverley Station puts you in the city center and below the TI. To get from the train station to the TI and the city bus stop for my recommended B&Bs, either take the many stairs (at the top,

TI is to your left; see "Sleeping," page 318, for directions to B&B neighborhood by bus) or walk up the ramp that surfaces on Waverley Bridge (bus to B&Bs around the block on North Bridge). Luggage storage is near platform 1 (£3.50/6 hrs, £4.50/6-24 hrs, daily 7:00–22:45).

Both Scottish Citylink and National Express buses use the bus station two blocks north of the train station on St. Andrew Square in the New Town.

Edinburgh's slingshot-of-an-airport is 10 miles northwest of the center and well-connected by taxi (£18, 30 min) and by shuttle bus with Waverley Bridge (LRT "Airline" bus #100, £3.30, or £4.20 with all-day "Airsaver" city-bus pass, 6/hr, 30 min, roughly 5:00–24:00). Flight info: tel. 0131/333-1000, bmi british midland tel. 0870-607-0555, British Airways tel. 0845-773-3377, Aer Lingus tel. 0845-084-444.

Helpful Hints

Sunday Activities: Many sights close on Sunday, but there's still a lot to do: You can take a Royal Mile walking tour or a city bus tour; visit Edinburgh Castle, St. Giles Cathedral, Holyrood Palace, or the Royal Botanic Gardens; and climb Arthur's Seat. An open-air market, including antiques, is held every Sunday from 10:00 to 16:00 at New Street Car Park near the train station. The Georgian House and National Gallery are open Sunday afternoon.

Internet Access: It's a cinch to get plugged in. The easyInternetcafé, with 450 terminals, is a block from the National Gallery (daily 7:00–23:00, 58 Rose Street, go through Caffè Nero and upstairs). At the TI, you'll find Connect@edinburgh (Mon–Sat 9:00–19:00, until 20:00 July–Aug, Sun 10:00–17:00, shorter hours off-season, as you enter TI head back to the left down a corridor). The Internet Café is southeast of the castle between Victoria Street and Grassmarket (daily 10:00-23:00, also has cheap phone cards, 98 Westbow, tel. 0131/226-5400).

Late-Night Pharmacy: Try Boots at 48 Shandwick Place (Mon–Fri until 21:00, tel. 0131/225-6757).

Car Rental: Consider Avis (5 West Park Place, tel. 0131/337-6363, airport tel. 0131/344-3900), Europcar (24 East London Street, tel. 0131/557-3456, airport tel. 0131/333-2588), Hertz (10 Picardy Place, tel. 0131/556-8311, airport tel. 0131/333-3494), or Budget (airport tel. 0131/333-1926).

Getting around Edinburgh

Nearly all of Edinburgh's sights are within walking distance of each other.

City **buses** are handy and inexpensive (about 80p/ride, buy tickets on bus, LRT transit office at Old Town end of Waverley Bridge has schedules and route maps, tel. 0131/555-6363). Tell the driver where you're going, have change handy (most buses require exact change; you

Edinburgh

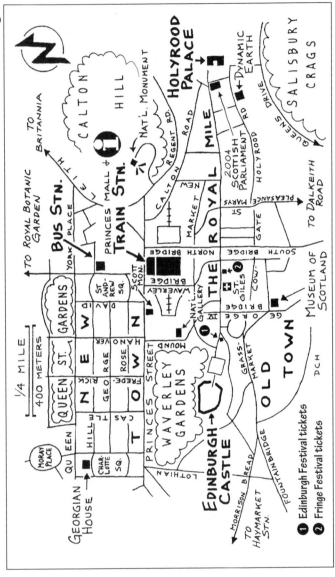

lose any excess), take your ticket as you board, push the stop button as you near your stop (so your stop isn't skipped), and exit from the middle door. Two companies handle the city routes: LRT (or Lothian) does most of it and First does the rest (e.g., to get from the city center to the recommended B&Bs on Dalkeith Road, you can catch LRT buses #14, #30, and #33 or First bus #86). Day passes sold by each company are valid only on their buses (£2.50, or £1.80 after 9:30 weekdays and all day weekends, buy from driver). Buses run from about 6:00 to 23:00.

Taxis are reasonable and easy to flag down (average ride between downtown and B&B district-£5).

BUS TOURS

Edinburgh

Three different 60-minute, hop-on, hop-off bus tours, all operated by Lothian Buses, circle the town center and stop at the biggies—Waverley Bridge, the castle, Royal Mile, Georgian New Town, and Princes Street—with an informative narration and pickups about every 10 to 15 minutes. You can hop on and off with one ticket all day. Hop on at any stop or go to Waverley Bridge to comparison-shop between your bus-tour options.

Two of the tours have live guides: Mac Tours' City Tour and Guide Friday's Edinburgh Tour. Their routes, cost, and frequency are virtually the same—the main difference is that Mac Tours runs vintage buses (£8.50, tickets give 10 percent discount off castle admission, valid 24 hours, buy on bus or on Waverley Bridge, tel. 0131/220-0770). The City Sightseeing Tours have a recorded narration and cost £1 less.

All three tours offer £13 combo-tickets that include their Britannia Tour, a hop-on, hop-off route that stops at the Royal Botanic Garden, docks, and the *Britannia* royal yacht (£8.50, *Britannia* admission extra, departs Waverley Bridge every 15-30 min, live guide, tel. 0131/220-0770). If your main interest is seeing the *Britannia,* you're better off taking a regular bus (see *Britannia,* page 313).

On sunny days they go topless (the buses), but they also suffer from traffic noise and congestion. Buses run year-round. First and last buses leave Waverley Bridge around 9:15 and continue until 19:00 mid-June through early September (last buses leave earlier off-season).

The Countryside

Many companies run day trips to regional sights. Study the brochures at the TI's rack.

Heart of Scotland Tours offers minibus day trips of the Highlands, including Loch Ness and Legends (£30, Wed, Sat & Sun, depart from 25 Waterloo Place near Waverley Station, reserve at least 1 day ahead by phone or online, 10 percent discount with this book, fewer tours off-season, tel. 0131/558-8855, www.heartofscotlandtours.co.uk).

Haggis Backpackers runs cheap day trips (£21, choose between distillery visit and northern Highlands or Loch Lomond and southern Highlands) and overnight trips for young backpackers (3 days-£80, 6 days-£140, hostels extra), but welcomes travelers of any age who want a quick look at the bonnie countryside (office hours: Mon–Sat 9:00–18:00, summer Sun 13:00-18:00, 60 High Street, at Blackfriars Street, tel. 0131/557-9393, www.radicaltravel.com).

SIGHTS

Edinburgh Castle

The fortified birthplace of the city 1,300 years ago, this imposing symbol of Edinburgh, rated ▲▲▲, sits proudly on a rock high above the city. While the castle has been both a fort and a royal residence since the 11th century, most of the buildings today are from its more recent use as a military garrison. This fascinating and multifaceted sight deserves several hours of your time (£8.50, April–Oct daily 9:30–18:00, Nov–March daily 9:30–17:00, last entrance 45 min before closing, cafeteria, tel. 0131/225-9846; consider avoiding the long uphill walk from the nearest city-bus stop by taking a cab to the castle gate).

Entry Gate: Start with the wonderfully droll 20-minute guided introduction tour (free with admission, departs 2-4 times/hr from entry, see clock for next departure; few tours run off-season). The audioguide is excellent, with four hours of quick digital dial descriptions (£3, pay at ticket office, pick up at entry gate before meeting the live guide). The clean WC at the entry annually wins "British Loo of the Year" awards (marvel at the plaques near men's room), but they use a one-way mirror showing the sink area in the women's room (women: pop your head into office near men's room to complain or make sure mirror is curtained).

In the castle there are five essential stops: Crown Jewels, Royal Palace, Scottish National War Memorial, St. Margaret's Chapel (with a city view), and the excellent National War Museum of Scotland. The first four are at the highest and most secure point—on or near the castle square, where your introductory guided tour ends. The War Museum is 50 yards below by the cafeteria and big shop.

1. Crown Jewels: The line of tourists leads from the square directly to the jewels. Skip this line and enter the building around to the left (next to WC), where you'll get to the jewels via a wonderful "Honors of Scotland" exhibition about the crown jewels and how they survived the harrowing centuries.

Scotland's **Crown Jewels** are older than England's. While Oliver Cromwell destroyed England's, the Scots hid theirs successfully. Longtime symbols of Scottish nationalism, they were made in Edinburgh—of Scottish gold, diamonds, and gems—in 1540 for a 1543 coronation. They were last used to crown Charles II in 1651. When the Act of Union, which dissolved Scotland's parliament into England's to create the United Kingdom in 1707, was forced upon the Scots, part of the deal was that they could keep their jewels locked up in Edinburgh. They remained hidden for more than 100 years. In 1818 Walter Scott and a royal commission rediscovered the jewels intact.

The **Stone of Scone** sits plain and strong next to the jewels. This big gray chunk of rock is the coronation stone of Scotland's ancient kings (ninth century). Swiped by the English, it sat under the coronation chair at Westminster Abbey from 1296 until 1996. With major fanfare, Scotland's treasured Stone of Scone returned to Edinburgh on Saint Andrew's Day, November 30, 1996. Talk to the guard for more details.

2. The Royal Palace (facing castle square under the flagpole) has two historic yet unimpressive rooms (through door reading 1566) and the Great Hall (separate entrance from the same castle square). Remember, Scottish royalty lived here only when safety or protocol required. They preferred the **Holyrood Palace** at the bottom of the Royal Mile. Enter the **Mary Queen of Scots room,** where in 1566 the queen gave birth to James VI of Scotland, who later became King James I of England. The **Presence Chamber** leads into **Laich Hall** (Lower Hall), the dining room of the royal family.

The **Great Hall** was the castle's ceremonial meeting place in the 16th and 17th centuries. In modern times it was a barracks and a hospital. While most of what you see is Victorian, two medieval elements survive: the fine hammer-beam roof and the big iron-barred peephole (above fireplace on right). This allowed the king to spy on his partying subjects.

3. The Scottish National War Memorial commemorates the 149,000 Scottish soldiers lost in World War I, the 58,000 lost in World War II, and the 750 lost in British battles since. Each bay is dedicated to a particular Scottish regiment. The main shrine, featuring a green Italian-marble memorial that contains the original WWI rolls of honor, actually sits upon an exposed chunk of the castle rock. Above you, the archangel Michael is busy slaying the dragon. The bronze frieze accurately shows the attire of various wings of Scotland's military. The stained glass starts with Cain and Abel on the left and finishes with a celebration of peace on the right. If the importance of this place is hard to understand, consider that one out of every three adult Scottish men died in World War I.

4. St. Margaret's Chapel, the oldest building in Edinburgh, is dedicated to Queen Margaret, who died here in 1093 and was sainted in 1250. Built in 1130 in the Romanesque style of the Norman invaders, it is wonderfully simple, with classic Norman zigzags decorating the round arch that separates the tiny nave from the sacristy. Used as a powder magazine for 400 years, very little survives. You'll see an 11th-century gospel book of St. Margaret's and small windows featuring St. Margaret,

St. Columba (who brought Christianity to Scotland via Iona), and William Wallace (the brave defender of Scotland). The place is popular for weddings and, since it seats only 20, it's particularly popular with brides' fathers.

Mons Meg—a huge and once-upon-a-time frightening 15th-century siege cannon that fired 330-pound stones nearly two miles—stands in front of the church.

Belly up to the banister (outside the chapel below the cannon) to enjoy the great view. Below you are the guns—which fire the one o'clock salute—and a sweet little line of doggie tombstones, the soldiers' pet cemetery. Beyond stretches the Georgian New Town (read the informative plaque).

5. The National War Museum of Scotland thoughtfully covers four centuries of Scottish military history. Instead of the usual musty, dusty displays of endless armor, this museum has an interesting mix of short films, uniforms, weapons, medals, mementos, and eloquent excerpts from soldiers' letters. A pleasant surprise just when you thought your castle visit was about over, this rivals any military museum you'll see in Europe.

When leaving the castle, turn around and look back at the gate. There stand King Robert the Bruce (on the left, 1274–1329) and Sir William Wallace (Braveheart—on the right, 1270–1305). Wallace (recently famous, thanks to Mel Gibson) fought long and hard against English domination before being executed in London—his body cut to pieces and paraded through the far corners of jolly olde England. Bruce beat the English at Bannockburn in 1314. Bruce and Wallace still defend the spirit of Scotland. The Latin inscription above the gate between them reads (basically) "What you do to us...we will do to you."

Along the Royal Mile

These are listed in walking order, from top to bottom. (Bus #35 runs along the Mile, handy for going up after you've hit bottom.)

▲▲▲Royal Mile—This is one of Europe's most interesting historic walks. Start at the top and amble down to the palace. The Royal Mile, which consists of a series of four different streets—Castlehill, Lawnmarket, High Street, and Canongate (each with its own set of street numbers)—is actually 200 yards longer than a mile. And every inch is packed with shops, cafés, and lanes leading to tiny squares. As you walk, remember that originally there were two settlements here, divided by a wall: Edinburgh lined the ridge from the castle at the top. The lower end, Canongate, was outside the wall until 1856. By poking down the many side alleys, you'll find a few rough edges of a town well on its way to becoming a touristic mall. See it now. In a few years tourists will be slaloming through the postcard racks on bagpipe skateboards.

Royal Mile Terminology: A "close" is a tiny alley between two buildings (originally with a door that closed it at night). A close usually leads to a "court" or courtyard. A "land" is a tenement block of apartments. A "pend" is an arched gateway. A "wynd" is a narrow winding lane. And "gate" is from an old Scandinavian word for street.

Royal Mile Walking Tours: Mercat Tours offers 90-minute guided walks of the Mile—more entertaining than historic (£6, daily at 10:30, from Mercat Cross on the Royal Mile, tel. 0131/557-6464). The guides, who enjoy making a short story long, ignore the big sights and take you behind the scenes with piles of barely historic gossip, bully-pulpit Scottish pride, and fun but forgettable trivia. They also offer a variety of other tours. In August only, the Voluntary Guides Association leads free tours of Edinburgh; call for a schedule (tel. 0131/664-7180 or 0131/556-8854).

Castle Esplanade—At the top of the Royal Mile, the big parking lot leading up to the castle was created as a military parade ground in 1816. It's often cluttered with bleachers under construction for the Military Tattoo—a spectacular massing of the bands that fills the square nightly for most of August (see "Edinburgh Festival," page 314). At the bottom, on the left (where the square hits the road), a plaque above the tiny witch's fountain memorializes 300 women who were accused of witchcraft and burned here. Scotland burned more witches per capita than any other country—17,000 between 1479 and 1722. But in a humanitarian gesture, rather than burning them alive as was the custom in the rest of Europe, Scottish "witches" were strangled to death before they were burned. The plaque shows two witches: one good and one bad. (For 90 minutes of this kind of Royal Mile trivia, take the guided tour described above.)

Camera Obscura—A big deal when built in 1853, this observatory topped with a mirror reflected images onto a disc before the wide eyes of people who had never seen a photograph or captured image. Today you can climb 100 steps for an entertaining 15-minute demonstration (3/hr). At the top enjoy the best view anywhere of the Royal Mile. Then work your way down through three floors of illusions, holograms, and early photos. This is a big hit with kids (£5.95, April–Oct daily 9:30–18:00, July–Aug until 19:30, Nov–March 10:00–17:00, tel. 0131/226-3709).

Scotch Whisky Heritage Centre—This touristy ambush is designed only to distill £7.50 out of your pocket. You get a video history, a short talk, and a little whiskey-keg train-car ride before downing a free sample and finding yourself in the shop 50 minutes later. Those in a hurry are offered the unadvertised quickie—a sample and a whiskey-keg ride for £3.50. People do seem to enjoy it, but that might have something to do with the sample (daily 9:30–17:30, tel. 0131/220-0441).

The Hub (Tolbooth Church)—This neo-Gothic church (1844), with the tallest spire in the city, is now the Hub, Edinburgh's Festival Ticket and Information Centre. From here, Johnston Terrace leads

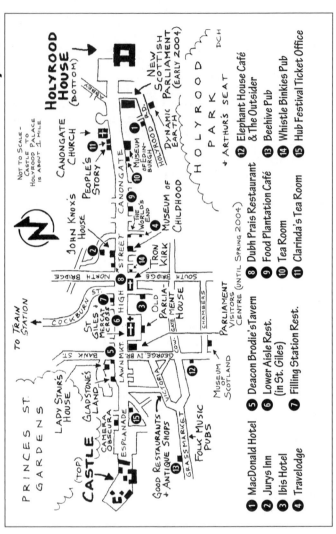

Royal Mile

1 MacDonald Hotel
2 Jurys Inn
3 Ibis Hotel
4 Travelodge
5 Deacon Brodie's Tavern
6 Lower Aisle Rest. (in St. Giles)
7 Filling Station Rest.
8 Dubh Prais Restaurant
9 Food Plantation Café
10 Tea Room
11 Clarinda's Tea Room
12 Elephant House Café & The Outsider
13 Beehive Pub
14 Whistle Binkies Pub
15 Hub Festival Ticket Office

down to Grassmarket street's lively pub scene (see "Nightlife," page 316).

▲▲**Gladstone's Land**—Take a good look at this typical 16th- to 17th-century merchant's house, complete with a lived-in furnished interior and guides in each room who love to talk (£3.50, mid-April–Oct Mon–Sat 10:00–17:00, Sun 14:00–17:00, last entry at 16:30, closed Nov–mid-April). For a good Royal Mile photo, lean out the upper-floor window (or simply climb the curved stairway outside the museum to the left of the entrance). Notice the snoozing pig outside the front door. Just like every house has a vacuum cleaner today, in the 14th century a snorting rubbish collector was a standard feature of any well-equipped house.

▲**Writers' Museum at Lady Stair's House**—This interesting house, built in 1622, is filled with well-described manuscripts and knickknacks of Scotland's three greatest literary figures: Robert Burns, Sir Walter Scott, and Robert Louis Stevenson. It's worth a few minutes for anyone and is fascinating for fans (free, Mon–Sat 10:00–17:00, closed Sun). Wander around the courtyard here. Edinburgh was a wonder in the 17th and 18th centuries. Tourists came here to see its skyscrapers, which towered 10 stories and higher. No city in Europe was so densely populated as "Auld Reekie."

Deacon Brodie's Pub—A decent place for a light meal (see "Eating," page 322). Read the story of its notorious namesake on the wall facing Bank Street. Then check out both sides of the hanging signpost.

Visitors Centre of the Scottish Parliament—Until the new Scottish Parliament building opens, possibly in early 2004 (near Holyrood Palace), this center will show models of the new building and explain how the Scottish Parliament works (free, Mon–Fri 10:00–17:00, Tue–Thu opens at 9:00, closed Sat–Sun, catercorner to Deacon Brodie's on George IV Bridge). You can sign up at the Visitors Centre to witness the Scottish Parliament's debates in their temporary quarters, a few steps north of the Royal Mile, tucked away in Mylnes Court, across from the Hub (debates usually Wed 14:30–17:30, Thu 9:30–12:30 & 14:30–17:30, tel. 0131/ 348-5411). When the new Parliament building opens, this Visitors Centre will close (for updates, see www.scottish.parliament.uk).

Heart of Midlothian—Near the street in front of the cathedral, find the outline of a heart in the brickwork. This marks the spot of a gallows and a prison now long gone. Traditionally, locals stand on the rim of the heart and spit into it. Hitting the middle brings good luck. Go ahead...do as the locals do.

▲▲**St. Giles Cathedral**—Wander through Scotland's most important church. Stepping inside, find John Knox's statue. Look into his eyes for 10 seconds from 10 inches away. Knox, the great reformer and founder of austere Scottish Presbyterianism, first preached here in 1559. His insistence that every person should be able to read the word of God gave Scotland an educational system 300 years ahead of the rest of Europe. For this reason it was Scottish minds that led the way in math, science, medicine, engineering, and so on. Voltaire called Scotland "the intellectual capital of Europe."

Knox preached Calvinism. Consider that the Dutch and the Scots were about the only nations to embrace this creed of hard work, thrift, and strict ethics. This helps explain why the English and the Scottish are so different (and why the Dutch and the Scots—both famous for their thriftiness and industriousness—are so much alike).

Speaking of intellects, look up at the modern window filling the West Wall celebrating Scotland's favorite poet, Robert Burns. It was made in 1985 by an Icelandic artist (Leifur Breidfjord).

The oldest parts of the cathedral—the four massive central pillars—date from 1120. After the English burnt the cathedral in 1385, it was rebuilt bigger and better than ever, and in 1495 its famous crown spire was completed. During the Reformation—when Knox preached here (1559-72)—the place was simplified and whitewashed. Before this, with the emphasis on holy services provided by priests, there were lots of little niches. With the new focus on sermons rather than rituals, the floor plan was opened up and the grand pulpit took center stage. The organ (1992, Austrian-built) is one of the best in Europe and comes with a glass panel in the back for peeking into the mechanism.

The neo-Gothic **Chapel of the Knights of the Thistle** (in the far right corner, from 1911), with its intricate wood carving, was built in two years entirely with Scottish material and labor. Find the angel tooting the bagpipes (from inside chapel, above the door to the right). The Scottish crown steeple from 1495 is a proud part of Edinburgh's skyline (Mon–Sat 9:00–17:00, May–Sept Mon–Fri until 19:00, Sat until 17:00, Sun 13:00–17:00 year-round; ask about concerts—some are free, usually Thu at 13:10, especially in the spring; café and WC downstairs; see "Eating," page 322, tel. 0131/225-9442).

John Knox is buried out back—austerely, under the parking lot, at spot 44. The statue among the cars shows King Charles II riding to a toga party back in 1685.

Parliament House—Stop in to see the grand hall with its fine 1639 hammer-beam ceiling and stained glass. This hall housed the Scottish Parliament until the Act of Union in 1707 (explained in history exhibition under the big stained-glass depiction of the initiation of the first Scottish High Court in 1532). It now holds the law courts and is busy with wigged and robed lawyers hard at work in the old library (peek through the door) or pacing the hall deep in discussion. The friendly doorman is helpful (free, public welcome Mon–Fri 9:00–17:00, best action midmornings Tue–Fri, open-to-the-public trials 10:00–16:00—doorman has day's docket, entry behind St. Giles Cathedral near parking spot 21).

Mercat Cross—This chunky pedestal, on the downhill side of St. Giles, holds a slender column topped with a white unicorn. Royal proclamations have been read here since the 14th century. The tradition survives. In 1952, three days (traditionally the time it took for a horse to speed here from London) after the actual event, a town crier heralded the news that England had a new queen. Today Mercat Cross is the meeting point of various walking tours—both historic and ghostly. Pop into the police information center, a few doors downhill, for a little local law-and-order history (free, May–Aug daily 10:00–21:30, less off-season).

Tron Kirk—This fine old building, used as a sales base for a local walking-tour company, sits over an old excavation site and houses a free Old Town history display.

Cockburn Street—Across from Tron Kirk, this street was cut through High Street's dense wall of medieval skyscrapers in the 1860s to give easy access to the Georgian New Town and the train station. Notice how the sliced buildings were thoughtfully capped with facades in a faux-16th-century Scottish baronial style. In medieval times, only tiny lanes (like the Fleshmarket Lane just uphill from Cockburn Street) interrupted the long line of Royal Mile buildings. Continue downhill to the old half-timbered building jutting out (John Knox House). Across the street is the...

▲**Museum of Childhood**—This five-story playground of historical toys and games is rich in nostalgia and history (free, Mon–Sat 10:00–17:00, closed Sun). Just downhill is a fragrant fudge shop offering delicious free samples.

▲**John Knox House**—Fascinating for Reformation buffs, this fine 16th-century house offers a well-explained look at the life of the great reformer (£2.25, Mon–Sat 10:00–17:00, closed Sun, 43 High Street, tel. 0131/556-9579). While some contend Knox never actually lived here, preservationists called it "his house" to save it from the wrecking ball in 1850. All or parts of the museum will be closed for construction periodically during 2004.

The World's End—For centuries, a wall halfway down the Royal Mile marked the end of Edinburgh and the beginning of Canongate, a community associated with the Holyrood Abbey. Today, where the mile hits St. Mary's and Jeffrey streets, High Street becomes Canongate. Just below John Knox House (at #43) notice the hanging sign showing the old gate. At the intersection, find the brass bricks that trace the gate (demolished in 1764). Look down St. Mary's Street to see a surviving bit of that old wall. Then, entering Canongate, you leave what was Edinburgh...

▲**People's Story**—This interesting exhibition traces the lot of the working class through the 18th, 19th, and 20th centuries (free, Mon–Sat 10:00–17:00, closed Sun, tel. 0131/529-4057). Curiously, while this museum is dedicated to the proletariat, immediately around the back is the tomb of Adam Smith—the author of *Wealth of Nations* and the father of modern capitalism (1723-1790).

▲**Museum of Edinburgh**—Another old house full of old stuff, this one is worth a look for its early Edinburgh history and handy ground-floor WC. Don't miss the original copy of the National Covenant (written in 1638 on an animal skin), sketches of pre-Georgian Edinburgh (which show a lake, later filled in to become Princes Street Gardens when New Town was built), and early golf balls (free, Mon–Sat 10:00–17:00, closed Sun).

White Horse Close—Step into this 17th-century courtyard (bottom of Canongate, on the left, a block before Holyrood Palace). It was from here that the Edinburgh stagecoach left for London. Eight days later, the horse-drawn carriage pulled into its destination: Scotland Yard. Across the street is the new Parliament building.

▲**Scottish Parliament Building**—Scotland's parliament originated in 1293, was dissolved by England in 1707, and returned in 1999. Their extravagant, and therefore controversial, new digs at the base of the Royal Mile next to Holyrood Palace are slated to open in 2004. For a conversation starter, ask a local what he or she thinks about the building's architect, expense, design, and so on.

You can sign up to witness the Scottish Parliament's debates as it creates Scottish history in its temporary quarters off the Royal Mile in Mylnes Court across from the Hub (free, see "Visitors Centre," page 307), and eventually, in its new building after it opens.

▲**Holyrood Palace**—A palace since the 14th century, this marks the end of the Royal Mile. The queen spends a week in Scotland each summer, during which this is her official residence and office. The abbey—part of a 12th-century Augustinian monastery—stood here first. It was named for a piece of the cross brought here as a relic by queen-then-saint Margaret. Scotland's royalty preferred living here to the blustery castle on the rock, and gradually the palace grew.

The building, rich in history and decor, is filled with elegantly furnished rooms and a few dark older rooms with glass cases of historic bits and Scottish pieces that Scots find fascinating. Bring the palace to life with the included one-hour audioguide. You'll learn which of the kings featured in the 110 portraits lining the Great Gallery are real and which are fictional, what touches were added to the bed chambers to flatter King Charles II, and why the exiled Comte d'Artois took refuge in the palace. You'll also hear a goofy reenactment of the moment when conspirators, dispatched by Mary Queen of Scots' jealous second husband, stormed into the queen's chambers and stabbed her male secretary. You can select the audio you want to hear by punching in the room number (if the rooms aren't yet numbered, ask the docent stationed in the room for the secret code).

The new **Queen's Gallery** features rotating exhibits of drawings from the royal collection (see Cost and Hours, below).

After exiting, you're free to stroll through the ruined abbey and the queen's gardens. Hikers: Note that the palace is near the trail up Arthur's Seat.

Cost and Hours: £7.50 for palace, £4 for Queen's Gallery, £10 joint admission for both, daily 9:30–18:00, Nov–April until 16:30, last admission 45 min before closing (palace guidebook-£4.50, tel. 0131/556-7371). The palace is closed when the queen is at home and whenever a prince drops in.

Dynamic Earth—This immense exhibit tells the story of our planet and fills several underground floors under a vast Gore-Tex tent appropriately pitched at the base of the Salisbury Crags. It's designed for younger kids and does the same thing an American science exhibit would do—but with a charming Scottish accent. Standing in a time tunnel, you watch time rewind from Churchill to dinosaurs to that first big bang. After several short films on stars, tectonic plates, and ice caps, you're free to wander past salty pools, a re-created rain forest, and various TV screens. End your visit with a 12-minute video finale (£8.45, family deals, April–Oct daily 10:00–18:00, Nov–March Wed–Sun 10:00–17:00, last ticket sold 70 min before closing, on Holyrood Road, between the palace and mountain, tel. 0131/550-7800).

▲▲▲**Museum of Scotland**—This huge museum has amassed more historic artifacts than everything I've seen in Scotland combined. It's all wonderfully displayed with fine descriptions offering a best-anywhere hike through the history of Scotland: prehistoric, Roman, Viking, the "birth of Scotland," all the way to life in the 20th century. Free audioguides offer a pleasant (if slow) description of various rooms and exhibits and even provide mood music for your wanderings (free, Mon–Sat 10:00–17:00, Tue until 20:00, Sun 12:00–17:00, 60-min introduction and highlights tours offered throughout the day, 2 long blocks south of Royal Mile from St. Giles Church, Chambers Street, off George IV Bridge, tel. 0131/247-4422, www.nms.ac.uk).

The **Royal Museum,** next door, fills a fine iron-and-glass Industrial Age building (built to house the museum in 1851) with all the natural sciences as it "presents the world to Scotland." It's great for schoolkids, but of no special interest to foreign visitors (free, same hours as Museum of Scotland). The famous statue of Greyfriars Bobby (Edinburgh's favorite dog—a terrier immortalized by Disney—who stood by his master's grave for 14 years) is across the street. Every business nearby is named for the pooch that put the fidelity into Fido.

More Bonnie Wee Sights
▲**Georgian New Town**—Cross Waverley Bridge and walk through Georgian Edinburgh. According to the 1776 plan, it was three streets (Princes, George, and Queen) flanked by two squares (St. Andrew and Charlotte), woven together by alleys (Thistle and Rose). George Street—20 feet wider than the others (so a four-horse carriage could make a U-turn)—was the main drag. And, while Princes Street has gone down-market, George Street still maintains its old grace. The entire elegantly planned New Town—laid out when George was king—celebrated the hard-to-sell notion that Scotland was an integral part of the United Kingdom. The streets and squares are named after the British royalty (Hanover was the royal family surname). Even Thistle and Rose streets are emblems of the two happily paired nations. Rose Street,

SCOTTISH WORDS

aye	yes	**inch, innis**	island
ben	mountain	**inver**	river, mouth
bonnie	beautiful	**kyle**	strait
cairn	pile of stones	**loch**	lake
cellotape	Scotch tape	**neeps**	turnips
creag	rock, cliff	**tattie**	potato
haggis	rich assortment of oats and sheep organs stuffed into a chunk of sheep intestine, liberally seasoned, boiled, and eaten mostly by tourists. Usually served with "neeps and tatties." Tastier than it sounds.		

mostly pedestrian-only, is famous for its rowdy pubs. Where it hits St. Andrew Square, Rose Street is flanked by the venerable Jenners department store and a Sainsbury supermarket. Sprinkled with popular restaurants and bars, stately New Town is turning trendy.

▲▲**Georgian House**—This refurbished Georgian house, set on Edinburgh's finest Georgian square, is a trip back to 1796. A volunteer guide in each of the five rooms shares stories and trivia. Start your visit with two interesting videos (£5, April–Oct daily 10:00–17:00, March & Nov–Dec 11:00–15:00, closed Jan–Feb, videos total 30 min and cover architecture and Georgian lifestyles, shown in the basement, 7 Charlotte Square, tel. 0131/226-3318). A walk down George Street after your visit here can be fun for the imagination.

▲▲**National Gallery of Scotland**—This elegant neoclassical building has a delightfully small but impressive collection of European masterpieces, from Raphael, Titian, and Peter Paul Rubens to Thomas Gainsborough, Claude Monet, and Vincent van Gogh. And it offers the best look you'll get at Scottish paintings. The gallery's free, but investing £2 in the fine audioguide makes the museum's highlights yours as well (daily 10:00–17:00, Thu until 19:00, tel. 0131/624-6200). After your visit, if the sun's out, enjoy a wander through Princes Street Gardens.

Royal Scottish Academy—Next to the National Gallery, this new museum opened in August 2004 with a major Monet exhibit (generally daily 10:00–17:00, Thu until 19:00, but hours and cost vary per exhibit, tel. 0131/624-6200, www.nationalgalleries.org).

Princes Street Gardens—This grassy park, a former lake bed, separates Edinburgh's New and Old Towns and offers a wonderful escape from the city. Once the private domain of the local wealthy, it was opened to the public in about 1870, not as a democratic gesture, but because it was thought that allowing the public into the park would increase sales for the Princes Street department stores. There are plenty of free concerts and country dances in the summer and the oldest floral clock in the world. Join the local office workers for a picnic lunch break.

▲**Sir Walter Scott Monument**—Built in 1840, this elaborate, neo-Gothic monument honors the great author, one of Edinburgh's many illustrious sons. Scott, who died in 1832, is considered the father of the romantic historical novel. The 200-foot monument shelters a marble statue of Scott and his dog Maida, surrounded by busts of 16 great Scottish poets and 64 characters from his books. Scott was a great dog lover. Of the 30 dogs he had in his lifetime, his favorite was the deer-hound Maida. Climb 287 steps for a fine view of the city (£2.50, March–Oct Mon–Sat 9:00–18:00, Sun 10:00–18:00, Nov–Feb daily 10:00–15:00, tel. 0131/529-4068).

Royal Botanic Garden—Britain's second-oldest botanical garden, established in 1670 for medicinal herbs, is now one of Europe's best (free, March and Sept–Oct 9:30–18:00, April–Aug 9:30–19:00, Nov–Feb 9:30–16:00, 90-min "rain forest to desert" tours April–Sept daily at 11:00 and 14:00 for £2.50, 1 mile north of center at Inverleith Row, tel. 0131/552-7171).

Near Edinburgh

▲**Britannia**—This much-revered vessel, which carted around Britain's royal family for more than 40 years and 900 voyages before being retired in 1997, is permanently moored at Edinburgh's Port of Leith. It's open to the public and worth the 15-minute bus or taxi ride from the center. After watching a video about the ship, wander through the museum filled with fascinating royal-family-afloat history. Then, armed with your included audioguide, hike the stairs to the ship's top deck and begin working your way down. You'll tour the bridge, dining room, and living quarters, and follow in the historic footsteps of such notables as Churchill, Gandhi, and Reagan. It's easy to see how the royals must have loved the privacy this floating retreat offered (£8, April–Sept daily 9:30–18:00, Oct–March daily 10:00–17:00, last ticket sold 1.5 hrs before closing; to get to ship from Edinburgh, catch Lothian bus #22, #34, or #35 at Waverley Bridge—£2.50 round-trip, cheap café on site, tel. 0131/555-5566, www.royalyachtbritannia.co.uk).

Edinburgh Crystal—Blowing, molding, cutting, polishing, and engraving, the Edinburgh Crystal Company glassworks tour smashes anything you'll see in Venice (£3.50, daily 10:00–16:30). There is a shop full of "bargain" second-quality pieces, a video show, and a cafeteria. Take Lothian Bus #37 or #37A from South Bridge, or drive 10 miles south of town on A701 to Penicuik. You can schedule a more expensive VIP tour (£10) where you actually blow and cut glass (tel. 01968/675-128).

ACTIVITIES

▲▲**Arthur's Seat Hike**—A 45-minute hike up the 822-foot volcanic mountain (surrounded by a fine park overlooking Edinburgh) starts from the Holyrood Palace and rewards you with a commanding view. You can drive up most of the way from behind (follow the one-way street from the palace, park by the little lake) or run up like they did in *Chariots of Fire.* Hikers: From the parking lot (immediately south of Holyrood Palace), you'll see two trails going up. For an easier grade, take the wide path to the left and skip the steeper path that begins with steps and skirts the base of the cliffs. You can also hike up to the seat from the Dalkeith B&B neighborhood. Take the road (Holyrood Park Road) that borders the Commonwealth pool, turn right (on Queen's Drive), and continue to a small car park. From here, it's a 20-minute hike.

Brush Skiing—If you'd rather be skiing, the Midlothian Ski Centre in Hillend has a hill on the edge of town with a chairlift, two slopes, a jump slope, and rentable skis, boots, and poles. While you're actually skiing over what seems like a million toothbrushes, it feels like snow skiing on a slushy day. Beware: Local doctors are used to treating an ailment called "Hillend Thumb"—thumbs dislocated when people fall here and get tangled in the brush (£7.50/first hr, then £3/hr, includes gear, Mon–Fri 9:30–21:00, Sat-Sun 9:30–19:00, closed last 2 weeks of June, probably closed if it snows, LRT bus #4 from Princes Street—garden side, tel. 0131/445-4433).

▲**Royal Commonwealth Games Swimming Pool**—This immense pool is open to the public, with a well-equipped fitness center (£6, includes swim), sauna (£6.70 extra), and a coffee shop overlooking the pool (Pool admission only-£3.50, Mon–Fri 6:00–21:30, Sat 6:00–7:45 & 10:00–16:30, Sun 10:00–16:30, closed 9:00–10:00 every Wed, no towels or suit rentals, tel. 0131/667-7211).

More Hikes—You can hike along the river (called Water of Leith) through Edinburgh. Locals favor the stretch between Roseburn and Dean Village, but the 1.5-mile walk from Dean Village to the Royal Botanic Garden is also good. This and other hikes are described in the TI's *Walks in and around Edinburgh* (ask for the free one-page flier, not their £2 guide to walks).

Shopping—The streets to browse are Princes Street (the elegant old Jenners department store is nearby on Rose Street, at St. Andrew's Square), Victoria Street (antiques galore), Nicolson Street (south of the Royal Mile for a line of interesting second-hand stores), and the Royal Mile (touristy but competitively priced). Shops are usually open from 9:00 to 17:30 (later on Thu, some closed Sun).

Edinburgh Festival

One of Europe's great cultural events, Edinburgh's annual festival turns the city into a carnival of culture. There are enough music, dance, art, drama, and multicultural events to make even the most jaded traveler drool with excitement. Every day is jammed with formal and spontaneous fun. A number of festivals—official, fringe, book, film, and jazz and blues—rage simultaneously for about three weeks each August, with the Military Tattoo starting a week earlier (the best overall Web site is www.edinburghfestivals.co.uk). Many city sights run on extended hours, and those that normally close on Sunday (Writers' Museum, Museum of Edinburgh, People's Story, and Museum of Childhood) open in the afternoon. It's a glorious time to be in Edinburgh.

The official festival (Aug 15–Sept 4 in 2004) is the original, more formal, and most likely to get booked up first. Major events sell out well in advance. The ticket office is at the Hub, located in a former church (with café, ATM, and WC) near the top of the Royal Mile (tickets-£4–55, booking from mid-April on, office open Mon–Sat 10:00–17:00 or longer, in Aug until 20:00 plus Sun 10:00–17:00, tel. 0131/473-2000, fax 0131/473-2003). You can also book online at www.eif.co.uk.

The less-formal **Fringe Festival** features "on the edge" comedy and theater (Aug 8–30 in 2004, ticket/info office just below St. Giles Cathedral on the Royal Mile, 180 High Street, tel. 0131/226-0026, bookings tel. 0131/226-0000, can book online from mid-June on, www.edfringe.com). Tickets are usually available at the door, but popular shows can sell out.

Other summer festivals: jazz and blues (tel. 0131/467-5200, www.jazzmusic.co.uk), film (tel. 0131/229-2550, www.edfilmfest.org.uk), and books (tel. 0131/228-5444, www.edbookfest.co.uk).

The **Military Tattoo** is a massing of the bands, drums, and bagpipes with groups from all over what was the British Empire. Displaying military finesse with a stirring lone-piper finale, this grand spectacle fills the castle esplanade nightly except Sunday, normally from a week before the festival starts until a week before it finishes (Aug 6–28 in 2004). Shows occur Monday through Friday at 21:00 and on Saturdays at 19:30 and 22:30 (£9–30, CC, booking starts in Dec, Fri–Sat shows sell out first; office open Mon–Fri 10:00–16:30, during Tattoo open until show time and Sat 10:00–22:30 and Sun 12:00–17:00; 33 Market Street, behind—and south of—Waverley train station, tel. 0131/225-1188, www.edinburgh-tattoo.co.uk). If nothing else, it is a really big show.

If you do manage to hit Edinburgh during the festival, book a room far in advance and extend your stay by a day or two. While Fringe tickets and most Tattoo tickets are available the day of the show, you may want to book a couple of official events in advance. Do it directly by telephone, leaving your credit-card number. Pick up your ticket at the office the day of the show. Several publications—including the festival's official schedule, the *Edinburgh Festivals Guide Daily, The List,* the *Fringe Program,* and the *Daily Diary*—list and evaluate festival events.

NIGHTLIFE

▲**Ghost Walks**—These walks are an entertaining and cheap night out (offered nightly, usually around 19:00 and 21:00, easy socializing for solo travelers). The theatrical and creatively staged **Witchery Tours,** the most established of the ghost tours, offer two different walks: "Ghosts and Gore" and "Murder and Mystery" (£7, 90 min, reservations required, leave from the top of the Royal Mile near castle esplanade, tel. 0131/225-6745, www.witcherytours.com).

▲▲**Literary Pub Tour**—This two-hour walk is interesting even if you think Sir Walter Scott was an arctic explorer. You'll follow the witty dialogue of two actors as they debate whether the great literature of Scotland was the creative recreation of fun-loving louts fueled by a love of whiskey or high art. You'll wander from the Grassmarket, over Old Town to New Town, with stops in three pubs as your guides share their takes on Scotland's literary greats. The tour meets at the Beehive Pub on Grassmarket (£8, book online and save £1, nightly in summer at 19:30, April–May & Oct Thu–Sun, Nov–March Fri; call 0131/226-6665 to confirm, www.scot-lit-tour.co.uk).

▲**Scottish Folk Evenings**—These £35 to £40 dinner shows, generally for tour groups intent on photographing old cultural clichés, are held in huge halls of expensive hotels. (Prices are bloated to include 20 percent commissions.) Your "traditional" meal is followed by a full slate of swirling kilts, blaring bagpipes, and Scottish folk dancing with an "old-time music hall" emcee. If you like Lawrence Welk, you're in for a treat. You can sometimes see the show without dinner for about two-thirds the price. The TI has fliers on all the latest venues.

Prestonfield House offers its Scottish folk evening with or without dinner Sunday to Friday (£21 for show only from 20:00–22:00, £33 includes four-course meal at 19:00, Priestfield Road, a 7-min walk from Dalkeith Road B&Bs, tel. 0131/668-3346, www.prestonfieldhouse.com).

▲▲**Folk Music in Pubs**—Edinburgh used to be a good place for folk music, but in the last few years, pub owners—out of economic necessity—are catering to twenty-somethings more interested in beer drinking than traditional music. Pubs that were regular venues for folk music have gone pop. Especially on weekends, you're unlikely to find much live folk music. The monthly *Gig Guide* (free at TI and various pubs, www.gigguide.co.uk) lists most of the live-music action. **Whistle Binkies** still offers nightly ad-lib traditional music, which can start as early as 19:30 or as late as 24:00 and goes until the wee hours (just off the Royal Mile on South Bridge, another entrance on Niddry Street, tel. 0131/557-5114, for a line-up see www.whistlebinkies.com).

Grassmarket (below the castle) is sloppy with live music and rowdy people spilling out of the pubs and into what was once upon a time a busy market square. It's fun to just wander through Grassmarket late at

Edinburgh, Our Neighborhood

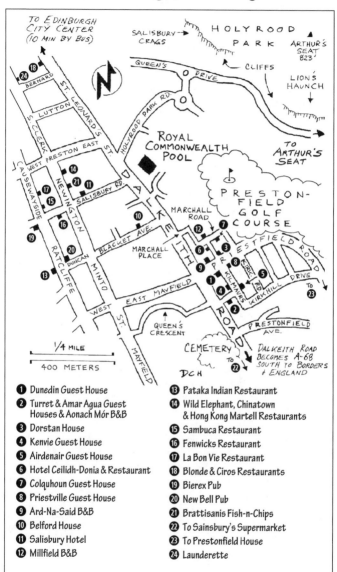

TO EDINBURGH CITY CENTER (10 MIN BY BUS)

SALISBURY CRAGS

HOLYROOD PARK

ARTHUR'S SEAT 823'

CLIFFS

LION'S HAUNCH

QUEEN'S DRIVE

BERNARD ST.

LUTTON

S. CLERK

ST. LEONARD'S ST.

HOLYROOD PARK RD.

WEST PRESTON EAST ST.

ROYAL COMMONWEALTH POOL

TO ARTHUR'S SEAT

PRESTON-FIELD GOLF COURSE

MARCHALL ROAD

CAUSEWAYSIDE

NEWINGTON

SALISBURY RD.

BLACKET AVE.

MARCHALL PLACE

WESTFIELD ROAD

RATCLIFFE

MINTO

DUNCAN

EAST MAYFIELD

KILMAURS

KIRKHILL

KIRK

DRIVE

WEST ST.

MAYFIELD

QUEEN'S CRESCENT

CEMETERY

PRESTONFIELD AVE.

DCH

DALKEITH ROAD BECOMES A-68 SOUTH TO BORDERS & ENGLAND

¼ MILE

400 METERS

1. Dunedin Guest House
2. Turret & Amar Agua Guest Houses & Aonach Mór B&B
3. Dorstan House
4. Kenvie Guest House
5. Airdenair Guest House
6. Hotel Ceilidh-Donia & Restaurant
7. Colquhoun Guest House
8. Priestville Guest House
9. Ard-Na-Said B&B
10. Belford House
11. Salisbury Hotel
12. Millfield B&B
13. Pataka Indian Restaurant
14. Wild Elephant, Chinatown & Hong Kong Martell Restaurants
15. Sambuca Restaurant
16. Fenwicks Restaurant
17. La Bon Vie Restaurant
18. Blonde & Ciros Restaurants
19. Bierex Pub
20. New Bell Pub
21. Brattisanis Fish-n-Chips
22. To Sainsbury's Supermarket
23. To Prestonfield House
24. Launderette

night. **Finnegan's Wake** has live music—often Irish rock—nightly (starts at 22:00, Sat not very Irish, Sun very Irish, a block off Grassmarket at 9 Victoria Street, tel. 0131/226-3816). Also consider **Biddy Mulligan** (Thu, Fri, Sun, tel. 0131/220-1246) and **White Hart Inn** (Sun, Mon, Thu, tel. 0131/226-2806), among others. By the music and crowds you'll know where to go and where not to. Have a beer and follow your ear.

Theater—Even outside of festival time, Edinburgh is a fine place for lively and affordable theater. Pick up *The List* for a complete rundown of what's on (£2.20 at newsstands).

SLEEPING

Off Dalkeith Road

These recommendations are south of town near the Royal Common-wealth Pool, just off Dalkeith Road. This comfortable and safe neighborhood is a 20-minute walk or 10-minute bus ride from the Royal Mile. All listings are non-smoking, on quiet streets, a two-minute walk from a bus stop, and well-served by city buses. B&Bs are unlikely to accept bookings for one-night stays in August. Some B&Bs offer Internet access, usually for a fee.

Near the B&Bs you'll find plenty of eateries (see "Eating," page 322) and easy free parking.

The Sun Dial **launderette** is along the bus route to the city center at 13 South Clerk Street (open daily, evening hours unpredictable, call to check, last wash 75 min before closing, opposite Queens Hall, tel. 0131/667-0549).

To reach the hotel neighborhood from the train station, TI, or Scott Monument, cross Princes Street and wait at the **bus stop** under the small C&A sign on the department store (80p; LRT buses #14, #30, and #33, or First bus #86; tell driver your destination is "Dalkeith Road;" red bus: exact change or pay more; green bus: makes change; ride 10 min to first or second stop—depending on B&B—after the pool, push the button, exit middle door). These buses also stop at the corner of North Bridge and High Street on the Royal Mile. Buses run from 6:00 to 23:00, and after 9:00 on Sunday morning. **Taxi** fare between the station or Royal Mile and the B&Bs is about £5.

B&Bs off Dalkeith Road

$$ **Dunedin Guest House** (dun-EE-din)—bright, plush, and elegantly Scottish, with seven huge rooms—is a fine value (S-£25–40, Db-£50–80, family rooms for up to 5, power showers, 8 Priestfield Road, tel. 0131/668-1949, fax 0131/668-3636, reservations@dunedinguesthouse .co.uk, Marsella Bowen).

SLEEP CODE

(£1 = about $1.60, country code: 44, area code: 0131)
Sleep Code: **S** = Single, **D** = Double/Twin, **T** = Triple, **Q** = Quad, **b** = bathroom, **s** = shower only, **no CC** = Credit Cards not accepted. You can assume credit cards are accepted unless otherwise noted.

To help you sort easily through these listings, I've divided the rooms into three categories based on the price for a standard double room with bath (during high season):

$$$ Higher Priced—Most rooms £80 or more.
$$ Moderately Priced—Most rooms between £50–80.
$ Lower Priced—Most rooms £50 or less.

The advent of big, cheap hotels has made life tough for B&Bs. Still, book ahead, especially in August when the annual festival fills Edinburgh. Conventions, school holidays, and weekends can make finding a room tough at almost any time of year. For the best prices, book directly rather than through the TI, which charges a higher room fee and levies a £3 booking fee. "Standard" rooms, with toilets and showers a tissue-toss away, save you £10 a night.

Room prices in this section are usually listed as a range, from low season (winter) to high season (July–Sept). I have not listed the higher "festival prices," which are limited to August. Prices get soft off-season, for longer visits, and sometimes for midweek stays outside of summer.

$$ Turret Guest House is teddy-on-the-beddy cozy, with a great bay-windowed family room and a vast breakfast menu that includes haggis and vegetarian options (8 rooms, S-£23–37, D-£46–56, Db-£56–74, £2/person discount with this book and cash, Internet access, 8 Kilmaurs Terrace, tel. 0131/667-6704, fax 0131/668-1368, www.turretguesthouse .co.uk, contact@turretguesthouse.co.uk, Jimmy & Fiona Mackie).

$$ Amar Agua Guest House, next door to Turret, is an inviting Victorian home away from home (7 rooms, S-£25–35, Db-£44–70, 3 percent more with CC, Internet access, 10 Kilmaurs Terrace, tel. 0131/ 667-6775, fax 0131/667-7687, www.amaragua.co.uk, rickstevesguest @amaragua.co.uk, run by energetic young couple Dawn-Ann and Tony Costa).

$$ Dorstan House is more hotelesque, with all the comforts, but still friendly and relaxed. Several of its 14 thoughtfully decorated rooms are on the ground floor (S-£20–30, Sb-£30–50, Ds-£40–60, Db-£50–70, family rooms, self-catering flat, laundry service available, 7 Priestfield Road, tel. 0131/667-6721, fax 0131/668-4644, www.dorstan-hotel.demon.co.uk, reservations@dorstan-hotel.demon.co.uk, Richard and Maki Stott).

$$ Kenvie Guest House, well run by Dorothy Vidler, comes with six pleasant rooms and lots of personal touches (1 small twin-£44, D-£46, Db-£54, family deals, 3 percent more with CC, 16 Kilmaurs Road, tel. 0131/668-1964, fax 0131/668-1926, www.kenvie.co.uk, dorothy @kenvie.co.uk).

$$ Airdenair Guest House, offering views, homemade scones, and other delicious sweets (made by the owner's mom and dad), has five attractive rooms with a lofty above-it-all feeling (Sb-£25–35, Db-£50–60, Tb-£75–90, 2 percent more with CC, 29 Kilmaurs Road, tel. 0131/668-2336, www.airdenair.com, jill@airdenair.com, Jill & Doug McLennan).

$$ Hotel Ceilidh-Donia is recently refurbished with 14 cheery, tricked-out rooms—computer hook-ups, strong showers, dimmer switches—a pleasant back deck, and a fine restaurant (Sb-£25–50, Db-£45–80, prices with this book through 2004, free Internet access for guests and diners, laundry service available, 14 Marchhall Crescent, tel. 0131/667-2743, www.hotelceilidh-donia.co.uk, reservations@hotelceilidh -donia.co.uk, Max & Annette).

$$ Colquhoun Guest House, in an elegant building, has seven fine rooms, several on the ground floor (S-£25–28, D-£44, Db-£56, family room, no CC, 5 Marchhall Road, tel. & fax 0131/667-8481, grace @colquhounhouse.freeserve.co.uk, run by amazing Grace McAinsh).

$$ Priestville Guest House has all the comforts of home, from VCRs and a video library to Internet access in the lobby (D-£40–54, Db-£44–60, 3 percent more with CC, family rooms available, 10 Priestfield Road, tel. & fax 0131/667-2435, www.priestville.com, bookings@priestville.com, Trina and Colin Warwick).

$$ Ard-Na-Said B&B is an elegant 1875 Victorian house with a comfy lounge and five classy rooms (S-£23–40, Db-£46–80, four-poster Db-£56–90, family room, 3 percent more with CC, 5 Priestfield Road, tel. 0131/667-8754, www.ardnasaid.freeserve.co.uk, Jim and Olive Lyons).

$$ Aonach Mór has seven simple, pleasant rooms (S-£18–30, D-£40–50, Db-£40–60, family rooms, Internet access, complimentary welcome drink with this book, 14 Kilmaurs Terrace, tel. 0131/667-8694, www.aonachmor.com, info@aonachmor.com, keen Ross and Kathleen Birnie).

$$ Belford House is a tidy, homey place offering seven good rooms and a warm welcome (D-£40–44, Db-£50–54, family deals, 5 percent off with cash, 13 Blacket Avenue, tel. 0131/667-2422, fax

0131/667-7508, www.belfordguesthouse.com, tom@belfordguesthouse
.com, Tom Borthwick).

$$ The Salisbury, more like a hotel than its neighbors, fills a classy
old Georgian building with eight rooms, a large lounge, and a dumb-
waiter in the breakfast room (Sb-£30–35, D-£50–58, Db-£50–60, 5
percent off with cash and this book, free parking, 45 Salisbury Road, tel.
& fax 0131/667-1264, www.salisburyguesthouse.co.uk, brenda-wright
@btconnect.com, Brenda Wright).

$ Millfield B&B, run graciously by Liz Broomfield, is thought-
fully furnished with antique class, a rare sit-and-chat ambience, and a
comfy TV lounge. Since the showers are down the hall, you'll get spa-
cious rooms and great prices (S-£22–25, D-£40–44, T-£50–60, no CC,
reconfirm reservation by phone, 12 Marchhall Road, tel. & fax 0131/
667-4428). Decipher the breakfast prayer by Robert Burns. Then try
the "Taste of Scotland" breakfast option. See how many stone (14
pounds) you weigh in the elegant throne room.

Big, Modern Hotels

The last three of these listings are cheap as hotels go and offer more
comfort than character. The first one's a splurge. In each case I'd skip
the institutional breakfast and eat out.

$$$ MacDonald Hotel, my only fancy listing, is an opulent four-
star splurge down the street from the new Parliament building. With its
classy marble-and-wood decor, fitness center, and pool, it's hard to leave.
On a gray winter day in Edinburgh, this could be worth it. Prices can
vary wildly (157 rooms, Db-£110, includes breakfast, near bottom of
Royal Mile, across from Dynamic Earth, Holyrood Road, tel. 0131/550-
4500, fax 0131/550-4545, www.macdonaldhotels.co.uk).

$$$ Jurys Inn, a cookie-cutter place with 186 dependably com-
fortable rooms, is capably run and well-located a short walk from the
station (Sb, Db, Tb all £95 Fri–Sat, £75 Sun–Thu, much cheaper in off-
season, breakfast-£9, 2 kids sleep free, non-smoking rooms, some views,
pub/restaurant, on quiet street just off Royal Mile, 43 Jeffrey Street, tel.
0131/200-3300, fax 0131/200-0400, www.jurys.com).

$$ Ibis Hotel, mid-Royal Mile behind Tron Kirk, is well-run and
perfectly located. It has 98 soulless but clean and comfy rooms
drenched in prefab American charm (Db-£50–70, top price July–Aug,
discounted in off-season, lousy continental breakfast-£5, non-smoking
rooms, elevator, 6 Hunter Square, tel. 0131/240-7000, fax 0131/240-
7007, h2039@accor-hotels.com).

$ Travelodge, the cheapest hotel in the center, has 193 no-
nonsense, central rooms all decorated in dark blue. All rooms are the
same and suitable for two adults with two kids or three adults. While
sleepable, it has a cheap feel with a quickly revolving staff (Sb, Db, Tb
all £50 except £70 Fri–Sun June–Sept, breakfast-£7, 33 St. Mary's

Street, a block off the Royal Mile, tel. 08700-850-950, www
.travelodge.co.uk).

Away from the Center

$$ The characterless **Travel Inn,** the biggest hotel in Edinburgh, has a
mediocre location a mile west of the Royal Mile, but has a great price.
Each of its 280 rooms is modern and comfortable, with a sofa that folds
out for two kids if necessary (Db-£53–57 for 2 adults and up to 2 kids
under 15, breakfast-£4.50–6.50, elevators, non-smoking rooms, week-
ends booked long in advance, near Haymarket station west of the castle
at 1 Morrison Link, tel. 0131/228-9819, fax 0131/228-9836, www
.travelinn.co.uk).

Hostels

Edinburgh's hostels are well-run and open to all, but are scruffy and
don't include breakfast. They do offer Internet access, laundry facilities,
and £11–13 bunk beds in 8- to 16-bed single-sex dorms (about a £9–12
savings over B&Bs).

$ **Castle Rock Hostel** is hip and easygoing, offering cheap beds,
plenty of friends, and a great central location just below the castle and
above the pubs with all the folk music (15 Johnston Terrace, tel.
0131/225-9666).

Their sister hostels are nearly across the street from each other:

$ **High Street Hostel** (laundry-£2.50, kitchen, 8 Blackfriars Street,
just off High Street/Royal Mile, tel. 0131/557-3984) and **Royal Mile
Backpackers** (105 High Street, tel. 0131/557-6120).

For more regulations and less color, try the two IYH hostels:
$ **Bruntsfield Hostel** (6–12 beds/room, near golf course, 7 Brunts-
field Crescent, buses #11, #15, #16, and #17 from Princes Street, tel.
0131/447-2994) and **Edinburgh Hostel** (4–10 beds/room, 5-min walk
from Haymarket station, 18 Eglinton Crescent, tel. 0131/337-1120).

EATING

Along the Royal Mile

Historic pubs and doily cafés with reasonable, unremarkable meals
abound. Here are some handy, affordable places for a good bite to eat
(listed in downhill order).

Deacon Brodie's Tavern serves soup, sandwiches, and snacks on
the ground floor and good £8 meals upstairs in the restaurant. As in all
Edinburgh pubs, kids are allowed only in the restaurant section (daily
12:00–22:00, tel. 0131/225-6531). Or munch prayerfully in the **Lower
Aisle** restaurant under St. Giles Cathedral (Mon–Fri 9:00–16:30, Sun
10:00–13:30, closed Sat except in Aug).

The **Filling Station,** a big noisy bar decorated with car parts, has an American-type menu, serves good burgers, and rocks at night (daily 12:00–23:30, later on weekends, 235 High Street, near North Bridge, tel. 0131/226-2488).

Dubh Prais Scottish Restaurant—the only serious restaurant on this list—is a dressy little place that fills a cellar 10 steps and a world away from the High Street bustle. The owner-chef promises to serve Scottish fayre at its very best. The only thing not Scottish here is the wine list and some of the guests (£8.50 2-course lunches Tue–Fri 12:00–14:00, £27 dinners Tue–Sat 18:30–22:30, closed Sun–Mon, reservations smart at night, opposite Crowne Plaza at 123b High Street, tel. 0131/557-5732).

Food Plantation has good, inexpensive, fresh sandwiches to eat in or take out (Mon–Fri 8:30-19:00, Sat 9:00-17:00, Sun 11:00-19:00, Internet access, 274 Canongate).

The **Tea Room** serves light lunches, scones, and fine tea in yellow elegance (Thu–Tue 10:30–16:30, off-season closed Wed, next to Museum of Edinburgh at 158 Canongate).

Clarinda's Tea Room, near the bottom of the Royal Mile, is a charming and tasty place to relax after touring the Mile or palace (Mon-Sat 9:00–16:45, Sun 10:00–16:45, 69 Canongate, tel. 0131/557-1888).

For a break from the touristic grind just off the top end of the Royal Mile, consider the **Elephant House,** where locals browse newspapers in the stay-awhile back room, listen to classic rock, and sip coffee or munch a light meal (daily 8:00–23:00, 2 blocks south of Royal Mile near Museum of Scotland at 21 George IV Bridge, tel. 0131/220-5355).

The Outsider, up the block, is a sleek spot serving stuffed pitas and stir-fry dishes (£10–15, daily 12:00–24:00, 15 George IV Bridge, tel. 0131/226-3131).

Grassmarket Street, below the castle, is lined with lots of eateries and noisy pubs. This is the place for live music and absorbent food.

The New Town

Princes Mall Food Court, below the TI and above the station, is a circus of sticky fast-food joints littered with paper plates and shoppers (Mon–Sat 8:30–18:00, Thu until 19:00, Sun 11:00–17:00). If you'd prefer pubs, browse nearby Rose Street.

The Dome Restaurant serves decent meals around a classy bar and under the elegant 19th-century skylight dome of what was a fancy bank. With soft jazz and dressy, white-tablecloth ambience, it feels a world apart (£12 lunches until 17:00, £17 dinners until 24:00, daily 12:00–24:00, modern cuisine, borderline smoky, open for a drink anytime under the dome or in the adjacent Art Deco bar, 14 George Street, tel. 0131/624-8624). Notice the facade of this former bank building—the various ways to make money fill the pediment with all the nobility of classical gods.

The **Undercroft,** in the basement of St. Andrew's church, is the

Edinburgh's New Town

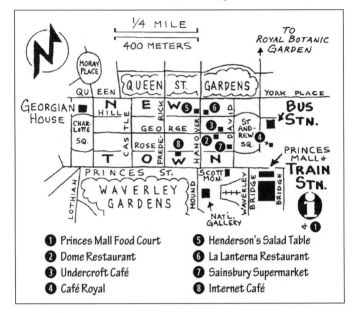

¼ MILE
400 METERS

TO ROYAL BOTANIC GARDEN

MORAY PLACE

GEORGIAN HOUSE

QUEEN ST. GARDENS

YORK PLACE

QUEEN

N HILL

CHARLOTTE SQ.

E GEORGE

ROSE

T O W N

PRINCES ST.

BUS STN.

ST ANDREW SQ.

PRINCES MALL & TRAIN STN.

WAVERLEY GARDENS

SCOTT MON.

NATL. GALLERY

❶ Princes Mall Food Court
❷ Dome Restaurant
❸ Undercroft Café
❹ Café Royal

❺ Henderson's Salad Table
❻ La Lanterna Restaurant
❼ Sainsbury Supermarket
❽ Internet Café

cheapest place in town for lunch (£1 sandwich or soup and roll, Mon–Fri 12:00–14:00, closed Sat–Sun, on George Street, just off St. Andrew Square).

Café Royal is a movie producer's dream pub—the perfect fin de siècle setting for a coffee, beer, or light meal (parts of *Chariots of Fire* were filmed in here). Drop in, if only to admire the 1880 tiles featuring famous inventors (daily noon–14:00 & 19:00–late, 2 blocks from Princes Mall on West Register Street, tel. 0131/556-4124).

A generation of New Town vegetarians have munched hearty cuisine and salads at **Henderson's Salad Table and Wine Bar** (£7, Mon–Sat 8:00–22:45, closed Sun, non-smoking section, strictly vegetarian, pleasant live music nightly in Wine Bar, always jazz on weekends, between Queen and George streets at 94 Hanover Street, tel. 0131/225-2131). Henderson's has two different seating areas, but both use the same self-serve cafeteria line. They also run **Henderson's Bistro** upstairs with table service.

Local office workers pile into the friendly and family-run **La Lanterna** for good Italian food (Mon–Sat 12:00–14:00 & 17:15–22:00, closed Sun, dinner reservations wise, 2 blocks off Princes Street, 83 Hanover Street, tel. 0131/226-3090).

Supermarket: The glorious **Sainsbury** supermarket, with a tasty assortment of take-away food and specialty coffees, is just one block from the Sir Walter Scott Monument and the lovely picnic-perfect Princes Street Gardens (Mon–Sat 7:00–22:00, Sun 10:00–20:00, on corner of Rose Street, on St. Andrew Square, across the street from Jenners, the classy department store).

Dalkeith Road Area, Near Your B&B

All these places are within a 10-minute walk of the recommended B&Bs. Most are on or near the intersection of Newington and East Preston Streets. For locations, see map on page 317.

Ethnic Restaurants: **Pataka Indian and Bengali Restaurant,** a 10-table "Indian bistro" with attentive service and great food, is understandably popular with locals. Portions are big, but not overly spicy, and prices are small. This tight little restaurant can be a bit smoky (£7 dishes, daily 12:00–14:00 & 17:30–23:30, also offers take-away, 190 Causewayside, tel. 0131/668-1167).

Wild Elephant serves decent Thai food to locals amid decor imported from Thailand, including a pagoda bar (£6–10, daily 17:00-23:00, also does take-away, 21 Newington Road, tel. 0131/662-8822).

Up the block, you'll find a couple of Chinese-food options: **Chinatown** (£6–9, Tue–Fri 12:00–14:00 & 17:30–23:00, Sat–Sun 17:30–23:30, closed Mon, reservations smart on weekend nights, take-away food 25 percent cheaper, 13 Newington Road, tel. 0131/662-0555) and **Hong Kong Martell** (daily from 12:00, 7 Newington Road, tel. 0131/668-4437).

Sambuca dishes up pizza and pasta in a lively bistro (£8–10 dishes, Mon–Sat 12:30–14:30 & 17:00–late, Sun 17:00–10:00, 103 Causewayside, tel. 0131/667-3307).

Scottish/French Restaurants: Several classy little eight-table places feature "Auld Alliance" cuisine—Scottish cooking with a French flair (seasoned with a joint historic disdain for England). They offer small menus with three or four items per course for two- or three-course meals (about £10 for a 2-course lunch, £20 for a 3-course dinner). These popular places take credit cards, and reservations are smart on weekend evenings. Many offer less-expensive meals outside of weekends.

Fenwicks is cozy and reliable, with tasty food and no French fries (main course-£13–16, daily 12:00–14:00, dinner 18:00–late, 15 Salisbury Place, tel. 0131/667-4265).

La Bon Vie Restaurant is candlelit chic with perhaps the most enticing menu (two-course dinner-£10–18, daily 12:00–14:00 & 18:00-22:00, call ahead to make sure they're open for lunch, 49 Causewayside, tel. 0131/667-1110).

Blonde Restaurant, with a more eclectic and European menu, is less expensive and bigger than the others with no set-price dinners (about £14 for 2 courses, good vegetarian options, Tue–Sun 12:00–14:30

& 18:00–22:00, closed Mon, 75 St. Leonard's Street, tel. 0131/668-2917).

Ciros Restaurant is a hardworking, well-established family affair (£15 2-course dinner, Tue–Sat 18:30–21:30, closed Sun–Mon; 93 St. Leonard's Street, tel. 0131/668-4207, run by Christine, Jean, and Stuart Stevenson).

Hotel Ceilidh-Donia serves well-prepared fish, meat, and vegetarian dishes in a flagstone-floored, high-ceilinged space with a small, friendly adjoining pub (£7–11, Mon–Fri eves plus Sun lunch 13:00–16:00, free Internet access to customers, within a block of most recommended B&Bs at 14 Marchhall Crescent, tel. 0131/667-2743).

Pubs: **Bierex,** a youthful pub, is the neighborhood favorite for modern dishes and camaraderie (£6 plates, daily 10:00–24:00, food served 10:00–21:00, Fri–Sat until 20:00, 132 Causewayside, tel. 0131/667-2335).

The **New Bell** serves up filling classics, from steak and salmon to haggis, in a tidy pub setting (£13 plates, Tue–Sun 17:30–22:30; 2-course £10 special 17:30–18:45; closed Mon, 233 Causewayside, tel. 0131/668-2868).

Cheaper Choices: **Brattisanis** is your basic fish-and-chips joint that serves lousy milk shakes and great haggis. Add a cheap touch of class by bringing in a beer or half bottle of wine from next door (daily 9:30–23:00, 87 Newington Road, tel. 0131/667-5808).

On Dalkeith Road, the huge Commonwealth Pool's noisy **café** has snacks for hungry swimmers and budget travelers alike (Mon–Fri 10:00–18:00, Sat–Sun 11:00–17:00, pass the entry without paying).

Supermarket: The nearest supermarket, **Sainsbury,** is a 10-minute walk or a quick bus ride down Dalkeith Road away from town in the Cameron Toll shopping complex (Mon–Sat 7:30–22:00, Sun 8:00–19:00, tel. 0131/666-5200). There's also a **Tesco** between the Dalkeith Road B&B neighborhood and the Royal Mile (Mon–Sat 7:00–midnight, Sun 9:00–22:00, 5 long blocks south of the Royal Mile, on Nicolson, just south of intersection with West Richmond Street).

TRANSPORTATION CONNECTIONS

By train to: Inverness (7/day, 4 hrs), **Oban** (3/day, change in Glasgow, 4.5 hrs), **York** (2/hr, 2.5 hrs), **London** (hrly, 5 hrs), **Durham** (hrly, 2 hrs, less frequent in winter), **Newcastle** (hrly, 1.5 hrs), **Keswick,** the Lake District (south past Carlisle to Penrith, then catch bus to Keswick, 6/day, fewer Sun, 40 min), **Birmingham** (6/day, 4.5 hrs), **Crewe** (6/day, 3.5 hrs), **Bristol,** near Bath (hrly, 6-7 hrs). Train info: tel. 08457-225-125, www.gner.co.uk.

By bus to: Oban (4/day, 4 hrs, not on Sun), **Fort William** (1/day, 4 hrs), **Inverness** (hrly, 4 hrs), **Blackpool** (Fri, Sat, Mon only, requires change in Glasgow, 5 hrs), **York** (1/day at 9:45, 5 hrs). For bus info, call Scottish Citylink (tel. 08705-505-050, www.citylink.co.uk) or National Express (tel. 08705-808-080). You can get info and tickets at the bus desk inside the Princes Mall TI.

Route Tips for Drivers

Arriving in Edinburgh from the north: Rather than drive through downtown Edinburgh to the recommended B&Bs, circle the city on the A720 City Bypass road. Approaching Edinburgh on the M9, take the M8 (direction: Glasgow) and quickly get onto the A720 City Bypass (direction: Edinburgh South). After four miles you'll hit a roundabout. Ignore signs directing you into Edinburgh North and stay on A720 for 10 more miles to the next and last roundabout, named Sheriffhall. Exit the roundabout on the first left (A7 Edinburgh). From here it's four miles to the B&B neighborhood (see "Arriving from the south," below, and B&B neighborhood map, page 317).

   Arriving from the south: Coming into town on A68 from the south, take the *A7 Edinburgh* exit off the roundabout. A7 becomes Dalkeith Road. If you see the huge swimming pool, you've gone a couple of blocks too far (avoid this by referring to B&B neighborhood map).

   Leaving Edinburgh, heading south: It's 100 miles from Edinburgh to Hadrian's Wall; to Durham it's another 50 miles. From Edinburgh, Dalkeith Road leads south and eventually becomes A68 (handy Cameron Toll supermarket with cheap gas is on the left as you leave Dalkeith Town, 10 min south of Edinburgh; gas and parking behind store). A68 takes you to Hadrian's Wall in two hours. You'll pass Jedburgh and its abbey after one hour. (For one last shot of shop-Scotland, there's a coach tour's delight just before Jedburgh, with kilt makers, woolens, and a sheepskin shop.) Across from Jedburgh's lovely abbey is a free parking lot, a good visitors center, and public toilets (20p to pee). The England/Scotland border is a fun, quick stop (great view, ice cream, and tea caravan). Before Hexham, roller-coaster two miles down A6079 to B6318, following the Roman wall westward. (See "Hadrian's Wall," on page 292 of the Durham chapter for more driving instructions.)

OBAN, ISLANDS, AND HIGHLANDS

Filled with more natural and historical mystique than people, the Highlands are where Scottish dreams are set. Legends of Bonnie Prince Charlie swirl around crumbling castles as pipers in kilts swirl around tourists. The harbor of Oban is a fruit crate of Scottish traditions, and the wind-bitten Hebrides islands are just a hop, skip, and jump away.

The Highlands are cut in two by the impressive Caledonian Canal, with Oban at one end and Inverness at the other. The major sights cluster along the scenic 120-mile stretch between these two towns. Oban is a fine home base for western Scotland, and Inverness makes a good overnight stop on your way through eastern Scotland.

Planning Your Time

While Ireland has more charm and Wales has better sights, this area provides your best look at rural Scottish culture. There are a lot of miles, but they're scenic, the roads are good, and the traffic is light. In two days you can get a feel for the area with the car hike described below. To do the islands, you'll need more time. Iona is worthwhile but adds a day to your trip. Generally, the region is hungry for the tourist dollar, and everything overtly Scottish is designed to woo the tourist. You'll need more than this quick visit to get away from that.

The charm of the Highlands deserves more time and a trip farther north (ideally to the Isle of Skye, see below). But with a car and two days to connect the Lake District and Edinburgh, this blitz of a tour is more interesting than two more days in England.

Day 1: 9:00-Leave Lake District (see Castlerigg Stone Circle if you haven't yet), 12:00-Rest stop on Loch Lomond, then joyride on, 13:00-Lunch in Inveraray, 16:00-Arrive in Oban, tour whiskey distillery, and drop by the TI, 20:00-Have dinner with music at McTavish's Kitchens or dinner with class at The Studio.

Day 2: 9:00-Leave Oban, 10:00-Visit Glencoe museum and the valley's Visitors Centre, 12:00-Drive to Fort William and follow Caledonian Canal to Inverness, stopping at Fort Augustus for a wander around the locks and at Loch Ness to take care of any monster business, 16:00-Visit the evocative Culloden Battlefield near Inverness, 17:00-Drive south, 20:00-Set up in Edinburgh.

With more time, spend a second night in Oban and tour Iona, or sleep in Inverness or Pitlochry, both fun and entertaining towns.

Oban

Oban, called the "gateway to the isles," is a busy little ferry-and-train terminal with no important "sights" but a charming shiver-and-bustle vitality that gives you a feel for small-town Scotland. Wind, boats, gulls, layers of islands, and the promise of a wide-open Atlantic beyond give it a rugged and salty charm.

ORIENTATION

(area code: 01631)

Oban's business action, just a couple of streets deep, stretches along the harbor and its promenade. Everything is close together, and the town seems eager to please its many visitors. There's live, touristy music nightly in several bars and restaurants; woolen and tweed are perpetually on sale (tourist shops open until 20:00 and on Sun); and posters announce a variety of day tours to Scotland's wild and rabbit-strewn western islands.

Tourist Information: The TI sells bus tickets and has brochures on everything from bike rental to golf courses to horseback riding to rainy-day activities as well as a fine bookshop (Mon–Sat 9:00–20:00, Sun 9:00–19:00, less Sept–June, Internet access, £3 room reservation fee, no WC, on Argyll Square, just off harbor a block from train station, tel. 01631/563-122, www.visitscottishheartlands.org). Wander through their exhibit on the area and pick up a few phones to hear hardy locals talk about their life on the wild, west edge of Scotland. Check the TI's "What's On" board for the latest on Oban's small-town evening scene (free live entertainment nightly at the Great Western Hotel, with a Scottish Night every Wed, tel. 01631/563-101).

Helpful Hints

Bike Rental: Try Oban Cycles (£8/half-day, £12.50/day, Mon–Sat 9:00–17:30, closed Sun but rentals can be arranged in advance, across from Tesco supermarket on Lochside Street, tel. 01631/566-996, www.obancycles.com).

Internet Access: Your cheapest bet is the library at The Esplanade and Dunollie Road (free, 10:00–13:00 & 14:00–17:00, closed Sun, Tue, and Sat afternoon, tel. 01631/571-444). Or try the TI (see above) or Oban Backpackers hostel (daily 10:00–19:00, near B&Bs on Breadalbane Street, tel. 01631/562-107).

Laundry: Oban Backpackers hostel provides same-day **laundry service** (guests-£2.50, otherwise £3.50, drop off by 9:00 for same-day service, 2-min walk from B&Bs, on Breadalbane Street, tel. 01631/562-107).

TOURS

Oban and Beyond

A couple of outfits offer 60- to 90-minute walking tours of Oban with the requisite nods to history, whiskey, and bagpipes. Both charge £5, depart from the TI, and can be booked through the TI: One is called simply Walking Tours (July–Aug Wed–Sun 10:00, 14:00, & 17:00, tel. 01631/570-638, Ewan) and the other is Tales on the Hoof (July–Aug Tue and Thu 11:00 & 14:00, tel. 01631/563-122, www.ansgeulaiche.co.uk).

For the best day trip from Oban, tour the Islands of Iona and Mull (offered daily May–Oct, fully described on page 337). Oban's tour companies offer an array of tours. You can spend an entire day on Mull. Those more interested in nature than church history will enjoy trips to the wildly scenic Isle of Staffa with Fingal's Cave. Trips to Treshnish Island brim with puffins, seals, and other sea critters.

On Sundays, Oban Backpackers offers an all-day Intro to Ancient Scotland tour that includes monuments, cairns, a castle, and Island of Seil (£18, departs 9:00 from hostel on Bredalbane Street, returns 18:30, tel. 01631/562-107).

SIGHTS

Oban

▲**West Highland Malt Scotch Whisky Distillery Tours**—The 200-year-old Oban Whisky Distillery produces more than 14,500 liters a week. They offer serious and fragrant 40-minute, £4 tours explaining the process from start to finish, with a free, smooth sample and a discount coupon for the shop. The exhibition that precedes the tour gives a quick, whiskey-centric history of Scotland. This is the handiest whiskey tour you'll see, just a block off the harbor and better than anything in Edinburgh (July–Sept Mon–Fri 9:30–19:30, Sat 9:30–17:00, Sun 12:00–17:00; April–June and Oct Mon–Sat 9:30–17:00, closed Sun; March and Nov Mon–Fri 10:00–17:00, closed Sat–Sun; Dec–Feb Mon–Fri 12:30–16:00, closed Sat–Sun; last tour one hour before closing, to avoid a wait, call to reserve a place, tel. 01631/572-004).

Oban

① To Glenburnie & Barriemore Hotels
& Kilchrenan House B&B
② Rowan Tree Hotel
③ Tanglin B&B, Strathlachlan, Raniven,
Gramarvin & Sand Villa Guest Houses
④ Oban Backpackers
⑤ IYHF Hostel
⑥ Jeremy Inglis' B&B
⑦ Oban Inn Rest. & Bowman Tours
⑧ Coasters Restaurant
⑨ The Lorne Pub
⑩ McTavish's Kitchens
⑪ The Studio Restaurant
⑫ To Manor House Hotel Rest.
⑬ The Kitchen Garden Deli & Café
⑭ Ee'usk Restaurant
⑮ Waterfront Restaurant
& Shellfish Shack
⑯ Cafe 41 Bistro
⑰ Whisky Distillery
⑱ To Supermarket & Bike Rental

McCaig's Tower—The unfinished "colosseum" on the hill overlooking the town was an "employ-the-workers-and-build-me-a-fine-memorial" project undertaken by an early Oban tycoon in 1900. While the structure itself is nothing to see close-up, a 10-minute hike through a Victorian residential neighborhood gets you to a peaceful garden and a mediocre view.

The Atlantis Sports and Leisure Center—Here you'll find an indoor swimming pool (with big water slide) and a rock-climbing wall (center open Mon–Fri 7:00–22:00, Sat–Sun 8:30–21:00, July–Aug closes Sat–Sun at 18:00, pool hours vary, call for the latest, pool: £2.70-adults, £1.70-kids ages 3-15, no towels or suits for rent, lockers-20p, on Dalriach Road 2 blocks above recommended B&Bs, tel. 01631/566-8000). The center's outdoor playground is free and open all the time.

Oban Lawn Bowling Club—The club has welcomed visitors since 1869. This elegant green is the scene of a wonderfully British spectacle of old men tiptoeing wishfully after their balls. It's fun to watch, and—if there's no match and the weather's dry—for £3 each you can rent shoes and balls and actually play (next to sports center on Dalriach Road).

Near Oban

Kerrera—Two miles south of Oban, this stark but very green island offers a quick, easy opportunity to get that romantic island experience (ferry-£3.00 round-trip, 50p for bikes, 15 ferries/day, at Gallanach's dock, tel. 01631/563-665, if no answer contact TI for info).

Isle of Seil—Enjoy a drive, a walk, some solitude, and the sea. Drive 12 miles south of Oban on A816 to B844 to the Isle of Seil, connected to the mainland by a bridge. Just over the bridge on the Isle of Seil is a pub called Tigh-an-Truish ("House of Trousers"). After a 1745 English law forbade the wearing of kilts on the mainland, Highlanders used this pub to change from kilts to trousers before crossing the bridge. The pub serves great meals to those in kilts or pants (March–Sept daily 12:30–17:00 & 18:00–20:30, drinks but not food served off-season, darts anytime, good seafood dish, crispy vegetables, tel. 01852/300-242). Five miles across the island, on a tiny second island and facing the open Atlantic, is Easdale, a historic, touristy, windy little slate-mining town—with a slate-town museum and incredibly tacky egomaniac's "Highland Arts" shop (shuttle ferry goes the 300 yards).

SLEEPING

Hotels

$$$ Glenburnie Hotel, a stately Victorian home on Oban's waterfront, has an elegant breakfast room overlooking the bay. Its spacious and comfortable rooms are furnished like plush living rooms (Sb-£30–37, Db-£60–80, good breakfast and views, non-smoking, parking, closed mid-Nov–mid-March, The Esplanade, tel. & fax 01631/562-089, www.glenburnie.co.uk, graeme.strachan@btinternet.com, Graeme and Allyson).

$$$ **Barriemore Hotel** is the last place on Oban's grand waterfront esplanade. It has a dark, woody, equestrian feel and 13 large, well-appointed rooms (Sb-£30–45, Db-£60–80, fine views, non-smoking, The Esplanade, tel. 01631/566-356, fax 01631/571-084, www .barriemore-hotel.co.uk, reception@barriemore-hotel.co.uk, Ina and Hamish Dawson). They serve elegant Scottish dinners (£11–17 main dish, Tue–Sun 18:00–21:00).

$$$ **Kilchrenan House,** the turreted former retreat of a textile magnate, has 10 tastefully-renovated, spacious rooms, most with bay views (Sb-£30–38, Db-£60–80, try for room 5, non-smoking, closed Dec–Jan, The Esplanade, tel. 01631/562-663, fax 01631/570-021, www.kilchrenanhouse.co.uk, info@kilchrenanhouse.co.uk, Alison and Kenny).

$$$ **Rowan Tree Hotel** is a group-friendly place with a tacky lobby, 24 basic, cleanser-clean rooms, and a central but quiet locale (Sb-£38–50, Db-£62–70, easy parking, George Street, tel. 01631/562-954, fax 01631/565-071).

Guest Houses

The following guest houses are well located on a quiet street two blocks off the harbor, three blocks from the center, and a 12-minute walk from the train station. By car, as you enter town, turn left after King's Knoll Hotel and take your first right onto Breadalbane Street. Each has parking from an alley behind the buildings.

$$ **Tanglin B&B** is a winner. Liz and Jim Montgomery offer a bright, non-smoking, homey place with an easygoing atmosphere (S-£18–20, D-£32, Db-£38–40, 5 rooms, flexible rates and family deals, no CC, 3 Strathaven Terrace, Breadalbane Street, tel. 01631/563-247, jimtanglin@aol.com).

$$ **Strathlachlan Guest House,** next door, offers a fine value and the Scottish hospitality of Rena Anderson. Each of the four rooms has a private adjacent bathroom, and they share a TV lounge (S-£16, D-£32, family deals, entirely smoke-free, no CC, 2 Breadalbane Street, tel. 01631/563-861).

$$ **Raniven Guest House,** with six tastefully decorated rooms, is friendly and a great value (Db-£40–50, no CC, non-smoking, 1 Strathlachlan Terrace, tel. 01631/562-713, Jessie Turnbull).

$$ **Gramarvin Guest House,** decorated in cool green and lavender tones, is also comfy and quiet (Db-£40–50, 5 rooms, family deals, non-smoking, no CC, Breadalbane Street, tel. 01631/564-622, www .gramarvin.co.uk, mary@gramarvin.co.uk, Mary).

$$ **Sand Villa Guest House** rents five cheery rooms but is a lesser

SLEEP CODE

(£1 = about $1.60, country code: 44, area code: 01631)
Sleep Code: **S** = Single, **D** = Double/Twin, **T** = Triple, **Q** = Quad, **b** = bathroom, **s** = shower only, **no CC** = Credit Cards not accepted. You can assume credit cards are accepted unless otherwise noted.

To help you sort easily through these listings, I've divided the rooms into three categories based on the price for a standard double room with bath (during high season):

$$$ **Higher Priced**—Most rooms £65 or more.
 $$ **Moderately Priced**—Most rooms between £30–65.
  $ **Lower Priced**—Most rooms £30 or less.

B&Bs offer a better value than the hotels.

value (Db-£40–50, Tb-£60, no CC, 4 Breadalbane Street, tel. 01631/562-803, http://holidayoban.co.uk, sandvilla@freeuk.com, Joyce).

Dorms and Hostels

Oban offers plenty of cheap dorm beds. Your choice: fun, orderly, or spacey.

$ Oban Backpackers is central, laid-back, and fun, with a wonderful sprawling public living room and 48 beds (£12/bed in July–Aug, £11 off-season when open, 6-12 bunks per room, closed Nov–March, Internet terminal, and £2.50 laundry service, £3.50 for non-guests, 10-min walk from station, on Breadalbane Street, tel. 01631/562-107).

$ The orderly **IYHF hostel,** on the waterfront esplanade, is in a grand building with 130 beds and smashing views of the harbor and islands (£12.50/bed, 4- to 10-bed rooms, 11 Db-£30, cheaper for youths under 18 and anyone off-season, great facilities and public rooms, Internet access, laundry machines, tel. 01631/562-025, oban@syha.org.uk).

$ Jeremy Inglis' spacey B&B, a block from the TI and train station, is least expensive and feels more like a commune than a youth hostel (£6.50/bed, no CC, 12 beds, 21 Airds Crescent, tel. 01631/565-065).

EATING

Oban has plenty of fun options. The downtown is full of cheap eateries and pubs serving decent grub: Consider the harborfront **Oban Inn,** the oldest building in town (£6, Mon–Sat 12:00–22:00, Sun from 12:30, stained glass coats-of-arms and comfy booth seating, 1 Stafford Street, tel. 01631/562-484) or **Coasters** (£5–9, daily 12:00–23:00, closed 15:00-17:00 off-season, good views but smoky, on Corran Esplanade, 1 block past William Street heading away from station, tel. 01631/566-881). Just off the main drag is **The Lorne,** a lively, friendly, high-ceilinged pub popular with locals (£7–12, food served Sun–Fri 12:00–14:30 & 17:00–21:00, Sat 12:00–21:00, Stevenson Street, tel. 01631/570-020).

To mix a sappy folk show inexpensively with dinner, gum haggis at **McTavish's Kitchens.** This huge eating hall is an Oban institution, which features live but tired folk music and dancing. This is your basic tourist trap filled with English vacationers. The food is inexpensive and edible (£7.50 for haggis, neeps, and tatties; £15 for a super Scottish multicourse menu). The piping, dancing, and singing occur nightly May through September (20:00–22:00, mostly a fiddle and two accordions, with precious little dancing and bagpiping, tel. 01631/563-064). The show costs £4 without a meal, £2 with dinner, or is free with dinner if you have a coupon from your B&B. No reservations are required. Nonsmokers get the best harbor views. Smokers sit closest to the stage.

Everyone's favorite "nice dinner out" is at **The Studio,** a small, tightly packed restaurant with 70s decor featuring serious, first-class Scottish cooking (£12 for a full Scottish meal until 18:30, £14 for 3-course meal after 18:30, or a pricey à la carte menu, April–Oct nightly 18:00-22:00, closed Nov–March, always make a reservation, intersection of Craigard Road and Albert Road, tel. 01631/562-030). It has great steaks, trout, and a prawn-and-clam chowder that hits the spot on a stormy day.

For a genteel dining experience—pricey but worthwhile for a waterfront splurge—eat at the well-polished **Manor House Hotel** (£29 five-course meal, nouveau cuisine, nightly 18:45–21:00, reservations in summer are wise, a short drive or taxi ride south of town on the waterfront, Gallanach Road, tel. 01631/562-087).

For soup, salad, or sandwiches, consider **The Kitchen Garden,** a deli and gourmet-foods store with a charming café upstairs (£2.50–7, Mon–Sat 9:00–17:30, Sun 11:00–17:00, closed Sun off-season, 14 George Street, tel. 01631/566-332).

Ee'usk (formerly The Fish Café), a stylish, family-run place on the waterfront, has tall tables, sweeping views, and fish dishes (£8–15, daily 11:00–16:00 & 18:00–22:00, North Pier, tel. 01631/565-666). You'll eat decent seafood at **The Waterfront Restaurant** (£15–20, daily 11:30–14:15 & 17:30–21:30, closed Jan–Feb, views of water and McCaig's Tower, #1 The Pier, tel. 01631/563-110).

Cafe 41 Bistro offers a relaxed BYOB option with an emphasis on Scottish and French cuisine (£11–16, Sun and Wed–Thu 18:30–20:45, Fri–Sat until 21:30, closed Mon–Tue, 41 Combie Street, tel. 01631/564-117).

For a seafood appetizer, drop by the green **Shellfish** shack at the ferry dock (often free salmon samples, inexpensive coffee, meal-sized salmon sandwiches, open until the boat unloads from Mull in the late afternoon—a pleasant way to cap off your day trip to the islands). Accept no substitutes—go for the green shack.

Supermarket: Tesco is a five-minute walk from the TI (Mon–Sat 8:00–22:00, Sun 9:00–20:00, WC in front by registers, Lochside Road).

TRANSPORTATION CONNECTIONS

Oban

Trains link Oban to the nearest transportation hub in **Glasgow** (3/day, 3 hrs, see below). Oban's small train station has lockers but no WC (ticket window open Mon–Sat 7:15–18:10, Sun 11:00–18:00). Train info: tel. 08457-484-950, www.gner.co.uk.

Ferries fan out from Oban to the **southern Hebrides** (see "The Islands of Iona and Mull," next page). Caledonian MacBrayne Ferry info: tel. 01631/566-688.

Buses, operated by Scottish Citylink (www.citylink.co.uk), run between Oban, Glencoe, and Inverness, but not on Sunday. **From Oban by bus to: Glencoe** (1/day, allow 8.5 hrs due to 6.5-hr lay-over in Tyndrum, £12.50 one-way), **Inverness** (3/day July–Aug, 2/day Sept–June, 4 hrs, transfer in Fort William, £12.70 one-way). Pay the driver cash or buy tickets in advance by calling Citylink at tel. 08705-505-050; or, even easier, drop by the TI. Buses arrive and depart in front of the Caledonian Hotel, across from the train station.

Glasgow

Glasgow, one of the region's major transportation hubs, has a bus station and two train stations, a seven-minute walk apart. Train info: tel. 08457-484-950.

A handy shuttle bus connects all three stations (50p, pay driver, or free if connecting between train stations, show train ticket to driver, Mon–Sat 7:00–22:00, Sun 10:00–22:00, every 10 min). All stations have pay WCs (20p).

If you need a place to stay in Glasgow, try **Hampton Court Hotel** in the city center (S-from £24, Sb-£28, Db-from £42, T-from £60, Tb-£66, non-smoking room, includes breakfast, 230 Renfrew Street, Glasgow, tel. 0141/332-6623, fax 0141/332-5885, www.hamptoncourt .activehotels.com, reception@hamptoncourt.activehotels.com).

Glasgow's Central Station by train to: Keswick in the Lake District (hrly, 2 hrs to Penrith, then catch a bus to Keswick, hrly except Sun 6/day, 40 min), **Stranraer** and ferry to Belfast (9/day, 2.5 hrs, change in Ayr), **Troon** and ferry to Belfast (2/hr, 40 min), **Preston** (hrly, 3 hrs, easy 30-min connection to Blackpool), **York** (12/day, 4 hrs, some changes), **London** (hrly, 6 hrs, some direct trains). The station is on Gordon Street, at the intersection with Renfield-Union Street. Lockers are at tracks 9–10 (£3–5/day depending on size).

Glasgow's Queen Street Station by train to: Oban (3/day, 3 hrs), **Inverness** (3/day, 3.5 hrs, more frequent with change in Perth), **Edinburgh** (4/hr, 1 hr).

Glasgow by bus to: Oban (3/day, 3 hrs), **Inverness** (hrly, 4 hrs, some transfer in Perth), **Edinburgh** (6/hr, 1.25 hrs). Buses depart from Buchanan Bus Station on Killermont Street, two blocks behind Queen Street Station. You can store luggage at the bus station (£2/2 hrs, £3/3–24 hrs, daily 6:30–22:30). Bus info: tel. 0870-608-2608, www .traveline.org.uk.

The Islands of Iona and Mull

For the best one-day look at the dramatic and historic Hebrides (HEB-rid-eez) islands around Oban, take the Iona/Mull tour from Oban (£27, Sun–Fri 10:00–17:40, Sat 10:30–19:00—but always confirm schedule). Bowman & MacDougall is the dominant and most established outfit. They offer a £2 discount on tours for anyone with this book (buy your ticket at the "Iona & Mull Tours" office, daily 8:00–18:00, no tours Nov–April, book 1 day ahead July–Sept, 3 Stafford Street facing harbor next to Oban Inn, tel. 01631/563-221, or 1 Queens Park Place near North Pier, tel. 01631/566-809, www.bowmanstours.co.uk).

Each morning, travelers gather on the Oban pier and pile onto the huge Oban–Mull ferry (40 min). On board, if it's a clear day, ask a local to point out Ben Nevis, the tallest mountain in Great Britain. The ferry has a fine cafeteria and a bookshop (though guidebooks are cheaper in Oban). Five minutes before landing on Mull, you'll see the striking Duart castle on the left.

Upon arrival in Mull, you'll find your tour company's bus for the entertaining and informative 35-mile bus ride across the Isle of Mull (75 min, single-lane road). All drivers spend the entire ride chattering away about life on Mull. They are hardworking local boys who make historical trivia fascinating—or at least fun.

The Isle of Mull, the third-largest in Scotland, has 300 scenic miles of coastline and castles and a 3,169-foot-high mountain. Called Ben More ("big hill" in Gaelic), it was once much bigger. The last active volcano in northern Europe, it was 10,000 feet tall—the entire island of Mull—before it blew. It's calmer now, and similarly, Mull has a notably laid-back population. My bus driver reported there are no deaths from stress and only a few from boredom.

On the far side of Mull the caravan of tour buses unloads at a tiny ferry town. The ferry takes about 200 walk-ons. Confirm clearly with the bus driver when to catch the boat off Iona for your return, then hustle off the bus and to the dock to avoid the 30-minute delay if you

HISTORY OF IONA

St. Columba, an Irish scholar, soldier, priest, and founder of monasteries, got into a small war over the possession of an illegally copied psalm book. Victorious but sickened by the bloodshed, Columba left Ireland, vowing never to return. According to legend, the first bit of land out of sight of his homeland was Iona. He stopped here in 563 and established the abbey.

Columba's monastic community flourished, and Iona became the center of Celtic Christianity. Iona missionaries spread the gospel through Scotland and North England, while scholarly monks established Iona as a center of art and learning. The *Book of Kells*—perhaps the finest piece of art from "Dark Ages" Europe—was probably made on Iona in the eighth century. The island was so important that it was the legendary burial place for ancient Scottish and even Scandinavian kings (including Shakespeare's Macbeth).

Slowly the importance of Iona ebbed. Vikings massacred 68 monks in 806. Fearing more raids, the monks evacuated most of Iona's treasures (including the *Book of Kells*, which is now in Dublin) to Ireland. Much later, with the Reformation, the abbey was abandoned, and most of its finely carved crosses were destroyed. In the 17th century, locals used the abbey only as a handy quarry for other building projects.

Iona's population peaked at about 500 in the 1830s. In the 1840s a potato famine hit. In the 1850s a third of the islanders emigrated to Canada or Australia. By 1900 the population was down to 210, and today it's only around 100.

But in our generation a new religious community has given the abbey new life. The Iona community is an ecumenical gathering of men and women who seek new ways of living the Gospel in today's world, with a focus on worship, peace and justice issues, and reconciliation.

don't make the first trip over. After the 10-minute ride, you wash ashore on sleepy Iona.

This tiny island, just three miles by 1.5 miles, is famous as the birthplace of Christianity in Scotland. You'll have about two hours here on your own before you retrace your steps; you'll dock back in Oban by about 17:40. While the day is spectacular when it's sunny, it's worthwhile in any weather.

A pristine light and a thoughtful peace pervade the stark, car-free island and its tiny community. While the present abbey, nunnery, and graveyard go back to the 13th century, much of what you'll see was rebuilt in the 19th century (£3 entry, tel. 01681/700-512). But with buoyant clouds bouncing playfully off of distant bluffs, sparkling white sand crescents, and lone tourists camped thoughtfully atop huge rocks just looking out to sea, it's a place perfect for meditation. Climb a peak—nothing's higher than 300 feet above the sea.

The village, Baile Mor, has shops, a restaurant/pub, enough beds, and a meager heritage center. The Finlay Ross Shop rents bikes (near ferry dock, £4.50/4 hrs, £8/day, tel. 01681/700-357).

SLEEPING

Iona
Enjoy the serenity of Iona by spending the night. When the day-trippers leave, you'll find that special peace. **$$$ Argyll Hotel,** built in 1867, sits proud and classy overlooking the waterfront, with basic rooms above a grassy yard and public spaces (15 rooms, Db-£60–104, dinner deals, Internet access, closed Nov–April, tel. 01681/700-334, fax 01681/700-510, www.argyllhoteliona.co.uk, reception@argyllhoteliona.co.uk).

$$$ Finlay B&B rents 11 no-charm rooms in front of the ferry dock (D-£49, Db-£53, reception at Finlay Ross Shop, tel. 01681/700-357, fax 01681/700-562, finlayross@ukgateway.net).

The Highlands: Oban to Inverness

Discover Glencoe's dark secrets in the Weeping Glen, where Britain's highest peak, Ben Nevis, keeps its head in the clouds. Explore the locks and lochs of the Caledonian Canal while the Loch Ness monster plays hide-and-seek. Hear the music of the Highlands in Inverness and the echo of muskets in Culloden, where the English put down Bonnie Prince Charlie and conquered the clans of the Highlands.

Getting Around the Highlands
The trains are scenic, but if schedules frustrate, take the bus. Two buses a day (three in summer) connect the towns from Oban to Inverness (4 hrs). Ask at the station to see how schedules work for sight-hopping, or rent a car (rental info at Oban and Inverness TIs). One great option is to ride with the mail carrier on the post bus. While locals do this to get somewhere, tourists do it to chat with the mail carrier—great gossip on the entire neighborhood! This costs only a few pounds and works well in remote spots like Glencoe. Ask at the post office (Fort William) or bus station for post-bus schedules and routes.

Oban, Islands, and Highlands

Glencoe

This valley is the essence of the wild, powerful, and stark beauty of the Highlands (and, I think, excuses the hurried tourist from needing to go north of Inverness). Along with its scenery, Glencoe offers a good dose of bloody clan history.

Glencoe town is just a line of houses. One is a tiny thatched early 18th-century croft house jammed with local history. The huggable **Glencoe and North Lorn Folk Museum,** staffed by enthusiastic volunteers, is filled with humble exhibits gleaned from the town's old closets and attics (which come to life when explained by a local). When one house was being rethatched, its owner found a cache of 200-year-old swords and pistols hidden there from the British Redcoats after the disastrous battle of Culloden (£2, Mon–Sat 10:00–17:30, closed Sun, tel. 01855/811-3140). See if you can scare up colorful Arthur Smith, one of the museum's trustees.

A mile into the dramatic valley on the A82, you'll find the new **Visitors Centre.** Built as a traditional *clachan,* or settlement, the Centre offers an exhibit on the surrounding landscape and local history. Take a touch-screen climb up a virtual mountain, or watch one of three videos: one on mountaineering, a "more interesting than it sounds" geology video, and 14 minutes on the 1692 massacre when the Redcoats killed sleeping MacDonalds and the valley got its nickname "The Weeping Glen" (£3.50, April–Aug daily 9:30–17:30; Sept–Oct daily 10:00–17:00; Nov–Feb Mon–Fri 10:00–16:00, closed Sat–Sun; March daily 10:00-16:00; café, WC, shop, tel. 01855/811-307). The nearest **TI** is in Ballachulish (bus timetables, room-booking service for a fee, café, shop, tel. 01855/811-296).

Walks: For a steep one-mile hike, climb the Devil's Staircase (trail leaves from A82, eight miles east of Glencoe). For a three-hour hike, ask at the Visitors Centre about the Lost Valley of the MacDonalds (trail leaves from A82, 3 miles east of Glencoe). For an easy walk from Glencoe, head to the mansion on the hill (over the bridge, turn left, fine loch views). Above Glencoe is a mansion built by Canadian Pacific Railway magnate Lord Strathcona for his wife, a Canadian Indian. She was homesick for the Rockies, so he had the grounds landscaped to represent the lakes, trees, and mountains of her home country. It didn't work, and they eventually returned to British Columbia. The house originally had 365 windows to allow a different view each day.

Glencoe's Burial Island and Island of Discussion: In the loch just outside Glencoe, notice the burial island—where the souls of those who "take the low road" are piped home. (Ask a local about "You take the high road, and I'll take the low road.") The next island was the Island of Discussion—where those in dispute went until they found agreement.

SLEEPING AND EATING

(£1 = about $1.60, country code: 44, area code: 01855)

Many find Glencoe more interesting than Oban for an overnight stop. Try the **$$ Mack-Leven House B&B** (Db-£36–40, family deals, smoke-free rooms, homey lounge, conservatory, no CC, Lorn Drive, Glencoe, tel. 01855/811-215, Mackintosh family) or **$$ Tulachgorm B&B** (D-from £32, no CC, soft prices off-season, non-smoking, on the main street in the village, tel. 01855/811-391, Ann Blake speaks English and Gaelic).

Nearby hotels and pubs serve food. Ask your B&B host for a recommendation. For evening fun, take a walk or ask your B&B host where to find music and dancing.

More Sights—Scottish Highlands

Ben Nevis—From Fort William, take a peek at Britain's highest peak, Ben Nevis (more than 4,400 feet). Thousands walk to its summit each year. On a clear day you can admire it from a distance. Scotland's only mountain cable cars can take you to a not-very-lofty 2,150-foot perch for a closer look (£7.50, July–Aug daily 9:30–18:00, Thu–Fri until 21:00, otherwise daily 10:00–17:00,15-min ride, signposted on A82, tel. 01397/705-825).

▲**Caledonian Canal**—Three lochs and a series of canals cut Scotland in two. Oich, Lochy, and Ness were connected in the early 1800s by the great British engineer Thomas Telford. Traveling between Fort William and Inverness (60 miles), you'll follow Telford's work—20 miles of canals and locks between 40 miles of lakes, raising ships from sea level to 51 feet (Ness), to 93 feet (Lochy), and to 106 feet (Oich).

While "Neptune's Staircase," a series of locks near Fort William, is cleverly named, the best lock stop is Fort Augustus, where the canal hits Loch Ness. In Fort Augustus, the Caledonian Canal Heritage Centre, three locks above the main road, gives a good rundown on Telford's work (free). Stroll to the top of the locks past several shops and eateries for a fine view.

Sleeping in Fort William: $$ Glenmorven Guest House is a friendly family-run place with views of Loch Linnhe (Db-£38–46, Union Road, Fort William, tel. & fax 01397/703-236, www.glenmorven.co.uk).

Loch Ness—I'll admit it: I had my zoom lens out and my eyes on the water. The local tourist industry thrives on the legend of the Loch Ness Monster. It's a thrilling thought, and there have been several seemingly reliable "sightings" (monks, police officers, and sonar images). The loch, 24 miles long, less than a mile wide, and the third deepest in Europe, is deepest near the Urquhart Castle. Most monster sightings are in this area.

The Nessie commercialization is so tacky that there are two "official" Loch Ness Exhibition Centres within 100 yards of each other. Each has a tour-bus parking lot and more square footage devoted to their kitschy shop than to the exhibit. The exhibits, while fascinating, are overpriced. The exhibition in the big stone mansion (closest to Inverness) is the better one, headed by a marine biologist who has spent more than 15 years researching lake ecology and scientific phenomena. With a 40-minute series of video bits and special effects, this exhibit explains the geological and historical environment that bred the monster story and the various searches (£5.95, July–Aug daily 9:30–20:30, June and Sept 9:30–18:30, Oct and April–May 9:30–17:30, Nov–March 10:00–16:00, tel. 01456/450-573, www.loch-ness-scotland.com). The other (closest to Oban) is a high school-quality photo report followed by the 30-minute *We Believe in the Loch Ness Monster* movie, which features credible-sounding locals explaining what they saw and a review of modern Nessie searches (£3.50, April–June daily 9:00–18:00, July–Aug 9:00–21:00, Sept–March 9:00–17:00, tel. 01456/450-342).

The nearby **Urquhart Castle** ruins are gloriously situated with a view of virtually the entire lake. Although its new Visitors Centre has a museum with castle artifacts, the castle itself is an overpriced empty shell swarming with tourists (£5.50, daily 9:30–18:30, July–Aug until 20:00, last entry 45 min before closing, tel. 01456/450-551).

▲**Culloden Battlefield**—Scottish troops under Bonnie Prince Charlie were defeated here by the English in 1746. This last land battle fought on British soil spelled the end of Jacobite resistance and the fall of the clans. Wandering the battlefield, you feel that something terrible occurred here. Locals still bring flowers and speak of "'46" as if it just happened.

The excellent Visitors Centre shows a stirring 16-minute audiovisual (2/hr). Wander through a furnished old cottage and the battlegrounds (£5, April–Oct daily 9:00–18:00, otherwise daily 11:00–16:00, closed Jan, June–Sept look for period actors and £4 guided tours—4/day, good tearoom, tel. 01463/790-607). Members of the City Sightseeing tour from Inverness receive a discount on the Visitors Centre entry (City Sightseeing tel. 01463/224-000).

Inverness

The only sizable town in the north of Scotland, with 42,000 people, Inverness is pleasantly located on the River Ness at the base of a castle (not worth a look) and has a free little museum (worth a look, Mon–Sat 9:00–17:00, closed Sun, cheap café). Check out the bustling pedestrian downtown or stroll the picnic-friendly riverside paths (several footbridges).

Tourist Information: At the centrally located TI, pick up activity and day-trip brochures and *What's On* for the latest showings in theater, music, and film (Mon–Sat 9:00–18:00, Sun 9:30–16:00, open as late as 20:00 in summer, less off-season, Internet access-£1/20 min, £2.50/hr, free WCs behind TI, Castle Wynd, tel. 01463/234-353, www .highlandfreedom.com).

Helpful Hints

Launderette: It's just across the Ness Bridge (£5-self-service, £8.90-same-day full-service, drop off by 12:00, Internet access, Mon–Fri 8:00–20:00, Sat 8:00–18:00, Sun 10:00–16:00, 17 Young Street, tel. 01463/242-507).

Internet Access: Mailboxes Etc., next door to the station, has Internet access and can mail your packages home (Mon–Fri 8:30–18:00, Sat

9:00–16:00, tel. 01463/234-700). The library behind the bus station offers free Internet access, but you have to reserve a time slot in advance (Mon and Fri 9:00–19:30, Tue and Thu 9:00–18:30, Wed 10:00–17:00, Sat 9:00–17:00, closed Sun). The launderette listed above also has Internet access.

SIGHTS

Folk Show—The **Scottish Showtime** evening is a fun-loving, hard-working, Lawrence Welk-ish show giving you all the clichés in a clap-along two-hour package. I prefer it to the big hotel spectacles in Edinburgh (usually June–Sept Mon–Fri at 20:30, no meals, £14, get £2 off if booked through TI, Spectrum Centre, Margaret Street, adjacent to bus station, tel. 0800-015-8001).

Day Trips—While thin on sights, Inverness is great for day trips. The biggest attraction is Loch Ness, a 20-minute drive southwest. All tours depart from and sell tickets at the TI.

For a bit of history and geology mixed in with your Loch Ness lore, consider **Discover Loch Ness,** with excursions that include Urquhart Castle, a cruise on the lake, and admission to the better Loch Ness exhibit (half day-£22, all day-£30; £12 half-day economy deal doesn't include cruise or admissions, economy stand-by tickets sometimes available for £10; all depart at 10:30, live guides, reserve ahead, tel. 0800-731-5564 or 01456/450-168, mobile 0786/753-2163, www.discoverlochness.com).

Jacobite's tours feature kids' activities. Its three-hour Exploration tour includes a minibus ride with live narration, a cruise with recorded narration, and a stop at the better Loch Ness exhibit (£12.50, departs 10:30, tel. 01463/233-999, www.jacobite.co.uk).

City Sightseeing runs 45-minute hop-on, hop-off tours of Inverness (£5, every 45 min from TI, recorded narration, 14 stops) and 90-minute "History of the Highlands" tours (£8.50, every 90 min from TI, includes Culloden Battlefield, Cawdor Castle, and Fort George, admission extra, live guide, tel. 01463/224-000, www.city-sightseeing.com).

Puffin Express offers day-long "Over the Sea to Skye" tours. The tour drives along Loch Ness and gives you a few hours on Skye; unfortunately, it goes only as far as the Sleat peninsula at the island's southern end (£25, departs from Castle Wynd in Inverness 9:30, mid-April–mid-Oct every Mon and Wed, also June–Aug Thu, sometimes also weekends, reservations recommended, tel. 01463/717-181, www.puffinexpress.co.uk).

Several other companies host daily excursions to Culloden battlefield, whiskey distilleries, 14th-century Cawdor Castle, and the nearby bay for dolphin-watching (information and booking for all at TI).

SLEEPING

(£1 = about $1.60, country code: 44, area code: 01463)

These rooms are all a 10- to 12-minute walk from the train station and town center. To get to the B&Bs from the station, either catch a taxi (£4) or walk: From the station, go left on Academy Street. At the first stoplight (the second if you're coming from the bus station), veer right onto Inglis Street in the pedestrian zone. Go up the Market Brae steps. At the top, turn right onto Ardconnel Street toward the B&Bs and hostels (except Ryeford).

$$ Craigside Lodge B&B is a treat. Its five spacious, cheery rooms share a cozy lounge with a great city view (Sb-£25, Db-£44, non-smoking, some street noise, just above Castle Street at 4 Gordon Terrace, tel. 01463/231-576, fax 01463/713-409, craigsidelodge@amserve.net, Janette and Wilf Skinner).

$$ Ardconnel House, with six rooms, is tasteful, spacious, and comfy with lots of extra touches (Sb-£30–35, Db-£48–54, family deals, non-smoking, car tours for 3–4 people-£18/hr, 21 Ardconnel Street, tel. & fax 01463/240-455, www.ardconnel-inverness.co.uk, ardconnel @tiscali.co.uk, friendly Isabel and Richard Cowe).

$$ Crown Guest House has six clean, simple rooms and a cheery blue-and-yellow breakfast room (S-£23, Sb-£25, Db-£50, family room-£60–69, 19 Ardconnel Street, tel. 01463/231-135, www.crownhotel -inverness.co.uk, kay@crownhotel-inverness.co.uk, Kay Frew).

$$ Melness Guest House has two fine rooms and a comfy lounge (Db-£52, less off-season, completely smoke-free, at 8 Old Edinburgh Road, tel. 01463/220-963, www.melnessie.co.uk, joy@melnessie.co.uk, Mrs. Joyce).

$$ Ryeford B&B has six flowery rooms with plush carpeting (Sb-£25, Db-£50, family deals, back room has fine garden view, above Market Brae steps, go left on Ardconnel Terrace to #21, vegetarian breakfast available, tel. 01463/242-871, ryeford@btinternet.com, Catriona and Simon Forsyth).

For inexpensive dorm beds near the center and a 12-minute walk from the train station, consider the friendly, side-by-side hostels on Culduthel Road.

$ Bazpackers Backpackers Hotel, a stone's throw from the castle, has 28 beds (beds-£11, D-£28, Internet access, laundry service, 4 Culduthel Road, tel. 01463/717-663).

$ The **Inverness Student Hotel's** 57 beds are often filled with groups doing the hop-on, hop-off bus circuit (£11–12 beds in six- to 10-bed rooms, breakfast-£1.90, Internet access, laundry service, 8 Culduthel Road, tel. 01463/236-556).

Inverness

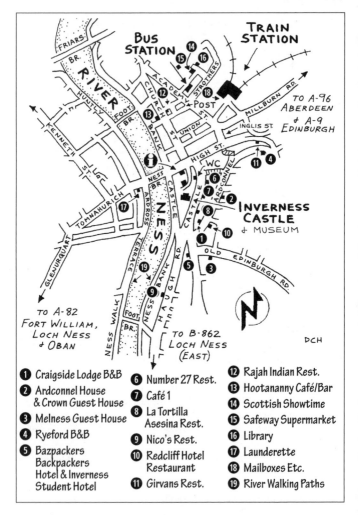

① Craigside Lodge B&B
② Ardconnel House & Crown Guest House
③ Melness Guest House
④ Ryeford B&B
⑤ Bazpackers Backpackers Hotel & Inverness Student Hotel
⑥ Number 27 Rest.
⑦ Café 1
⑧ La Tortilla Asesina Rest.
⑨ Nico's Rest.
⑩ Redcliff Hotel Restaurant
⑪ Girvans Rest.
⑫ Rajah Indian Rest.
⑬ Hootananny Café/Bar
⑭ Scottish Showtime
⑮ Safeway Supermarket
⑯ Library
⑰ Launderette
⑱ Mailboxes Etc.
⑲ River Walking Paths

EATING

You'll find a lot of traditional Highland fare—game, fish, lamb, and beef. Reservations are smart at most of these places, especially on summer weekends.

Several inviting eateries line Castle Street near the recommended B&Bs. The casual **Number 27**, a local favorite, is the Scottish version of

TGI Friday's with something for everyone—salads, burgers, seafood, and more (£5–12, daily 12:00–14:45 & 17:00–21:45, shorter hours off-season, generous portions, noisy adjacent bar, 27 Castle Street, tel. 01463/241-999). The trendy **Café 1,** a few doors up the same street, serves up local meaty dishes with a bistro flair (£8-15, lunch and early-bird dinner specials 18:00–21:30, Mon–Sat 12:00–14:00 & 18:00–22:00, closed Sun, 75 Castle Street, tel. 01463/226-200). The nearby **La Tortilla Asesina** is a lively Spanish tapas place offering an appealing late-night dining option (cold and hot tapas-£1–3.25, a few make a meal, daily 12:00–24:00, 99 Castle Street, tel. 01463/709-809).

For good seafood, consider **Nico's,** a buttoned-down, wood-beamed, candlelit restaurant a few minutes' walk beyond Castle Street (£13–29, nightly, reservations required, next to Glen Mhor Hotel on Haugh Road, tel. 01463/234-308).

The **Redcliff Hotel** restaurant is convenient (on the B&B street) for decent dinners in a bright, leafy sunroom (dinner-£10–15, daily 18:00–21:30, 1 Gordon Terrace, tel. 01463/232-767); the adjacent bar serves £4–6 pub grub (daily 12:00–14:00 & 17:00–21:30).

For sandwiches and tempting pastries, stop in the easygoing **Girvans** at the end of the pedestrian zone nearest the station (£4, Mon–Sat 9:00–21:00, Sun opens at 10:00, shorter hours off-season, 2 Stephens Brae, tel. 01463/711-900).

Rajah Indian Restaurant provides a tasty break from meat and potatoes with vegetarian options served in a classy red-velvet and white-linen atmosphere (£7–13 meals, 10 percent discount for take-out, Mon–Sat 12:00–23:00, Sun 15:00–23:00, just off Church Street at 2 Post Office Avenue, tel. 01463/237-190).

Hootananny serves simple food and features live local music every evening (£8–10, music begins at 21:30, traditional music every night except Sun, when it's contemporary, 67 Church Street, tel. 01463/712-973). Upstairs is Highland World, a touristy place where you can don a kilt, dance a reel, and speak Gaelic.

For groceries, a mega **Safeway** is next to the bus station (daily, WC, pharmacy).

TRANSPORTATION CONNECTIONS

By train to: Pitlochry (9/day, 1.5 hrs), **Edinburgh** (8/day, 3.5 hrs). ScotRail does a great sleeper service to **London** (£139 first class or £109 standard class for a private compartment with breakfast, not available Sat night, www.scotrail.co.uk). Consider dropping your car in Inverness and riding to London by train. Train info: tel. 08457-484-950.

By bus to: Oban (4/day July–Aug, 2/day Sept–June, 4 hrs, Mon–Sat only, one way-£12.70, transfer in Fort William), **Glencoe** (2/day July–Aug, fewer off-season, 2.5–3.5 hrs depending on layover,

Mon–Sat only, £12 one-way, transfer in Fort William), **Portree/Isle of Skye** (2/day, 3.25 hrs). The buses are run by Scottish Citylink; for schedules, see www.citylink.co.uk. Pay the driver cash or buy tickets in advance by calling Citylink at tel. 08705-505-050 or stopping by the Inverness bus station (Mon–Sat 8:30–18:30, Sun 9:00–18:30, daily luggage storage-£2–3/bag depending on size, 2 blocks from train station on Margaret Street, tel. 01463/233-371).

Isle of Skye

The rugged Isle of Skye has a reputation for tourist throngs and unpredictable weather ("Skye" means "cloud" in Old Norse)—but it offers some of Scotland's best scenery, and it rarely fails to charm visitors. Narrow, twisty roads wind you around Skye in the shadows of craggy, black, bald mountains. Skye seems to have a lot more sheep than people; 200 years ago, many human residents were forced to move off the island to make room for more livestock during the Highland Clearances.

Skye has some of the most ardently Gaelic Scots in Scotland—the island's Sleat peninsula is home to a rustic but important Gaelic college, and half of all island residents don't speak English as their first language. Here on Skye, you may just meet one of the very few Gaelic-speaking teenagers on the planet.

Getting Around the Isle of Skye

Once on the island, you'll do best to rent a car. Even if you're doing the rest of your trip by public transportation, a car rental is cheap and worthwhile to bypass the frustrating public-transportation options. Public buses connect the island's major towns, but service is skimpy on weekends and in the winter. Instead of renting a car elsewhere to drive to the island, rent on Skye to save on gas and bridge tolls. **Skye Car Rental** in Broadford is good (http://www.gael-net.co.uk/sutherld/0017_1.html).

SIGHTS

The island's capital and main population center is **Portree** (accommodations listed below), with a **TI** that can find you a room and give you ideas on how to spend your time here (just south of Bridge Street, tel. 01478/612-137). If you need to get out of the rain, Portree's **Aros Centre** offers a multimedia show about the island's history (£3.50, daily 9:00–18:00, open later July–Aug, a mile south of town center on Viewfield Road, tel. 01478/613-649, www.aros.co.uk).

The island's biggest attraction is the dramatic **Cuillin hills** along the southeast coast. The road to the seaside village of Glenbrittle gets you close to the most scenic stretch of this volcanic range.

The striking **Trotternish peninsula,** north of Portree, is packed with bizarre geological formations. There's good hiking around the spiky Old Man of Storr, and farther north you'll find Lealt Falls, Kilt Rock, the village of Staffin, and—at the island's northern tip—the ruins of Duntulm Castle.

To the west, near the village of Glendale, you'll discover fewer crowds, the Romantic renovation of **Dunvegan Castle** (£5.50, mid-March–Oct daily 10:00–17:30, Nov–mid-March daily 11:00–16:00, also hosts chamber music concerts, www.dunvegancastle.com), and a hardy but scenic hike to the **lighthouse** at Neist Point (half-mile footpath begins at end of Glendale-to-Waterstein road; rooms available—see below).

Consider a tour of the **Talisker Distillery** in Carbost (£3, July–Sept Mon–Sat 9:00–16:30, closed Sun, April–June and Oct Mon–Fri 9:00–16:30, closed Sat–Sun, Nov–March Mon–Fri 14:00–16:30, closed Sat–Sun, tel. 01478/614-308; good restaurant in town, listed below).

SLEEPING AND EATING

(£1 = about $1.60, country code: 44, area code: 01478)

Portree: There's not much to see here, but it's a convenient home base. Consider the 23-room **$$ Rosedale Hotel,** with a fine attached restaurant; try to get a harbor-view table (Sb-£47–50, Db-£76–90, Beaumont Crescent, tel. 01478/613-131, fax 01478/612-531, www.rosedalehotelskye .co.uk).

Waternish: Try the four-room **$$ Stein Inn,** built in 1790 and proudly claiming to be "the oldest inn on Skye" (£24.50–31 per person per night, tel. 01470/592-362, www.steininn.co.uk, angus.teresa@steininn .co.uk).

Glendale: For a scenic but remote setting on the northwestern fringe of the island, rent a room or a cottage at the **$ Neist Point Lighthouse** (rooms-£20/night per person, 2-bedroom cottage-£475/week, 3-bedroom cottage-£525/week, all rates less off-season; tel. & fax 01470/511-200, www.skye-lighthouse.com, info@skye-lighthouse.com).

Carbost: Consider splurging at **Three Chimneys Restaurant** (£42 for 3 courses, £48 for 4 courses, dinner nightly from 18:30, lunch March–Oct Mon–Sat 12:30–14:00, no lunch Sun, reservations recommended, call ahead to be sure they're open in winter, near Dunvegan Castle, tel. 01470/511-258, www.threechimneys.co.uk); they also rent six swanky, pricey suites next door (Db-£190).

TRANSPORTATION CONNECTIONS

By bus: Scottish CityLink buses are the best way to reach the island by public transportation (www.citylink.co.uk). Buses between Inverness and Portree run twice daily in both directions (3.25 hrs). There is no train station on the Isle of Skye; the closest one is across the Skye Bridge in Kyle of Lochalsh.

By car: The mainland town Kyle of Lochalsh is connected to the island town of Kyleakin by the controversial Skye Bridge—Europe's most expensive toll bridge (£5 per car each way—but the defiant local SKAT group refuses to pay; for the scoop, see www.skat.org.uk). Though the new bridge severely damaged B&B business in the towns it connects, it has been a boon for Skye tourism—making a quick visit to the island possible without having to wait on a ferry.

The island can also be reached from the mainland via a pair of car ferry crossings: Mallaig to Armadale (mid-July–Aug, operated by CalMac, www.calmac.co.uk) and Glenelg to Kylerhea (mid-April–Oct, sometimes no service Sun, Skye Ferry, www.skyeferry.co.uk).

Pitlochry

This likable tourist town, famous for its whiskey, makes an enjoyable overnight stop. Navigate easily by following the black directional signs to Pitlochry's handful of sights. The town also has plenty of forest walks (brochures at TI) and a salmon ladder that climbs alongside its lazy river (free viewing area—best in May, 10-min walk from town).

Tourist Information: The helpful **TI** provides train schedules and sells good maps for walks and scenic drives (May–Sept Mon–Sat 9:00–19:00, Sun 9:00–18:00, less off-season, no luggage storage, exit left from station, turn right on Atholl Road and walk 8 min to TI on left, tel. 01796/472-215).

SIGHTS

Distillery Tours—The cute **Edradour Scotch Distillery,** the smallest in Scotland, offers a free one-hour guided tour, a 10-minute audiovisual show, and, of course, a sample. Unlike the bigger distilleries, they allow you to take photos of the equipment (March–Oct Mon–Sat 9:30–18:00, Sun 11:30–17:00, less off-season, no tours Jan–Feb but shop is open, a lovely 40-min walk through the forest from downtown, tel. 01796/472-095).

The big, ivy-covered **Bell's Blair Athol Distillery** gives £4 hour-long tours with a wee taste at the end (2/hr, Easter–Sept Mon–Sat 9:30–17:00, June–Sept also Sun 12:00–17:00, off-season Mon–Fri 11:00–16:00, last tour starts at 16:00, half mile from town, tel. 01796/482-003).

Pitlochry Power Station—The station, adjacent to the salmon ladder, offers a mildly entertaining exhibit about hydroelectric power in the region (£2.50, April–Oct Mon–Fri 10:30–17:30, July–Aug open weekends, closed off-season, tel. 01796/473-152).

Theater—From May through October, the Pitlochry Festival Theatre presents a different play every night and concerts on some Sundays (both £15–20, purchase tickets at theater, tel. 01796/484-626, or at the TI). Some productions are staged outside in the newly-planted Scottish Plant Collector's Garden adjacent to the theater (the garden is also available for visits Mon–Sat 10:00–17:00, Sun 11:00–17:00).

SLEEPING

(£1 = about $1.60, country code: 44, area code: 01796)

$$ Try **Craigroyston House,** a quaint, large Victorian country house with eight smoke-free, Laura Ashley-style bedrooms run by the charming Gretta and Douglas Maxwell (Db-£40–60, family room, no CC, behind the TI and next to the church at 2 Lower Oakfield, tel. & fax 01796/472-053, www.craigroyston.co.uk, reservations@craigroyston .co.uk). Gretta can find you another B&B if her place is full.

$$ For drivers, **Donavourd Farmhouse B&B** offers a simple, rural option two miles south of town on the old A9 (Db-£36–44, no CC, dinner-£10, non-smoking, 10-min walk to Edradour Distillery, tel. 01796/472-254, www.donavourd.cx, Somersal Shepley).

$ The fine **hostel** is on Knockard Road (£11 bunks, Internet access, above main street, office open from 7:30–10:30 & 17:00–23:00, tel. 01796/472-308, fax 01796/473-729, pitlochry@syha.org.uk).

TRANSPORTATION CONNECTIONS

By train to: Inverness (9/day, 1.5 hrs), **Edinburgh** (6/day, 2 hrs). Train info: tel. 08457-484-950.

Route Tips for Drivers

Lake District to Oban (220 miles): From Keswick, take A66 for 18 miles to M6 and speed nonstop north (via Penrith and Carlisle), crossing Hadrian's Wall into Scotland. The road becomes the M74 south of Glasgow. To slip quickly through Glasgow, leave M74 at Junction 4 onto M73, following signs to M8/Glasgow. Leave M73 at Junction 2, exiting onto M8. Stay on M8 west through Glasgow, exit on Junction 30, cross Erskine Bridge (60p), and turn left on A82, following signs to Crianlarich and Loch Lomond. (For a scenic drive through Glasgow, take exit 17 off M8 and stay on A82 toward Dumbarton.) You'll soon be driving along scenic Loch Lomond. The first picnic turnout has the best lake views, benches, a park, and a playground. Halfway up the loch, at Tarbet, take the "tourist route" left onto A83, drive along Loch Long toward Inveraray via Rest-and-Be-Thankful Pass. (This colorful name comes from the 1880s, when second- and third-class coach passengers got out and pushed the coach and first-class passengers up the hill.) Stop in Inveraray, a lovely castle town on Loch Fyne. Park near the pier. (TI open April–Oct daily 9:00–17:00, July–Aug until 18:00, Nov–March Mon–Sat 10:00–15:00, Sun 11:00–15:00, tel. 01499/302-063.) The town jail, now a museum, is a "19th-century living prison" (£5.50, daily 9:30–18:00, last entry 17:00, tel. 01499/302-381). Leaving Inveraray, drive through a gate (at the Woolen Mill) to A819, through Glen Aray, and along Loch Awe. A85 takes you into Oban.

Oban to Glencoe (45 miles) to Loch Ness (75 miles) to Inverness (20 miles) to Edinburgh (150 miles): Barring traffic, you'll make great time on good, mostly two-lane roads. Be careful, but if you're timid about passing, diesel fumes and large trucks might be your memory of this drive. From Oban, follow the coastal A828 toward Fort William. After about 20 miles you'll see the photogenic Castle Staulker marooned on a lonely island. At Loch Leven and Ballachulish Village, leave A828, taking A82 into Glencoe. Drive through the village up the valley (Glencoe) for 10 minutes for a grand view and a chance to hear a bagpiper in the wind—Highland buskers. If you play the recorder (and no other tourists are there), ask to finger a tune while the piper does the hard work.

At the top of the valley you hit the vast Rannoch Moor—500 square and desolate miles with barely enough decent land to graze a sheep. Then make a U-turn and return through Glencoe. Continue north on A82, over the bridge, past Fort William toward Loch Ness. Follow the Caledonian Canal on A82 for 60 miles, stop at Loch Ness, and then continue on A82 to Inverness.

Leaving Inverness, follow signs to A9 (south toward Perth). Just as you leave Inverness, detour four miles east off A9 on B9006 to the Culloden Battlefield Visitors Centre. Back on A9 it's a wonderfully speedy, scenic highway (A9, M90, A90) all the way to Edinburgh (Inverness–Edinburgh, minimum 3 hrs).

For a scenic shortcut, head north only as far as Glencoe and then cut to Edinburgh via Rannoch Moor and Tyndrum. For directions to B&Bs, see the Edinburgh chapter (page 297).

APPENDIX

Britain was created by force and held together by force. It's really a nation of the 19th century. Its traditional industry, buildings, and the popularity of the notion of "Great" Britain are a product of the wealth derived from the empire that was at its peak through the Victorian era...the 19th century. Generally, the nice and bad stories are not true and the boring ones are. To best understand the many fascinating guides you'll encounter in your travels, have a basic handle on the sweeping story of this land.

What's So Great about Britain?

Regardless of the revolution we had 200 years ago, many American travelers feel that they "go home" to Britain. This most popular tourist destination has a strange influence and power over us. The more you know of Britain's roots, the better you'll get in touch with your own.

Geographically, the isle of Britain is small (about the size of Uganda or Idaho)—600 miles long and 300 miles at its widest point. Its highest mountain is 4,400 feet, a foothill by our standards. The population is a quarter that of the United States. At its peak in the mid-1800s, Britain owned one-fifth of the world and accounted for more than half of the planet's industrial output. Today, the empire is down to the isle of Britain itself and a few token and troublesome chunks, such as the Falklands, Gibraltar, and Northern Ireland.

Economically, Great Britain's industrial production is about 5 percent of the world's total. For the first time in history, Ireland has a higher per-capita income than Britain. Still, the economy is booming, and inflation, unemployment, and interest rates are all low.

Culturally, Britain is still a world leader. Her heritage, her culture, and her people cannot be measured in traditional units of power. London is a major exporter of actors, movies, and theater, of rock and classical music, and of writers, painters, and sculptors.

GET IT RIGHT

Americans tend to use "England," "Britain," and "U.K." inter-changeably, but they're not quite the same:

- **England** is the country occupying the southeast part of the island.
- **Britain** is the name of the island.
- **Great Britain** is the political union of the island's three countries, England, Scotland, and Wales.
- The **United Kingdom** adds a fourth country, Northern Ireland.
- The **British Isles** (not a political entity) also includes the independent nation of Ireland.
- The **British Commonwealth** is a loose association of posses-sions and former colonies (including Canada, Australia, and India) that profess at least symbolic loyalty to the Crown.

You can call the modern nation either the United Kingdom ("the U.K.") or just simply "Britain."

Ethnically, the British Isles are a mix of the descendants of the early Celtic natives (like Scots and Gaels, in Scotland, Ireland, and Wales) and descendants of the invading Anglo-Saxons who took south-east England in the Dark Ages. Cynics call the United Kingdom an English empire ruled by London, whose dominant Anglo-Saxon English (46 million) far outnumber their Celtic brothers and sisters (10 million).

Politically, Britain is ruled by the House of Commons, with some guidance from the mostly figurehead Queen and House of Lords. Just as the United States Congress is dominated by Democrats and Republicans, Britain's Parliament is dominated by two parties: Labor and Conservative ("Tories"). (George W. Bush would fit the Conservative Party and Bill Clinton the Labor Party like political gloves.)

The prime minister is the chief executive. He's not elected directly by voters; rather, he assumes power as the head of the party that wins a majority in parliamentary elections.

In the 1980s and early 1990s, Conservatives under Prime Minister Margaret Thatcher and John Major were in charge. As proponents of traditional, Victorian values—community, family, hard work, thrift, and trickle-down economics—they took a Reaganesque approach to Britain's serious social and economic problems.

In 1994, a huge Labor victory brought Tony Blair to the prime ministership. Labor began shoring up a social-service system (health care, education, the minimum wage) undercut by years of Conservative rule. Blair's Labor Party is "New Labor"—akin to Clinton's "New" Democrats—meaning they're fiscally conservative but attentive to the needs of the people. Conservative Party fears of old-fashioned, big-spending, bleeding-heart, Union-style liberalism have proved unfounded. The liberal Parliament is more open to integration with Europe.

Tony Blair—relatively young, family-oriented, personable, easy-going, and forever flashing his toothy grin—has been a respected and well-liked PM, but his popularity took a dive after he propelled the country into a war with Iraq.

Basic British History for the Traveler

When Julius Caesar landed on the misty and mysterious isle of Britain in 55 B.C, England entered the history books. The primitive Celtic tribes he conquered were themselves invaders, who had earlier conquered the even more mysterious people who built Stonehenge. The Romans built towns and roads and established their capital at Londinium. The Celtic natives in Scotland and Wales—consisting of Gaels, Picts, and Scots—were not subdued so easily. The Romans built Hadrian's Wall near the Scottish border as protection against their troublesome northern neighbors. Even today, the Celtic language and influence are strongest in these far reaches of Britain.

As Rome fell, so fell Roman Britain, a victim of invaders and internal troubles. Barbarian tribes from Germany and Denmark, called Angles and Saxons, swept through the southern part of the island, establishing Angle-land. These were the days of the real King Arthur, possibly a Christianized Roman general who fought valiantly, but in vain, against invading barbarians. The island was plunged into 500 years of Dark Ages—wars, plagues, and poverty—lit only by the dim candle of a few learned Christian monks and missionaries trying to convert the barbarians. The sightseer sees little from this Anglo-Saxon period.

Modern England began with yet another invasion. William the Conqueror and his Norman troops crossed the English Channel from France in 1066. William crowned himself king in Westminster Abbey (where all subsequent coronations would take place) and began building the Tower of London. French-speaking Norman kings ruled the country for two centuries. Then followed two centuries of civil wars, with various noble families vying for the crown. In one of the most bitter feuds, the York and Lancaster families fought the Wars of the Roses, so-called because of the white and red flowers the combatants chose as their symbols. Battles, intrigues, kings, nobles, and ladies imprisoned and executed in the Tower—it's a wonder the country survived its rulers.

England was finally united by the "third-party" Tudor family. Henry VIII, a Tudor, was England's Renaissance king. He was handsome, athletic, highly sexed, a poet, a scholar, and a musician. He was also arrogant, cruel, gluttonous, and paranoid. He went through six wives in 40 years, divorcing, imprisoning, or beheading them when they no longer suited his needs.

Henry also "divorced" England from the Catholic Church, establishing the Protestant Church of England (the Anglican Church) and setting in motion years of religious squabbles. He also "dissolved" the monasteries (around 1540), left just the shells of many formerly glorious abbeys dotting the countryside, and pocketed their land and wealth for the crown.

Henry's daughter, Queen Elizabeth I, who reigned for 45 years, made England a great trading and naval power (defeating the Spanish Armada) and presided over the Elizabethan era of great writers (such as William Shakespeare) and scientists (such as Francis Bacon).

The long-standing quarrel between England's divine-right kings and Parliament's nobles finally erupted into a civil war (1643). Parliament forces under the Protestant Puritan farmer Oliver Cromwell defeated—and beheaded—King Charles I. This civil war left its mark on much of what you'll see in England. Eventually, Parliament invited Charles' son to take the throne. This "restoration of the monarchy" was accompanied by a great colonial expansion and the rebuilding of London (including Christopher Wren's St. Paul's Cathedral), which had been devastated by the Great Fire of 1666.

Britain grew as a naval superpower, colonizing and trading with all parts of the globe. Admiral Horatio Nelson's victory over Napoleon's fleet at the Battle of Trafalgar secured her naval superiority ("Britannia rules the waves"), and ten years later, the Duke of Wellington stomped Napoleon on land at Waterloo. Nelson and Wellington—both buried in London's St. Paul's Cathedral—are memorialized by many arches, columns, and squares throughout England.

Economically, Britain led the world into the Industrial Age with her mills, factories, coal mines, and trains. By the time of Queen Victoria's reign (1837–1901), Britain was at its zenith of power, with a colonial empire that covered one-fifth of the world.

The 20th century was not kind to Britain. Two world wars devastated the population. The Nazi blitzkrieg reduced much of London to rubble. The colonial empire has dwindled to almost nothing, and Britain is no longer an economic superpower. The "Irish Troubles" are constant, as the Catholic inhabitants of British-ruled Northern Ireland fight for the independence their southern neighbors won decades ago. The war over the Falkland Islands in 1982 showed how little of the British Empire is left—and how determined the British are to hang on to what remains.

But the tradition (if not the substance) of greatness continues, presided over by Queen Elizabeth II, her husband Prince Philip, and Prince Charles. With economic problems, the marital turmoil of Charles and the late Princess Diana, and a relentless popular press, the royal

ROYAL LINEAGE

802–1066	Saxon and Danish kings
1066–1154	Norman invasion (William the Conqueror), Norman kings
1154–1399	Plantagenet
1399–1461	Lancaster
1462–1485	York
1485–1603	Tudor (Henry VIII, Elizabeth I)
1603–1649	Stuart (civil war and beheading of Charles I)
1649–1653	Commonwealth, no royal head of state
1653–1659	Protectorate, with Cromwell as Lord Protector
1660–1714	Restoration of Stuart monarchy
1714–1901	Hanover (four Georges, Victoria)
1901–1910	Edward VII
1910–present	Windsor (George V, Edward VIII, George VI, Elizabeth II)

family has had a tough time. But the queen has stayed above it all, and most British people still jump at an opportunity to see royalty. With the death of Princess Diana and the historic outpouring of grief, it's clear that the concept of royalty is still alive and well as Britain enters the third millennium.

Queen Elizabeth marked her 50th year on the throne in 2002 with a flurry of Golden Jubilee festivities. While many wonder who will succeed her, the case is fairly straightforward: The queen sees her job as a lifelong position, and legally, Charles (who wants to be king) cannot be skipped over for his son William. Given the longevity in the family (the Queen's mum, born in August of 1900, made it to 101 before she died in April 2002), Charles is in for a long wait.

Architecture in Britain

From Stonehenge to Big Ben, travelers are storming castle walls, climbing spiral staircases, and snapping the pictures of 5,000 years of architecture. Let's sort it out.

The oldest ruins—mysterious and prehistoric—date from before Roman times back to 3000 B.C The earliest sites, such as Stonehenge and Avebury, were built during the Stone and Bronze Ages. The remains from these periods are made of huge stones or mounds of earth, even man-made hills, and were created as celestial calendars and for worship or burial. Britain is crisscrossed with lines of these mysterious sights (ley lines). Iron Age people (600 B.C–A.D. 50) left desolate stone forts. The Romans thrived in Britain from A.D. 50 to 400, building cities, walls, and roads. Evidence of Roman greatness can be seen in lavish villas with ornate mosaic floors, temples uncovered beneath great English churches, and Roman stones in medieval city walls. Roman roads sliced across the island in straight lines. Today, unusually straight rural roads are very likely laid directly on these ancient roads.

As Rome crumbled in the fifth century, so did Roman Britain. Little architecture survives from Dark Ages England, the Saxon period from 500 to 1000. Architecturally, the light was switched on with the Norman conquest in 1066. As William earned his title "the Conqueror," his French architects built churches and castles in the European Romanesque style.

English Romanesque is called Norman (1066–1200). Norman churches had round arches, thick walls, and small windows; Durham Cathedral and the Chapel of St. John in the Tower of London are typical examples. The Tower of London, with its square keep, small windows, and spiral stone stairways, is a typical Norman castle. You'll see plenty of Norman castles—all built to secure the conquest of these invaders from Normandy.

Gothic architecture (1200–1600) replaced the heavy Norman style with light, vertical buildings, pointed arches, soaring spires, and bigger windows. English Gothic is divided into three stages. Early English (1200–1300) features tall, simple spires; beautifully carved capitals; and elaborate chapter houses (such as the Wells Cathedral). Decorated Gothic (1300–1400) gets fancier, with more elaborate tracery, bigger windows, and ornately carved pinnacles, as you'll see at Westminster Abbey. Finally, the Perpendicular style (1400–1600, also called "rectilinear") returns to square towers and emphasizes straight, uninterrupted vertical lines from ceiling to floor, with vast windows and exuberant decoration, including fan-vaulted ceilings (King's College Chapel at Cambridge). Through this evolution, the structural ribs (arches meeting at the top of the ceilings) became more and more decorative and fanciful (the most fancy being the star vaulting and fan vaulting of the Perpendicular style).

As you tour the great medieval churches of England, remember that nearly everything is symbolic. For instance, on the tombs, if the figure has crossed legs, he was a Crusader. If his feet rest on a dog, he died at home, but if the legs rest on a lion, he died in battle. Local guides and books help us modern pilgrims understand at least a little of what we see.

Wales is particularly rich in English castles, which were needed to subdue the stubborn Welsh. Edward I built a ring of powerful castles in Wales, including Conwy and Caernarfon.

Gothic houses were a simple mix of woven strips of thin wood, rubble, and plaster called wattle and daub. The famous black-and-white Tudor, or half-timbered, look came simply from filling in heavy oak frames with wattle and daub.

The Tudor period (1485–1560) was a time of relative peace (the Wars of the Roses were finally over), prosperity, and renaissance. Henry VIII broke with the Catholic Church and "dissolved" (destroyed) the monasteries, leaving scores of England's greatest churches as gutted shells. These hauntingly beautiful abbey ruins (Glastonbury, Whitby, and Tintern) surrounded by lush lawns are now pleasant city parks.

Although few churches were built during the Tudor period, this was a time of house and mansion construction. Heating a home was becoming popular and affordable, and Tudor buildings featured small square windows and many chimneys. In towns where land was scarce, many Tudor houses grew up and out, getting wider with each over-hanging floor.

The Elizabethan and Jacobean periods (1560–1620) were followed by the English Renaissance style (1620–1720). English architects mixed Gothic and classical styles, then Baroque and classical styles. Although the ornate Baroque never really grabbed England, the classical style of the Italian architect Andrea Palladio did. Inigo Jones (1573–1652), Christopher Wren (1632–1723), and those they inspired plastered England with enough columns, domes, and symmetry to please a Caesar. The Great Fire of London (1666) cleared the way for an ambitious young Wren to put his mark on London forever with a grand rebuilding scheme, including the great St. Paul's Cathedral and more than 50 other churches.

The celebrants of the Boston Tea Party remember England's Georgian period (1720–1840) for its lousy German kings. Georgian architecture was rich and showed off by being very classical. Grand orna-mental doorways, fine cast-ironwork on balconies and railings, Chippendale furniture, and white-on-blue Wedgwood ceramics graced rich homes everywhere. John Wood Jr. and Sr. led the way, giving the trendsetting city of Bath its crescents and circles of aristocratic Georgian row houses. "Georgian" is English for "neoclassical."

The Industrial Revolution shaped the Victorian period (1840–1890) with glass, steel, and iron. England had a huge new erector set (so did France's Mr. Eiffel). This was also a Romantic period, reviving the "more Christian" Gothic style. London's Houses of Parliament are neo-Gothic—just 100 years old but looking 700, except for the telltale modern precision and craftsmanship. Whereas Gothic was stone or concrete, neo-Gothic was often red brick. These were England's glory days, and there was more building in this period than in all previous ages combined.

The architecture of modern times obeys the formula "form follows function"—it worries more about your needs than your eyes. England treasures its heritage and takes great pains to build tastefully in historic districts and to preserve its many "listed" buildings. With a booming tourist trade, these quaint reminders of its past—and ours—are becoming a valuable part of the British economy.

British TV

British television is so good—and so British—that it deserves a mention as a sightseeing treat. After a hard day of castle climbing, watch the telly over tea in the living room of your village B&B.

England has five channels. BBC-1 and BBC-2 are government regulated, commercial free, and traditionally highbrow. Channels 3, 4, and 5 are private, are a little more Yankee, and have commercials—but those commercials are clever and sophisticated and provide a fun look at England. Broadcasting is funded by a £100-per-year-per-household tax. Hmmm, 40 cents per day to escape commercials and public-television pledge drives.

Britain is about to leap into the Digital Age ahead of the rest of the TV-watching world. Ultimately every house will enjoy literally hundreds of high-definition channels with no need for cable or satellites. Right now it's high subscription rates that are slowing the transition.

Whereas California "accents" fill our airwaves 24 hours a day, homogenizing the way our country speaks, England protects and promotes its regional accents by its choice of TV and radio announcers. Commercial-free British TV, while looser than it used to be, is still careful about what it airs and when.

American programs (such as *Friends, Oprah,* and trash-talk shows) are very popular. The visiting viewer should be sure to tune the TV to a few typical English shows, including a dose of English situation- and political-comedy fun and the top-notch BBC evening news. Quiz shows are taken very seriously here (where *Who Wants to Be a Millionaire* originated). Michael Parkinson is the Johnny Carson of Britain for late-night talk. For a tear-filled, slice-of-life taste of British soap dealing in all the controversial issues, see the popular *Brookside, Coronation Street,* or *Eastenders.*

Let's Talk Telephones

Here's a primer on making direct phone calls. For information specific to Britain, see "Telephones" in the Introduction.

Making Calls within a European Country: About half of all European countries—including Britain—use area codes; the other half uses a direct-dial system without area codes.

In countries that use area codes (such as Austria, Britain, Finland, Germany, Ireland, Netherlands, and Sweden), you dial the local number when calling within a city, and you add the area code if calling long distance within the country.

To make calls within a country that uses a direct-dial system (Belgium, the Czech Republic, Denmark, France, Italy, Portugal, Norway, Spain, and Switzerland), you dial the same number whether you're calling across the country or across the street.

Making International Calls: You always start with the international access code (011 if you're calling from America or Canada, or 00 from virtually anywhere in Europe), then dial the country code of the country you're calling (see chart below).

What you dial next depends on the phone system of the country you're calling. If the country uses area codes, drop the initial zero of the area code, then dial the rest of the number.

Countries that use direct-dial systems (no area codes) vary in how they're accessed internationally by phone. For instance, if you're making an international call to the Czech Republic, Denmark, Italy, Norway, Portugal, or Spain, simply dial the international access code, country code, and phone number. But if you're calling Belgium, France, or Switzerland, drop the initial zero of the phone number. Example: To call a Paris hotel (tel. 01 47 05 49 15) from London, dial 00, 33 (France's country code), then 1 47 05 49 15 (phone number without the initial zero).

International Access Codes
When dialing direct, first dial the international access code of the country you're calling from. For the United States and Canada, it's 011. All European countries use "00" as their international access code.

Country Codes
After you've dialed the international access code, dial the code of the country you're calling.

Austria—43
Belgium—32
Britain—44
Canada—1
Croatia—385
Czech Rep.—420
Denmark—45
Estonia—372
Finland—358
France—33
Germany—49
Gibraltar—350
Greece—30
Hungary—36

Ireland—353
Italy—39
Morocco—212
Netherlands—31
Norway—47
Poland—48
Portugal—351
Slovenia—386
Spain—34
Sweden—46
Switzerland—41
Turkey—90
United States—1

European Calling Chart

Just smile and dial, using this key:
AC = Area Code, LN = Local Number.

European Country	Calling long distance within...	Calling from the U.S.A./ Canada to...	Calling from a European country to...
Austria	AC + LN	011 + 43 + AC (without the initial zero) + LN	00 + 43 + AC (without the initial zero) + LN
Belgium	LN	011 + 32 + LN (without initial zero)	00 + 32 + LN (without initial zero)
Britain	AC + LN	011 + 44 + AC (without initial zero) + LN	00 + 44 + AC (without initial zero) + LN
Czech Republic	LN	011 + 420 + LN	00 + 420 + LN
Denmark	LN	011 + 45 + LN	00 + 45 + LN
Estonia	LN	011 + 372 + LN	00 + 372 + LN
Finland	AC + LN	011 + 358 + AC (without initial zero) + LN	00 + 358 + AC (without initial zero) + LN
France	LN	011 + 33 + LN (without initial zero)	00 + 33 + LN (without initial zero)
Germany	AC + LN	011 + 49 + AC (without initial zero) + LN	00 + 49 + AC (without initial zero) + LN
Gibraltar	LN	011 + 350 + LN	00 + 350 + LN From Spain: 9567 + LN
Greece	LN	011 + 30 + LN	00 + 30 + LN

European Country	Calling long distance within...	Calling from the U.S.A./ Canada to...	Calling from a European country to...
Ireland	AC + LN	011 + 353 + AC (without initial zero) + LN	00 + 353 + AC (without initial zero) + LN
Italy	LN	011 + 39 + LN	00 + 39 + LN
Morocco	LN	011 + 212 + LN (without initial zero)	00 + 212 + LN (without initial zero)
Netherlands	AC + LN	011 + 31 + AC (without initial zero) + LN	00 + 31 + AC (without initial zero) + LN
Norway	LN	011 + 47 + LN	00 + 47 + LN
Portugal	LN	011 + 351 + LN	00 + 351 + LN
Spain	LN	011 + 34 + LN	00 + 34 + LN
Sweden	AC + LN	011 + 46 + AC (without initial zero) + LN	00 + 46 + AC (without initial zero) + LN
Switzerland	LN	011 + 41 + LN (without initial zero)	00 + 41 + LN (without initial zero)
Turkey	AC (if no initial zero is included, add one) + LN	011 + 90 + AC (without initial zero) + LN	00 + 90 + AC (without initial zero) + LN

- The instructions above apply whether you're calling a fixed phone or cell phone.

- The international access codes (the first numbers you dial when making an international call) are 011 if you're calling from the U.S.A./Canada, or 00 if you're calling from anywhere in Europe.

- To call the U.S.A. or Canada from Europe, dial 00, then 1 (the country code for the U.S.A. and Canada), then the area code and number. In short, 00 + 1 + AC + LN = Hi, Mom!

Useful Numbers in Britain
Emergency (police and ambulance): 999
Operator Assistance: 100
Directory Assistance: 192 (20p from phone booth, otherwise expensive)
International Info: 153 (20p from phone booth, £1.50 otherwise)
International Assistance: 155
United States Embassy: 55 Upper Brook Street, London, tel. 020/7499-9000, www.usembassy.org.uk
Eurostar (Chunnel Info): 08705-186-186 (www.eurostar.com)
Trains to all points in Europe: 08705-848-848 (www.raileurope.com)
Train information for trips within England: 0845-748-4950

Telephone Directory
Note: Understand the various prefixes: 09 numbers are as expensive as phone sex. Prefixes 0845 (4p/min, 2p evenings and weekends) and 0870 (8p/min, 4p evenings and weekends) are local calls nationwide. And 0800 numbers are toll free. If you have questions about a prefix, call 100 for free help.

London's Airports and Airlines
Airports
For online information on the first three airports, check www.baa.co.uk.
Heathrow (flight info): 0870-000-0123
Gatwick (general info): 01293-535353 or 0870-000-2468 for all airlines, except British Airways—0870-551-1155 (flights) or 0845-773-3377 (booking)
Stansted (general info): 0870-000-0303.
Luton (general info): 01582/405-100 (www.london-luton.com)

Airlines
Aer Lingus: 0845-084-4777, 0845-084-4444 (www.aerlingus.ie)
Air Canada: 0870-524-7226, 020/8751-1331 (www.aircanada.ca)
Alitalia: reservations 0870-544-8259, Heathrow 020/8745-5812, (www.alitalia.it)
American: 020/8750-1048 (www.aa.com)
British Airways: reservations 0870-850-9850, flight info 0870-551-1155 (www.britishairways.com), cool voice-activated system
bmi british midland: reservations 0870-607-0555, info 020/8745-7321 (www.flybmi.com)
Continental Airlines: 0800-776-464, 01293/511-581 (www.continental .com)
KLM Royal Dutch Airlines: 0870-507-4074 (www.klm.com)
Lufthansa: 020/8750-3300 (www.lufthansa.co.uk)

2004

JANUARY
S	M	T	W	T	F	S
				1	2	3
4	5	6	7	8	9	10
11	12	13	14	15	16	17
18	19	20	21	22	23	24
25	26	27	28	29	30	31

FEBRUARY
S	M	T	W	T	F	S
1	2	3	4	5	6	7
8	9	10	11	12	13	14
15	16	17	18	19	20	21
22	23	24	25	26	27	28
29						

MARCH
S	M	T	W	T	F	S
	1	2	3	4	5	6
7	8	9	10	11	12	13
14	15	16	17	18	19	20
21	22	23	24	25	26	27
28	29	30	31			

APRIL
S	M	T	W	T	F	S
				1	2	3
4	5	6	7	8	9	10
11	12	13	14	15	16	17
18	19	20	21	22	23	24
25	26	27	28	29	30	

MAY
S	M	T	W	T	F	S
						1
2	3	4	5	6	7	8
9	10	11	12	13	14	15
16	17	18	19	20	21	22
23/30	24/31	25	26	27	28	29

JUNE
S	M	T	W	T	F	S
		1	2	3	4	5
6	7	8	9	10	11	12
13	14	15	16	17	18	19
20	21	22	23	24	25	26
27	28	29	30			

JULY
S	M	T	W	T	F	S
				1	2	3
4	5	6	7	8	9	10
11	12	13	14	15	16	17
18	19	20	21	22	23	24
25	26	27	28	29	30	31

AUGUST
S	M	T	W	T	F	S
1	2	3	4	5	6	7
8	9	10	11	12	13	14
15	16	17	18	19	20	21
22	23	24	25	26	27	28
29	30	31				

SEPTEMBER
S	M	T	W	T	F	S
			1	2	3	4
5	6	7	8	9	10	11
12	13	14	15	16	17	18
19	20	21	22	23	24	25
26	27	28	29	30		

OCTOBER
S	M	T	W	T	F	S
					1	2
3	4	5	6	7	8	9
10	11	12	13	14	15	16
17	18	19	20	21	22	23
24/31	25	26	27	28	29	30

NOVEMBER
S	M	T	W	T	F	S
	1	2	3	4	5	6
7	8	9	10	11	12	13
14	15	16	17	18	19	20
21	22	23	24	25	26	27
28	29	30				

DECEMBER
S	M	T	W	T	F	S
			1	2	3	4
5	6	7	8	9	10	11
12	13	14	15	16	17	18
19	20	21	22	23	24	25
26	27	28	29	30	31	

Ryanair (cheap fares): 0870-333-1231 (www.ryanair.com)
Scandinavian Airlines System (SAS): 0870-607-27727
(www.scandinavian.net)
United Airlines: 0845-844-4777, 07626/915-500 (www.ual.com)
US Airways: 0845-600-3300 (www.usairways.com)
Virgin Express: 020/7744-0004 (www.virgin-express.com)

London Heathrow Car Rental Agencies
Avis: 0870-0100-287
Budget: 0800-181-181, 020/8750-2520
Europcar: 0870-607-5000, 020/8897-0811
Hertz: 0870-599-6699, 020/8897-2072
National: 0870-600-6666, 020/87502-800

PUBLIC HOLIDAYS AND FESTIVALS

Great Britain (including banks and some sights) closes down on these holidays: January 1 (New Years Day, Britain), January 2 (New Year's Holiday, Scotland), Easter Sunday and Monday (April 11 and 12 in 2004), May 3 (May Day, Britain), May 31 (Spring Holiday, Britain), August 30 (Late Summer Holiday, Britain), November 1 (All Saints' Day, Britain), and December 25 and 26.

For specifics on festivals, visit www.travelbritain.org, www .londontouristboard.com, www.eif.co.uk (Edinburgh festival), and www.whatsonwhen.com.

Here's a partial list of events:

February

York	mid-Feb	**Jorvik Viking Festival** (costumed warriors, battles)

March

Bath	early March	**Literature Festival**
York	mid- to late March	**Late Music Festival**

May

Bath	early to mid-May	**Annual Spring Flower Show** (displays, food, music, dancers)
Keswick	mid-May	**Jazz Festival**
Bath	mid- to late May	**International Music Festival**
London	mid- to late May	**Chelsea Flower Show**
Bath	late May to early June	**Fringe Festival** (alternative music, dance, theater)

June

Keswick	early to mid-June	**Beer Festival** (music, shows)
Liverpool	mid-June	**Mersey River Festival** (maritime festival)
London	mid-June	**Trooping the Color** (military bands & pageantry)
Edinburgh	mid- to late June	**Royal Highland Show** (Scottish county fair)
London	last Monday	**Wimbeldon** begins

July

Greenwich	early to mid-July	**Greenwich and Docklands Arts Festival**
York	early to mid-July	**Early Music Festival**
Llangollen	early to mid-July	**International Eisteddfod** (folk songs, dances)
Liverpool	late July	**Merseyside International Street Festival** (music, dance, theater)

August

Cambridge	early Aug	**Folk Festival** (acoustic music, food)
Edinburgh	through Aug	**Military Tattoo** (massing of bands)
Edinburgh	mid-Aug	**Fringe Festival** (off-beat theater and comedy)
Edinburgh	mid- to late Aug	**Edinburgh Festival** (music, dance, shows)
London	late Aug	**Notting Hill Carnival**
Blackpool	Sept 3–Nov 7 in 2004	**Illuminations** (waterfront light festival)

November

York	late Nov to early Dec	**St. Nicholas Fayre** (markets, music, entertainment)
Britain	Nov 5	**Guy Fawkes Day** (fireworks, effigy burning of traitor "Guy Fawkes")

December

Keswick	early Dec	**Victorian Fayre** (music, dance, carolers)
Edinburgh	Dec 31–Jan 2	**Hogmanay** (music, street theater, carnival)

Temperature Conversion

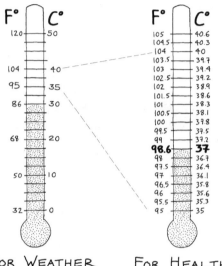

FOR WEATHER   FOR HEALTH

Climate
The first line is the average low temperature, the second line is the average high, and the third line is the number of days with no rain.

	J	F	M	A	M	J	J	A	S	O	N	D
LONDON												
	36°	36°	38°	42°	47°	53°	56°	56°	52°	46°	42°	38°
	43°	44°	50°	56°	62°	69°	71°	71°	65°	58°	50°	45°
	16	15	20	18	19	19	19	20	17	18	15	16
CARDIFF (South Wales)												
	35°	35°	38°	41°	46°	51°	54°	55°	51°	46°	41°	37°
	45°	45°	50°	56°	61°	68°	69°	69°	64°	58°	51°	46°
	13	14	18	17	18	17	17	16	14	15	13	13
YORK												
	33°	34°	36°	40°	44°	50°	54°	53°	50°	44°	39°	36°
	43°	44°	49°	55°	61°	67°	70°	69°	64°	57°	49°	45°
	14	13	18	17	18	16	16	17	16	16	13	14

| J | F | M | A | M | J | J | A | S | O | N | D |

EDINBURGH

34°	34°	36°	39°	43°	49°	52°	52°	49°	44°	39°	36°
42°	43°	46°	51°	56°	62°	65°	64°	60°	54°	48°	44°
14	13	16	16	17	15	14	15	14	14	13	13

Metric Conversion (approximate)

1 inch = 25 millimeters

1 foot = 0.3 meter

1 yard = 0.9 meter

1 mile = 1.6 kilometers

1 centimeter = 0.4 inch

1 meter = 39.4 inches

1 kilometer = .62 mile

32 degrees F = 0 degrees C

82 degrees F = about 28 degrees C

1 ounce = 28 grams

1 kilogram = 2.2 pounds

1 quart = 0.95 liter

1 square yard = 0.8 square meter

1 acre = 0.4 hectare

Weights and Measures

1 British pint = 1.2 U.S. pints

1 imperial gallon = 1.2 U.S. gallons or about 4.5 liters

1 stone = 14 pounds (a 168-pound person weighs 12 stone)

28 degrees Centigrade = 82 degrees Fahrenheit

Shoe sizes = about .5 to 1.5 sizes smaller than in the United States

Numbers and Stumblers

• Europeans write a few of their numbers differently than we do. 1 = 𝟣, 4 = 𝟦, 7 = 𝟋. Learn the difference or miss your train.

• In Europe, dates appear as day/month/year, so Christmas is 25/12/04.

• Commas are decimal points and decimals commas. A dollar and a half is $1,50, and there are 5.280 feet in a mile.

• When pointing, use your whole hand, palm down.

• When counting with fingers, start with your thumb. If you hold up your first finger to request one item, you'll probably get two.

• What Americans call the second floor of a building is the first floor in Europe.

• Europeans keep the left "lane" open for passing on escalators and moving sidewalks. Keep to the right.

British-Yankee Vocabulary

advert advertisement

afters dessert

anticlockwise counterclockwise

aubergine eggplant

banger sausage

bangers and mash sausage and mashed potatoes

bank holiday legal holiday

bap hamburger-type bun

billion a thousand of our billions (a million million)

biro ballpoint pen

biscuit cookie

black pudding sausage made from dried blood

bloody damn

bobby policeman ("copper" is more common)

Bob's your uncle there you go (with a shrug), naturally

bomb success

bonnet car hood

boot car trunk

braces suspenders

bridle way path for walkers, bikers, and horse riders

brilliant cool

bubble and squeak cold meat fried with cabbage and potatoes

bum bottom or "backside"

candy floss cotton candy

caravan trailer

car boot sale temporary flea market with car trunk displays (a good place to buy back your stolen goods)

cat's eyes road reflectors

ceilidh (KAY-lee) informal evening of song and folk fun (Scottish and Irish)

cheap and nasty cheap and bad quality

cheerio good-bye

chemist pharmacist

chicory endive

chips french fries

chock-a-block jam-packed

cider alcoholic apple cider

clearway road where you can't stop

coach long-distance bus

concession discounted admission

cos romaine lettuce

cotton buds Q-tips

courgette zucchini

craic (crack) good conversation (Irish and spreading to England)

crisps potato chips

cuppa cup of tea

dear expensive

dicey iffy, risky

digestives round graham crackers

dinner lunch or dinner

diversion detour

donkey's years until the cows come home

draughts checkers

draw marijuana

dual carriageway divided highway (four lanes)

elvers baby eels

face flannel washcloth

fag cigarette

fagged exhausted

faggot meatball

fanny vagina

fell hill or high plain

first floor second floor

football soccer

force waterfall (Lake District)

fortnight two weeks

Frogs French people

Full Monty The whole shebang. Everything.

gallery balcony

gammon ham

gangway aisle

gaol jail (same pronunciation)

give way yield

glen narrow valley

goods wagon freight truck

grammar school high school

half eight 8:30 (not 7:30)

heath open treeless land

holiday vacation

homely likable or cozy

hoover vacuum cleaner

ice lolly Popsicle

interval intermission

ironmonger hardware store

jacket potato baked potato

jelly Jell-O

Joe Bloggs John Doe

jumble sale, rummage sale

jumper sweater

just a tick just a second

keep your pecker up be brave

kipper smoked herring
knackered exhausted (Cockney: cream crackered)
knickers ladies' panties
knocking shop brothel
knock up wake up or visit
ladybird ladybug
lady fingers okra
left luggage baggage check
lemon squash lemonade
let rent
loo toilet or bathroom
lorry truck
mac mackintosh coat
mate buddy (boy or girl)
mean stingy
mews courtyard stables, often used as cottages
mobile (MOH-bile) mobile phone
nappy diaper
natter talk and talk
neep Scottish for turnip
nought zero
noughts & crosses tic-tac-toe
off license store selling take-away liquor
pasty crusted savory (usually meat) pie
pavement sidewalk
petrol gas
pillar box postbox
pissed (rude), paralytic, bevvied, wellied, popped up, trollied, ratted, rat-arsed, pissed as a newt drunk
pitch playing field
plaster Band-Aid
publican pub manager
public convenience toilets
public school private "prep" school (Eton)
put a sock in it shut up
queue line
queue up line up
quid pound (money, worth about $1.50)
randy horny
redundant, made fired
Remembrance Day Veterans' Day
return ticket round trip
ring up call (telephone)
roundabout traffic circle
rubber eraser
sanitary towel sanitary pad
sausage roll sausage wrapped in a flaky pastry

Scotch egg hard-boiled egg wrapped in sausage meat
self-catering apartment with kitchen
sellotape Scotch tape
serviette napkin
single ticket one-way ticket
sleeping policeman speed bumps
smalls underwear
snogging kissing, cuddling
solicitor lawyer
starkers buck naked
starters appetizers
sticking plaster Band-Aid
sticky tape Scotch tape
stone 14 pounds (weight)
subway underground pedestrian passageway
sultanas golden raisins
surgical spirit rubbing alcohol
suss out figure out
swede rutabaga
ta thank you
taxi rank taxi stand
telly TV
theatre live stage
tick a check mark
tight as a fish's bum cheapskate (water-tight)
tights panty hose
tin can
tipper lorry dump truck
to let for rent
top hole first rate
top up refill a drink
torch flashlight
towpath path along a river
Tube subway
twee quaint, cute
underground subway
vegetable marrow summer squash
verge grassy edge of road
verger church official
way out exit
wee urinate
Wellingtons, wellies rubber boots
whacked exhausted
witter on gab and gab
yob hooligan
zebra crossing crosswalk
zed the letter "z"

Road Scholar Feedback for Great Britain 2004

We're all in the same travelers' school of hard knocks. Your feedback helps us improve this guidebook for future travelers. Please fill this out (or use the online version at www.ricksteves.com/feedback), attach more info or any tips/favorite discoveries if you like, and send it to us. As thanks for your help, we'll send you our quarterly travel newsletter free for one year. Thanks! **Rick**

Of the recommended accommodations/restaurants used, which was:

Best _____

      Why? _____

Worst _____

      Why? _____

Of the sights/experiences/destinations recommended by this book, which was:

Most overrated _____

      Why? _____

Most underrated _____

      Why? _____

Best ways to improve this book:

_____

_____

I'd like a free newsletter subscription:

_____ Yes   _____ No   _____ Already on list

_____
Name

_____
Address

_____
City, State, Zip

_____
E-mail Address

Please send to: ETBD, Box 2009, Edmonds, WA 98020

Faxing Your Hotel Reservation

Use this handy form for your fax or find it online at
www.ricksteves.com/reservation. Photocopy and fax away.

One-Page Fax

To: _____ @ _____
        hotel   fax

From: _____ @ _____
          name   fax

Today's date: ___ / ___ / ___
                   day   month   year

Dear Hotel _____,

Please make this reservation for me:

Name: _____

Total # of people: _____ # of rooms: _____ # of nights: _____

Arriving: ___ / ___ / ___ My time of arrival (24-hr clock): _____
             day   month   year   (I will telephone if I will be late)

Departing: ___ / ___ / ___
               day   month   year

Room(s): Single___ Double___ Twin___ Triple___ Quad___

With: Toilet___ Shower___ Bath___ Sink only___

Special needs: View___ Quiet___ Cheapest___ Ground Floor___

Credit card: Visa___ MasterCard___ American Express___

Card #: _____

Expiration date:_____

Name on card: _____

After you confirm my reservation, you may charge me for the first night as a
deposit. Please fax, e-mail, or mail me confirmation of my reservation, along
with the type of room reserved, the price, and whether the price includes
breakfast. Please also inform me of your cancellation policy. Thank you.

_____
Signature

_____
Name

_____
Address

_____
City   State   Zip Code   Country

_____
E-mail Address

INDEX

ABOUT THE AUTHOR

RICK STEVES

 RICK STEVES is on a mission: to help make European travel accessible and meaningful for Americans. Rick has spent 100 days every year since 1973 exploring Europe. He's researched and written 24 travel guidebooks. He writes and hosts the public television series *Rick Steves Europe*, now in its seventh season. With the help of his hardworking staff of 60 at Europe through the Back Door, Rick organizes and leads tours of Europe and offers an information-packed Web site (www.ricksteves.com). Rick, his wife (and favorite travel partner) Anne, and their two teenage children, Andy and Jackie, call Edmonds, just north of Seattle, home.

FREE-SPIRITED TOURS FROM
Rick Steves
Small Groups
Great Guides
Guaranteed Prices
No Grumps

Free, fresh travel tips, all year long.

Visit **www.ricksteves.com**
to get Rick's free
64-page newsletter... and more!

Rick Steves

COUNTRY GUIDES 2004

Best of Europe
Best of Eastern Europe
France
Germany, Austria & Switzerland
Great Britain
Ireland
Italy
Scandinavia
Spain & Portugal

CITY GUIDES 2004

Amsterdam, Bruges & Brussels
Florence & Tuscany
London
Paris
Provence & The French Riviera
Rome
Venice

MORE EUROPE FROM RICK STEVES

Europe 101
Europe Through the Back Door 2004
Mona Winks
Postcards from Europe

More Savvy. More Surprising. More Fun.

PHRASE BOOKS & DICTIONARIES

French, Italian & German
French
German
Italian
Portuguese
Spanish

VHS RICK STEVES' EUROPE

The Best of Ireland
Bulgaria, Eastern Turkey, Slovenia
    & Croatia
The Heart of Italy
London & Paris
Prague, Amsterdam & the Swiss Alps
Romantic Germany & Berlin
Rome, Caesar's Rome, Sicily
South England, Heart of England & Scotland
Southwest Germany & Portugal
Travel Skills Special
Venice & Veneto 2003

DVD RICK STEVES' EUROPE

Rick Steves' Europe
    All Thirty Shows 2000-2003
Britain & Ireland
Exotic Europe
Germany, the Swiss Alps
    & Travel Skills
Italy

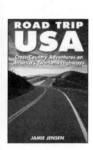